KINGS, RULERS,
AND STATESMEN

KINGS, RULERS, AND STATESMEN

Original Edition Compiled and Edited by
L. F. WISE and E.W. EGAN

Updated and Revised by
MARK HILLARY HANSEN, Ph.D.

STERLING PUBLISHING CO., INC.
NEW YORK

Library of Congress Cataloging-in-Publication Data Available

10   9   8   7   6   5   4   3   2   1

Published by Sterling Publishing Co., Inc.
387 Park Avenue South, New York, NY 10016
Revised Edition Copyright © 2005 Sterling Publishing Co., Inc.
Originally published and © 1967 by Sterling Publishing Co., Inc.
Distributed in Canada by Sterling Publishing
C/o Canadian Manda Group, 165 Dufferin Street
Toronto, Ontario, Canada M6K 3H6
Distributed in Great Britain by Chrysalis Books PLC
The Chrysalis Building, Bramley Road, London W10 6SP, England
Distributed in Australia by Capricorn Link (Australia) Pty Ltd.
P.O. Box 704, Windsor, NSW 2756, Australia

For information about custom editions, special sales, premium and
corporate purchases, please contact Sterling Special Sales Department
at 800-805-5489 or specialsales@sterlingpub.com.

Manufactured in the United States of America
All Rights Reserved

Sterling ISBN 13: 978-1-4027-2592-0
ISBN 10: 1-4027-2592-2

In memory of

Harry William Hansen
and
Mary Geraldine Hansen,

whose love of people from different lands showed
the true meaning of multiculturalism.

THE PLAN OF THIS VOLUME

The information in this volume is arranged alphabetically and chronologically according to various geographical, political, and historical criteria. The governing principle of organization is the roster of nation-states admitted to the United Nations as of the year 2005, which alone are listed by both the common name and, in parentheses, the official title. The reader will thus be able to determine whether a given entry represents a sovereign state recognized by the United Nations.

The contents-index follows the alphabetical and page order of the book. However, since certain subheadings relate to more than one general heading, numerous cross-references have been provided for geographically specific terms in the body of the text as well.

Important modern dependent states are included—Puerto Rico, for example—and follow the general alphabetical order. Defunct states with all or most of their territory now part of a single modern state are listed alphabetically under the heading of the modern state. In general, these subordinate territories appear alphabetically after the complete chronology of the major state which absorbed them—for example, Brittany, Burgundy, Champagne, etc., come after the chronology of France from Frankish times to the 5th Republic. Such states, along with the names of dynasties and historical periods are listed in the contents-index, with the geographic terms also cross-referenced in the body of the text.

For convenience, the following are also cross-referenced: former names of countries, e.g., Siam (*See* Thailand); geographical terms for areas formerly composed of many small states not well known to the average reader, e.g., Asia Minor; and countries where there is a geographical link, but not a clear historical and cultural link, e.g., Mauritania (*See* Morocco). Popular names, e.g., Holland, appear as cross-references.

Brief commentaries appear at the beginning of, and interspersed throughout, the chronological tables, providing such contextualizing information as: the origin of the country or the circumstances of its gaining independence; changes in government; and, in the case of defunct states, the causes of its fall. Further commentary is intended to place a human face on what might otherwise appear as a sterile recitation of facts.

Countries speaking major international languages written in the Latin alphabet are furnished with a translation key, since some monarchs are listed in the text under the English form of their Christian name, others under the native form. These countries are: Austria, Belgium, Brazil, France, Germany, Italy, Luxembourg, Monaco, Portugal, and Spain.

No attempt has been made to impart uniformity to names transliterated from Arabic, Chinese, and certain other languages. Since there is no universally accepted system of rendering these names in English, and since the data contained in this book originated from many different sources, Hussein and Hosein, Abdul and Abd-al, for example, may share the same page.

Decisions had to be made whether to list certain countries separately or under the general heading of another, e.g., Antioch. The fact that the modern city of Antioch is historically part of Syria, but currently part of Turkey, influenced the decision to list the Crusader Principality of Antioch separately.

The primary criterion for inclusion of personages in these lists is the holding of office as head of government. In some cases, such as constitutional monarchies, ceremonial heads of state have been listed as well. No claim is made, however, as to absolute accuracy in those numerous cases where the distinction between *de facto* and *de jure* authority is by no means clear. Indeed, such matters constitute legitimate grounds for debate, the settling of which lies beyond the purpose of this volume.

EDITORS' NOTE

This volume is an updated and revised version of the most complete listing of kings, rulers, and statesmen ever brought together under one cover. It is intended to serve the student and researcher by furnishing a starting point and guide to provide the general reader with a tool to quickly find the place of a given historical personage in the chronology of that leader's country. In this book are listed rulers and statesmen representing all modern independent states, some modern dependencies and protectorates of special interest, and significant states of the past, sovereign and semisovereign, the records of whose governments have survived. It also lists, in the case of the many nation-states emerging, material that is not available elsewhere in book form.

No claim is made that this volume is complete. There are obvious gaps in history which have been recognized by the compilers, and there are undoubtedly other gaps which kind readers will call to our attention. An attempt has been made to include all important personages and a large number of lesser ones, with available dates of birth, death, and tenure of office. Where the interests of clarity were served by indicating relationships between one person and another, these have been noted.

Perhaps most importantly, this book does not purport to address questions regarding the "legitimacy" of the governors or governments listed. In general, a given government's self-characterization has been taken at face value. Where editorial judgment was unavoidable in characterizing a given regime, the path deemed least controversial was chosen.

CONTENTS

KINGS, RULERS,
AND STATESMEN

Abyssinia *See* Ethiopia

Afghanistan (Islamic Republic of Afghanistan)

Once belonging to the Parthian, Sassanian, Mogul, and Persian empires, Afghanistan became an independent state in 1747.

1747–1773	Amir	Ahmad Shah	b. 1724 d. 1773
1773–1793	Amir	Timur Shah, son of Ahmad Shah	b. 1746 d. 1793
1793–1800	Amir	Zaman Mirza (Zaman Shah), son of Timur	deposed 1800
1800–1803	Amir	Mahmud Shah, son of Timur	deposed 1803
1803–1810	Amir	Shuja-ul-Mulk, son of Timur	
1810–1818	Amir	Mahmud Shah	
1818–1826		*Anarchy with Various Independent Khanates*	
1826–1839	Amir	Dost Mohammed Khan	deposed 1839 b. 1793 d. 1863
1839	Shah	Shuja	assassinated 1842
1839–1842	Shah	Akbar Khan, son of Dost Mohammed	d. 1849
1842–1863	Amir	Dost Mohammed	d. 1863
1863–1866	Amir	Ali Khan, son of Dost Mohammed	b. 1825 d. 1879
1866	Amir	Ufzul	d. 1867
1866–1869	Amir	Azim	d. 1869
1869–1879	Amir	Sher Ali Khan	
1879	Amir	Yakub Khan, son of Sher Ali	abd. 1879 b. 1849 d. 1923
1880–1901	Amir	Abdir Rahman Khan, grandson of Dost Mohammed	b. 1845 d. 1901
1901–1919	King	Habibullah, son of Abdir Rahman	b. 1872 assassinated 1919
1919–1929	King	Amanullah Khan	abdicated 1929 b. 1892 d. 1951
1929	King	Habibullah	executed 1929
1929–1933	King	Nadir Shah, cousin of Amanullah	b. 1880 assassinated 1933
1933–1973	King	Zahir Shah, son of Nadir Shah	b. 1914
1973–1978	President	Sardar Mohammad Daoud	assassinated
1978–1979	Marxist leader	Nur Muhammad Taraki	deposed
1979	Marxist leader	Hafizullah Amin	killed
1979–1986	Marxist leader	Babrak Karmal	deposed
1986–1992	Marxist leader	Muhhamad Najibullah	
1992–2001		*Rule of the Mujahidin and the Taliban Overthrown*	
2001–2004		*Transitional Government with New Constitution*	
2004–	President	Hamid Karzai	

Albania (Republic of Albania) *See also* Epirus

1443–1468	National leader	Scanderbeg (Iskender Bey)	b. 1403? d. 1468
1468–1912		*Under Turkish Suzerainty*	
1914	King	Wilhelm Zu Wied	b. 1876 d. 1945
1914	First Minister	Essad Pasha	b. 1863 assassinated 1920
1914–1916	President	Essad Pasha	

After a period of internal disorder and Italian, Yugoslav, and other foreign interventions, Albania gained its independence in 1921.

1922–1924	Prime Minister	Ahmed bey Zogu	b. 1895 d. 1961
1925–1928	President	Ahmed bey Zogu	
1928–1946	King	Zog I (Ahmed bey Zogu)	

Occupied by Italy from 1939 to 1943

Occupied by Germany from 1943 to 1944

1944–1985	Stalinist dictator	Enver Hoxha	died
1985–1991		*Unstable Communist Government Voted Out*	
1992–1997	President	Sali Ram Berisha	resigned
1997–2002		*Transition to Democracy*	
2002–	President	Alfred Moisiu	

Algeria (People's Democratic Republic of Algeria) *See also* Numidia

Algeria was annexed to France in 1842 and became independent in 1962.

1962–1965	President	Ahmed Ben Bella	
1965–1978	President	Houari Boumedienne	died
1979–1992	President	Chadli Bendjedid	resigned
1992	President	Mohamed Boudiaf	assassinated
1992–1995		*General disorder*	
1995–1999	President	Liamine Zeroual	resigned
1999–	President	Abdelaziz Bouteflika	

Andorra (Principality of Andorra)

Andorra was created as a principality in 1278 with nominal co-heads of state: the Bishop of Urgel, Spain, and the head of the French government (formerly the King of France and now the President of the French Republic). The two co-princes are represented by viguiers. Under the constitution, democratically adopted in 1993, the co-princes and their local representatives are retained while an executive head of government is established.

1994–	Head of Government	Marc Forne Molne	

Angola (Republic of Angola)

Colonized by the Portuguese in 1575, the nation gained independence in 1975, and has been governed by the successful MPLA (Popular Movement for the Liberation of Angola).

1979–	President	José Eduardo dos Santos	

Annam *See* Vietnam

Antigua and Barbuda (Official U.N. Name)

A member of the British Commonwealth, full independence was gained in 1981.

1981–1994	Prime Minister	Vere Cornwall Bird	retired
1994–2004	Prime Minister	Lester Bird	party voted out
2004–	Prime Minister	Baldwin Spencer	

Antioch *See also* Syria; Turkey

The Principality of Antioch was founded by the Crusader Bohemond, son of Robert Guiscard.

1098–1111	Prince	Bohemond I	b. 1056 d. 1111
1111–1131	Prince	Bohemond II	
1131–1163	Princess	Constance (co-ruler)	d. 1163
1131–1149	Prince	Raymond (co ruler)	d. 1149
1163–1201	Prince	Bohemond III	
1201–1233	Prince	Bohemond IV	
1233–1251	Prince	Bohemond V	
1251–1268	Prince	Bohemond VI	
		Fell to Egyptian Mamelukes in 1268	

Apulia and Calabria *See* Italy

Arabia *See* Bahrain; Kuwait; Oman; Qatar; Saudi Arabia; United Arab Emirates; Yemen

Aragon, Kingdom of *See* Spain

Argentina (Argentine Republic)

Argentina was discovered in 1516 by Spain, which ruled it from 1553 to 1816. It was then controlled by a junta from 1810.

1826–1827	President	Bernardino Rivadavia	b. 1780	d. 1845
1827–1828	President	Vicente López y Planes	b. 1784	d. 1856
1828–1835		*Period of anarchy*		
1835–1852	Dictator	Juan Manuel de Rosas	b. 1793	d. 1877
1854–1860	President	Justo José de Urquiza	b. 1800	d. 1870
1860–1861	President	Santiago Derqui	b. 1846	d. 1891
1861	President	Juan Esteban Pedernera	b. 1796	d. 1886
1862–1868	President	Bartolomé Mitre	b. 1821	d. 1906
1868–1874	President	Domingo Faustino Sarmiento	b. 1811	d. 1888
1874–1880	President	Nicolás Avellaneda	b. 1837	d. 1885
1880–1886	President	Julio A. Roca	b. 1843	d. 1914
1886–1890	President	Miguel Juárez Celmán	b. 1844	d. 1909
1890–1892	President	Carlos Pellegrini	b. 1846	d. 1906
1892–1895	President	Luis Sáenz Peña	b. 1822	d. 1907
1895–1898	President	José Evaristo Uriburu	b. 1831	d. 1914
1898–1904	President	Julio A. Roca		
1904–1906	President	Manuel Quintana	b. 1835	d. 1906
1906–1910	President	José Figueroa Alcorta	b. 1860	d. 1931
1910–1914	President	Roque Sáenz Peña	b. 1851	d. 1914
1914–1916	President	Victorino de la Plaza	b. 1840	d. 1919
1916–1922	President	Hipólito Irigoyen	b. 1852	d. 1933
1922–1928	President	Marcelo Torcuato de Alvear	b. 1868	d. 1942
1928–1930	President	Hipólito Irigoyen		
1930–1932	President	José Felix Uriburu	b. 1868	d. 1932
1932–1938	President	Agustín P. Justo	b. 1878	d. 1943
1938–1941	President	Roberto M. Ortiz	b. 1886	d. 1942
1941–1943	President	Ramón S. Castillo	b. 1873	d. 1944
1943–1944	President	Pedro Ramírez	b. 1884	d. 1962
1944–1946	President	Edelmiro J. Farrell	b. 1887	
1946–1955	President	Juan Domingo Perón	b. 1895	
1955	President	Eduardo Lonardi	b. 1896	d. 1956
1955–1958	President	Pedro Eugenio Aramburu		
1958–1962	President	Arturo Frondizi		
1962–1963	President	José Maria Guido		

1963–1966	President	Arturo Umberto Illia
1966–1970	President	Juan Carlos Ongania
1970–1971	President	Roberto Levingston
1971–1973	President	Alejandro Lanusse
1973–1973	President	Héctor Cámpora
1973–1974	President	Juan Domingo Perón
1974–1976	President	Isabel Martínez Perón
1976–1981	President	Roberto Viola
1981–1982	President	Leopoldo Fortunato Galtieri
1982–1983	President	Reynaldo Benito Antonio Bignone
1983–1989	President	Raul Alfonsín
1989–1999	President	Carlos Menem
1999–2001	President	Fernando de la Rua
2001	President	Adolfo Rodriguez Saa
2002–2003	President	Eduardo Duahalde
2003–	President	Nestor Kirchner

Armenia (Republic of Armenia)

Under Median, Persian, and Macedonian rule until 331 B.C. and then under the Seleucids until 301 B.C., Armenia emerged as an independent kingdom around 200 B.C.

189 B.C.–	King	Artaxias	
?	King	Guras	
?	King	Tigranes I	
c. 100	King	Artavasdes II	
94–56	King	Tigranes II	d. 56
		Became Vassal-state of Rome in 66 B.C.	
c. 30	King	Artavasdes III	

■ Arscacid Dynasty (From A.D. 63)

The Arscacid dynasty was under Byzantines, Persians, and Arabs.

? –216	King	Vagarshak
217–?	King	Tiridates II
252–?	King	Artavasdes (Parthian puppet)
287–?	King	Tiridates III
330–339	King	Khosrov II
428–?	King	Artaxias IV

■ Bagratid Dynasty

By 1022 Armenia had split into several principalities and came under Byzantine, Seljuk, Mongol, and eventually Ottoman rule. The state of Lesser Armenia, west of the Taurus Mountains, remained independent.

885–?	King	Ashot I
922??	King	Ashot II the Iron
952–977	King	Ashot III

■ Lesser Armenia

In 1375 Lesser Armenia fell to the Mamelukes and later to the Ottomans.

1092–1100	Prince Constantine I		
1100–1129	Prince	Thoros I	
1129–1139	Prince	Leo I	
1145–1168	Prince	Thoros II	
1170–1175	Prince	Mleh	
1187–1219	King	Leo II	
1219–1226	Queen	Zabel	
1226–1269	King	Hayton	
1320–1342	King	Leo V	
1342–1344	King	Guy of Lusignan	
1344–?	King	Constantine IV	
?–1374	King	Constantine V	assassinated 1374

■ Modern Armenia

The northern part of Armenia came under Russian rule in 1813. In 1917 Russian Armenia broke free and joined the Transcaucasian Republic with Georgia and Azerbaijan. It became a separate state in 1918.

1918–1920	Premier	R. I. Kachaznuni
	Foreign Minister	A. I. Khatisian
		In 1920 Armenia was invaded by the Soviet Army and became a republic of the Soviet Union. Armenians voted overwhelmingly for independence from the Soviet Union in 1991.
1991–1998	President	Levon Ter-Petrossian
1998–	President	Robert Kocharian

Aruba

Seceding from the Netherlands Antilles to become an autonomous member of the Kingdom of the Netherlands in 1986, Aruba has full autonomy in all customary spheres of government except defense, foreign affairs, and the supreme judiciary.

1986–1989	Prime Minister	Henny Eman
1989–1994	Prime Minister	Nelson O. Oduber

1994–2001	Prime Minister	Henny Eman
2001–	Prime Minister	Nelson O. Oduber

Asia Minor *See* Bithynia; Cappadocia; Hittite Empire; Lydia; Pergamum; Pontus; Turkey

Assyria

Assyria flourished from about 2500 B.C. It was first ruled by priest-kings.

1410–1393 B.C.	King	Ashur-nadir-ahe	
1392–1381	King	Enib-Adad	
1380–1341	King	Ashur-yuballidh	
1340–1326	King	Enlil-nirari	
1325–1311	King	Arik-den-ili	
1310–1281	King	Adadnirari I	
1280–1261	King	Shalmaneser I, great-great-grandson of Ashur-yuballidh	
1260–1232	King	Tukulti-Ninurta I, son of Shalmaneser I	
1231–1214	King	Ashur nasir pal I	
1213–1208	King	Ashur-nirari III	
1207–1203	King	Bel-Kudur-uzur	
1202–1176	King	Ninurta-apal-ekur I	
1175–1141	King	Ashur-dan I	
1140–1138	King	Ninurta-tutulti-Assur	
1137–1128	King	Mutakkil-Nusku	
1127–1116	King	Ashur-res-isi	
1115–1103	King	Tiglath-pileser I	
1102–1093	King	Ninurta-apal-ekur II	
1092–1076	King	Ashur-bel-kala I	
1075–1069	King	Enlil-rabi	
1061–1056	King	Enriba-Adad	
1055–1050	King	Shamshi-Adad IV	d. 103
1049–1031	King	Ashurnasirpal I	
1030–1019	King	Shalmaneser II	
1018–1013	King	Ashur-nirari IV	
1012–995	King	Ashur-rabi II	
994–967	King	Ashur-res-isi II	
956–934	King	Tiglath-pileser II	
933–912	King	Assur-dan II	

911–891	King	Adadnirari II	
890–885	King	Tukulti-Ninurta II, son of Adadnirari II	
884–860	King	Ashurnasirpal II	
859–825	King	Shalmaneser III, son of Ashurnasirpal II	
824–812	King	Shamshi-Adad V, son of Shalmaneser III	
811–783	King	Adadnirari III, son of Shamshi-Adad V	
782–773	King	Shalmaneser IV	
772–764	King	Ashur-dan III	
763–755	King	Hadad-nirari IV	
754–747	King	Ashur-nirari V	
746–728	King	Tiglath-pileser III (Pul)	d. 728
727–722	King	Shalmaneser V	d. 722
722–705	King	Sargon II	killed 705
705–682	King	Sennacherib, son of Sargon II	murdered 682

Sennacherib, after a stormy reign, is noted for the destruction of Babylon. He was murdered by his sons.

681–668	King	Esarhaddon, son of Sennacherib	d. 668
668–626	King	Ashurbanipal, son of Esarhaddon	d. 626
632–629	King	Ashur-etil-ilani	
629–612	King	Sin-sar-iskun, brother of Ashur-etil-ilani	

The Assyrian capital fell to the Scythians in 612 B.C.

Asturias *See* Spain

Australia (Commonwealth of Australia)

No known organized government existed in Australia prior to British settlement. The Commonwealth of Australia was established in 1901.

■ Colony of New South Wales (Founded in 1788)

1788–1792	Captain-General	Captain Arthur Philip, R.N.
1792–1794	Administrator	Major Francis Grose
1794–1795	Administrator	Captain William Patterson
1795–1800	Governor	Captain John Hunter, R.N.
1800–1806	Governor	Captain Philip Gidley King, R.N.
1806–1808	Governor	Captain William Bligh, R.N.
1808	Administrator	Lt.-Colonel George Johnston
1808–1809	Administrator	Major Joseph Foveaux
1809	Administrator	Colonel William Patterson

1810–1821	Governor	Major-General Lachlan Macquarie
1821–1825	Governor	Major-General Sir Thomas Brisbane
1825	Administrator	Lt.-Colonel William Stewart
1825–1831	Governor	Lt.-General Ralph Darling
1831	Administrator	Colonel Patrick Lindesay
1831–1837	Governor	Sir Richard Bourke
1837–1838	Administrator	Lt.-Colonel Kenneth Snodgrass
1838–1846	Governor	Sir George Gipps
1846	Administrator	Sir Maurice Charles O'Connell
1846–1851	Governor	Sir Charles Augustus Fitz Roy
1851–1855	Captain-General	Sir Charles Augustus Fitz Roy
1855–1861	Captain-General	Sir William Thomas Denison
1861	Administrator	Lt.-Colonel J. F. Kempt
1861–1867	Captain-General	Sir John Young (later Baron Lisgar)
1867–1868	Administrator	Sir Trevor Chute
1868–1872	Governor	Earl of Belmore
1872	Administrator	Sir Alfred Stephen
1872–1879	Governor	Sir Hercules Robinson (later Baron Rosmead)
1879	Administrator	Sir Alfred Stephen
1879–1885	Governor	Lord Augustus William Spencer Loftus
1885	Administrator	Sir Alfred Stephen
1885–1890	Governor	Baron Carrington
1890–1891	Administrator	Sir Alfred Stephen
1891–1893	Governor	Earl of Jersey
1893	Administrator	Sir Frederick Darley
1893–1895	Governor	Sir Robert William Duff
1895	Administrator	Sir Frederick Darley
1895–1899	Governor	Viscount Hampden
1899–1901	Governor	Earl Beauchamp

Entered Commonwealth of Australia in 1901

■ Colony of Tasmania (Dependency of New South Wales from 1803 to 1825)

1825–1836	Lieutenant-Governor	Colonel George Arthur
1836–1837	Administrator	Lt.-Colonel Kenneth Snodgrass
1837–1843	Lieutenant-Governor	Sir John Franklin
1843–1846	Lieutenant-Governor	Sir John Eardley-Wilmot
1846–1847	Administrator	Charles Joseph La Trobe

1847–1855	Lieutenant-Governor	Sir William Thomas Denison
1855–1861	Governor-in-Chief	Sir Henry Edward Fox Young
1861–1862	Administrator	Colonel Thomas Gore Browne
1862–1868	Governor	Colonel Thomas Gore Browne
1868–1869	Administrator	Lt.-Colonel W. C. Trevor
1869–1874	Governor	Charles Du Cane
1874–1875	Administrator	Sir Francis Smith
1875–1880	Governor	Frederick Aloysius Weld
1880	Administrator	Sir Francis Smith
1880–1881	Administrator	Sir John Henry Lefroy
1881–1886	Governor	Sir George Strahan
1886	Administrator	Chief Justice W. R. Giblin
1886–1887	Administrator	Sir William Dobson
1887–1892	Governor	Sir Robert Crookshank Hamilton
1892–1893	Administrator	Sir William Dobson
1893–1900	Governor	Viscount Gormanston

Entered Commonwealth of Australia in 1901

■ Colony of Western Australia

1829–1832	Lieutenant-Governor	Captain James Stirling, R.N.
1832	Governor	Captain James Stirling, R.N.
1832–1833	Administrator	Captain F. C. Irwin
1833–1834	Administrator	Captain Richard Daniell
1834	Administrator	Captain Picton Beete
1834–1839	Governor	Sir James Stirling
1839–1846	Governor	John Hutt
1846–1847	Governor	Lt.-Colonel Andrew Clarke
1847–1848	Governor	Lt.-Colonel F. C. Irwin
1848–1855	Governor	Captain Charles Fitzgerald
1855–1862	Governor	Arthur Edward Kennedy
1862	Administrator	Lt.-Colonel John Bruce
1862–1868	Governor	John Stephen Hampton
1868–1869	Administrator	Lt.-Colonel John Bruce
1869–1875	Governor	Frederick Aloysius Weld
1875	Administrator	Lt.-Colonel E. D. Harvest
1875–1877	Governor	William C. F. Robinson
1877	Lieutenant-Governor	Lt.-Colonel E. D. Harvest
1877–1878	Lieutenant-Governor	Sir Harry St. George Ord

1878–1880	Governor	Sir Harry St. George Ord
1880–1883	Governor	Sir William F. C. Robinson
1883	Administrator	Henry Thomas Wrenfordsley
1883–1889	Governor	Sir Frederick Napier Broome
1889–1890	Administrator	Sir Malcolm Fraser
1890–1895	Governor	Sir William C. F. Robinson
1895	Administrator	Sir Alexander Campbell Onslow
1895–1900	Governor	Sir Gerard Smith
1900–1901	Administrator	Sir Alexander Campbell Onslow

Entered Commonwealth of Australia in 1901

■ Colony of South Australia (Colony established in 1836)

1836–1838	Governor	Captain John Hindmarsh, R.N.
1838	Administrator	George Milner Stephen
1838–1841	Resident Commissioner	Lt.-Colonel George Gawler
1841–1845	Governor	Captain George Grey
1845–1848	Lieutenant-Governor	Lt.-Colonel Frederick Holt Robe
1848–1854	Lieutenant-Governor	Sir Henry Edward Fox Young
1854–1855	Administrator	Boyle Travers Finiss
1855–1862	Captain-General	Sir Richard Graves MacDonnell
1862–1868	Governor	Sir Dominick Daly
1868–1869	Administrator	Lt.-Colonel Francis Gilbert Hamley
1869–1873	Governor	Sir James Ferguson
1872–1873	Administrator	Sir Richard Davies Hanson
1873–1877	Governor	Sir Anthony Musgrave
1877	Administrator	Chief Justice S. J. Way
1877	Administrator	Sir W. W. Cairns
1877	Administrator	Chief Justice. S. J. Way
1877–1883	Governor	Sir William Francis Drummond Jervois
1883	Administrator	Chief Justice S. J. Way
1883–1889	Governor	Sir William C. F. Robinson
1889	Administrator	Chief Justice S. J. Way
1889–1895	Governor	Earl of Kintore
1895	Administrator	Chief Justice S. J. Way
1895–1899	Governor	Sir Thomas Fowell Buxton
1899–1900	Governor	Baron Tennyson

Entered Commonwealth of Australia in 1901

■ Colony of Victoria (Detached from New South Wales in 1851)

1851–1854	Lieutenant-Governor	Charles Joseph La Trobe
1854	Administrator	John Vesey Fitzgerald
1854–1855	Lieutenant-Governor	Sir Charles Hotham
1855	Governor-in-Chief	Sir Charles Hotham
1856	Administrator	Major-General Edward Macarthur
1856–1863	Governor-in-Chief	Sir Henry Barkly
1863–1866	Governor	Sir Charles Henry Darling
1866	Administrator	Brigadier-General G. J. Carey
1866–1873	Governor	Sir John Manners-Sutton
1873–1879	Governor	Sir George Ferguson Bowen
1879–1884	Governor	Marquess of Normanby
1884	Administrator	Sir William Foster Stawell
1884–1889	Governor	Sir Henry Brougham Loch
1889	Administrator	Sir William C. F. Robinson
1889–1895	Governor	Earl of Hopetoun
1895	Administrator	Sir John Madden
1895–1900	Governor	Baron Brassey
1900–1901	Administrator	Sir John Madden

Entered Commonwealth of Australia in 1901

■ Colony of Queensland (Detached from New South Wales in 1859)

1859–1868	Governor-in-Chief	Sir George Ferguson Bowen
1868	Administrator	Sir Maurice Charles O'Connell
1868–1871	Governor	Colonel Samuel Wensley Blackall
1871	Administrator	Sir Maurice Charles O'Connell
1871–1874	Governor	Marquess of Normanby
1874–1875	Administrator	Sir Maurice Charles O'Connell
1875–1877	Governor	William Wellington Cairns
1877	Administrator	Sir Maurice Charles O'Connell
1877–1883	Governor	Sir Arthur Edward Kennedy
1883	Administrator	Sir Arthur Hunter Palmer
1883–1888	Governor	Sir Anthony Musgrave
1888–1889	Administrator	Sir Arthur Hunter Palmer
1889–1895	Governor	Sir Henry Wylie Norman
1895–1896	Administrator	Sir Arthur Hunter Palmer
1896–1900	Governor	Baron Lamington

Entered Commonwealth of Australia in 1901

■ Commonwealth
Governors-General and Administrators

1901–1903	Governor-General	Lord Linlithgow, Earl of Hopetoun	b. 1860 d. 1908
1902–1903	Governor-General (acting)	Hallam Tennyson, Baron Tennyson	
1903–1904	Governor-General	Hallam Tennyson, Baron Tennyson	b. 1852 d. 1928
1904–1908	Governor-General	Henry Stafford Northcote, Baron Northcote	b. 1846 d. 1911
1908–1911	Governor-General	Earl of Dudley (William Humble Ward)	b. 1867 d. 1932
1909–1910	Governor-General (acting)	Viscount Chelmsford	b. 1868 d. 1933
1911–1914	Governor-General	Thomas Denman, Baron Denman	b. 1874 d. 1954
1914–1920	Governor-General	Viscount Novar of Raith	b. 1860 d. 1934
1920–1925	Governor-General	Baron Forster of Lepe	b. 1866 d. 1936
1925–1930	Governor-General	Baron Stonehaven	b. 1874 d. 1941
1930–1931	Administrator	Baron Somers	b. 1887 d. 1944
1931–1936	Governor-General	Sir Isaac Alfred Isaacs	b. 1885 d. 1948
1936–1945	Governor-General	Baron Gowrie (Alexander Gore Arkwright Hore-Ruthven)	b. 1872 d. 1955
1938	Governor-General	Baron Huntingfield (in absence of Lord Gowrie)	b. 1883
1944–1945	Governor-General	Sir Winston J. Dugan	b. 1877 d. 1951
1945–1947	Governor-General	Prince Henry, Duke of Gloucester	b. 1900
1947	Governor-General	Sir Winston J. Dugan	
1947–1953	Governor-General	Sir William John McKell	b. 1891
1951	Officer-Administrator	Sir John Northcott	b. 1890
1953–1960	Governor-General	Sir William Slim	b. 1891

Field Marshal Viscount Slim took command of the 14th ("forgotten") Army in Burma in 1943 and led them to victory over the Japanese.

1956	Administrator	Sir John Northcott	
1959	Administrator	Sir Reginald Alexander Dallas Brooks	b. 1896
1960–1961	Governor-General	William Shepherd, Viscount Dunrossil	b. 1893 d. 1961
1961	Administrator	Sir Reginald Alexander Dallas Brooks	
1961–1965	Governor-General	Viscount De L'Isle	b. 1909
1965–1969	Governor-General	Lord Casey of Berwick	b. 1890 d. 1976
1969–1974	Governor-General	Sir Paul Meernaa Caedwalla Hasluck	b. 1905 d. 1993
1974–1977	Governor-General	Sir John Robert Kerr	b. 1914 d. 1991
1977–1982	Governor-General	Sir Zelman Cowen	b. 1919
1982–1989	Governor-General	Sir Ninian Stephen	b. 1923
1989–1996	Governor-General	William George Hayden	b. 1933
1996–2001	Governor-General	Sir William Patrick Deane	b. 1931

2001–2003	Governor-General	Rev. Dr. Peter Hollingworth	b. 1935
2003–	Governor-General	Michael Jeffrey	b. 1937

Prime Ministers

1901–1903	Prime Minister	Sir Edmund Barton	b. 1849 d. 1920
1903–1904	Prime Minister	Alfred Deakin	b. 1856 d. 1919
1904	Prime Minister	J. C. Watson	b. 1867 d. 1941
1904–1905	Prime Minister	Sir George Reid	b. 1845 d. 1918
1905–1908	Prime Minister	Alfred Deakin	
1908–1909	Prime Minister	Andrew Fisher	b. 1862 d. 1928
1909–1910	Prime Minister	Alfred Deakin	
1910–1913	Prime Minister	Andrew Fisher	
1913–1914	Prime Minister	Sir Joseph Cook	b. 1860 d. 1947
1914–1915	Prime Minister	Andrew Fisher	
1915–1923	Prime Minister	William Morris Hughes	b. 1864 d. 1952
1923–1929	Prime Minister	Stanley Melbourne, Viscount Bruce	b. 1883
1929–1932	Prime Minister	James Henry Scullin	b. 1876 d. 1953
1932–1939	Prime Minister	Joseph Aloysius Lyons	b. 1879 d. 1939
1939	Prime Minister	Sir Earle Page	b. 1880 d. 1961
1939–1941	Prime Minister	Robert Gordon Menzies	b. 1894 d. 1978
1941	Prime Minster	Arthur William Fadden	b. 1894 d. 1973
1941–1945	Prime Minister	John Curtin	b. 1885 d. 1945
1945 (1 week)	Prime Minister	Francis Michael Forde	b. 1890 d. 1983
1945–1949	Prime Minister	Ben Chifley	b. 1885 d. 1951
1949–1966	Prime Minister	Robert Gordon Menzies	
1966–1967	Prime Minister	Harold Holt	b. 1908 d. 1967
1967–1968	Prime Minister	John McEwan	b. 1900 d. 1980
1968–1971	Prime Minister	John Grey Gorton	b. 1911 d. 2002
1971–1972	Prime Minister	William McMahon	b. 1908 d. 1988
1972–1975	Prime Minister	Gough Whitlam	b. 1916
1975–1983	Prime Minister	John Malcolm Fraser	b. 1930
1983–1991	Prime Minister	Robert James Lee Hawke	b. 1929
1991–1996	Prime Minister	Paul John Keating	b. 1944
1996–	Prime Minister	John Winston Howard	b. 1939

Austria (Republic of Austria)

Austria owes its name and its beginnings to Charlemagne, who set up his easternmost conquests in 788 as the East Mark, later Oesterreich (East Realm).

English versions of the names of rulers of German-speaking states are:

Albert–Adalbert, Albrecht	Frederick–Friedrich	Louis–Ludwig
Charles–Karl	George–Georg	Maurice–Moritz
Ernest–Ernst	Henry–Heinrich	Philip–Philipp
Eugene–Eugen	Joseph–Josef	William–Wilhelm
Francis–Franz	John–Johann	

■ House of Babenberg

976–994	Margrave	Leopold I	
994–1018	Margrave	Henry I, son of Leopold I	
1018–1055	Margrave	Adalbert, son of Leopold I	
1055–1075	Margrave	Ernst, son of Adalbert	
1075–1096	Margrave	Leopold II, son of Ernst	
1096–1136	Margrave	Leopold III, the Pious, son of Leopold II	canonized 1485
1136–1141	Margrave	Leopold IV, son of Leopold III	
1141–1156	Margrave	Henry II, brother of Leopold IV	b. 1114 d. 1177
1156–1177	Duke	Henry II, grandfather of Leopold VI	
1177 1194	Duke	Leopold V, son of Henry II	
1194–1198	Duke	Frederick I, son of Leopold V	
1198–1230	Duke	Leopold VI, the Glorious, brother of Frederick I	b. 1176 d. 1230
1230–1246	Duke	Frederick II, brother of Leopold VI	
1246–1248		*Given to the Empire.*	
1248–1250	Duke	Hermann von Baden, nephew-in-law of Frederick II	
1250–1253		*Anarchy with Several Claimants*	
1253–1276	King	Ottokar II of Bohemia	b. 1230? killed 1278

■ Habsburg Dynasty

The Counts of Habsburg were originally in Switzerland from 1023 to 1276.
The dynasty ruled Austria—and much more—from 1276 to 1918.

1276–1282	Duke	Rudolf I, son of Albert IV of Habsburg	b. 1218 d. 1291
		Rudolf I was a comparatively unimportant German count who was made king by the Electors of the Rhine to counter the influence of the King of Bohemia. His descendants ruled Austria for 642 years.	
1282–1308	Duke	Albert I, son of Rudolf I	b. 1250? murdered 1308
1308–1330	Duke	Frederick, son of Albert I	b. 1286? d. 1330

1308–1326	Co-regent	Leopold I, son of Albert I	b. 1290? d. 1326
1330–1358	Duke	Albert II, son of Albert I	
1330–1339	Co-regent	Otto, son of Albert I	
1358–1365	Duke	Rudolf, son of Albert II	
1358–1397	Duke	Albert III, son of Albert II	
1365–1379	Co-regent	Leopold III, son of Albert II	b. 1351 killed 1386

Austria Divided between Albert III and Leopold III in 1379

■ Line of Albert

1379–1395	Duke	Albert III	
1397–1404	Duke	Albert IV, son of Albert III	
1404–1439	Duke	Albert V, son of Albert IV (Holy Roman Emperor 1438)	b. 1397 d. 1439
1440–1457	Duke	Ladislaus, son of Albert V	

■ Line of Leopold

1379–1386	Duke	Leopold III	
1386–1406	Duke	William, son of Leopold III	
1386–1411	Duke	Leopold IV, son of Leopold III	
1406–1424	Duke	Ernst, son of Leopold III	
1457–1463	Duke	Albert VI, brother of Frederick	
1457–1493	Archduke	Frederick V, cousin of Ladislaus (Holy Roman Emperor 1440)	b. 1415 d. 1493
1493–1519	Archduke	Maximilian, son of Frederick V	b. 1459 d. 1519
1519–1522	Archduke	Charles, grandson of Maximilian I (Holy Roman Emperor 1519)	b. 1500 d. 1558
1519–1564	Archduke	Ferdinand, brother of Charles (Holy Roman Emperor 1556)	b. 1503

(See Holy Roman Empire for the period 1564–1806)

1804–1835	Emperor	Francis I (Holy Roman Emperor 1792)	b. 1768 d. 1835
1835–1848	Emperor	Ferdinand I, son of Francis I abdicated 1848	b. 1793 d. 1875
1848–1916	Emperor	Francis Joseph, nephew of Ferdinand I	b. 1830 d. 1916

Francis Joseph was partly educated by Metternich. After revoking the constitution, he bore the entire responsibility of governing his vast domains personally. His rule was generally oppressive and absolutist, but he genuinely wanted peace. He experienced tragedy in his personal life, as his wife was assassinated and his son Rudolf committed suicide.

| 1916–1918 | Emperor | Charles I, grand-nephew of Francis Joseph | b. 1887 d. 1922 |

Austria Became a Republic in 1918

| 1920–1928 | President | Michael Hainisch | b. 1858 d. 1940 |

| 1928–1938 | President | Wilhelm Miklas | b. 1872 d. 1956 |

Annexed by Germany in 1938

| 1938–1939 | German Governor-General | Arthur Jon Seyss-Inquart | b. 1892 hanged 1946 |

Second Republic Established in 1945

1945–1950	President	Karl Renner	b. 1870 d. 1950
1951–1957	President	Theodor Körner	b. 1873 d. 1957
1957–1965	President	Adolf Schärf	b. 1890 d. 1965
1965–1974	President	Franz Jonas	b. 1899 d. 1974
1974–1986	President	Rudolf Kirchschläger	b. 1915 d. 2000
1986–1992	President	Kurt Waldheim	b. 1918
1992–2004	President	Thomas Klestil	b. 1932
2004–	President	Heinz Fischer	b. 1938

■ Statesmen

| 1753–1792 | Chancellor | Wenzel Anton von Kaunitz | b. 1711 d. 1794 |
| 1821–1848 | Chancellor | Klemens Wenzel Nepomuk Lothar von Metternich | b. 1773 d. 1859 |

Metternich had complete control of Austrian affairs for forty years. He negotiated the marriage between Marie Louise and Napoleon and presided at the Congress of Vienna. Even during the last eight years of his life, he continued to influence events.

1868–1870	Prime Minister	Eduard von Taaffe	b. 1833 d. 1895
1879–1893	Prime Minister	Eduard von Taaffe	
1919–1920	Chancellor	Karl Renner	b. 1870 d. 1950
1932–1934	Chancellor	Engelbert Dollfuss	b. 1892 assassinated 1934
1934–1938	Chancellor	Kurt Edler von Schuschnigg	b. 1897
1945–1953	Chancellor	Leopold Figl	b. 1902 d. 1965
1953–1961	Chancellor	Julius Raab	b. 1891 d. 1964
1961–1964	Chancellor	Alfons Gorbach	b. 1898
1964–1970	Chancellor	Josef Klaus	b. 1910 d. 2001
1970–1983	Chancellor	Bruno Kreisky	b. 1911 d. 1990
1983–1986	Chancellor	Fred Sinowatz	b.1929
1986–1997	Chancellor	Franz Vranitzky	b. 1937
1997–2000	Chancellor	Viktor Klima	b. 1947
2000–	Chancellor	Wolfgang Schussel	b. 1945

Azerbaijan (Republic of Azerbaijan)

Called Atropatene by the Greeks, Azerbaijan was ruled by the Macedonians and Persians prior to the 7th century. It fell to the Byzantines, the Arabs (642), the Seljuks (11th century), the Mongols (1236 to 1498), and the Persians until annexed by Russia in 1813. It was part of the Transcaucasian Republic from 1917 to 1918, when it declared independence.

1918–1919	Chief of State	Khan Khoiski	d. 1920
1919–1920	Chief of State	Nazim Beg Usubekov	

Conquered by Russian Army and Made a Soviet Republic in 1920
Declared Independence from the U.S.S.R. in 1991

1991–1992	President	Ayaz Mutalibov
1992–1993	President	Abulfez Elchibey
1993–2003	President	Heydar Aliyev
2003–	President	Ilham Aliyev

Aztec Civilization *See* Mexico

Babylonia

The Babylonian Empire united the territories of several city-states, one being Akkad. The most famous rulers of Akkad were Sargon I (c. 2637–2582 B.C.) and Naram-Sin (c. 2550 B.C.).

■ First Dynasty

2049–2036 B.C.	King	Sumuabi
2035–2000	King	Sumu-la-ilu, son of Sumuabi
1967–1948	King	Sin-muballit
1947–1905	King	Hammurabi (or Hammurapi or Khammurabi)
1904–1867	King	Samsu-iluna
1866–1839	King	Abeshuh
1838–1802	King	Ammi-ditana
1801–1781	King	Ammi-zaduga
1780–1750	King	Samsuditana

Unknown Dynasty of Eleven Kings

■ Kassite Dynasty 1746–1171

1521–1503 B.C.	King	Burnaburiash I
1502–1484	King	Kashtiliash II
1483–1465	King	Agum III
1445–1427	King	Karaindash
1344–1320	King	Kurigalza III

1319–1294	King	Nazimaruttash II	
1293–1277	King	Kadashman-Turgu	
1276–1271	King	Kadashman-Enlil II	
1270–1263	King	Kudur-Enlil	
1262–1250	King	Sagarakti-Suriash	
1249–1242	King	Kastiash III	
1232–1203	King	Adad-shum-nasir	
1202–1188	King	Melishipah II	
1187–1175	King	Merodach (Marduk)-baladan I	
1174	King	Zabada-sum-iddin	
1173–1171	King	Enlil-nadin-ahe	

■ Elamite Dynasty 1170–730

1170–1153	King	Merodash (Marduk)-shapik-zer	
1152–1147	King	Ninurta-nadin-shumi	
1146–1123	King	Nebuchadnezzar	
1123–1117	King	Enlil-nadin-apli	
1116–1101	King	Merodach (Marduk)-nadin-ahe	
1100–1092	King	Itti-Marduk-balatu	
1091–1084	King	Merodach (Marduk)-shapik-zer-mati	
1083–1062	King	Adad-apal-iddin	
990–955	King	Nabo-mukin-apli	
954	King	Ninurta-kudur-usur	
953–942	King	Marbiti-ahe-iddin	
941–901	King	Samas-mudaminiq	
900–886	King	Nabo-shum-ukin	
885–852	King	Nabo-apal-iddin	
851–828	King	Merodach (Marduk)-zakir-shum	
827–815	King	Merodach (Marduk)-balatsuiqbi	
814–811	King	Bau-ahe-iddin	
802–763	King	Eriba-Marduk	
747–734	King	Nabonassar	d. 734
734–733	King	Nadinu	
752–730	King	Ukin-zer	
729–728	King	Tiglathpileser III (of Assyria)	
727–723	King	Shalmaneser V (of Assyria)	
722–710	King	Merodach (Marduk)-baladan III	d. 710??

710–705	King	Sargon II (of Assyria)	
705–682	King	Sennacherib, son of Sargon II (of Assyria)	

■ New Babylonian Empire

625–605	King	Nabopolassar	
605–562	King	Nebuchadnezzar II, son of Nabopolassar	d. 562
562–560	King	Evil-Merodach (Amel-Marduk), son of Nebuchadnezzar II	d. 560
559–556	King	Nergal-shar-usur	
556–539	King	Nabonidus	d. about 539
539–538	King	Belshazzar, son of Nabonidus	killed 538

Fell to the Persians in 538 B.C.

Bahamas (Commonwealth of The Bahamas)

The first Royal Governor, a former pirate named Woodes Rogers, brought law and order to The Bahamas in 1718 when he expelled the buccaneers who had used the islands as hideouts. Full independence within the Commonwealth of Nations came in 1973.

1973–1992	Prime Minister	Lynden Oscar Pindling	b.1930 d. 2000
1992–2002	Prime Minister	Hubert Alexander Ingraham	b. 1947
2002–	Prime Minister	Perry Gladstone Christie	b. 1943

Bahrain (Kingdom of Bahrain)

An Arab state under British protection since 1861, Bahrain is a sheikhdom whose present ruler is the eleventh since the dynasty was founded in 1782.

1961–1999	Sheikh	Isa bin Sulman Al Khalifah	b. 1933
1999–	Sheikh	Hamad bin Isa Al Khalifa	

Bangladesh (People's Republic of Bangladesh)

Bangladesh gained its independence from Pakistan in December of 1971.

1972–1975	Prime Minister	Sheikh Mujibur Rahman	assassinated 1975
1975–1981	Military dictator/Pres.	Ziaur Rahman ("Zia")	assassinated 1981
1982–1990	Military dictator/Pres.	Hussain Mohammed Ershad	resigned 1991
1991–1996	Prime Minister	Khaleda Zia	
1996–2001	Prime Minister	Sheikh Hasina	
2001–	Prime Minister	Khaleda Zia	

Barbados (Official U.N. Name)

A British colony from 1605 to 1966, Barbados is now an independent Dominion of the Commonwealth.

1959–1966	Governor	Sir John Montague Stow	b. 1911
1966	Governor-General	Sir John Montague Stow	
1966	Prime Minister	E. W. Barrow	
1976–1985	Prime Minister	J.M.G. Adams	
1985–1986	Prime Minister	Bernard St. John	
1986–1987	Prime Minister	E.W. Barrow	
1987–1994	Prime Minister	Erskine Sandiford	
1994–	Prime Minister	Owen Arthur	

Basutoland *See* Lesotho

Bavaria *See* Germany

Bechuanaland *See* Botswana

Belarus (Republic of Belarus)

Prior to absorption by Lithuania in the 14th century, Belarus consisted of the independent duchies of Smolensk, Polotsk, and Turov. By the 18th century, most of Belarus was under Russian rule. An independent republic was proclaimed in 1918.

1918–1921	President	Piotra Kreuceuski

Following World War I, the country was partitioned between Poland and Russia, with the eastern part becoming the Byelorussian Soviet Socialist Republic. The western part was regained following World War II. Independence from the Soviet Union was declared in 1991.

1994–	President	Alexander Lukashenko

Belgium (Kingdom of Belgium)

English versions of the names of rulers of French-speaking states are:

Baldwin-Baudouin	John-Jean	Philip-Philippe
Francis-François	James-Jacques	Rudolph-Rodolphe
Henry-Henri	Odo-Eudes	Stephen-Etienne
Hugh-Hugues	Peter-Pierre	Theobald-Thibaut
William-Guillaume		

No authentic information is available for the period before Baldwin I.

862–878	Count of Flanders	Baldwin I (Bras de fer)	d. 879

878–918	Count of Flanders	Baldwin II, son of Baldwin I	
918–950	Count of Flanders	Arnulf I, son of Baldwin II	
950–961	Count of Flanders	Baldwin III, son of Arnulf I	
961–964	Count of Flanders	Arnulf I (again)	
964–989	Count of Flanders	Arnulf II	
989–1035	Count of Flanders	Baldwin IV	
1036–1067	Count of Flanders	Baldwin V, son of Baldwin IV	d. 1067
1067–1070	Count of Flanders	Baldwin VI, son of Baldwin V	
1070–1071	Count of Flanders	Arnulf III, brother of Baldwin VI	
1071–1093	Count of Flanders	Robert I, brother of Baldwin VI	b. 1013? d. 1093
1093–1111	Count of Flanders	Robert II, son of Robert I	d. 1111
1111–1119	Count of Flanders	Baldwin VII, son of Robert II	b. 1058 d. 1119
1119–1127	Count of Flanders	Charles the Good, cousin of Baldwin VII	b. 1083? murdered 1127
1127–1128	Count of Flanders	William Clito, grandson of William I of England	
1128–1157	Count of Flanders	Didrik of Alsace, grandson of Robert I	abdicated 1157 d. 1177
1157–1191	Count of Flanders	Philip, son of Didrik of Alsace	
1171–1195	Count of Flanders	Baldwin VIII	b. 1150 d. 1195
1191	Countess	Margareta (wife of Baldwin of Hainault), sister of Philip	
1195–1206	Count	Baldwin IX (Emperor of Constantinople)	b. 1171 murdered 1205?
1206–1244	Countess	Joanna, daughter of Baldwin IX	
1212–1233	Co-regent	Ferdinand of Portugal, husband of Joanna	
1244–1280	Countess	Margaret, daughter of Joanna	b. 1200? d. 1280
1280–1305	Count	Guy de Dampierre, son of Margaret	d. 1305
1305–1322	Count	Robert III of Béthune, son of Guy de Dampierre	b. 1240 d. 1322
1322–1337	Count of Flanders	Louis I de Nevers, grandson of Robert of Béthune	b. 1304? killed 1346
1336–1345	Governor	Jacob van Artevelde	b. 1290? d. 1345
1346–1384	Count	Louis II de Male, son of Louis de Nevers	b. 1330 d. 1384

Louis II was wounded at Crécy, where his father was killed
fighting with the French against the English under Edward III.
His reign was a continuous struggle with the communes,
and he was aided by the French in subduing the towns.

1384–1405	Countess	Margaret, wife of Philip of Burgundy, daughter of Louis II de Male	b. 1350 d. 1405

Belgium was under Burgundy from 1384 to 1477 and under the
Habsburgs from 1477 to 1795. It was united with France from 1795 to
1814 and with Holland from 1815 to 1830. It became an independent
kingdom in 1830.

■ House of Saxe-Coburg

1831–1865	King	Leopold I, son of Francis Frederick, Duke of Saxe-Coburg-Saalfield	b. 1790 d. 1865
1865–1909	King	Leopold II, son of Leopold I	b. 1835 d. 1909

Leopold II was a great world-traveler. He financed Stanley's expedition to the Congo, and five years later was granted personal sovereignty over the Congo. However, his cruel treatment of the Congolese led Belgium to annex the territory.

1909–1934	King	Albert I, nephew of Leopold II	b. 1875 killed 1934
1934–1951	King	Leopold III, son of Albert I abdicated 1951	b. 1901
1951–1993	King	Baudouin, son of Leopold III	b. 1930 d. 1993
1993–	King	Albert II, brother of Baudouin	b. 1934

■ Statesmen

1944–1945	Prime Minister	Hubert Pierlot	b. 1883
1945	Prime Minister	Achille Van Acker	b. 1898
1945–1946	Prime Minister	Achille Van Acker	
1946	Prime Minister	Paul Henri Spaak	b. 1899
1946	Prime Minister	Achille Van Acker	
1946–1947	Prime Minister	Camille Huysmans	b. 1871
1947–1949	Prime Minister	Paul Henri Spaak	
1949–1950	Prime Minister	Gaston Eyskens	b. 1905
1950	Prime Minister	Jean Duvieusart	b. 1900
1950–1952	Prime Minister	Joseph Pholien	b. 1884
1952–1954	Prime Minister	Jean Van Houtte	b. 1907
1954–1958	Prime Minister	Achille Van Acker	
1958	Prime Minister	Gaston Eyskens	
1958–1960	Prime Minister	Gaston Eyskens	
1960–1961	Prime Minister	Gaston Eyskens	
1961–1965	Prime Minister	Théodore Lefevre	
1965	Prime Minister	Pierre Harmel	
1965–1968	Prime Minister	Paul Vanden Boeynants	b. 1919 d. 2001
1968–1973	Prime Minister	Gaston Eyskens	b. 1905 d. 1988
1973–1974	Prime Minister	Edmond Leburton	b. 1915 d. 1997
1974–1978	Prime Minister	Leo Tindemans	b. 1922
1978–1979	Prime Minister	Paul Vanden Boeynants	
1979–1981	Prime Minister	Wilfried Martens	b. 1936
1981	Prime Minister	Mark Eyskens	b. 1933

1981–1992	Prime Minister	Wilfried Martens	
1992–1999	Prime Minister	Jean-Luc Dehaene	b. 1940
1999–	Prime Minister	Guy Verhofstadt	b. 1953

Belize (Official U.N. Name)

Formerly known as British Honduras, this member of the Commonwealth of Nations officially adopted its present name in 1973, prior to gaining full independence in 1981.

1981–1984	Prime Minister	George Cadle Price
1984–1989	Prime Minister	Manuel Esquivel
1989–1993	Prime Minister	George Cadle Price
1993–1998	Prime Minister	Manuel Esquivel
1998–	Prime Minister	Said Musa

Benin (Republic of Benin)

As the seat of one of the great African medieval kingdoms called Dahomey, Benin witnessed the arrival of Europeans in the 1700s. Under French administration from 1892 to 1958, Benin became an independent republic within the French Community until 1960, when it became fully independent outside the Community.

■ Rulers of Dahomey

? –1620	King	Gangnihessou
1620–1645	King	Dakodonou
1645–1685	King	Houegbadja
1685–1708	King	Akaba
1732–1774	King	Tegbessou
1774–1789	King	Kpengla
1789–1797	King	Agonglo
1797–1818	King	Adandozan
1818–1856	King	Ghezo
1856–1889	King	Glele
1889–1894	King	Behanzin

■ Independent Nation

1957–1959	Prime Minister	Sorou-Migan Apithy	b. 1913
1959–1961	Prime Minister	Hubert Maga	b. 1916
1961–1963	President	Hubert Maga	
		Provisional Military Government from 1963 to 1964	
1964–1965	President	Sorou-Migan Apithy	deposed
1965–1967	President	Christophe Soglo	

1967–1967	Head of State	Iropa Maurice Kouandété
1967–1968	Head of State	Alphonse Amadou Alley
1968–1969	Head of State	Émile Derlin Henri Zinsou
1969–1970	Directory Chairman	Paul-Émile de Souza
1970–1972	Chair, Presidential Council	Coutoucou Hubert Maga
1972	Chair, Presidential Council	Justin Ahomadegbé-Tomêtin
1972–1991	President	Mathieu Kérékou
1991–1996	President	Nicéphore Dieudonné Soglo
1996–	President	Mathieu Kérékou

Bermuda (Official U.N. Name)

1973–1975	Premier	Edward Richards
1975–1977	Premier	John Henry Sharpe
1977–1982	Premier	David Gibbons
1982–1995	Premier	John W. Swan
1995–1997	Premier	David Saul
1997–1998	Premier	Pamela Meridith Gordon
1998–2003	Premier	Jennifer Felicity Smith
2003–	Premier	Alex Scott

Bhutan (Kingdom of Bhutan)

A decentralized theocracy by tradition and a monarchy since 1907, Bhutan is in the process of becoming a constitutional monarchy with representative government. A Protectorate under the aegis of the British and Indian governments, Bhutan was admitted to the United Nations in 1971.

1907–1926	King	Ugyen Wangchuck		d. 1926
1926–1952	King	Jigme Wangchuck		
1952–1972	King	Jigme Dorji Wangchuck		d. 1972
1972–	King	Jigme Singye Wanchuck	b. 1955	

Biafra *See* Nigeria

Bithynia

Bithynia is in western Asia Minor near the Bosporus.

383–382 B.C.	King	Doedalsus	d. 382
381 378	King	Botyrus	d. 378

378–328	King	Bias	d. 328
328–281	King	Zipoetes	d. 281
281–245	King	Nicomedes I	d. 245
245–229	King	Zelas	d. 229
229–186	King	Prusias I	d. 186
186–149	King	Prusias II	d. 149
149–92	King	Nicomedes II	d. 92
92–74	King	Nicomedes III	d. 74

Nicomedes III willed his realm to Rome after it was merged with Pontus.

Bohemia *See* Czech Republic

Bolivia (Republic of Bolivia)

Boliva declared independence in 1825.

1825–1826	President	Simón Bolívar	b. 1795 d. 1830
1826–1828	President	Antonio José de Sucre	b. 1795 assassinated 1830
1828	President (provisional)	Pedro Blanco	
1829–1839	President	Andrés Santa Cruz	b. 1792? d. 1865
1839–1841	President	José Miguel de Velasco	
1841–1848	President	José Ballivián	b. 1804 d. 1852
1848	President	Eusebio Guilarte	
1848–1855	President	Manuel Isidoro Belzú	
1855–1857	President	Jorge Córdoba	
1857–1861	Dictator	José María Linares	b. 1810 d. 1861
1861–1864	President	José María de Achá	
1865–1871	Dictator	Mariano Melgarejo	b. 1818 d. 1871
1871–1872	President	Agustín Morales	b. 1810 assassinated 1872
1873–1874	President	Adolfo Ballivián	b. 1831 d. 1874
1874–1876	President	Tomás Frías	b. 1804 d. 1882
1876–1880	President	Hilarión Daza	b. 1840 killed 1894
1880–1884	President	Narciso Campero	b. 1815 d. 1896
1884–1888	President	Gregorio Pacheco	
1888–1892	President	Aniceto Arce	b. 1824 d. 1906
1892–1896	President	Mariano Baptista	b. 1832 d. 1907
1896–1899	President	Severo Fernández Alonso	

1899–1904	President	José Manuel Pando	b. 1848? d.1917
1904–1909	President	Ismael Montes	b. 1861 d. 1933
1909–1913	President	Eliodoro Villazón	
1913–1917	President	Ismael Montes	
1917–1920	President	José Gutiérrez Guerra (provisional junta, 1920–1921)	
1921–1925	President	Bautista Saavedra	b. 1870 d. 1939
1925–1926	President (provisional)	Felipe Guzmán	
1926–1930	President	Hernando Siles	b. 1881 d. 1942
1930–1931	President (provisional)	Carlos Blanco Galindo	
1931–1934	President	Daniel Salamanca	b. 1869 d. 1935
1934–1936	President	José Luis Tejada Sorzano	b. 1881 d. 1938
1936–1937	President	José David Toro	
1937–1939	President	Germán Busch	d. 1939
1939–1940	President (provisional)	Carlos Quintanilla	
1940–1943	President	Enrique Peñaranda	b. 1892
1943–1946	President	Gualberto Villarroel	lynched 1946
1946–1947	President (provisional)	Tomás Monje Gutierrez	
1947–1949	President	Enrique Hertzog	
1949–1951	President	Mamerto Urriolagoitia	
1951–1952	President	Hugo Ballivián Rojas	
1952–1956	President	Victor Paz Estenssoro	
1956–1960	President	Hernán Siles Zuazo	
1960–1964	President	Victor Paz Estenssoro	
1964–1965	President	Rene Barrientos Ortuño	
1965–1966	Co-President	Alfredo Ovardo Candia	
1966–1969	President	Rene Barrientos Ortuño	
1969–1970	President	Alfredo Ovando Candía	
1970–1971	President	Juan José Torres Gonzáles	
1971–1978	President	Hugo Banzer Suarez	
1978–1980		*Political Instability*	
1980–1981	Military dictator	Luis Garcia Meza	
1981–1982		*Various Military Leaders*	
1982–1985	President	Hernan Siles Zuazo	
1985–1989	President	Victor Paz Estenssoro	
1989–1993	President	Jaime Paz Zamora	

1993–1997	President	Gonzalo Sanchez de Lozada
1997–2001	President	Hugo Banzer Suarez
2001–2002	President	Jorge Quiroga
2002–	President	Gonzalo Sanchez de Lozada

Bosnia and Herzegovina (Official U.N. Name)

Bosnia and Herzegovina was occupied by Austria in 1878.

1878	Governor	Josef von Philippovich Philippsberg	b. 1819 d. 1889
1878–1881	Governor	Wilhelm Nikolaus, Herzog von Württemberg	b. 1828 d. 1896
1881–1882	Governor	Freiherr Hermann Dahlen-Orlaburg	b. 1828 d. 1887
1882–1903	Governor	Johann von Appel	b. 1826 d. 1906
1903–1907	Governor	Freiherr Eugen von Albori	b. 1838 d. 1915
1907–1909	Governor	Freiherr Anton von Winzor	b. 1844 d. 1910
		Annexed by Austria-Hungary in 1908	
1909–1911	Governor	Freiherr Marian von Varesanin-Vares	b. 1847 d. 1917
1911–1914	Governor	Oskar Potiorek	b. 1853 d. 1933
1915–1918	Governor	Freiherr Stefan von Sarkotic-Lovcen	b. 1858 d. 1939

Became part of Yugoslavia in 1918

The contemporary state was admitted to the United Nations in 1992, but a stable form of government was only achieved with the Dayton Peace Accords of 1995. The Presidency in Bosnia and Herzegovina is held by a triumvirate consisting of a Bosniak, a Serb, and a Croat, each of whom is chosen by direct popular elections held on a rotating basis of four-year terms.

1996–1998	Tri-Presidency	Alija Izetbegovic, Momcilo Krajisnik, Kresimir Zubak
1998–2000	Tri-Presidency	Alija Izetbegovic, Zivco Radisic, Ante Jelavic
2000–2001	Tri-Presidency	Halid Genjac, Zivco Radisic, Ante Jelavic
2001–2002	Tri-Presidency	Beriz Belkic, Zivco Radisic, Jozo Krizanovic
2002–2003	Tri-Presidency	Mirko Sarovic, Dragan Covic, Sulejman Tihic
2003–	Tri-Presidency	Borislav Paravac, Dragan Covic, Sulejman Tihic

Botswana (Republic of Botswana)

Formerly the British Protectorate of Bechuanaland, Botswana became an independent republic in 1966.

1966–1980	President	Sir Seretse Khama	b. 1921
1980–1998	President	Ketumile Masire	
1998–	President	Festus Mogae	

Brazil (Federative Republic of Brazil)

After three centuries of Portuguese rule, Brazil became independent as an Empire in 1822 under a member of the Portuguese royal house of Braganza. Brazil became the first nation in the Western Hemisphere to have a female head of state as the heir to the throne, Princess Isabel, who was regent from 1887 to 1888. During that brief period, Princess Isabel left an indelible mark on Brazilian history by promoting and signing the "Golden Law" that abolished slavery "forever."

English versions of the names of rulers of Portuguese-speaking states are:

Charles-Carlos	Ferdinand-Fernando	John-João
Denis-Diniz	Henry-Enrique	Michael-Miguel
Edward-Duarte	James-Diogo	Peter-Pedro

1549–1553	Governor-General	Martin Alfonso da Souza	
1553–1556	Governor-General	Duarte da Costa	
1556–1570	Governor-General	Mem de Sá	b. 1500? d. 1572
1570–1572	Governor-General	Luis de Brito de Almeida; Antônio de Salema	
1572–1577	Governor-General	Luis de Brito de Almeida	
1577–1580	Governor-General	Lourenço da Veiga	
1580–1583	Governor-General	Cosme Rangel	
1583–1587	Governor-General	Manuel Teles Barreto	
1587–1591	Governor-General	Antônio Barreiros; Cristóvão de Barros	
1591–1602	Governor-General	Francisco de Souza	
1602–1608	Governor-General	Diogo Botelho	
1608–1612	Governor-General	Diogo de Menezes e Siqueira	
1612–1617	Governor-General	Gaspar de Souza	
1617–1621	Governor-General	Luiz de Souza	
1621–1624	Governor-General	Diogo de Mendonça Furtado	
1624	Governor-General	Mathias de Albuquerque	d. 1646
1624	Governor-General	Francisco Nunes Marinho d'Eça	
1624–1626	Governor-General	Francisco de Moura Rolim	
1626–1635	Governor-General	Diogo Luis de Oliveira	
1635–1639	Governor-General	Pedro da Silva	
1639	Governor-General	Fernando Mascarenhas, Count of Tôrre	
1639–1640	Governor-General	Vasco Mascarenhas, Count of Óbidos	
1640–1641	Governor-General	Jorge Mascarenhas, Marquis of Montalvão (1st Viceroy of Brazil)	
1641–1642	Governor-General	Bispo D. Pedro; Luis Barbalho; Provedor-Mor Lourenço Brito Correia	
1642–1647	Governor-General	Antônio Teles da Silva	
1647–1650	Governor-General	Antônio Teles de Menezes, Count of Vila Pouca de Aguiar	
1650–1654	Governor-General	João Rodrigues de Vasconcelos, Count of Castelo Melhor	
1654–1657	Governor-General	Jerônimo de Ataíde, Count of Atouguia	
1657–1663	Governor-General	Francisco Barreto	

1663–1667	Governor-General	Vasco Mascarenhas, Count of Óbidos (2nd Viceroy of Brazil)
1667–1671	Governor-General	Alexandre de Souza Freire
1671–1675	Governor-General	Afonso Furtado de Castro de Mendonça, Viscount of Barbacena
1675–1678	Governor-General	Desembargador Agostinho de Azevedo Monteiro; Alvaro de Azevedo; Antônio Guedes Brito
1678–1682	Governor-General	Roque da Costa Barreto
1682–1684	Governor-General	Antônio de Souza Meneses
1684–1687	Governor-General	Antônio Luís de Souza, Marquis of Minas
1687–1688	Governor-General	Mathias da Cunha
1688–1690	Governor-General	Manuel da Ressureição
1690–1694	Governor-General	Antônio Luiz Gonçalves da Câmara Coutinho
1694–1702	Governor-General	João Lencastro
1702–1708	Governor-General	Rodrigo da Costa
1708–1710	Governor-General	Luis César de Meneses
1710–1711	Governor-General	Lourenço de Almada
1711–1714	Governor-General	Pedro de Vasconcelos de Souza

■ Viceroys

1711–1714	Viceroy	Marquês de Angeja (3rd Viceroy of Brazil)
1718–1719	Viceroy	Sancho de Faro, Count of Vimieiro
1719–1720	Viceroy	Sebastião Monteiro de Vide; Desembargador Caetano de Brito e Figueiredo; João de Araújo e Azevedo
1720–1735	Viceroy	Vasco Fernandes César de Meneses, Count of Sabugosa
1735–1749	Viceroy	André de Melo e Castro, Count of Galveias
1749–1754	Viceroy	Luiz Pedro Peregrino de Carvalho Meneses e Ataíde, Count of Atouguia
1754–1755	Viceroy	José Botelho de Mattos; Manuel Antônio de Cunha Soto Maior; Lourenço Monteiro
1755–1760	Viceroy	Marços de Noronha, Count of Arcos
1760	Viceroy	Antônio d' Almeida Soares e Portugal, Count of Avintes and Marquis of Lavradio
1760–1763	Viceroy	Tomás Rubi de Barros Barreto; José Carvalho de Andrada; Barros e Alvim
1763–1767	Viceroy	Antônio Alvares da Cunha, Count of Cunha
1767–1769	Viceroy	Antônio Rolim de Moura
1769–1778	Viceroy	Luiz de Almeida, Marquis of Lavradio
1778–1790	Viceroy	Luiz de Vasconcelos e Souza
1790–1801	Viceroy	José Luiz de Castro, Count of Resende
1801–1806	Viceroy	José Fernandes de Portugal e Castro
1801–1806	Viceroy	José Fernandes de Portugal e Castro

1806–1808	Viceroy	Marcos de Noronha e Brito, Count of Arcos	

As a result of the Napoleonic invasion of the Iberian peninsula,
the king and the entire court fled to Rio de Janeiro, which became
the seat of Portuguese government between 1808 and 1821.
Brazil was raised to the status of a Kingdom.

1815–1821	King	John VI	
1821–1822	Prince-Regent	Dom Pedro, son of John VI	b. 1798 d. 1834

Brazil declared its independence from Portugal in 1822
and was established as a monarchy, with the Prince-Regent
becoming the nation's first ruler.

1822–1831	Emperor	Pedro I	Abdicated

Because the heir to the throne was only five years old, the nation
was governed by a series of regents, during a period which came
to be known as the "Minority of Dom Pedro II."

1831	Regent	José Joaquim Carneiro de Campos; Marquis de Caravelas; Nicolau Pereira de Campos Vergueiro; Francisco de Lima e Silva	b. 1785 d. 1853
1831–1835	Regent	José da Costa Carvalho, (afterwards Viscount and Marquis of Montalvão); João Bráulio Muniz; Francisco de Lima e Silva	
1835–1837	Regent	Diogo Antônio Feijó	
1837–1840	Regent	Pedro de Araújo Lima, (afterwards Viscount and Marquis of Olinda)	
1840-1889	Emperor	Dom Pedro II	b. 1826 d. 1891

Under pressure from the military, Dom Pedro II abdicated in 1889
and went into exile.

Brazil Declared a Republic in 1889

1889–1891	President	Marshall Deodoro da Fonseca	b. 1827 d. 1892
1891–1894	President	Marshall Floriano Peixoto	b. 1842 d. 1895
1894–1896	President	Prudente José de Morais Barros	b. 1841 d. 1902
1896–1897	President	Manuel Vitorino Pereira	
1898–1900	President	Manuel Ferraz de Campos Salles	b. 1846 d. 1913
1900	President	Francisco de Assis Rosa e Silva	
1900–1902	President	Manuel Ferraz de Campos Salles	
1902–1906	President	Francisco de Paula Rodrigues Alves	b. 1848 d. 1919
1906–1909	President	Affonso Augusto Moreira Penna	b. 1847 d. 1909
1909–1910	President	Nilo Peçanha	b. 1867 d. 1924
1910–1914	President	Hermes Rodrigues da Fonseca	b. 1855 d. 1923
1914–1917	President	Wenceslão Braz Pereira Gomes	b. 1868
1917	President	Urbano Santos da Costa Araujo	
1917–1918	President	Wenceslão Braz Pereira Gomes	
1918–1919	President	Delfim Moreira da Costa Ribeiro	

1919–1922	President	Epitácio da Silva Pessôa	b. 1865 d. 1942
1922–1926	President	Arthur da Silva Bernardes	b. 1875 d. 1955
1926–1930	President	Washington Luiz Pereira de Souza	b. 1869 d. 1957
1930	President elect	Júlio Prestes de Albuquerque	
1930	President	Augusto Tasso Fragoso	
1930–1945	President	Getúlio Dornelles Vargas	b. 1883 d. 1954
1945–1946	President (provisional)	José Linhares	
1946–1951	President	Eurico Gaspar Dutra	b. 1885
1951–1954	President	Getúlio Dornelles Vargas	
1954–1955	President	João Café Filho	
1955	President (acting)	Carlos Coimbra da Luz	
1955	President	Nereu de Oliveira Ramos	
1956–1960	President	Juscelino Kubitschek de Oliveira	b. 1922
1960	President	Ranieri Mazzilli	
1960–1961	President	Juscelino Kubitschek de Oliveira	
1961	President	Jānio da Silva Quadros	
1961–1964	President	João Belchior Marques Goulart	b. 1918
1964	President	Ranieri Mazzilli	
1964–1967	President	Humberto de Alencar Castelo Branco	b. 1900 d. 1967
1967–1969	President	Arthur Costa e Silva	
1969–1969	Military Junta	Aurélio de Lyra Tavaros, Mácio de Souza e Mello, Augusto Rademaker	
1969–1974	President	Emílio Garrrastazú Medici	
1974–1979	President	Ernesto Geisel	
1979–1985	President	João Baptista de Oliveira Figueiredo	
1985–1990	President	José Sarney	
1990–1992	President	Fernando Collor de Mello	
1992–1994	President	Itamar Franco	
1994–2002	President	Fernando Henrique Cardoso	
2002–	President	Luiz Inacio "Lula" da Silva	

Britanny *See* France

Brunei Darussalam (Negara Brunei Darussalam)

Between the fifteenth and seventeenth centuries, Brunei was the seat of an empire that covered the entire island of Borneo and the Philippine Islands. A British protectorate from 1888 until its full independence in 1984, Brunei has been ruled by the same family for over six centuries. The current constitution was adopted in 1959.

1405–1415	Sultan	Muhammad

1415–1425	Sultan	Ahmad
1425–1433	Sultan	Sharif Ali
1433–1473	Sultan	Sulaiman
1473–1521	Sultan	Bolkiah
1521–1575	Sultan	Abdul Kahar
1575–1600	Sultan	Saifal Rijal
1600–1605	Sultan	Shah Berunai
1605–1619	Sultan	Hassan
1619-1649	Sultan	Abdul Jalilul Akhbar
1649-1652	Sultan	Abdul Jalilul Jabbar
1625–1660	Sultan	Muhammad Ali
1660–1673	Sultan	Abdul Mubin
1673–1690	Sultan	Muyiddin
1690–1705	Sultan	Nassaruddin
1705–1730	Sultan	Hussin Kamaluddin
1730–1745	Sultan	Muhammad Alauddin
1745–1762	Sultan	Hussin Kamaluddin
1762–1796	Sultan	Omar Ali Sifuddien
1796–1807	Sultan	Muhammad Tajuddin
1806–1807	Sultan	Muhammad Jamalul Alam I
1807–1829	Sultan	Muhammad Kanzal Alam
1825–1828	Sultan	Muhammad Alam
1829–1852	Sultan	Omar Ali Saifuddien II
1852–1885	Sultan	Abdul Momin
1885–1906	Sultan	Hashim Jalilul Alam Aqamaddin
1906–1924	Sultan	Muhummad Jamalul Alam II
1924–1950	Sultan	Ahmad Tajuddin
1950–1967	Sultan	Omar Ali Saifuddin III
1967–	Sultan	Hassanal Bolkiah

Brunswick *See* Germany

Bulgaria (Republic of Bulgaria)

852–893	Tsar	Boris I (Michael Simeon)	d. 907
893–927	Tsar	Simeon I, son of Boris	d. 927
927–969	Tsar	Peter, son of Simeon I	

969–972	Tsar	Boris II	
		Conquered by Byzantine Empire from 972 to 1186	
976–1014	Prince	Samuel	
1014–1015	Prince	Gabriel Radomir	
1015–1018	Prince	John Vladislav	
1186–1197	Tsar	Peter Asen	d. 1197
1186–1196	(Co-regent)	John Asen I, brother of Peter	d. 1196
1197–1207	Tsar	Kaloyan, brother of Peter	d. 1207
1218–1241	Tsar	John Asen II, son of John Asen I	

John Asen II was the most powerful ruler of Bulgaria. He conquered Albania, Epirus, Thrace, and Macedonia; assumed the title of Tsar of the Greeks and Bulgars; and is considered to have ruled wisely and well. During his reign, trade, art, and industry flourished, and many churches and monasteries were founded.

1241–1246	Tsar	Kaliman I	
1246–1257	Tsar	Michael Asen	
1257–1258	Tsar	Kaliman II	
1258–1277	Tsar	Constantine Asen	murdered 1277
1278–1279	Tsar	Ivaljo	
1279–1280	Tsar	Ivan III Asen	

A feudal system followed the extinction of the Asen dynasty in 1280.

1280–1292	Tsar	George I Terter	
1292–1300	Tsar	Smilitz	
1300	Tsar	Caka	
1300–1322	Tsar	Theodore Svetoslav	
1322–1323	Tsar	George II Terter	
1322–1330	Tsar	Michael	killed 1330
1330–1331	Tsar	Ivan II Stephen	
1330–1371	Tsar	Ivan I Alexander	
1365–1393	Tsar	Ivan III Shishman	

Under Turkish rule from 1396 to 1878
Made a Principality under Turkish Suzerainty in 1878

1879–1886	Prince	Alexander Joseph of Battenberg, nephew of Alexander II of Russia abdicated 1886	b. 1857 d. 1893
1887–1908	Prince	Ferdinand of Saxe-Coburg-Gotha	b. 1861 d. 1948

Became an Independent Kingdom in 1908

1908–1918	King	Ferdinand I	abdicated 1918
1918–1943	King	Boris III, son of Ferdinand I	b. 1894 d. 1943
1943–1944	Regent	Cyril, brother of Boris II	b. 1895 executed 1945

1943–1946	King	Simeon II, son of Boris II	b. 1937 abdicated 1946
		Became a Communist Republic in 1946	
1946–1947	Chair, Prov. Presidency	Vasil Kolarov	
1947–1950	Chair, Presidium	Mincho Neychev	
1950–1958	Chair, Presidium	Georgi Damyanov	
1958–1964	Chair, Presidium	Dimitur Vurbanov	
1964–1971	Chair, Presidium	Georgi Girovoski	
1971–1989	Chair, State Council	Todor Zhivkov	
1989–1990	Chair, State Council	Petur Mladenov	
1990	President	Petur Mladenov	
1990	Acting President	Stanko Georgiev	
1990	Acting President	Nikolay Todorov	
1990–1997	President	Zhelyu Zhelev	
1997–2002	President	Petur Stoyanov	
2002–	President	Georgi Purvanov	

Burkina Faso *Formerly* Upper Volta

The French colony of Upper Volta was established in 1919, with the French relying on indigenous leadership of the Mossi, who had dominated the region to the end of the 19th century. National independence was achieved in 1960, with the current official name being adopted in 1984.

1959–1966	President	Maurice Yaméogo	b. 1920
1966–	Chief of State	Lt.-Col. Sangoule Lamizana	

Burma (Union of Burma) *Also known as* Myanmar

Burma consisted of separate states until King Alompra united them into one empire.

1753–1760	King	Alompra (or Alaungpaya)	b. 1711 d. 1760
1853–1878	King	Mindon Min	d. 1878
1878–1885	King	Thibaw (or Theebaw), son of Mindon Min deposed 1885	b. 1858 d. 1916
		Upper and Lower Burma Became a Province of British India in 1886	
1886–1887	Chief Commissioner	Sir Charles Edward Bernard	b. 1873 d. 1901
1887–1889	Chief Commissioner	Charles Haukes Todd Crosthwaite	b. 1835 d. 1915
1889–1890	Chief Commissioner	Antony Patrick MacDonnell, later 1st Baron MacDonnell of Swinford	b. 1844 d. 1925
1890–1892	Chief Commissioner	Alexander Mackenzie	b. 1842 d. 1902
1892	Chief Commissioner	Donald Mackenzie Smeaton	b. 1848 d. 1910
1892–1897	Chief Commissioner	Sir Frederick William Richards Fryer	b. 1845 d. 1922
1897–1903	Lieutenant-Governor	Sir Frederick William Richards Fryer	
1903–1905	Lieutenant-Governor	Sir Hugh Shakespear Barnes	b. 1853 d. 1940

1905–1910	Lieutenant-Governor	Sir Herbert Thirkell White	b. 1855 d. 1931
1910–1913	Lieutenant-Governor	Sir Harvey Adamson	b. 1854 d. 1941
1913	Lieutenant-Governor	Sir George Watson Shaw	b. 1858 d. 1931
1913–1915	Lieutenant-Governor	Sir Harvey Adamson	
1915–1917	Lieutenant-Governor	Sir Spencer Harcourt Butler	b. 1869 d. 1938
1917–1918	Lieutenant-Governor	Walter Francis Rice	d. 1941
1918–1922	Lieutenant-Governor	Sir Reginald Henry Craddock	b. 1864 d. 1937
1923–1927	Governor	Sir Spencer Harcourt Butler	
1927–1930	Governor	Sir Charles Alexander Innes	b. 1874 d. 1959
1930–1931	Governor	Sir Joseph Augustus Moung Gyi	b. 1872 d. 1955
1932–1935	Governor	Sir Hugh Lansdowne Stephenson	b. 1871 d. 1941
1935	Governor	Thomas Couper	b. 1878 d. 1954
1936–1939	Governor	Sir Archibald Douglas Cochrane	b. 1885 d. 1958
1939	Governor	Sir Walter Booth-Graveley	b. 1882
1941–1946	Governor	Sir Reginald Hugh Dorman-Smith	b. 1899
		Invaded by the Japanese in 1941	
1946–1948	Governor	Sir Hubert Elvin Rance	b. 1898
		Union of Burma Founded in 1948	
1948–1952	President	Sao Shwe Thaike	
1952–1957	President	Ba U	b. 1887
1957–1962	President	U Win Maung	b. 1916
1962	President	Sama Duwa Sinwa Nawng	b. 1915
1962–1981	Chair, Rev. Council	Ne Win (Maung Shu Maung)	b. 1911
1981–1988	President	San Yu	
1988	President	Sein Lwin	
1988	Acting President	Aye Ko	
1988	President	Maung Maung	
1988–1992	Chair, Council	Saw Maung	
1992–1997	Chair, Council	Than Shwe	

■ Statesmen

1948–1956	Prime Minister	U Nu	b. 1907
1957–1958	Prime Minister	U Nu	
1958–1960	Prime Minister	Ne Win	
1960–1962	Prime Minister	U Nu	
1962–1974	Prime Minister	Ne Win	b. 1911 d. 2002
1974–1977	Prime Minister	Sein Win	b. 1929

1977–1988	Prime Minister	Maung Maung Kha	b. 1920 d. 1995
1988	Prime Minister	Tun Tin	b. 1930
1988–1992	Prime Minister	Saw Maung	b. 1928 d. 1997
1992–2003	Prime Minister	Than Shwe	b. 1933
2003–2004	Prime Minister	Khin Nyunt	b. 1939
2004–	Prime Minister	Soe Win	b. 1949

Burundi (Republic of Burundi)

Formerly a German colony and Belgian trusteeship, Burundi became an independent state in 1962.

1962–1966	Ruler	Mwambutsa IV, Mwami of Burundi	b. 1912
1966–	Ruler	Charles, son of Mwambutsa IV	b. 1947
1961–	Prime Minister	Prince Louis Rwagasore, son of Mwambutsa IV	assassinated 1961
1961–1963	Prime Minister	Pierre Muhirwa, son-in-law of Mwambutsa IV	
1963–1964	Prime Minister	Pierre Ngendandumwe	
1964–1965	Prime Minister	Albin Nyamoya	
1965	Prime Minister	Pierre Ngendandumwe	assassinated 1965
1965–1966	Prime Minister	Joseph Bamina	
		Republic Proclaimed in 1966	
1966–	President	Michel Micombero	
1966–?	President	Michel Micombero	b. 1939?
1976–1981	President	Jean-Baptiste Bagaza	
1987–1993	President	Pierre Buyoya	
1993	President	Melchior Ndadaye	Assassinated
1994	President	Cyprien Ntaryamira	Killed in plane crash
1994–1996	President	Sylvestre Ntibantunganya	
1996–2003	President	Pierre Buyoya	
2003–	President	Domitien Ndayizeye	

Byelorussia *See* Belarus

Byzantine Empire *See* Roman Empire

Caliphate of the East

622–632	Caliph	Mohammed	b. 571 d. 632
632–634	Caliph	Abu Bekr, father-in-law of Mohammed	b. 573 d. 634
634–644	Caliph	Omarl, father-in-law of Mohammed	b. 581? assassinated 644

| 644–656 | Caliph | Othman bin Affan, son-in-law of Mohammed | b. 574 ? assassinated 656 |
| 656–661 | Caliph | Ali, cousin and son-in-law of Mohammed | b. 600 ? assassinated 661 |

■ Omayyad Dynasty

661–680	Caliph	Muawiyah	d. 680
680–683	Caliph	Yazid I, son of Muawiyah	d. 683
683	Caliph	Muawiyah II, son of Yazid I	d. 683
684–685	Caliph	Marwan I	d. 685
685–705	Caliph	Abd al-Melik, son of Marwan I	b. 646? d. 705
705–715	Caliph	Walid I, son of Abd al-Melik	b. 675? d. 715
715–717	Caliph	Suleiman, son of Abd al-Melik	d. 717
717–720	Caliph	Omar II, nephew of Abd al-Melik	d. 720
720–724	Caliph	Yazid II, son of Abd al-Melik	d. 724
724–743	Caliph	Hisham I, son of Abd al-Melik	d. 743
743–744	Caliph	Walid II, son of Yazid II	d. 744
744	Caliph	Yazid III, son of Walid I	d. 744
744	Caliph	Ibrahim, son of Walid I	
744–750	Caliph	Marwan II, nephew of Abd al-Melik	d. 750
750		*End of Arab Dynasty*	

■ Bbassid Dynasty (Persian)

750–754	Caliph	Abu'l- Abbas, descendant of Abbas, uncle of Mohammed	b. 721? d. 754
754–775	Caliph	Abu-djafar El-mansur, brother of Abu'l-Abbas	
775–785	Caliph	Mohammed al-mahdi, son of Abu-djafar Al-mansur	
785–786	Caliph	Musa al-hadi, son of Mohammed al-mahdi	
786–809	Caliph	Harun al-Rashid, brother of Musa al-hadi	b. 764? d. 809
809–813	Caliph	Mohammed al-amin, son of Harun al-Rashid	
813–833	Caliph	Abdullah-al-mamun, son of Harun al-Rashid	
833–842	Caliph	El-mutasim-billah, brother of Abdallah-al-mamun	
842–847	Caliph	Harum al-wathik-billah, son of Al-mutasim-billah	
847–861	Caliph	Djafar al-mutawakkil, brother of Harun al-wathik-billah	
861–862	Caliph	Mohammed al-muntasir-billah, son of Djafar al-mutawakkil	
862–866	Caliph	Ahmed al-mustain-billah, grandson of Harun al-wathik-billah	
866–869	Caliph	Mohammed al-mutazz-billah, son of Djafar al-mutawakkil	
869–870	Caliph	Mohammed al-muhtadi-billah, son of Harun al-wathik-billah	
870–892	Caliph	Ahmed al-mutamid ala'llah, son of Djafar al-mutawakkil	
892–902	Caliph	Ahmed al-mutadid-billah, nephew of Ahmed al-mutamid ala'llah	

902–908	Caliph	Ali al-muktafi-billah, son of Ahmed al-mutadid-billah	
908–932	Caliph	Djafar al-muktadir-billah, brother of Ali al-muktafi-billah	
932–934	Caliph	Mohammed al-kahir-billah, brother of Djafar al-muktadir-billah	
934–940	Caliph	Ahmed ar-radi-billah, son of Djafar al-muktadir-billah	
940–944	Caliph	Ibrahim al-muttaki-billah, son of Djafar al-muktadir-billah	
944–946	Caliph	Al-Mustakfi billah, son of Ali al-muktafi-billah	
946–974	Caliph	Al-Muti, son of Djafar al-muktadir-billah	
974–991	Caliph	Al-Tai li-amrillah, son of El-Muti	
991–1031	Caliph	Al-Kadir-billah, grandson of Djafar al-muktadir-billah	
1031–1075	Caliph	Al-Ka-im, son of Al-Kadir-billah	
1075–1094	Caliph	Al-Muktadi, grandson of Al-Ka-im	
1094–1118	Caliph	Al-Mustazhi-billah, son of Al-Muktadi	
1118–1135	Caliph	Al-Mustarshir-billah, son of Al-Mustazhi-billah	
1135–1136	Caliph	Al-Raschid, son of Al-Mustarshir-billah	
1136–1160	Caliph	Al-Muktafi, son of Al-Mustarshir-billah	
1160–1170	Caliph	Al-Muktanijd-billah, son of Al-Muktafi	
1170–1180	Caliph	Al-Mustadi, son of Al-Mukstanijd-billah	
1180–1225	Caliph	Al-Nasir, son of Al-Mustadi	
1225–1226	Caliph	Al-Zahir, son of Al-Nasir	
1226–1242	Caliph	Al-Munstansir	
1242–1258	Caliph	Al-Mustasin-billah	

Dynasty Overthrown by Mongols in 1258

Cambodia (Kingdom of Cambodia)

The Kingdom of Cambodia reached its apogee of power around 1000 as the Khmer Empire. A long decline began in the 15th century. In 1863 Cambodia became a French protectorate until 1954, when independence was gained. Below are listed the better known monarchs since independence from France in 1953. Under the Constitution of 1993 (amended in 1999), Cambodia is a constitutional monarchy with the king as head of state who appoints the prime minister.

802 ?–850	King	Jayavarman II	d. 850
850–877	King	Jayavarman III	
877–889	King	Indravarman I	
889–900	King	Yasovarman I	
928–942	King	Jayavarman IV	
944–968	King	Rajendravarman II	
968–1001	King	Jayavarman V	
1002–1050	King	Suryavarman I	
1050–1066	King	Udayadityavarman II	

1066–1080	King	Harshavarman III	
1080–1107	King	Jayavarman VI	
1107–1113	King	Dharanindravarman I	
1113–1150	King	Suryavarman II	
1181–1218?	King	Jayavarman VII	b. 1125 d. 1218?
1941–1955	King	Norodom Sihanouk (abdicated)	b. 1922
1955–1960	King	Norodom Suramarit (joint ruler)	d. 1960
1955–1960	Queen	Kossamak (joint ruler)	
1960	Chief of State	Norodom Sihanouk	
1960–1970	Chief of State	Norodom Sihanouk	
1970–1975	Military dictator	Lon Nol	
1975–1979	Prime Minister	Pol Pot	
1979–1992	Vietnam client	Heng Samrin	
1992–1993	Chair, Council of State	Chea Sim	
1993–	King	Norodom Sihanouk	

Cameroon (Republic of Cameroon)

An independent republic since 1960, portions of the original territory seceded to become part of Nigeria.

1960–1982	President	Ahmadou Ahidjo
1982–	President	Paul Biya

Canada (Official U.N. Name)

■ French Colony

1608–1629	Lieutenant-Governor of Quebec	Samuel de Champlain	b. 1567? d. 1635
1629	Governor	Samuel de Champlain	
1633–1635	Governor	Samuel de Champlain	
1636–1648	Governor	Charles Huault de Montmagny	
1648–1651	Governor	Louis D'Ailleboust de Coulonge	
1651–1656	Governor	Jean de Lauzon	
1658–1661	Governor	Pierre de Voyer, Vicomte D'Argenson	
1661–1663	Governor	Pierre Dubois, Baron D'Avaugour	
1663–1665	Governor	Augustin de Saffray Mésy	
1665–1672	Governor	Daniel de Rémy de Courcelle	
1672–1682	Governor	Louis de Buade, Comte de Palluau et de Frontenac	b. 1620 d. 1698
1682–1685	Governor	Le Febvre de La Barre	

1685–1689	Governor	Jacques-René de Brisay, Marquis de Denonville	
1689–1698	Governor	Louis de Buade, Comte de Palluau et de Frontenac	
1699–1703	Governor	Louis Hector de Callières Bonnevue	b. 1646 d. 1703
1703–1725	Governor	Philippe de Rigaud, Marquis de Vaudreuil	b. 1643 d. 1725
1714–1716	Governor	Claude de Ramesay	
1726–1747	Governor	Charles Beauharnois, Marquis de La Galissonnière, Rolland	
1749–1752	Governor	Jacques Pierre de Taffanel, Marquis de La Jonquière	b. 1680 d. 1753
1752–1755	Governor	Duquesne, Marquis de Menneville	
1755–1760	Governor	Pierre de Rigaud, Marquis de Vaudreuil-Cavagnal	b. 1698 d. 1765
1760–1763	Head of English Military Government	Jeffrey Amherst	b. 1717 d. 1797

■ British Colony

The French colony became a possession of Great Britain by the Treaty of Paris in 1763.

1763–1768	Governor	James Murray	b. 1721 d. 1794
1768–1778	Governor	Sir Guy Carleton, Baron Dorchester	b. 1724 d. 1808
1778–1786	Governor	Sir Frederick Haldimand	b. 1718 d. 1791
1786–1796	Governor	Sir Guy Carleton	
1797–1807	Governor	Robert Prescott	
1807–1811	Governor	Sir James Henry Craig	b. 1748 d. 1812
1811–1815	Governor	Sir George Prevost	b. 1767 d. 1816
1816–1818	Governor	Sir John Coape Sherbrooke	b. 1764 d. 1830
1818–1819	Governor	Charles Lennox, Duke of Richmond	b. 1764 d. 1819
1819–1828	Governor	George Ramsay, Earl of Dalhousie	b. 1770 d. 1838
1831–1835	Governor	Lord Aylmer	
1835–1838	Governor	A. A. Gosford	
1838	Governor	John George Lambton, Earl of Durham	b. 1792 d. 1840
1838–1839	Governor	Sir John Colborne	b. 1778 d. 1863
1839–1841	Governor	Charles Edward Poulett Thomson	b. 1799 d. 1841
1841–1843	Governor	Sir Charles Bagot	b. 1781 d. 1843
1843–1845	Governor	Sir Charles Theophilus Metcalfe	b. 1785 d. 1846
1846–1847	Governor	Charles Murray, Earl of Cathcart	b. 1783 d. 1859
1847–1854	Governor	James Bruce, Earl of Elgin	b. 1811 d. 1863
1854–1861	Governor	Sir Edmund Walker Head	b. 1805 d. 1868
1861–1867	Governor	Charles Stanley Monck	b. 1819 d. 1894

In 1867 Canada was granted a constitution as a Dominion.
Monck became the first Governor-General of Canada.

■ Governors-General (Since Confederation 1867)

1867–1868	Governor-General	Charles Stanley, Viscount Monck	b. 1819 d. 1894
1868–1872	Governor-General	John Young, Lord Lisgar	b. 1807 d. 1876
1872–1878	Governor-General	Frederick Temple Hamilton Temple Blackwood, Marquis of Dufferin and Ava	b. 1826 d. 1902
1878–1883	Governor-General	John Douglas Sutherland Campbell, Marquis of Lorne	b. 1826 d. 1902
1883–1888	Governor-General	Henry Charles Keith Petty-Fitzmaurice, Marquis of Lansdowne	b. 1845 d. 1927
1888–1893	Governor-General	Frederick Arthur Stanley, Lord Stanley of Preston	b. 1841 d. 1908
1893–1898	Governor-General	Sir John Campbell Gordon, Earl of Aberdeen	b. 1847 d. 1934
1898–1904	Governor-General	Gilbert John Elliot-Murray-Kynynmound, Earl of Minto	b. 1845 d. 1914
1904–1911	Governor-General	Albert Henry George, Earl Grey	b. 1851 d. 1917
1911–1916	Governor-General	Arthur William Patrick Albert Wettin, Field Marshal H.R.H. Duke of Connaught	b. 1850 d. 1942
1916–1921	Governor-General	Victor Christian William, Duke of Devonshire	b. 1868 d. 1938
1921–1926	Governor-General	Julian Hedworth George Byng, General The Lord Byng of Vimy	b. 1862 d. 1935
1926–1931	Governor-General	Freeman Freeman-Thomas, Viscount Willingdon of Ratton	b. 1866 d. 1941
1931–1935	Governor-General	Vere Brabazon Ponsonby, Earl of Bessborough	b. 1880 d. 1956
1935–1940	Governor-General	John Buchan, Lord Tweedsmuir of Elsfield	b. 1875 d. 1940
1940–1946	Governor-General	Alexander Augustus Frederick William Alfred George Cambridge, Major-General The Earl of Athlone	b. 1874 d. 1957
1946–1952	Governor-General	Harold Rupert Leofric George Alexander, Field Marshal Viscount Alexander of Tunis	b. 1891
1952–1959	Governor-General	Vincent Massey	b. 1887
1959–1967	Governor-General	Major-General Georges Philias Vanier	b. 1888 d. 1967
1967–1974	Governor-General	Daniel Roland Michener	b. 1900
1974–1979	Governor-General	Edward Schreyer	
1984–1990	Governor-General	Jeanne Sauvé	
1990–1995	Governor	Ramon John Hnatyshyn	
1995–1999	Governor	Roméo LeBlanc	
1999–2005	Governor	Addrienne Clarkson	
2005–	Governor	Michaëlle Jean	

■ Prime Ministers (Since Confederation 1867)

L = Liberal   C = Conservative

The Conservative Party assumed the formal name Progressive Conservative in 1942. In 2003 a realignment of various conservative political groups occurred, with the current Conservative Party being the result of a merger between the Progressive Conservative Party and the Canadian Alliance.

1867–1873	Prime Minister	Sir John Alexander Macdonald (C)	b. 1815 d. 1891
1873–1878	Prime Minister	Alexander Mackenzie (L)	b. 1822 d. 1892
1878–1891	Prime Minister	Sir John Alexander Macdonald (C)	
1891–1892	Prime Minister	Sir John Joseph Caldwell Abbott (C)	b. 1821 d. 1893
1892–1894	Prime Minister	Sir John Sparrow David Thompson (C)	b. 1844 d. 1894
1894–1896	Prime Minister	Sir Mackenzie Bowell (C)	b. 1823 d. 1917
1896	Prime Minister	Sir Charles Tupper (C)	b. 1821 d. 1915
1896–1911	Prime Minister	Sir Wilfrid Laurier (L)	b. 1841 d. 1919
1911–1920	Prime Minister	Sir Robert Laird Borden (C)	b. 1854 d. 1937
1920–1921	Prime Minister	Arthur Meighen (Unionist)	b. 1874 d. 1960
1921–1926	Prime Minister	William Lyon Mackenzie King (L)	b. 1874 d. 1950
1926	Prime Minister	Arthur Meighen (C)	
1926–1930	Prime Minister	William Lyon Mackenzie King (L)	
1930–1935	Prime Minister	Richard Bedford Bennett, (Viscount Bennett, 1941) (C)	b. 1870 d. 1947
1935–1948	Prime Minister	William Lyon Mackenzie King (L)	
1948–1957	Prime Minister	Louis Stephen St. Laurent (L)	b. 1882 d. 1973
1957–1963	Prime Minister	John Diefenbaker (C)	b. 1895 d. 1979
1963–1968	Prime Minister	Lester Bowles Pearson (L)	b. 1897 d. 1972
1968–1979	Prime Minister	Pierre Elliot Trudeau (L)	b. 1919 d. 2000
1979–1980	Prime Minister	Charles Joseph Clarke (C)	b. 1939
1980–1984	Prime Minister	Pierre Elliot Trudeau (L)	
1984–1984	Prime Minister	John Napier Turner (L)	b. 1929
1984–1993	Prime Minister	M. Brian Mulroney (C)	b. 1939
1993–1993	Prime Minister	A. Kim Campbell (C)	b. 1947
1993–2003	Prime Minister	Jean Chrétien (L)	b. 1934
2003–	Prime Minister	Paul Martin (L)	b. 1938

■ British Columbia

1858–1864	Governor	Sir James Douglas
1864–1869	Governor	Frederick Seymour
1869–1871	Governor	Anthony Musgrave

■ Newfoundland

Newfoundland was discovered by John Cabot in 1497 and was taken possession by Sir Humphrey Gilbert in 1583.

1729–1731	Governor	Henry Osborne	d. 1771
1731	Governor	Captain Clinton	b. 1686 d. 1761
1732	Governor	Captain Falkenham	

1733	Governor	Lord Muskerry	d. 1769
1735–1737	Governor	Fitzroy Henry Lee	
1738	Governor	Captain Vanbrugh	d. 1753
1739	Governor	Henry Medley d. 1747	
1740	Governor	Lord George Graham	
1741–1743	Governor	Thomas Smith	d. 1762
1742	Governor	John Byng	b. 1704 d. 1757
1744	Governor	Charles Hardy	b. 1716 d. 1780
1746	Governor	Richard Edwards	d. 1773
1748	Governor	Charles Watson	
1749	Governor	George Brydges, Lord Rodney	b. 1719 d. 1792
1750	Governor	Francis W. Drake	d. 1780
1753	Governor	Hugh Bonfoy	d. 1762
1755–1756	Governor	Richard Dorril	d. 1762
1757–1760	Governor	Richard Edwards	
1761	Governor	James Webb	d. 1761
1762–1764	Governor	Lord Thomas Graves	b. 1725 d. 1802
1764	Governor	Sir Hugh Palliser	b. 1722 d. 1796
1769	Governor	John Byron	b. 1723 d. 1786
1772	Governor	Molyneaux, Lord Shuldham	d. 1798
1775	Governor	Robert Duff	d. 1787
1776–1778	Governor	John Montague	b. 1719 d. 1795
1779	Governor	Richard Edwards	d. 1794
1782–1786	Governor	John Campbell	b. 1720 d. 1790
1786–1789	Governor	Rear Admiral Elliott	d. 1808
1790–1792	Governor	Mark Milbanke	b. 1725 d. 1805
1792	Governor	Sir R. King	b. 1730 d. 1806
1794–1796	Governor	Sir James Wallace	b. 1731 d. 1803
1797	Governor	William Waldegrave, Lord Radstock	b. 1753 d. 1825
1800	Governor	Sir Charles Morice Pole	b. 1757
1802	Governor	Lord James Gambier	b. 1756 d. 1833
1804	Governor	Sir Erasmus Gower	d. 1814
1807–1810	Governor	Admiral Holloway	b. 1742 d. 1826
1810–1813	Governor	Sir John Thomas Duckworth	b. 1748 d. 1817
1813–1816	Governor	Sir Richard Godwin Keats	b. 1757 d. 1834
1817	Governor	Sir Francis Pickmore	
1818–1824	Governor	Sir Chas. Hamilton	b. 1767 d. 1849
1825–1834	Governor	Sir Thos. Cochrane	b. 1789

1834–1841	Governor	Sir H. Prescott	b. 1783 d. 1874
1841–1846	Governor	Sir John Harvey	b. 1778 d. 1852
1847–1852	Governor	Sir J. Gaspard LeMarchant	b. 1803 d. 1874
1852–1855	Governor	Ker Baillie Hamilton	
1855	Governor	Charles Henry Darling	b. 1809 d. 1870
1857	Governor	Sir Alexander Bannerman	b. 1783 d. 1864
1864	Governor	Sir Anthony Musgrave	b. 1828 d. 1888
1869	Governor	Sir Stephen John Hill	b. 1808 d. 1891
1876	Governor	Sir John Hawley Glover	b. 1829 d. 1885
1881	Governor	Sir Henry Fitz-Harding Maxse	b. 1830 d. 1883
1884	Governor	Sir John Hawley Glover	
1886	Governor	Sir George W. Des Voeux	b. 1834 d. 1909
1887	Governor	Sir Henry A. Blake	b. 1840 d. 1918
1889–1895	Governor	Sir Terrence N. O'Brien	b. 1830 d. 1903
1895–1898	Governor	Sir Herbert H. Murray	b. 1829 d. 1904
1898–1901	Governor	Sir Henry Edward McCallum	b. 1852 d. 1919
1901–1904	Governor	Sir Cavendish Boyle	b. 1849 d. 1916
1904–1909	Governor	Sir William McGregor	b. 1846 d. 1919
1909–1913	Governor	Sir Ralph C. Williams	b. 1848 d. 1927
1913–1917	Governor	Sir Walter E. Davidson	b. 1859 d. 1923
1917–1922	Governor	Sir Charles A. Harris	b. 1855 d. 1947
1922–1928	Governor	Sir William L. Alderdyce	
1928–1932	Governor	Sir John Middleton	
1932–1936	Governor	Sir David Murray Anderson	
1936–1946	Governor	Sir Humphrey Thomas Walwyn	
1946–1949	Governor	Sir Gordon A. MacDonald	

Newfoundland became the tenth province of the Dominion of Canada in 1949.

■ Nova Scotia

Nova Scotia was ceded to Britain in 1713.

1710–1713	Governor	Samuel Vetch	b. 1668 d. 1732
1713–1715	Governor	Francis Nicholson	b. 1655 d. 1728
1715–1717	Governor	Samuel Vetch	
1753–1760	Governor	Charles Lawrence	b. 1709 d. 1760
1760–1763	Governor	Jonathan Belcher	b. 1710 d. 1776
1776–1778	Governor	Mariot Arbuthnot	b. 1711 d. 1794
1778–1781	Governor	Richard Hughes	b. 1729? d. 1812

1781–1782	Governor	Sir Andrew Snop Hamond	b. 1738 d. 1828
1783–1786	Governor	Edmund Fanning	b. 1737 d. 1818
1786–1791	Governor	John Parr	b. 1725 d. 1791
1792–1808	Governor	John Wentworth	b. 1737 d. 1820
1808–1811	Governor	Sir George Prevost	b. 1767 d. 1816
1811–1816	Governor	Sir John Coape Sherbrooke	b. 1764 d. 1830
1816–1820	Governor	George Ramsay, Earl of Dalhousie	b. 1770 d. 1838
1820–1828	Governor	Sir James Kempt	b. 1764 d. 1854
1828–1834	Governor	Sir Peregrine Maitland	b. 1777 d. 1854
1834–1840	Governor	Sir Colin Campbell	b. 1776 d. 1847
1840–1846	Governor	Viscount Falkland	b. 1803 d.1884
1846–1852	Governor	Sir John Harvey	b. 1778 d. 1852
1852–1858	Governor	Sir John Gaspard Le Marchant	b. 1803 d. 1874
1858–1863	Governor	Sir George Augustus Constantine Phipps, Earl of Mulgrave	b. 1819 d. 1890
1864–1865	Governor	Sir Richard Graves MacDonnell	b. 1814 d. 1881
1865–1867	Governor	Sir F. W. Williams	b. 1800 d. 1883

Became a Province of the Dominion of Canada in 1867

■ **Vancouver Island**

1849–1851	Governor	Richard Blanshard	
1851–1864	Governor	Sir James Douglas	b. 1803 d. 1877
1864–1866	Governor	Arthur Edward Kennedy	

United with British Columbia in 1866

■ **Nunavut**

Although technically a territory within Canada, Nunavut enjoys a unique degree of autonomy under the 1999 Land Claims Agreement that established its legal existence. The ancestral homeland of the Inuit People, it encompasses a territory twice the size of Ontario.

| 1999– | Premier | Paul Okalik |

Cape Verde (Republic of Cape Verde)

Independent from Portugal since 1975, Cape Verde is not a cape but a collection of ten islands and islets about 300 miles off the Atlantic coast from Africa.

1975–1991	President	Aristides Pereira
1991–2001	President	António Manuel Mascarenhas Gomes Monteiro
2001–	President	Pedro Verona Rodrigues Pires

Cappadocia

Cappadocia, situated in eastern Anatolia, emerged as an independent kingdom in the 3rd century B.C., after being successively under the rules of Persia, Macedonia, and Syria.

c. 250 B.C.	King	Ariarathes IV	
190	King	Ariarathes V	
	King	Mithridates	
	King	Ariarathes VI	
	King	Ariarathes VII	
	King	Ariarathes VIII	
?90–63	King	Ariobarzanes I	d. 63
63–51	King	Ariobarzanes II	d. 51
51–42	King	Ariobarzanes III	d. 42
34 –A.D. 17	King	Archelaus	d. A.D. 17

Became a Roman Province in 17 A.D.

Carthage

Carthage began as a Phoenician colony in what is now Tunisia around 900 B.C. It rose to be a great empire.

c. 400 B.C.	Suffete (head of oligarchic council)	Mago	
c. 250	Soldier and Statesman	Hamilcar Barca	d. 228
c. 250	Leader of aristocratic faction	Hanno	
221–183?	General and Chief Magistrate	Hannibal	b. 247 d. 183??
?–221	General and Statesman	Hasdrubal	d. 229

Carthage was conquered finally by Rome in 146 B.C.
Its home territory became the Roman province of Africa.

Central African Republic (Official U.N. Name)

The Central African Republic was the French colony Ubangi Shari (Oubangui-Chari) from 1910 to 1958. It became an autonomous republic within the French Community in 1958 and fully independent in 1960.

1959–1965	President	David Dacko
1966–1976	President	Jean-Bedel Bokassa
1976–1979	Emperor	Bokassa I
1979–1981	President	David Dacko
1981–1993	President	Andre Kolingba
1993–2003	President	Ange-Felix Patasse
2003–	President	François Bozizé-Yangouvonda

Central American Federation

Costa Rica, Guatemala, Honduras, Nicaragua, and El Salvador were united under Spanish rule; became independent in 1821; came under Mexican rule from 1821 to 1823; and then regained independence as the Central American Federation from 1823 to 1838, when the Federation dissolved.

| 1825–1829 | President | Manuel José Arce (deposed) | d. 1847 |
| 1830–1838 | President | Francisco Morazón (Federation dissolved in 1838) | b. 1799 d. 1842 |

Chad (Republic of Chad)

The former French Overseas Territory of Chad became an independent republic in 1960.

1960–1975	President	François Tombalbaye
1975–1979	President	Felix Malloum
1979–1981	President	Goukouni Oueddei
1981–1990	President	Habre
1990–	President	Idriss Deby

Champagne *See* France

Chile (Republic of Chile)

Settled by Spaniards from 1540 to 1565, Chile declared independence in 1810.

?–1541		*Araucanian Indians*	
1541–1554	Conqueror	Pedro de Valdivia	b. 1510 killed 1554
1557–1561	Conqueror	García Hurtado de Mendoza (conquest resumed)	
1561–1609		*Spanish Conquest Continued Apathetically*	
1609–1778		*Administered by Spanish governors as part of the Peruvian Vice-royalty.*	
1778–1810		*Under Charles III (Spain), Chile became captaincy general, autonomous of Peru.*	
1788–1795	Governor	Ambrosio O'Higgins, later Marquis of Orsono. An Irish immigrant, father of Bernardo O'Higgins.	b. 1720? d. 1801
1796–1801	Viceroy	Marquis of Osorno	
		Declared Independence in 1810	
1811–1813	Dictator	José Miguel Carrera	b. 1785 killed 1821
1813–1814	Dictator	Bernardo O'Higgins	b. 1776 d. 1842
1814–1818		*War*	
		In 1814 royalist armies from Peru reconquered Chile, but were finally defeated in a decisive battle by Gen. José de San Martín with the help of Argentine troops. San Martín was offered the dictatorship of Chile as a reward, but proclaimed O'Higgins "Supreme Director" instead.	
1823–1826	President	Ramón Freire	b. 1787 d. 1851

1826–1828	President	Manuel Blanco Encalada	b. 1790 d. 1876
1828–1831	President	Francisco A. Pinto	b. 1785 d. 1858
1831–1841	President	Joaquín Prieto	b. 1786 d. 1854
1841–1851	President	Manuel Bulnes	b. 1799 d. 1866
1851–1861	President	Manuel Montt	b. 1809 d. 1880
1861–1871	President	José Joaquín Peréz	b. 1801 d. 1889
1871–1876	President	Federico Errázuriz Zañartu	b. 1825 d. 1877
1876–1881	President	Aníbal Pinto	b. 1825 d. 1884
1881–1886	President	Domingo Santa María	b. 1825 d. 1889
1886–1891	President	José Manuel Balmaceda	b. 1838 d. 1891
1891–1896	President	Jorge Montt	b. 1847 d. 1922
1896–1901	President	Federico Errázuriz Echaurren	b. 1850 d. 1901
1901–1906	President	Germán Riesco	b. 1854 d. 1916
1906–1910	President	Pedro Montt	b. 1848 d. 1910
1910–1915	President	Ramón Barros Luco	b. 1835 d. 1919
1915–1920	President	Juan Luis Sanfuentes	b. 1858 d. 1930
1920–1925	President	Arturo Alessandri Palma	b. 1868 d. 1951
1925	President	Luis Altamirano	d. 1936
1925 1927	President	Emiliano Figueroa Larrain	
1927–1931	President	Carlos Ibáñez del Campo	b. 1877 d. 1960
1931–1932	President	Juan Estaban Montero	b. 1879 d. 1952
1932	President	Carlos Dávila Espinoza	d. 1957
1932–1938	President	Arturo Allessandri Palma	
1938–1942	President	Pedro Aguirre Cerda	b. 1879 d. 1946
1942–1946	President	Juan Antonio Ríos	b. 1888 d. 1946
1946–1952	President	Gabriel González Videla	b. 1898
1952–1958	President	Carlos Ibáñez del Campo	
1958–1964	President	Jorge Alessandri Rodriguez	b. 1896
1964–1970	President	Eduardo Frei	b. 1911
1970–1973	President	Salvador Allende	
1973–1990	President	Augusto Pinochet	
1990–1994	President	Patricio Aylwin	
1994–2000	President	Eduardo Frei Ruiz-Tagle	
2000–	President	Ricardo Lagos Escobar	

China (People's Republic of China)

An Empire from the 23rd century B.C. until A.D. 1912, when it became a republic, China's recent history has been dominated by the establishment of the People's Republic of China by Mao Tse Tung in the aftermath of World War II.

■ Imperial Dynasties

2205–1766 B.C.	Dynasty	Hsia	
1766–1122	Dynasty	Shang (or Yin)	
1122–255	Dynasty	Chou (or Chow)	
255–206	Dynasty	Ch'in (or Ts'in)	
202 B.C.–A.D. 9	Dynasty	Han, Earlier	
25–220	Dynasty	Han, Later	
220–264	Dynasty	Wei	
265–317	Dynasty	Chin or Tsin (Western)	
317–419	Dynasty	Chin or Tsin (Eastern)	
420–479	Dynasty	Sung (Liu Sung)	
479–502	Dynasty	Ch'I (Tsi)	
502–557	Dynasty	Liang	
557–589	Dynasty	Ch'en (Chen)	
589–618	Dynasty	Sui	
618–907	Dynasty	T'ang (Tang)	
618–626	Emperor	Kao-tsu	
627–649	Emperor	Tai-tsung, son of Kao-tsu	
650–683	Emperor	Kao-tsung, son of Tai-tsung	
684–704	Emperor	Wu-hou, consort of Tai-tsung	
713–755	Emperor	Ming-huang	
756–762	Emperor	Su-tsung, son of Ming-huang	
763–779	Emperor	Tai-tsung	
750–804	Emperor	To-tsung	
907–1125	Dynasty	Liang	
923–936	Dynasty	T'ang	
936–946	Dynasty	Chin	
947–950	Dynasty	Han	
951–960	Dynasty	Chou	
960–1127	Dynasty	Sung (all China)	
1127–1280	Dynasty	Sung (in South China)	
		Mongol Invasion of North China from 1127 to 1280	
1206–1280	Dynasty	Yüan (in North China)	
1260–1294	Emperor	Kublai Khan	b. 1216? d. 1294

1280–1368	Dynasty	Yüan	
1368–1644	Dynasty	Ming	
1368–1398	Emperor	Hung-wu	b. 1328 d. 1398
1403–1424	Emperor	Yung-lo	b. 1359 d. 1424
1426–1435	Emperor	Hsüan-te	
1488–1505	Emperor	Hung-his	
1522–1566	Emperor	Chia-ching	d. 1566
1573–1619	Emperor	Wan-li	b. 1563 d. 1620
1644–1912	Dynasty	Ch'ing or Ta Ch'ing (Manchu)	

■ Rulers of Ch'ing Dynasty

1644–1661	Emperor	Shih-tsu (Shun-chih)	b. 1638 d. 1661
1662–1722	Emperor	K'ang-hsi, son of Shih-tsu	b. 1654 d. 1722
1723–1735	Emperor	Yung-cheng, son of K'ang-hsi	b. 1678 d. 1735
1736–1796	Emperor	Ch'lien-lung, son of Yung-cheng	b. 1711 d. 1799
1796–1820	Emperor	Jen-tsung, Chia-ch'ing, son of Ch'lien-lung	b. 1760 d. 1820
1820–1850	Emperor	Hsüan-tsung, Tao-kuang, son of Jen-tsung, Chia-ch'ing	b. 1782 d. 1850
1851–1861	Emperor	Wen-tsung, Hsien-feng, son of Hsüan-tsung, Tao-kuang	b. 1831 d. 1861
1862–1875	Emperor	Ki-tsiang, T'ung-chi, son of Wen-tsung, Hsien-feng	b. 1856 d. 1875
1862–1873	Regent	Tsu-hsi, wife of Wen-tsung, Hsien-feng	b. 1835 d. 1908
1875–1889	Empress	Tsu-hsi	
1875–1908	Emperor	Tsai-tien, Kuang-hsü, cousin of Ki-tsiang, T'ung-chi	b. 1871 d. 1908
1898–1908	Empress	Tsu-hsi	
1908–1912	Emperor	P'u-yi, Hsüan-t'ung, nephew of Tsai-tien, Kuang-hsü (Emperor of Manchukuo in 1934)	abdicated 1912 b. 1906

■ Republic

1912–1913	Provisional President	Yüan-Shih-k'ai	b. 1859 d. 1916
1913–1916	President	Yüan-Shih-k'ai	
1916–1917	President	Li-Yüan-hung	b. 1864 d. 1928
1917–1925	Head of Government in Canton	Sun Yat-sen	b. 1867 d. 1925
1917–1918	President	Feng Kuo-chang	
1918–1922	President	Su Shi-chang	
1922–1923	President	Li-Yüan-hung	
1923–1924	Provisional President	Ts'ao K'un	b. 1862 d. 1938

1924–1926	President	Tuan Ch'i-jui	b. 1864 d. 1936
1927–1931	President (in Nanking)	Chiang Kai-shek	b. 1886
1932–1943	President	Lin Sen	b. 1867? d.1943

■ People's Republic of China

1949–1976	Chairman	Mao Tse-tung	b. 1893 d. 1976
1949–1976	Premier	Chou En-lai	b. 1898? d. 1976
1976–1980	Premier	Hua Guofeng	
1980–1987	Premier	Zhao Ziyang	
1987–1998	Premier	Li Peng	
1998–2003	Premier	Zhu Rongji	
2003–	Premier	Wen Jiabao	

■ Hong Kong (Hong Kong Special Administrative District)

Hong Kong was ceded to Britain by China in 1842 and remained a crown colony until 1997.

1843–1844	Governor	Sir Henry Pottinger	b. 1789 d. 1856
1844–1848	Governor	Sir John Francis Davis	
1848–1854	Governor	Sir Samuel George Bonham	
1854–1859	Governor	Sir John Bowring	b. 1792 d. 1872
1859–1866	Governor	Sir Hercules George Robert Robinson, Baron Rosmead	b. 1824 d. 1897
1866–1872	Governor	Sir Richard Graves MacDonnell	
1872–1877	Governor	Sir Arthur Edward Kennedy	
1877–1883	Governor	Sir John Pope Hennessy	
1883–1887	Governor	Sir George Ferguson Bowen	b. 1821 d. 1899
1887–1891	Governor	Sir George William Des Voeux	b. 1834 d. 1909
1891–1898	Governor	Sir William Robinson	b. 1836 d. 1912
1898–1904	Governor	Sir Henry Arthur Blake	b. 1840 d. 1918
1904–1907	Governor	Sir Matthew Nathan	b. 1862 d. 1939
1907–1912	Governor	Sir Frederick John Dealtry Lugard, Baron Lugard	b. 1858 d. 1945

An energetic colonial administrator, Lord Lugard did much to abolish slave trading and build up the British dominions during his long service as a commissioner and governor.

1912–1919	Governor	Sir Francis Henry May	b. 1860 d. 1922
1919–1925	Governor	Sir Reginald Edward Stubbs	b. 1876 d. 1947
1925–1930	Governor	Sir Cecil Clementi	b. 1875 d. 1947
1930–1935	Governor	Sir William Peel	b. 1875 d. 1945
1935–1937	Governor	Sir Andrew Caldecott	b. 1884 d. 1951

1937–1941	Governor	Sir Geoffry Alexander Stafford Northcote	b. 1881 d. 1948
1941–1947	Governor	Sir Mark Aitchison Young	b. 1886
1947–1958	Governor	Sir Alexander William George Herder Grantham	b. 1899
1958–1964	Governor	Sir Robert Brown Black	b. 1906
1964–1971	Governor	Sir David Clive Crosbie Trench	b. 1915
1971–1982	Governor	Lord Crawford Murray MacLehose	b. 1917 d. 2000
1982–1986	Governor	Sir Edward Youde	b. 1924 d. 1986
1986–1992	Governor	Lord David Wilson	b. 1935
1992–1997	Governor	Chris Patten	b. 1944

In 1997 sovereignty over Hong Kong reverted to the People's Republic of China. The first Chief Executive of the Hong Kong Special Administrative Region, Tung Chee-hwa, was reelected to a second term of office under a system that is partly appointive and partly representative.

1997–2005	Chief Executive	Tung Chee-hwa	b. 1937
1997–2005	Chief Executive	Tung Chee Hwa (2 terms)	b. 1937
2005	Chief Executive (acting)	Donald Tsang	b. 1944
2005	Chief Executive (acting)	Henry Tang	b. 1953
2005–	Chief Executive	Donald Tsang	b. 1944

■ Macau

A trading outpost of the Portuguese Empire as early as the 1500s, Macau became an uncontested colony in 1887. One century later, an agreement was reached to restore sovereignty to the People's Republic of China as a Special Administrative Region.

1999–	Chief Executive	Edmund Ho

■ Manchuria

Manchuria was part of China until the fall of the Chinese Empire in 1911.

1911–1928	Military Governor	Chang Tso-lin	b. 1873 assassinated 1928
1928–1932	Military Governor	Chang Hsueh-liang, son of Chang Tso-lin	b. 1898

Manchuria Occupied by Japan from 1930 to 1932

■ Manchukuo

The Japanese established a puppet state in Manchuria in 1932 under the name of Manchukuo.

1932–1934	Chief Executive	Henry Pu-yi (Hsüan T'ung)	b. 1906
		(See China)	
1934–1945	Emperor	Kang Teh (Hsüan T'ung)	
		Part of China since 1945	

Colombia (Republic of Colombia)

? –1536	Tipa (Chief)	Nemenquene, chief of Chibcha Indians at Bogota	
1499–1536		*Discovery and Partial Conquest by Spain*	
1536–1541	Conqueror	Gonzalo Jimenez de Quesada	b. 1500? d. 1579
		The greatest of the conquistadores, Gonzalo subdued the mighty Chibcha Indian nation, assuring full control of the land. In 1538 he founded Santa Fé (now Bogotá) and, reminded of his native land, named Colombia "New Granada."	
1542–1549		*Spain Continued Conquest and Colonization*	
1549–1717		*King of Spain Made New Granada an* Audiencia	
		The state was to be governed by presidents who would also have authority as captains-general.	
1717–1810		*Colombia became the Vice-Royalty of New Granada, which encompassed what is modern-day Venezuela, Panama, and Ecuador.*	
? –1810	Viceroy	Antonio de Amar	
1810–1821	President	Simón Bolívar	
		A revolt for independence, headed by Simón Bolívar, broke out in 1810. At the end of a series of fierce battles, Colombia overcame the Spanish and declared itself the Republic of Greater Colombia in 1819. Bolívar was proclaimed president in 1821.	
1821–1828	Vice-President	Francisco de Paula Santander	b. 1792 d. 1840
		A commander of the warriors of the plains during the revolution, Santander helped Bolívar win the decisive battle at Boyacá and was named vice-president. He capably administered the country during the president's frequent absences, but, believing in constitutional government, Santander revolted against Bolívar and was suspended from office. Accused of attempting to assassinate Bolívar, Santander was banished. After Bolívar's death in 1830, Greater Colombia dissolved, and Santander was recalled to serve as the first President of Colombia, which was renamed New Granada.	
1831		*Republic of New Granada Organized*	
1832–1836	President	Francisco de Paula Santander	
1836–1840	President	José Ignacio de Marquez	
1840–1844	President	Pedro Alcantara Herron	
1844–1849	President	Tomás Cipriano de Mosquera	b. 1798 d. 1878
1849–1853	President	Jose Hilario Lopez	
1853–1857	President	Jose Maria Obando	
1857–1861	President	Mariano Ospina Rodriguez	
		Adopted Name of United States of Colombia in 1863	
1861–1863	Dictator	Tomás Cipriano de Mosquera	b. 1798 d.1878
1863	President	Froilán Largacha	

1863–1864	President	Tomás Cipriano de Mosquera	
1864	President (acting)	Juan Agustín Uricoechea	
1864–1866	President	Manuel Murillo Toro	
1866	President (acting)	José María Rojas Garrido	
1866–1867	President	Tomás Cipriano de Mosquera	
1867–1868	President (acting)	Santos Acosta	
1868–1870	President	Santos Gutiérrez	
1868–1869	President (acting)	Salvador Camacho Roldán	
1869–1870	President	Santiago Pérez	b. 1830 d. 1900
1870–1872	President	Eustorgio Salgar	
1872–1874	President	Manuel Murillo Toro	
1874–1876	President	Santiago Pérez	
1876–1878	President	Aquileo Parra	
1878–1880	President	Julián Trujillo	b. 1829 d. 1884
1880–1882	President	Rafael Núñez	b. 1825 d. 1894
1882	President	Francisco Javier Zaldúa	d. 1882
1882	President (acting)	Climacho Calderón	
1882–1884	President	José Eusebio Otálora	
1884	President (acting)	Ezequiel Hurtado	
1884–1886	President	Rafael Núñez	

Became Republic of Colombia in 1885

1886	President (acting)	José María Campo Serrano	
1887	President	Eliseo Payán	
1887–1888	President	Rafael Núñez	
1888–1892	President	Carlos Holguín	
1892–1896	President	Miguel Antonio Caro	b. 1843 d. 1909
1896	President	Guillermo Quintero Calderón	
1896–1898	President	Miguel Antonio Caro	
1898	President (acting)	José Manuel Marroquín	b. 1827 d. 1908
1898–1900	President	Manuel Antonio Sanclemente	
1900–1904	President	José Manuel Marroquin	
1904–1908	President	Rafael Reyes	b. 1850? d.1921
1908	President	Euclides de Angulo	
1908–1909	President	Rafael Reyes	
1909	President (acting)	Jorge Holguín	
1909–1910	President	Ramón González Valencia	
1910–1914	President	Carlos E. Restrepo	b. 1867 d. 1937
1914–1918	President	José Vicente Concha	

1918–1921	President	Marco Fidel Suárez	
1921–1922	President (acting)	Jorge Holguín	
1922–1926	President	Pedro Nel Ospina	
1926–1930	President	Miguel Abadía Méndez	b. 1867 d. 1947
1930–1934	President	Enrique Olaya Herrera	
1934–1938	President	Alfonso López	b. 1886 d. 1959
1938–1942	President	Eduardo Santos	b. 1888
1942–1945	President	Alfonso López	
1945–1946	President	Alberto Lleras Camargo	b. 1906
1946–1950	President	Mariano Ospina Pérez	b. 1891
1950–1953	President	Laureano Gómez	b. 1889
1951–1953	President (acting)	Roberto Urdaneta Arbeláez	b. 1890
1953–1957	Dictator	Gustavo Rojas Pinilla	b. 1900
1957–1958	President (acting)	Gabriel Paris	
		Military Junta from 1957 to 1958	
1958–1962	President	Alberto Lleras Camargo	
1962–1966	President	Guillermo-León Valencia	b. 1909 d. 1971
1966–1970	President	Carlos Lleras Restrepo	b. 1908 d. 1994
1970–1974	President	M. E. Pastrana Borrero	b. 1923 d. 1997
1974–1978	President	Alfonso López Michelsen	b. 1913
1978–1982	President	Julio César Turbay Ayala	b. 1916
1982–1986	President	Belisario Betancur Cuartas	b. 1923
1986–1990	President	Virgilio Barca Vargas	b. 1921 d. 1997
1990–1994	President	César Augusto Gaviria Trujillo	b. 1947
1994–1998	President	Ernesto Samper Pizano	b. 1950
1998–2002	President	Andrés Pastrana Arango	b. 1954
2002–	President	Álvaro Uribe	b. 1952

Comoros (Union of Comoros)

This archipelago-nation in the Indian Ocean declared its independence from France in 1975, although one of its islands, Mayotte, remains under French administration. The central government has not enjoyed considerable stability since that time. At present, the nation is ruled by President Azali Assoumani, a former army colonel.

Congo (Democratic Republic of Congo)

The state of Congo was founded in 1885. It was a Belgian colony from 1908 to 1960. It became an independent state in 1960.

1960–1965	President	Joseph Kasavubu	
1965–1997	President	Mobutu Sese Seko	b. 1930 d. 1997

| 1997–2001 | President | Laurent Désiré Kabila | b. 1939 d. 2001 |
| 2001– | President | Joseph Kabila | b. 1971 |

Congo (Republic of the Congo)

Congo was the former French colony of Moyen-Congo. It became a member state of the French Community in 1958 and fully independent in 1960.

1960–1963	President	Fulbert Youlou	b. 1917
1963–1968	President	Alphonse Massamba-Débat	b. 1921
		Instability	
1969–1977	President	Marien Ngouabi	b. 1938 d. 1977
1977–1979	President	Jacques Joachim Yhombi-Opango	
1979–1979	President	Jean-Pierre Thystere Tchicaya	
1979–1992	President	Denis Sassou-Nguesso	
1992–1997	President	Pascal Lissouba	
1997–	President	Denis Sassou-Nguesso	

Costa Rica (Republic of Costa Rica)

Costa Rica has been an independent republic since 1821. It was part of the Confederation of Central America from 1824 to 1838.

1847–1849	President	José María Castro ("Founder of the Republic")	b. 1818 d. 1893
1859	President	Juan Mora	
1859–1863	President	Jose Montealegre	
1863–1866	President	J. Jiménez	
1866–1868	President	José María Castro	
1868–1871	Governor	J. Jiménez	
1871	President	Vicente Quadra	
1871–1876	President	Tomás Guardia	b. 1832 d. 1882
1876	President	Aniceto Esquivel	
1876	President	Vicente Herrera	
1877–1882	Dictator	Tomás Guardia	
1882–1885	President	Próspero Fernández	b. 1834 d. 1885
1885–1890	President	Bernardo Soto	
1890	President	J. J. Rodriguez	
1893–1902	President	Rafael Iglesias	
1902–1906	President	Ascensión Esquivel	
1906–1910	President	Cleto González Víquez	
1910–1914	President	Ricardo Jiménez Oreamuno	b. 1859 d. 1945
1914–1917	President	Alfredo González Flores	

1917–1919	President	Federico Tinoco Granados	
1919–1920	President (provisional)	Francisco Aguilar Barquero	
1920–1924	President	Julio Acosta	b. 1872 d. 1954
1924–1928	President	Ricardo Jiménez Oreamuno	
1928–1932	President	Cleto González Viquez	
1932–1936	President	Ricardo Jiménez Oreamuno	
1936–1940	President	León Cortés Castro	b. 1882 d. 1946
1940–1944	President	Rafael Angel Calderón Guardia	b. 1900
1944–1948	President	Teodoro Picado Michalski	
1948–1949	President	José Figueres Ferrer	
1949–1953	President	Otilia Ulate	
1953–1958	President	José Figueres Ferrer	
1958–1962	President	Mario Echandi Jimenez	
1962–1966	President	Francisco J. Orlich Bolmarich	
1966–1970	President	José Joaquin Trejos Fernández	
1974–1978	President	Daniel Oduber Quirós	
1978–1982	President	Rodrigo Carazo Odio	
1982–1986	President	Luis Alberto Monge Alvarez	
1986–1990	President	Oscar Arias Sánchez	
1990–1994	President	Rafael Angel Calderón	
1994–1998	President	José María Figueres Olsen	
1998–2002	President	Miguel Ángel Rodrigues Echeverría	
2002–		Abel Pacheco de la Espriella	

Côte d'Ivoire (Republic of Côte d'Ivoire)

Côte d'Ivoire was a French colony from 1893 to 1958 and an autonomous republic within the French Community from 1958 to 1960, when it gained full independence.

1960–1993	President	Félix Houphouët-Boigny	b. 1905
1993–1999	President	Henri Konan Bedie	
1999–2002	President	General Guei	
2002–	President	Laurent Gbagbo	

Croatia (Republic of Croatia)

Croatia was under Hungary from 1091; under Turkey from 1526; part of France from 1809 to 1813; and under Austria-Hungary until 1918, when it became part of Yugoslavia. Croatia declared independence in 1941.

1941–1944	Dictator	Ante Pavelich	b. 1889 d. 1959

Kingdom Created by Italy

| 1941–1943 | King | Aimone of Spoleto | abdicated |

Croatia came under German control until the end of World War II,
when it was reincorporated into Yugoslavia as part of the Soviet bloc.
Independence from Yugoslavia was achieved in 1991.
The Dayton Peace Accords of 1995 brought a peaceful settlement
to a civil war against the Serbs.

1991–1999	President	Franjo Tudjman	d. 1999
1999–2000	Acting President	Vlatko Pavletic	
2000–2000	Acting President	Zlatko Tomcic	
2000–	President	Stjepan "Stipe" Mesic	

Cuba (Republic of Cuba)

Cuba was under Spanish rule from 1492 to 1898, except when under British occupancy from 1762 to 1763.

■ Spanish Governors

1834–1838	Governor	Miguel de Tacón	b. 1777 d. 1855
1838–1840	Governor	Joaquín Ezpeleta y Enrille	
1840–1841	Governor	Pedro Téllez de Girón	
1841–1843	Governor	Gerónimo Valdé y Sierra	
1843	Governor (provisional)	Francisco Javier de Ulloa	
1843–1848	Governor	Leopoldo O'Donnell, Count of Lucena	b. 1809 d. 1867
1848–1850	Governor	Federico Roncalí, Count of Alcoy	
1850–1852	Governor	José Gutiérrez de la Concha	
1852–1853	Governor	Valentín Cañedo Miranda	
1853–1854	Governor	Juan de la Pezuela	
1854–1859	Governor	José Gutiérrez de la Concha	
1859–1862	Governor	Francisco Serrano y Domínguez, Duque de la Torre	b. 1810 d. 1885
1862–1866	Governor	Domingo Dulce y Garay	
1866	Governor	Francisco Lersundi	
1866–1867	Governor	Joaquín del Manzano y Manzano	
1867	Governor	Blas Villate y de la Hera, Count of Balmaseda	b. 1825 d. 1882
1867–1869	Governor	Francisco Lersundi	
1869	Governor	Domingo Dulce y Garay	
1869	Governor (provisional)	Filipe Ginovés del Espinar	
1869–1870	Governor	Antonio Caballero y Fernández de Rodas	
1870–1872	Governor	Blas Villate y de la Hera, Count of Balmaseda	
1872–1873	Governor	Francisco Ceballos y Vargas	

1873	Governor	Cándido Pieltain y Jove-Huelgo	
1873–1874	Governor	Joaquín Jovellar y Soler	
1874–1875	Governor	José Gutiérrez de la Concha	
1875	Governor (provisional)	Buenaventura Carbó	
1875–1876	Governor	Blas Villate y de la Hera, Count of Balmaseda	
1876–1878	Governor	Joaquin Jovellar y Soler	
1876–1879	Governor	Arsenio Martínez de Campos	
1879	Governor (provisional)	Cayetano Figueroa y Garahondo	
1879–1881	Governor	Ramón Blanco y Erenas	
1881–1883	Governor	Luis Prendergast y Gordon	
1883	Governor (provisional)	Tomás de Reyna y Renya	
1883–1884	Governor	Ignacio María del Castillo	
1884–1886	Governor	Ramón Fajardo y Izquierdo	
1886–1887	Governor	Emilio Calleja e Isasi	
1887–1889	Governor	Sabás Marín y González	
1889–1890	Governor	Manuel Salamanca y Negrete	
1890	Governor (provisional)	José Sanchez Gómez	
1890	Governor	José Chinchilla y Díez de Oñate	
1890–1892	Governor	Camilo Polavieja y del Castillo	
1892–1893	Governor	Alejandro Rodríguez Arias	
1893	Governor (provisional)	José Arderius y García	
1893–1895	Governor	Emilio Calleja e Isasi	
1895–1896	Governor	Arsenio Martínez de Campos	
1896	Governor	Sabás Marín y González	
1896–1897	Governor	Valeriano Weyler y Nicolau	
1897–1898	Governor	Ramón Blanco y Erenas	
1898	Governor	Adolfo Jimenez Castellanos	

■ First American Intervention

1899	Military Governor	John Rutter Brooke	b. 1838 d. 1926
1899–1902	Military Governor	Leonard Wood	b. 1860 d. 1927

■ Cuban Republic

1902–1906	President	Tomás Estrada Palma	b. 1835 d. 1908

■ Second American Intervention

1906	Governor (provisional)	William Howard Taft	b. 1857 d. 1930
1906–1909	Governor (provisional)	Charles Edward Magoon	b. 1861 d. 1920

■ Cuban Republic Restored

1909–1913	President	José Miguel Gómez	b. 1858 d. 1921
1913–1921	President	Mario Garciá Menocal	b. 1866 d. 1941
1921–1925	President	Alfredo Zayas y Alfonso	b. 1861 d. 1934
1925–1933	President	Gerardo Machado y Morales	b. 1871 d. 1939
1933	President (provisional)	Carlos Manuel de Céspedes y Quesada, son of Carlos Manuel de Céspedes	b. 1871 d. 1939
		Provisional Junta	
1933–1934	President (provisional)	Ramón Grau San Martín	
1934–1935	President (provisional)	Carlos Mendieta	b. 1873 d. 1960
1935–1936	President (provisional)	José A. Barnet y Vinageras	
1936	President	Miguel Mariano Gómez y Arias, son of José Miguel Gómez	
1936–1940	President	Federico Laredo Bru	b. 1875 d. 1946
1940–1944	President	Fulgencio Batista y Zaldívar	b. 1901
1944–	President	Ramón Grau San Martín	
1948–1952	President	Carlos Prío Socarrás	
1952–1959	President	Fulgencio Batista y Zaldívar	
1959	President (provisional)	Manuel Urrutia Lleo	
1959–	Communist Dictator	Fidel Castro Ruz	b. 1927

Cyprus (Republic of Cyprus)

Cyprus was under Turkish rule until it was annexed to Britain from 1914 to 1925. It was then a British crown colony from 1925 to 1960. It became an independent sovereign republic in 1960.

1960–1974	President	Archbishop Makarios III	b. 1913
1974–1974	President	Nikos Sampson	

1974–1974	President	Glaukos Clerides
1977–1988	President	Spyros Kyprianou
1988–1993	President	Giorgios Vassiliou
1993–2003	President	Glaukos Clerides
2003–	President	Tassos Papadopoulos

Cyrenaica *See* Libya

Czech Republic (Official U.N. Name)

BOHEMIA
■ Přemyslid Dynasty

871–894	Count	Borivoj I	
894–895	Count	Spithnjew I, son of Borivoj	
895–912	Duke	Spithnjew I	
912–926	Duke	Vratislav I, son of Borivoj	
926–928	Regent	Drahomire, von Stoder, widow of Vratislav I	
928–935	Duke	Wenceslaus (Wenzel) the Holy, son of Vratislav I	b. 908 murdered 935
935–967	Duke	Boleslaus (Boleslav) I, brother of Wenceslaus the Holy	d. 967
967–999	Duke	Boleslaus (Boleslav) II, son of Boleslaus I	d. 999
999–1003	Duke	Boleslaus (Boleslav) III, son of Boleslaus II	d. 1037
1003–1035	Duke	Vladivoj of Poland	
1035–1055	Duke	Bretislav I	
1055–1061	Duke	Spithnjew II, son of Bretislav I	
1061–1092	Duke	Vratislav II, son of Bretislav I	
1092–1100	Duke	Bretislav II	
1100–1107	Duke	Borivoj II	
1107–1109	Duke	Swartopluk	
1100–1140		*Internal Conflicts*	
1109–1125	Duke	Ladislas I	
1125–1140	Duke	Sobjislaw	
1140–1158	Duke	Ladislas II	
1158–1173	King	Ladislas II	
1173–1197		*Internal Conflicts*	
1197–1230	King	Ottokar I, son of Ladislas II	d. 1230
1230–1253	King	Wenceslaus (Wenzel) I, son of Ottokar I	b. 1205 d. 1253
1253–1278	King	Ottokar II, son of Wenceslaus I	b. 1230? killed 1278

1278–1305	King	Wenceslaus (Wenzel) II, son of Ottokar II	b. 1271 d. 1305
1305–1306	King	Wenceslaus (Wenzel) III, son of Wenceslaus II	b. 1289 d. 1306
1306–1307	King	Rudolph, son of Albert, King of the Romans	d. 1307
1307–1310	King	Henry, Duke of Carinthia	d. 1335

■ Luxemburg Dynasty

1310–1346	King	John the Blind, brother-in-law of Wenceslaus III	b. 1296 killed 1346
1346–1378	King	Charles, son of John the Blind	b. 1316 d. 1378
		(See Holy Roman Empire*)*	
1378–1419	King	Wenceslaus (Wenzel) IV, (Holy Roman Emperor), son of Charles	b. 1361 d. 1419
1419–1436		*Hussite Wars*	
1419–1437	King	Sigismund of Hungary, brother of Wenceslaus IV	b. 1368 d. 1437

■ Habsburg (and other) Dynasties

1437–1439	King	Albert of Austria, son-in-law of Sigismund of Hungary	b. 1397 d. 1439
1440–1457	King	Ladislas Posthumus, son of Albert	b. 1440 d. 1457
1458–1471	King	George of Podebrad	b. 1420 d. 1471
1469	Rival King	Matthias of Hungary	
1471–1516	King	Ladislas II, (Vladislav), nephew of Ladislas Posthumus	b. 1456 d. 1516
1516–1526	King	Louis, son of Vladislav	b. 1506 killed 1526
1526–1564	King	Ferdinand I of Austria, son-in-law of Louis	b.1503 d. 1564
1526–1918		*Bohemia United with Austria under Hapsburgs*	
1619–1620	King	Frederick V of the Palatinate	b. 1596 d. 1632
		Part of Czechoslovakia since 1918	

■ Republic

The republic was founded in 1918.

1918–1935	President	Tomáš Garrigue Masaryk	b. 1850 d. 1937

A strong critic of Austrian policies, Masaryk escaped from Austria at the beginning of the First World War and became president of the revolutionary Czechoslovak National Council, which was recognized in 1918 as the de facto *government of the new state.*

1935–1938	President	Eduard Beneš	b. 1884 d. 1948
1938	President	Jan Syrovy	b. 1885
1938–1939	President	Emil Hácha	b. 1872 d. 1945
1939		*Annexed by Germany in 1939*	
1939–1945	President (in London)	Eduard Beneš	

1945–1948	President	Eduard Beneš	
1948		*Communist Regime Established in 1948*	
1948–1953	President	Klement Gottwald	b. 1896 d. 1953
1953–1957	President	Antonín Zapotocky	b. 1884 d. 1957
1957–1968	President	Antonín Novotny	b. 1904 d. 1975

■ Protectorate of Bohemia and Moravia

1939–1943	German Protector	Konstantin von Neurath	b. 1873 d. 1956
1939–1945	President	Emil Hácha	

■ Statesmen

1918–1919	Premier	Karel Kramár	b. 1860 d. 1937
1919–1920	Premier	Vlastimil Tusar	b. 1880 d. 1924
1920–1921	Premier	Jan Cerny	b. 1874 d. 1959
1921–1922	Premier	Eduard Beneš	
1922–1925	Premier	Antonín Svehla	b. 1873 d. 1933
1925–1926	Premier	Antonín Svehla	
1926	Premier	Jan Cerny	
1926–1929	Premier	Antonín Svehla	
1929–1932	Premier	Frantisek Udrzal	b. 1866 d. 1938
1932–1934	Premier	Jan Malypetr	b. 1873 d. 1947
1934–1935	Premier	Jan Malypetr	
1935–1937	Premier	Milan Hodza	b. 1878 d. 1944
1937–1938	Premier	Milan Hodza	
1938	Premier	Jan Syrovy	
1938–1939	Premier	Rudolf Beran	b. 1887 d. 1954
1940–1942	Premier *	Jan Srámek	b. 1870 d. 1956
1942–1945	Premier *	Jan Srámek	
1945–1946	Premier	Zdenek Fierlinger	b. 1891
1946–1948	Premier	Klement Gottwald	
1948–1953	Premier	Antonín Zápotocky	
1953–1954	Premier	Viliam Siroky	b. 1902
1954–1960	Premier	Viliam Siroky	
1960–1963	Premier	Viliam Siroky	
1963–1968	Premier	Jozef Lenárt	b. 1923
1968–1975	Premier	Ludvík Svoboda	

* Government in exile

1975–1989	Premier	Gustáv Husák	
1989–1989	Premier	Marián Calfa	
1989–1992	Premier	Václav Havel	
1992–1992	Premier	Jan Strásk	
1993–2003	Premier	Vaclav Havel	
2003–	Premier	Vaclav Klaus	

On January 1, 1993, the Czech Republic and the Republic of Slovakia were simultaneously and peacefully established as separate states.

Dahomey *See* Benin

Danzig *See* Poland

Denmark (Kingdom of Denmark)

c. 60 B.C.	King	Skiold (mythical character)	
A.D. 794–803	King	Sigfred (or Sigurd) Snogoje	
798 ?–810	King	Godfred	
810–812	King	Hemming, nephew of Godfred	
812–813	King	Harold Klak, nephew of Godfred	
819–822	King	Harold Klak, nephew of Godfred	
825–826	King	Harold Klak, nephew of Godfred	
827–854	King	Haarik (Eric) the Old, son of Godfred	
803–850	King	Hardicanute (Canute I)	

No authentic information is available for the period before 900.

900–950	King	Gorm the Old	
950–985	King	Harold Bluetooth, son of Gorm the Old	d. 988?
985–1014	King	Sweyn I Forkbeard, son of Harold Bluetooth	d. 1014

A Viking, Sweyn I raided England as a youth in 982 and 994. On a subsequent invasion, he forced Ethelred the Unready to flee the country and was declared King of England. He died suddenly at Gainsborough, Lincolnshire, after landing and capturing the town.

1014–1018	King	Harold, son of Sweyn Forkbeard	
1019–1035	King	Canute the Great, son of Sweyn Forkbeard	b. 1000 d. 1035
1035–1042	King	Canute III, son of Canute the Great	b. 1018 d. 1042
1042–1047	King	Magnus the Good, son of King Olav the Holy of Norway	b. 1024 d. 1047
1047–1074	King	Sweyn II Estrithson, nephew of Canute the Great	
1074–1080	King	Harold Hen, son of Sweyn Estrithson	d. 1080

1080–1086	King	Canute IV the Holy, son of Sweyn Estrithson	b. 1040 killed 1086
1086–1095	King	Oluf I Hunger, son of Sweyn Estrithson	d. 1095
1095–1103	King	Eric I Evergood, son of Sweyn Estrithson	d. 1103
1104–1134	King	Niels, son of Sweyn Estrithson	d. 1134
1134–1137	King	Eric II Emune the Memorable, son of Eric Evergood	d. 1137
1137–1146	King	Eric III Lam	d. 1146
1146–1157	King	Sweyn III Grade, son of Eric Emune	d. 1157
1157	King	Knud III Magnussen, son of Magnus Nielsen	d. 1157
1157–1182	King	Valdemar I the Great, son of Knud Lavard	b. 1131 d. 1182
1182–1202	King	Canute VI, son of Valdemar I the Great	b. 1163 d. 1202
1202–1241	King	Valdemar II the Victorious, son of Valdemar I the Great	b. 1170 d. 1241
1241–1250	King	Eric IV Ploughpenny, son of Valdemar II the Victorious	b. 1216 d. 1250
1250–1252	King	Abel, son of Valdemar II the Victorious	d. 1252
1252–1259	King	Christopher I, son of Valdemar II the Victorious	b. 1219 d. 1259
1259–1286	King	Eric V Klipping, son of Christopher I	b. 1249 d. 1286
1286–1319	King	Eric VI Maendved, son of Eric Klipping	b. 1274 d. 1319
1320–1332	King	Christopher II, son of Eric Klipping	b. 1276 d. 1332
1340–1375	King	Valdemar IV Atterdag, son of Christopher II	b. 1320 d. 1375
1376–1387	King	Oluf II, grandson of Valdemar Atterdag	b. 1370 d. 1387
1387–1412	Queen	Margrete, daughter of Valdemar IV Atterdag	b. 1353 d. 1412

Known as "Semiramis of the North," Queen Margrete conquered Sweden and brought about the Union of Kalmar in 1397, providing for a perpetual union of the three crowns. However, Sweden left the Union in 1523, and Norway in 1814.

1412–1439	King	Eric VII of Pomerania, grand-nephew of Margrete	b. 1382 d. 1459
1440–1448	King	Christopher III of Bavaria, nephew of Eric of Pomerania	b. 1416 d.1448
1448–1481	King	Christian I, son of Count Diderik the Happy of Oldenborg and Delmenhorst	b. 1426 d. 1481
1481–1513	King	Hans, son of Christian I	b. 1455 d. 1513
1513–1523	King	Christian II, son of Hans	b. 1481 d. 1559
1523–1533	King	Frederik I, son of Christian I	b. 1471 d. 1533
1534–1559	King	Christian III, son of Frederik I	b. 1503 d. 1559
1559–1588	King	Frederik II, son of Christian III	b. 1534 d. 1588
1588–1648	King	Christian IV, son of Frederik II	b. 1577 d. 1648
1648–1670	King	Frederik III, son of Christian IV	b. 1609 d. 1670
1670–1699	King	Christian V, son of Frederik III	b. 1646 d. 1699
1699–1730	King	Frederik IV, son of Christian V	b. 1671 d. 1730
1730–1746	King	Christian VI, son of Frederik IV	b. 1699 d. 1746
1746–1766	King	Frederik V, son of Christian VI	b. 1723 d. 1766

1766–1808	King	Christian VII, son of Frederik V	b. 1749 d. 1808
1808–1839	King	Frederik VI, son of Christian VII	b. 1768 d. 1839
1839–1848	King	Christian VIII, cousin of Frederik VI	b. 1786 d. 1848
1848–1863	King	Frederik VII, son of Christian VIII	b. 1808 d. 1863
1863–1906	King	Christian IX, son of William, Duke of Schleswig-Holstein-Sönderberg-Glücksborg	b. 1818 d. 1906
1906–1912	King	Frederik VIII, son of Christian IX	b. 1843 d. 1912
1912–1947	King	Christian X, son of Frederik VIII	b. 1870 d. 1947
1947–1972	King	Frederik IX, son of Christian X	b. 1899 d. 1972
1972–	King	Margrethe II	b. 1940

■ Statesmen

1643–1651	Steward of the Court	Corfitz Ulfeldt	b. 1606 d. 1664
1673–1676	Leading Minister	Peder Schumacher Griffenfeld	b. 1635 d. 1699
1746–1770	Master of the Royal Household	Adam Gottlob Moltke	b. 1710 d. 1792
1770–1772	Leading Minister	Johann Friedrich Von Struensee	b. 1737 d. 1772
1772–1784	Leading Minister	Ove Høegh-Guldberg	b. 1731 d. 1808

■ Prime Ministers

1781–1784	Prime Minister	Joachim Godske Moltke	b. 1746 d. 1818
1813–1818	Prime Minister	Joachim Godske Moltke	
1848–1852	Prime Minister	Adam Vilhelm Moltke	b. 1785 d. 1864
1852–1853	Prime Minister	Christian Albrecht Bluhme	b. 1794 d. 1866
1853–1854	Prime Minister	Andreas Sandø Ørsted	b. 1778 d. 1860
1854–1856	Prime Minister	Peter Georg Bang	b. 1797 d. 1861
1856–1857	Prime Minister	Carl C. G. Andrae	b. 1812 d. 1893
1857–1863	Prime Minister	Carl Christian Hall	b. 1812 d. 1888
1863–1864	Prime Minister	Ditlev Gothard Monrad	b. 1811 d. 1887
1864–1865	Prime Minister	Christian Albrecht Bluhme	b. 1797 d. 1866
1865–1870	Prime Minister	Christian Emil Frijs	b. 1817 d. 1896
1870–1874	Prime Minister	Ludvig Henrik C. H. Holstein	b. 1815 d. 1892
1874–1875	Prime Minister	Christian Andreas Fonnesbech	b. 1817 d. 1880
1875–1894	Prime Minister	Jacob B. S. Estrup	b. 1825 d. 1913
1894–1897	Prime Minister	K. T. Tage O. Reedtz-Thott	b. 1839 d. 1923
1897–1900	Prime Minister	Hugo Egmont Hørring	b. 1842 d. 1909
1900–1901	Prime Minister	Hannibal Sehested	b. 1842 d. 1924
1901–1905	Prime Minister	Johan Henrik Deuntzer	b. 1845 d. 1918

1905–1908	Prime Minister	Jens Christian Christensen	b. 1856 d. 1930
1908–1909	Prime Minister	Niels T. Neergaard	b. 1854 d. 1936
1909	Prime Minister	Johan Ludvig Holstein	b. 1839 d. 1912
1909–1910	Prime Minister	Carl Theodor Zahle	b. 1866 d. 1946
1910–1913	Prime Minister	Klaus Berntsen	b. 1844 d. 1927
1913–1920	Prime Minister	Carl Theodor Zahle	
1920	Prime Minister	C. J. Otto Liebe	b. 1860 d. 1929
1920	Prime Minister	Michael Petersen Friis	b. 1857 d. 1944
1920–1924	Prime Minister	Niels T. Neergaard	b. 1854 d. 1936
1924–1926	Prime Minister	Thorvald A. M. Stauning	b. 1873 d. 1942
1926–1929	Prime Minister	Thomas Madsen-Mygdal	b. 1876 d. 1943
1929–1942	Prime Minister	Thorvald A. M. Stauning	
1942	Prime Minister	Vilhelm Buhl	b. 1881 d. 1954
1942–1945	Prime Minister	Erik Scavenius	b. 1877 d. 1962
1945	Prime Minister	Vilhelm Buhl	
1945–1947	Prime Minister	Knud Kristensen	b. 1880 d. 1962
1947–1950	Prime Minister	Hans Hedtoft	b. 1903 d. 1955
1950–1953	Prime Minister	Erik Eriksen	b. 1902 d. 1972
1953–1955	Prime Minister	Hans Hedtoft	b. 1903 d. 1955
1955–1960	Prime Minister	Hans Chr. Hansen	b. 1906 d. 1960
1960–1962	Prime Minister	Viggo Kampmann	b. 1910 d. 1976
1962–1968	Prime Minister	Jens Otto Krag	b. 1914 d. 1978
1968–1971	Prime Minister	Hilmar Baunsgaard	b. 1920 d. 1989
1971–1972	Prime Minister	Jens Otto Krag	
1972–1973	Prime Minister	Anker Jorgensen	b. 1922
1973–1975	Prime Minister	Poul Hartling	b. 1914 d. 2000
1975–1982	Prime Minister	Anker Jorgensen	
1982–1993	Prime Minister	Poul Schluter	b. 1929
1993–2001	Prime Minister	Poul Nyrup Rasmussen	b. 1943
2001–	Prime Minister	Anders Fogh Rasmussen	b. 1953

Dijbouti (Republic of Dijbouti)

As the successor to French Somaliland, Dijbouti gained its independence in 1977.

1977–1999	President	Hassan Gouled Aptidon
1999–	President	Ismail Omar Guelleh

Dominica (Commonwealth of Dominica)

Dominica was granted independence by the United Kingdom in 1978.

1978–1979	Prime Minister	Patrick Rowland John
1979–1980	Prime Minister	Oliver James Seraphine
1980–1995	Prime Minister	Mary Eugenia Charles
1995–2000	Prime Minister	Edison Chenfil James
2000–2000	Prime Minister	Roosevelt "Rosie" Douglas
2000–2004	Prime Minister	Pierre Charles
2004	Acting Prime Minister	Osborne Riviere
2004–	Prime Minister	Roosevelt Skerrit

Dominican Republic (Dominican Republic)

The Dominican Republic became an independent state in 1821. The republic was founded in 1844.

1844–1848	President	Pedro Santana	b. 1801 d. 1864
1848–1849	President	Manuel Jimenez	
1849–1853	President	Buenaventura Baez	
1853–1856	President	Pedro Santana	
1856–1858	President	Buenaventura Baez	
1858–1861	President	Pedro Santana	
1861–1865	President	Pedro A. Pimentel	
1865	President	José Maria Cabral	
1865–1866	President	Buenaventura Baez	
1866–1868	President	José Maria Cabral	
1868–1874	President	Buenaventura Baez	
1874–1876	President	Ignacio Maria Gonzalez	
1876	President	Ulises Francisco Espaillat	
1876–1878	President	Ignacio Maria Gonzalez	
1878–1880	President	Gregorio Luperón	
1880–1882	President	Fernando Arturo de Meriño	
1882–1884	President	Ulises Heureaux	
1884–1887	President	Alejandro Woss y Gil	
1887–1899	President	Ulises Heureaux	
1899–1901	President	Horacio Vasquez	
1901–1903	President	Juan Isidro Jiménez	
1903–1904	President	Alejandro Woss y Gil	
1904–1905	President	Carlos Morales Lauguasco	
1905–1911	President	Ramón Cáceres	

1911–1912	President	Alfredo Victoria		
1912–1913	President	Adolfo A. Nouel		
1913–1914	President	José Bordas Valdés		
1914–1915	President	Ramón Báez		
1915–1916	President	Juan Isidro Jimenez		
1916	President	Francisco Henriquez y Carvajal		
1916–1924		*American Intervention and U.S. Military Government*		
1924–1930	President	Horacio Vasquez		
1930–1961	President and Dictator	Rafael Leonidas Trujillo	b. 1891	assassinated 1961
1961–1962	President	Joaquín Balaguer	b. 1907	d. 2002
1962–1963	President	Rafael F. Bonnelly		
1963	President	Juan Bosch		
1963	President	Emilio de los Santos		
1963–1965	President	Donald Reid Cabral		
1965–1966		*Military Junta*		
1966–1978	President	Joaquín Balaguer		
1978–1982	President	Antonio Guzmán Fernández		
1982–1982	President	Jacobo Majluta Azar		
1982–1986	President	Salvador Jorge Blanco		
1986–1996	President	Joaquín Balaguer		
1996–2000	President	Leonel Fernández Reyna		
2000–2004	President	Hipólito Mejía		
2004–	President	Leonel Fernández Reyna		

Dutch East Indies *See* Indonesia

East Timor (Democratic Republic of Timor-Leste)

Having originally gained its independence from Portugal in 1975, East Timor almost immediately found itself occupied by military forces from their much larger neighbor, Indonesia. Full independence was gained in 2002, with Kay Rala Xanana Gusmão serving as the first president.

Ecuador (Republic of Ecuador)

Ecuador became independent in 1830.

1830–1835	President	Juan José Flores	b. 1800	d. 1864
1835–1839	President	Vicente Rocafuerte	b. 1783	d. 1847
1839–1845	President	Juan José Flores		

1845–1850	President	Vicente Ramón Roca	b. 1790? d. 1850
1851	President	Diego Noboa	
1852–1856	President	José María Urvina (or Urbina)	b. 1808 d. 1891
1856–1859	President	Francisco Robles	b. 1811 d. 1893
1861–1865	President	Gabriel García Moreno, son-in-law of Flores	b. 1821 assassinated 1875
1865–1867	President	Gerónimo Carrión	b. 1812 d. 1873
1868–1869	President	Javier Espinosa	
1869–1875	President	Gabriel García Moreno	
1875–1876	President	Antonio Borrero	
1876–1883	President	Ignacio de Veintemilla	b. 1830 d. 1909
1883–1888	President	José María Plácido Caamaño	b. 1838 d. 1901
1888–1892	President	Antonio Flores	
1892–1895	President	Luis Cordero	
1897–1901	President	Eloy Alfaro	b. 1864 murdered 1912
1901–1905	President	Leonidas Plaza Gutierrez	
1905–1906	President	Lizardo Garcia	
1907–1911	President	Eloy Alfaro	
1911	President	Emilio Estrada	
1912–1916	President	Leonidas Plaza Gutierrez	
1916–1920	President	Alfredo Baquerizo Moreno	b. 1859 d. 1951
1920–1924	President	Jose Luis Tamayo	
1924–1925	President	Gonzalo S. Cordoba	
1925–1926		*Provisional Junta*	
1926–1931	President	Isidro Ayora	
1931	President (provisional)	Luis A. Larrea Alba	
1931–1932	President (provisional)	Alfredo Baquerizo Moreno	
1932		*Period of Revolution*	
1932	President (provisional)	Alberto Guerrero Martinez	
1932–1933	President	Juan de Dios Martinez Mera	
1933–1934	President (provisional)	Abelardo Montalvo	
1934–1935	President	José María Velasco Ibarra	
1935	President (provisional)	Antonio Pons	
1935–1937	President (provisional)	Federico Páez	

1937–1938	President (provisional)	G. Alberto Enriquez	
1938	President (provisional)	Manuel María Borrero	
1938–1939	President (provisional)	Aurelio Mosquera Narvaez	d. 1939
1938–1939	President	Aurelio Mosquera Narvaez	
1940	President	Andres F. Cordova	
1940–1944	President	Carlos Alberto Arroyo del Río	b. 1893
1944–1947	President	José María Velasco Ibarra	
1947		*Military Coup*	
1948–1952	President	Galo Plazo Lasso	
1952–1956	President	Camilo Ponce Enríquez	
1956–1960	President	José María Velasco Ibarra	
1961–1963	President	Carlos J. Arosemena	(Exiled)
1963–1966		*Military Junta*	
1966–1966	Interim President	Clemente Yerovi Indaburu	b. 1904
1966–1968	Interim Pres./ President	Otto Arosemena Gómez	d. 1981
1968–1972	President	José María Velasco Ibarra	
1972–1976	President	Guillermo A. Rodrígez Lara	b. 1923
1976–1979		*Superior Council*	
1979–1981	President	Jaime Roldós Aguilera	d. 1981
1981–1984	President	Oswaldo Hurtado Larrea	b. 1939
1984–1988	President	León Esteban Febres Cordero Rivadeneyra	b. 1931
1988–1992	President	Rodrigo Borja Cevallos	b. 1935
1992–1996	President	Sixto Alfonso Durán-Ballén Cordovez	b. 1921
1996–1997	President	Abdalá Jaime Bucaram Ortiz	b. 1952
1997–1998	Interim President	Fabián Ernesto Alarcón Rivera	b. 1947
1998–2000	President	Jamil Mahuad Witt	b. 1949
2000–2003	President	Gustavo Naboa Bejerano	b. 1937
2003–2005	President	Lucio Gutierrez Borbúa	b. 1957
2005–	President	Alfredo Palacio	b. 1939

Egypt (Arab Republic of Egypt)

THE OLD KINGDOM

3400 B.C.	King	Menes (united north and south kingdoms)

- *3400–2980 B.C., 1st and 2nd (Thinite) Dynasties*

- *2980–2900 B.C., 3rd (Memphite) Dynasty*

	King	Zoser
	King	Seris
about 2920	King	Snefru (or Sneferu)

- *2900–2750 B.C., 4th (Memphite) Dynasty*

2900–2877	King	Cheops (Khufu)
	King	Dedefré
	King	Chephren (Khafré)
2800	King	Menkure (Mycerinus)

- *2750–2625 B.C., 5th (Memphite) Dynasty*

	King	Weserkef (Userkaf)
	King	Sahure, brother of Weserkef
	King	Nefererkere, brother of Weserkef

- *2625–2475 B.C., 6th (Memphite) Dynasty*

	King	Teti
	King	Weserkere (Userkere)
2590–2570	King	Pepi (Pheops) I Merire
2566–2476	King	Pepi (Pheops) II Neferkere, son of Pepi I
	King	Mereme II

- *2475–2445 B.C., 7th and 8th (Memphite) Dynasties*

"The Age of Misrule"

THE MIDDLE KINGDOM

- *2445–2160 B.C., 9th and 10th (Heracleopolitan) Dynasties*

	King	Kheti (Achthoés)

- *2160–2000 B.C., 11th (Theban) Dynasty*

	King	Mentuhotep I
	King	Mentuhotep II

	King	Mentuhotep III
	King	Mentuhotep IV
	King	Mentuhotep V

■ 2000–1788 B.C., 12th (Theban) Dynasty

2000–1970	King	Amenemhet I
1970–1938	King	Sesostris I, son of Amenemhet I
1938–1903	King	Amenemhet II, son of Sesostris I
1903–1887	King	Sesostris II, son of Amenemhet II
1887–1849	King	Sesostris III, son of Sesostris II
1849–1801	King	Amenemhet III, son of Sesostris III
1801–1792	King	Amenemhet IV, son of Amenemhet III
1792–1788	Princess	Sebeknefrure

THE HYKSOS or "SHEPHERD KINGS"
■ 1788–1580 B.C., 13th to 17th Dynasties

THE NEW KINGDOM
■ 1580–1350 B.C., 18th (Diospolite) Dynasty

1580–1557	Ring	Ahmosi I (Amasis)
1557–1540	Ring	Amenhotep I, son of Ahmosi I
1540–1505	Ring	Thotmes I (Tuthmosis), son of Amenhotep I
1505–1501	Ring	Thotmes II, son of Thotmes I
1501–1498	Queen	Hatsepsut, (co-ruler) daughter of Thotmes II
1501–1447	King	Thotmes III, (co-ruler) brother of Hatshepsut
1447–1420	King	Amenhotep II, son of Thotmes III
1420–1411	King	Thotmes IV, son of Amenhotep II
1411–1375	King	Amenhotep III, son of Thotmes IV
1375–1358	King	Amenhotep IV (Aknaton), son of Amenhotep III
1358–1357	King	Sakere, son-in-law of Amenhotep IV (Aknaton)
1357–1351	King	Tutankhamen, son-in-law of Sakere
1351–1350	Queen	Eje

■ 1350–1215 B.C., 19th (Diospolite) Dynasty

1350–1315	King	Horemheb
1315–1314	King	Rameses I

1313–1292	King	Seti, son of Rameses I
1292–1225	King	Rameses II, son of Seti I
1225–1215	King	Merneptah, son of Rameses II
1215–1212	King	Seti II
1215–1209	Rival Regent	Siptak

■ *1198–1150 B.C., 20th (Diospolite) Dynasty*

1198	King	Setnacht
1198–1167	King	Rameses III
1167–1161	King	Rameses IV
1161–1142	King	Rameses V-VIII
1142–1123	King	Rameses IX
	King	Rameses X
1118–1090	King	Rameses XII

The high priests of Ammon were in power from 1150 to 1090.

■ *1090–945 B.C., 21st (Tarite) Dynasty*

■ *945–745 B.C., 22nd (Bubastite) Dynasty*

■ *745–718 B.C., 23rd (Tanite) Dynasty*

■ *718–712 B.C., 24th (Saite) Dynasty*

718–712	King	Bocchoris of Sais

■ *712–663 B.C., 25th (Ethiopian) Dynasty*

712–700	King	Sabaka
700–688	King	Sabataka
688–663	King	Taharka, nephew of Shabaka

■ *663–525 B.C., 26th (Saite) Dynasty*

670–663	King	Cecho I (Assyrian vassal)
663–603	King	Psammetichus, son of Nech I
609–593	King	Nech II, son of Psammetichus
593–588	King	Psammetichus II, son of Nech II

569–525	King	Ahmosi II (Amasis II)	
525	King	Psammetichus III, son of Ahmosi II	

■ 523–332 B.C., Egypt under Persia

332–323	Conqueror	Alexander III the Great	b. 356 d. 323

■ Greek Epoch (Transition to A.D.)

323–285 B.C.	King	Ptolemy I, Soter	b. 367? d. 283
285–247	King	Ptolemy II, Philadelphus, son of Ptolemy I	b. 309 d. 247
247–221	King	Ptolemy III, Euergetes, son of Ptolemy II	b. 282? d. 221
221–203	King	Ptolemy IV, Philopator, son of Ptolemy III	b. 244? d. 203
203–180	King	Ptolemy V, Epiphanes, son of Ptolemy IV	b. 210? d. 180
180–144	King	Ptolemy VI, Philometor, son of Ptolemy V	b. 186? killed 144
144–117	King	Ptolemy VII, Euergetes II, son of Ptolemy V	b. 184? d. 117
117–108	King	Ptolemy VIII, Lathyrus, son of Ptolemy VII	d. 81
88–80	King	Ptolemy VIII	
108–89	King	Ptolemy IX, Alexander I, son of Ptolemy VII	killed 89
81–80	Queen	Berenice, daughter of Ptolemy VIII	murdered 80
81	King	Ptolemy X, Alexander II, son of Ptolemy IX	b. 105? killed 80
81–51	King	Ptolemy XI, Auletes, son of Ptolemy VIII	b. 95? d. 51
51–30	Queen (joint ruler)	Cleopatra VII, daughter of Ptolemy XI	b. 69 suicide 30
51–47	King	Ptolemy XII, son of Ptolemy XI	b. 61 drowned 47
47–44	King	Ptolemy XIII, brother of Cleopatra VII	b. 58? murdered 44
44–30	King	Ptolemy XIV, Cesarion, son of Cleopatra VII and Julius Caesar	b. 47 murdered 30
30 B.C.–A.D. 640		*Roman Province*	
640		*Arab Conquest*	
868–884	King	Ahmed ibn-Tulun	b. 835 d. 884

■ 868–884, Tulunid Dynasty

■ 935–969, Ikhshidites

■ 969–1171, Fatimidites Dynasty (14 Caliphs)

1171–1193	Sultan	Saladin	b. 1137 d. 1193

■ *1171–1250, Ayuyubid Dynasty*

1260–1382		Bahri Mamelukes (24 sultans)	
1260–1277	Mameluke Sultan	Bibars I	b. 1233 d. 1277
1291–1341	Mameluke Sultan	Nasir	b. 1284 d. 1341
1382–1517	Mameluke Sultan	Burji Mamelukes (23 sultans)	
1382–1399		Baruk	
1501–1516		Kansuh-el-Ghury	

Egyptian Caliphate Extinguished by Ottoman Conquest in 1517

■ Turkish Rule

1805–1849	Viceroy	Mohammed Ali	b. 1769 d. 1849
1849–1854	Viceroy	Abbas I, grandson of Mohammed Ali	b. 1813 Assassinated 1854
1854–1863	Viceroy	Said Pasha, son of Mohammed Ali	b. 1822 d. 1863
1863–1879	Khedive	Ismail Pasha, grandson of Mohammed Ali	b. 1830 d. 1895
1879–1892	Khedive	Mohammed Tewfik Pasha, son of Ismail Pasha	b. 1852 d. 1892
1892–1914	Khedive	Abbas II Hilmi, son of Tewfik Pasha	b. 1874 d. 1944

British Protectorate Established in 1914

■ British Rule

British Occupation from 1882 to 1922

1879–1883	Consul General	Sir Edward Bladwin Malet	b. 1837 d. 1908
1883–1907	Consul General	Evelyn Baring, Earl of Cromer	b. 1841 d. 1917
1907–1911	Consul General	Sir John Eldon Gorst	b. 1861 d. 1911
1911–1916	Consul General	Horatio Herbert Kitchener, Earl Kitchener of Khartoum	b. 1850 d. 1916
1914–1916	High Commissioner	Sir Arthur Henry MacMahon	b. 1862 d. 1949
1916–1919	High Commissioner	Sir Francis Reginald Wingate	b. 1861 d. 1953
1919–1925	High Commissioner	Edmund Henry Hynman, Viscount Allenby	b. 1861 d. 1936
1925–1929	High Commissioner	George Ambrose Lloyd, Baron Lloyd of Dolobran	b. 1879 d. 1941
1929–1933	High Commissioner	Sir Percy Loraine	b. 1880
1934–1936	High Commissioner	Sir Miles Wedderburn Lampson	b. 1880
1914–1917	Sultan	Hussein Kemal, son of Ismail Pasha	b. 1853 d. 1917
1917–1922	Sultan	Ahmed Fuad Pasha, brother of Hussein Kemal	b. 1868 d. 1936
1922–1936	King	Ahmed Fuad (Fuad I)	
1936–1952	King	Farouk, son of Fuad I	b. 1920 d. 1965
1952–1953	King	Ahmed II, son of Farouk	b. 1950
1952–1953	Dictator	Mohammed Naguib	b. 1901

| 1953–1954 | President | Mohammed Naguib | |
| 1956–1958 | President | Gamal Abdel Nasser | b. 1918 |

■ Statesmen

1924	Prime Minister	Saad Zaghlul Pasha	b. 1852 d. 1927
1928	Prime Minister	Mustafa el-Nahas Pasha	b. 1879 d. 1965
1930	Prime Minister	Mustafa el-Nahas Pasha	
1936–1937	Prime Minister	Mustafa el-Nahas Pasha	
1942–1944	Prime Minister	Mustafa el-Nahas Pasha	
1950–1952	Prime Minister	Mustafa el-Nahas Pasha	
1952–1956	Prime Minister	Gamal Abdel Nasser	

In 1958 Egypt and Syria united to form the United Arab Republic. In 1961, when Syria seceded, Egypt retained the name United Arab Republic, which was later changed to the Arab Republic of Egypt.

■ United Arab Republic/Arab Republic of Egypt

1958–1970	President	Gamal Abdel Nasser	
1970–1981	President	Anwar el-Sadat	assassinated
1981–	President	Hosni Mubarak	

El Salvador (Republic of El Salvador)

El Salvador was part of the Spanish vice-royalty of Guatemala from 1526 to 1821. It joined the Central American Federation in 1821; obtained independence in 1821; and was occupied by Mexico from 1821 to 1823. It suffered from a period of anarchy until a republic was established in 1859.

1860–1863	President	Gerard Barrios	shot 1865
1863–1872	President	Francis Dueñas	
1872–1876	President	Gonzales	
1876–1885	President	Rafael Zaldívar	
1885–1890	President	Francisco Menéndez	d. 1890
1890–1894	President (provisional)	Carlos Ezeta	
1895–1899	President	Rafael Antonio Gutiérrez	
1899–1903	President	Tomás Regalado	b. 1864
1903–1907	President	Pedro José Escalón	
1907–1911	President	Fernando Figueroa	
1911–1913	President	Manuel Enrique Araújo	
1913–1914	President (acting)	Carlos Meléndez	

1914–1915	President (provisional)	Alfonso Quiñónez Molina	b. 1873 d. 1950
1915–1919	President	Carlos Meléndez	
1919–1923	President	Jorge Meléndez	
1923–1927	President	Alfonso Quiñónez Molina	
1927–1931	President	Pio Romero Bosque	
1931	President	Arturo Araújo	
1931–1934	President	Maximiliano Hernández Martínez	b. 1882
1934–1935	President (acting)	Andrés Ignacio Menéndez	
1935–1944	President	Maximiliano Hernández Martínez	
1944	President (acting)	Andrés Ignacio Menéndez	
1944	President	Osmin Aguirre Salinas	
1945–1949	President	Salvador Castenada Castro	
1949–1956	President	Oscar Osorio	
1956–1960	President	José María Lemus	
1960–1962	Head of Junta	Miguel Castillo	
1962	President (provisional)	Eusebio Rodolfo Cordon Cea	
1962–1967	President	Julio Adalberto Rivera	
1967–1972	President	Fidel Sanchez Fernandez	
1972–1977	President	Arturo Armando Molina Barraza	
1977–1979	President	Carlos Humberto Romero Mena	
1979–1980		*Military Junta*	
1980–1982	President	José Napoleón Duarte Fuentes	
1982–1984	President	Álvaro Alfredo Magaña Borja	
1984–1989	President	José Napoleón Duarte Fuentes	
1989–1994	President	Alfredo Félix Cristiani Bukard	
1994–1999	President	Armando Calderón Sol	
1999–2004	President	Francisco Guillermo Flores Pérez	
2004–	President	Elías Antonio Saca González	

England *See* United Kingdom

Epirus

Epirus corresponded roughly to modern-day Albania and northwestern Greece.

c. 500 B.C.	King	Admetus
	King	Arymbas

c. 400	King	Alcetas I	
	King	Neoptolemus	
	King	Arybbas	
−326	King	Alexander I	d. 326
	King	Neoptolemus II	
	King	Alcetas II	
	King	Aeacides	
295–272	King	Pyrrhus	b. 318 d. 272
272–	King	Alexander II	
	King	Ptolemy	
	King	Pyrrhus III	

Epirus was conquered by Rome in 167 B.C. and remained under Rome and its Byzantine successor states until occupied by the Albanians in the A.D. 14th century.

Equatorial Guinea (Republic of Equatorial Guinea)

Equatorial Guinea was granted its independence from Spain in 1968 as the result of a combination of internal nationalist pressure and efforts by the United Nations.

| 1968–1979 | President | Francisco Macias Nguema |
| 1979– | President | Teodoro Obiang Nguema |

Eritrea (State of Eritrea)

Eritea gained its military independence from Ethiopia in 1991 and was admitted to the United Nations in 1993. As of 2005, the nation was still in the process of establishing a permanent constitution, with Isaias Afwerki as the President of the State.

Estonia (Republic of Estonia)

Formerly a province of the Russian Empire, Estonia was an independent republic from 1918 to 1940 and under German occupation from 1941 to 1944.

1921–1924	Chief of State	Konstantin Päts	b. 1874
1927–1928	Chief of State	Jaan Tonisson	b. 1868
1928–1929	Chief of State	August Rei	
1929–1931	Chief of State	Otto Strandmann	b. 1875
1931–1933	Chief of State	Konstantin Päts	
1932	Chief of State	Karl Einbund (resigned)	
1934–1938	Dictator	Konstantin Päts	
1938–1940	Chief of State	Konstantin Päts	

Estonia was occupied and absorbed by the Soviet Union in 1944. Since regaining independence in 1991, Estonia has had eleven governments with seven prime ministers: Edgar Savisaar, Tiit Vähi, Mart Laar, Andres Tarand, Mart Siimann, Siim Kallas, and Juhan Parts.

Ethiopia (Federal Democratic Republic of Ethiopia)
See also Abyssinia

Ethiopia was divided into semi-independent parts until 1855.

1855–1868	King (Negus)	Theodore (Kasa)	b. 1818? suicide 1868
1868–1872		*Internal Struggles*	
1871–1889	Negus negusti	John II (Kassai)	b. 1832 killed 1889
1889–1911	Emperor	Menelik II, son of King of Shoa	b. 1844 d. 1913
1911–1916	Emperor	Lij Yasu, grandson of Menelik II	b. 1896 d. 1935
1916–1930	Empress	Waizero (Zauditu), daughter of Menelik II	b. 1876 d. 1930
1916–1930	Co-ruler	Ras Tafari, son of Ras Makonnen	b. 1891
1930–1936	Emperor	Haile Selassie (Ras Tafari)	b. 1892
1936–1941		*Italian Occupation*	
1941–1974	Emperor	Haile Selassie	Assassinated, 1975
1974–1975		*Military Junta*	
1975–1991	Military dictator	Mengistu Haile Miriam	
1991–1995		*Transitional Government*	
1995–	Prime Minister	Meles Zenawi	

Fiji (Republic of the Fiji Islands)

Fiji became independent as a member of the Commonwealth of Nations in 1970.

1970–1973	Governor-General	Robert Sidney Foster
1973–1987	Governor-General	George Cakobau
1987	Head of Interim (Military Govt.)	Sitiveni Rabuka
1987–1993	President	Penaia Ganilau
1993–2000	President	Kamisese Mara
2000	Head of Interim (Military Govt.)	Josaia Voreqe "Frank" Bainimarama
2000–	President	Josefa Iloilo

Finland (Republic of Finland)

No authentic information is available for the period before 1284. Finland was ruled by Sweden until 1808.

1284–1291	Duke	Bengt, son of Birger Jarl of Sweden		
1302–1318	Duke	Waldemar Magnusson, son of Magnus Ladulås, King of Sweden		
1322–1326	Duke	Matts Kettilmundsson		
1340–1348	Duke	Dan Niklinsson		
1353–1357	Duke	Bengt Algotsson		d. 1360
1357–1359	Duke	Erik Magnusson (Erik XII of Sweden)	b. 1339	d. 1359
1371–1386	Lagman	Bo Jonsson Grip		
1440–1448	Lagman	Karl Knutsson Bonde (in Finland)	b. 1409	d. 1470
1465–1467	Lagman	Karl Knutsson Bonde		
1457–1481	Lagman	Erik Axelsson Tott (in Viborg)		
1495–1496	Lagman	Knut Posse (in Viborg)		d. 1500
1497–1501	Lagman	Sten Sture the Elder, son of sister of Charles VIII	b. 1440?	d. 1503
1499–1511	Lagman	Erik Turesson Bielke (in Viborg)		
1520–1522	Junker	Thomas Wolf		
1556–1563	Duke	Johan		d. 1592
1561–1566	Governor	Gustav Fincke		d. 1566
1566–1568	Governor	Ivar Mansson Stiernkors		d. 1573
1568–1571	Governor	Hans Larsson Björnram		d. 1571
1571–1576	Governor	Henrik Klasson Horn		d. 1595
1576–1587	Governor	Klas Åkesson Tott		d. 1592
1587–1590	Governor	Axel Stensson Leijonhufvud		d. 1619
1591–1597	Governor	Klas Eriksson Fleming		d. 1597
1597–1599	Governor	Arvid Stålarm		d. 1620
1623–1631	Governor-General	Nils Bielke		d. 1639
1613–1633	Governor-General	Gabriel Bengtsson Oxenstierna		d. 1656
1637–1640	Governor-General	Per Brahe	b. 1602	d. 1680
1648–1654	Governor-General	Per Brahe		
1657–1659	Governor-General	Gustav Evertsson Horn		d. 1666
1664–1669	Governor-General	Herman Fleming		d. 1673
1710–1712	Governor-General	Karl Nieroth		d. 1712

During the 18th century, Finland was invaded and partially annexed by Russia. In 1808 the entire country became an autonomous Grand Duchy united with the Russian Crown.

1808–1809	Governor-General	Göran Magnus Sprengtporten	d. 1819
1809–1810	Governor-General	Mikael Barclay de Tolly	d. 1818
1810–1823	Governor-General	Fabian Steinheil	d. 1831

1823–1831	Governor-General	Arsenii Zakrevski	d. 1865
1831–1855	Governor-General	Prince Alexander Menshikov	b. 1787 d. 1869
1833–1847	Governor-General	Alexander A. Thesleff	d. 1847
1848–1854	Governor-General	Platon Rokassovski	d. 1869
1854–1855	Governor-General	Fredrik Wilhelm Berg	b. 1794 d. 1874
1854–1861	Governor-General	Fredrik Wilhelm Berg	
1861–1866	Governor-General	Platon Rokassovski	
1866–1881	Governor-General	Nikolai Adlerberg	b. 1819 d. 1892
1881–1897	Governor-General	Feodor Heiden	b. 1821 d. 1900
1897–1898	Governor-General	Stepan Gontscharov	d. 1912
1898–1904	Governor-General	Nikolaj Bobrikoff	b. 1839 assassinated 1904

*When in accordance with Nicholas I's policy of Russification,
General Bobrikoff began to rule dictatorially. The Finns
replied vigorously. Their "national strike" forced the
government to restore the power of the Finnish diet and
freedom of speech.*

1904–1905	Governor-General	Ivan M. Obolenski	d. 1910
1905–1908	Governor-General	Nikolaj N. Gerard	d. 1929
1908–1909	Governor-General	Vladimir K. Boeckmann	d. 1923
1909–1917	Governor-General	Frans A. Seyn	d. 1918
1917	Governor-General	Mikael Stahovich	d. 1923
1917	Governor-General	Nikolai Nekrasov	b. 1879
1811–1834	Minister Secretary	Robert Rehbinder	b. 1777 d. 1841
1834–1841	Minister Secretary	Robert Rehbinder	
1841–1842	Minister Secretary	Alexander Armfelt	b. 1794 d. 1876
1876–1881	Minister Secretary	Karl Knut Emil Stiernwall-Wallen	b. 1806 d. 1890
1881–1888	Minister Secretary	Theodor Bruun	b. 1822 d. 1888
1888–1891	Minister Secretary	Jonan Casimir Ehrnrooth	b. 1833 d. 1913
1891–1898	Minister Secretary	Waldemar Karl von Daehn	b. 1838 d. 1900
1898–1899	Minister Secretary	Victor Procopé	b. 1839 d. 1906
1899–1904	Minister Secretary	Vyacheslav von Pleve	b. 1846 d. 1904
1904–1905	Minister Secretary	Constantin Linder	b. 1836 d. 1908
1906–1913	Minister Secretary	Karl Fredrik August Langhoff	b. 1856 d. 1929
1913–1917	Minister Secretary	Vladimir Markov	b. 1859 d. 1919
1917	Minister Secretary	Carl Enckell	b. 1876
1822–1826	Prime Minister	Carl Erik Mannerheim	b. 1759 d. 1857
1826–1828	Prime Minister	Samuel Fredrik von Born	b. 1782 d. 1850
1828–1833	Prime Minister	Anders Henrik Falck	b. 1772 d. 1851
1833–1841	Prime Minister	Gustaf Hjärne	b. 1763 d. 1845

1841–1858	Prime Minister	Lars Gabriel von Haartman	b. 1789	d. 1859
1858–1882	Prime Minister	Johan Mauritz Nordenstam	b. 1802	d. 1882
1882–1885	Prime Minister	Edvard af Forselles	b. 1817	d. 1891
1885–1891	Prime Minister	Werner von Troil	b. 1833	d. 1900
1891–1900	Prime Minister	Sten Carl Tudeer	b. 1840	d. 1905
1900–1905	Prime Minister	Constantin Linder	b. 1836	d. 1908
1905	Prime Minister	Emil Streng	b. 1838	d. 1911
1905–1908	Prime Minister	Leo Mechelin	b. 1839	d. 1914
1908–1909	Prime Minister	Edvard Hjelt	b. 1855	d. 1921
1909	Prime Minister	August Hjelt	b. 1862	d. 1919
1909	Prime Minister	Andrej Virenius		
1909–1913	Prime Minister	Vladimir Markov	b. 1859	d. 1919
1913–1917	Prime Minister	Michael Borovitinov	b. 1874	
1917	Prime Minister	Andrej Virenius		
1917	Prime Minister	Oskari Tokoi	b. 1873	
1917	Prime Minister	Emil Nestor Setälä	b. 1864	d. 1955

Finland Became an Independent Republic in 1918

1918	Regent	Pehr Evind Svinhufvud	b. 1861	d. 1944
1918	Head of Red Government	Kullervo Manner	b. 1880	
1918	"King"	Frederick Charles of Hesse (monarchy not established)	b. 1868	d. 1940
1918–1919	Regent	Carl Gustaf Emil von Mannerheim	b. 1867	d. 1951
1919–1925	President	Kaarlo Juho Ståhlberg	b. 1865	d. 1952
1925–1931	President	Lauri Kristian Relander	b. 1883	d. 1942
1931–1937	President	Pehr Evind Svinhufvud		
1937–1940	President	Kyösti Kallio	b. 1873	d. 1940
1940–1944	President	Risto Heikki Ryti	b. 1889	d. 1956
1944–1946	President	Carl Gustaf Emil von Mannerheim		

Mannerheim, the "Liberator of Finland," served with distinction in the Russian army. After the Russian Revolution, he went to Finland and defeated the "Red Guards." He commanded the Finnish army against the Russians in 1939 and again after 1941.

1946–1956	President	Juho Kusti Paasikivi	b. 1870	d. 1956
1956–1982	President	Urho Kaleva Kekkonen	b. 1900	d. 1986
1982–1994	President	Mauno Koivisto	b. 1923	
1994–2000	President	Martti Ahtisaari	b. 1937	
2000–	President	Tarja Halonen	b. 1943	

Prime Ministers

1918	Prime Minister	Juho Kusti Paasikivi		
1918–1919	Prime Minister	Lauri Johannes Ingman	b. 1868	d. 1934
1919	Prime Minister	Kaarlo Castren	b. 1860	
1919–1920	Prime Minister	Juho Heikki Vennola	b. 1872	d. 1938
1920–1921	Prime Minister	Rafeal Erich	b. 1879	d. 1946
1921–1922	Prime Minister	Juho Heikki Vennola		
1922	Prime Minister	Aimo Kaarlo Cajander	b. 1879	
1922–1924	Prime Minister	Kyösti Kallio		
1924	Prime Minister	Aimo Kaarlo Cajander		
1924–1925	Prime Minister	Lauri Johannes Ingman		
1925	Prime Minister	Antti Agaton Tulenheimo	b. 1879	d. 1952
1925–1926	Prime Minister	Kyösti Kallio		
1926–1927	Prime Minister	Väinö Alfred Tanner	b. 1881	
1927–1928	Prime Minister	Juho Emil Sunila	b. 1875	
1928–1929	Prime Minister	Oskari Mantere	b. 1874	d. 1942
1929–1930	Prime Minister	Kyösti Kallio		
1930–1931	Prime Minister	Pehr Evind Svinhufvud		
1931–1932	Prime Minister	Juho Emil Sunila		d. 1936
1932–1936	Prime Minister	Toivo Mikael Kivimäki	b. 1886	
1936–1937	Prime Minister	Kyösti Kallio		
1937–1939	Prime Minister	Aimo Kaarlo Cajander		
1939–1940	Prime Minister	Risto Heikki Ryti		
1941–1943	Prime Minister	Johan Wilhelm Rangell	b. 1894	
1943–1944	Prime Minister	Edwin Linkomies	b. 1894	
1944	Prime Minister	Antti Hackzell	b. 1881	d. 1944
1944	Prime Minister	Urho Castren	b. 1886	
1944–1946	Prime Minister	Juho Kusti Paasikivi		
1946–1948	Prime Minister	Mauno Pekkala	b. 1890	d. 1952
1948–1950	Prime Minister	Karl-August Fagerholm	b. 1901	
1950–1953	Prime Minister	Urho Kaleva Kekkonen		
1953–1954	Prime Minister	Sakari Tuomioja	b. 1911	d. 1964
1954	Prime Minister	Ralf Törngren	b. 1900	d. 1961
1954–1956	Prime Minister	Urho Kaleva Kekkonen		
1956–1957	Prime Minister	K.-A. Fagerholm		
1957	Prime Minister	V. J. Sukselainen	b. 1906	
1957–1958	Prime Minister	Rainer von Fieandt	b. 1890	

1958	Prime Minister	Reino Kuuskoski	b. 1907
1958–1959	Prime Minister	K.-A. Fagerhohn	
1959–1961	Prime Minister	V. J. Sukselainen	
1961–1962	Prime Minister	Martti Miettunen	b. 1907
1962–1963	Prime Minister	Ahti Karjalainen	b. 1923
1963–1964	Prime Minister	Reino Lehto	b. 1898
1964–1966	Prime Minister	Johannes Virolainen	b. 1914
1966–1968	Prime Minister	Rafael Paasio	b. 1903 d. 1980
1968–1970	Prime Minister	Mauno Koivisto	b. 1923
1970–1970	Prime Minister	Teuvo Aura	b. 1912 d. 1999
1970–1971	Prime Minister	Ahti Karjalainen	b. 1923 d. 1990
1971–1972	Prime Minister	Teuvo Aura	
1972–1972	Prime Minister	Raphael Paasio	
1972–1975	Prime Minister	Kalevi Sorsa	b. 1930 d. 2004
1975	Prime Minister	Keijo Liinamaa	b. 1929 d. 1980
1975–1977	Prime Minister	Martti Miettunen	b. 1908 d. 2002
1977–1979	Prime Minister	Kalevi Sorsa	
1979–1982	Prime Minister	Mauno Koivisto	
1982–1987	Prime Minister	Kalevi Sorsa	
1987–1991	Prime Minister	Harri Holkeri	b. 1937
1991–1995	Prime Minister	Esko Aho	b. 1954
1995–2003	Prime Minister	Paavo Lipponen	b. 1941
2003	Prime Minister	Anneli Jaatteenmaki	b. 1955
2003–	Prime Minister	Matti Vanhanen	

Florence *See* Italy

France (French Republic)

English versions of the names of rulers of French-speaking states are:

Baldwin–Baudouin   Odo–Eudes
Francis–François   Peter–Pierre
Henry–Henri   Philip–Philippe
Hugh–Hugues   Rudolph–Rodolphe
John–Jean   Stephen–Etienne
James–Jacques   Theobald–Thibaut
William–Guillaume

▪ Gaul

Gaul was a Roman province from the 2nd century B.C. to A.D. 476.

462–486	Independent Roman Governor	Syagrius	b. 430? d. 496

▪ Merovingian Dynasty (First Frankish Dynasty)

No authentic information is available for the period before the Merovingians emerged.

420–428	King	Pharamond	
428–448	King	Clodio or Clodion	
448–458	King	Merovech or Mérovée	d. 456
458–481	King	Childeric I, son of Merovech	b. 437? d. 481
481–511	King	Clovis I, son of Childeric I	b. 456? d. 511
		Clovis married a Christian princess, who converted him to Christianity. He beat the Germans, as he believed, with God's help. He overthrew Syagrius and made his court in Paris.	
511–534	King	Thierry I of Austrasia, son of Clovis	d. 534
511–524	King	Clodomir of Neustria, son of Clovis	d. 524
511–558	Co-regent	Childebert I of Neustria, son of Clovis	d. 558
511–558	King of Soissons	Clothaire I of Neustria, son of Clovis	d. 561
534–548	King	Theodeberti of Austrasia, son of Thierry	d. 548
548–555	King	Theobald of Austrasia, son of Theodebert	d. 555
558–561	King	Clothaire I	
561–567	King	Charibert, son of Clothaire I	d. 567
561–593	King	Gontram of Burgundy, son of Clothaire I	d. 593
561–575	King	Sigebert I of Austrasia, son of Clothaire I	b. 535 assassinated
561–584	King	Chilperic I of Neustria, son of Clothaire I	d. 584
575–596	King	Childebert II of Austrasia, son of Sigebert of Austrasia	b. 570 d. 596
575–596	Regent	Brunhilde, consort of Sigebert of Austrasia	murdered 613
584–628	King	Clothaire II of Neustria, son of Chilperic of Neustria	d. 628
584–597	Regent	Fredegund, consort of Chilperic I of Neustria	d. 597
596–612	King	Theodebert II of Austrasia, son of Childebert II of Austrasia	d. 612
596–613	King	Thierry II of Burgundy, son of Childebert of Austrasia	d. 613
613	King	Sigebert II of Burgundy, son of Thierry of Burgundy	d. 613
613–628	King (whole kingdom)	Clothaire II of Austrasia and Burgundy	
628–639	King	Dagobert I, son of Clothaire of Austrasia and Burgundy	d. 639
639–656	King	Sigebert III of Austrasia, son of Dagobert I	d. 656
638–657	King	Clovis II of Neustria and Burgundy, son of Dagobert I	b. 632 d. 657

657–671	King	Clothaire III of Neustria and Burgundy, son of Clovis of Neustria and Burgundy	d. 671
663–673	King	Childeric II of Austrasia, son of Clovis II of Neustria and Burgundy	b. 653? d. 673
673–678	King	Dagobert II of Austrasia, son of Sigebert III of Austrasia	d. 678
673–691?	King	Thierry III of Neustria and Burgundy, son of Clovis II of Neustria and Burgundy	d. 691
678–691	King	Thierry III of Austrasia	
691–695	King	Clovis III of Neustria, son of Thierry III	b. 682 d. 695
695–711	King	Childebert III, son of Thierry III	d. 711
711–715	King	Dagobert III of Neustria, son of Childebert III	d. 715
715–720	King	Chilperic II, son of Childeric II of Austrasia	d. 720
717–719	King	Clothaire IV of Neustria	d. 719
720–737	King	Thierry IV, son of Dagobert III	d. 737
737–742		*Interregnum*	
742–751	King	Childeric III, son of Chilperic II	

■ Carolingian Dynasty (Second Frankish Dynasty)

628–639	Mayor of the Palace	Pepin I the Elder	d. 640 ?
687–714	Mayor of the Palace	Pepin II, son of Pepin the Elder	d. 714
714–741	Mayor of the Palace	Charles Martel, son of Pepin II	b. 689? d. 741
		In 732 the Arabs attacked Tours, the holy town of Gaul. Charles Martel won a major victory over the Arabs and ended the last great Arab invasion of the European continent.	
741–747	Mayor of the Palace	Carloman of Austrasia, son of Charles Martel	d. 754
741–751	Mayor of the Palace	Pepin the Short, son of Charles Martel	b. 714? d. 768
751–768	King	Pepin the Short (Pepin III)	
768–771	King	Carloman, son of Pepin III	d. 771
768–814	Joint Ruler	Charlemagne, son of Pepin III (Holy Roman Emperor, 800–814)	b. 742 d. 814
814–840	Joint Ruler	Louis I the Pious, son of Charlemagne	b. 778 d. 840
838–840		*Civil War*	
840–843	Joint Ruler	Lothair, Louis and Charles the Bald, sons of Louis I	
	Emperor	Lothair (*See* Italy)	
	King	Louis (*See* Germany)	
843–877	King	Charles I the Bald b. 823	d. 877
877–879	King	Louis II, son of Charles I the Bald	b. 846 d. 879
879–882	King	Louis III, son of Louis II	b. 863 d. 882
879–884	Co-regent	Carloman, brother of Louis III	d. 884

885–887	King	Charles II the Fat, son of Louis (*See* Germany)	b. 839	d. 891
888–898	King	Odo, Count of Paris		d. 898
893–922	King	Charles III the Simple, posthumous son of Louis II	b. 879	d. 929
922–923	Rival King	Robert, brother of Odo, Count of Paris		killed 923
923–936	King	Rudolf (see Burgundy), son-in-law of Robert		d. 937
936–954	King	Louis IV, son of Charles the Simple	b. 921?	d. 954
954–986	King	Lothair, son of Louis IV	b. 941	d. 986
986–987	King	Louis V, son of Lothair	b. 967?	d. 987

■ Frankish Dukes of the House of Capet

861–866	Duke	Robert the Strong, son-in-law of Louis the Pious		killed 866
866–886	Duke	Hugh the Abbot, brother of Robert the Strong		
866–886	Duke	Odo, Count of Paris, son of Robert the Strong		
889–923	Duke	Robert II, brother of Odo, Count of Paris	b. 865?	killed 923
923–936	Duke	Rudolf, brother-in-law of Robert II		d. 936
923–956	Duke	Hugh the Great, son of Robert, Count of Paris		d. 956
956–987	Duke	Hugh Capet, son of Hugh the Great	b. 938?	d. 996
		Duchy of Francia united with France.		

■ Kingdom of France: House of Capet

987–996	King	Hugh Capet		
996–1031	King	Robert II, son of Hugh Capet	b. 970?	d. 1031
1031–1060	King	Henry I, son of Robert II	b. 1008	d. 1060
1060–1108	King	Philip I, son of Henry I	b. 1052	d. 1108
1108–1137	King	Louis VI, son of Philip I	b. 1081	d. 1137
1137–1180	King	Louis VII, son of Louis VI	b. 1120	d. 1180
1180–1223	King	Philip II, son of Louis VII	b. 1165	d. 1223
1223–1226	King	Louis VIII, son of Philip II	b. 1187	d. 1226
1226–1270	King	Louis IX (St. Louis), son of Louis VIII	b. 1214	d. 1270
1270–1285	King	Philip III the Bold, son of Louis IX	b. 1245	d. 1285
1285–1314	King	Philip IV the Fair, son of Philip III	b. 1268	d. 1314
1314–1316	King	Louis X, son of Philip IV	b. 1289	d. 1316
1316	King	John I, posthumous son of Louis X	b. 1316	d. 1316
1316–1322	King	Philip V the Tall, son of Philip IV	b. 1294	d. 1322
1322–1328	King	Charles IV the Fair, son of Philip IV	b. 1294	d. 1328

■ House of Valois

1328–1350	King	Philip VI, nephew of Philip IV	b. 1293 d. 1350
1350–1364	King	John II the Good, son of Philip VI	b. 1319
1364–1380	King	Charles V the Wise, son of John II	b. 1337 d. 1380
1380–1422	King	Charles VI the Foolish, son of Charles V	b. 1368 d. 1422
1422–1461	King	Charles VII, son of Charles VI	b. 1403 d. 1461
1461–1483	King	Louis XI, son of Charles VII	b. 1423 d. 1483
1483–1498	King	Charles VIII, son of Louis XI	b. 1470 d. 1498
1498–1515	King	Louis XII, brother-in-law of Charles VIII	b. 1462 d. 1515
1515–1547	King	Francis I, second son of Louis XII	b. 1494 d. 1547
1547–1559	King	Henry II, son of Francis I	b. 1519 d. 1559
1559–1560	King	Francis II, son of Henry II	b. 1544 d. 1560
1560–1563	Regent	Catharine de' Medici, consort of Henry II	b. 1519 d. 1589
1560–1574	King	Charles IX, son of Henry II	b. 1550 d. 1574
1574–1589	King	Henry III, son of Henry II	b. 1551 assassinated 1589

■ House of Bourbon

1589–1610	King	Henry IV, son-in-law of Henry II	b. 1553 assassinated 1610
1610–1617	Regent	Marie de' Medici, consort of Henry IV	b. 1573 d. 1642
1610–1643	King	Louis XIII, son of Henry IV	b. 1601 d. 1643
1643–1651	Regent	Anne of Austria, consort of Louis XIII	b. 1601 d. 1666
1643–1715	King	Louis XIV, son of Louis XIII	b. 1638 d. 1715
1715–1723	Regent	Philip of Orleans, nephew of Louis XIV	b. 1674 d. 1723
1715–1774	King	Louis XV, great-grandson of Louis XIV	b. 1710 d. 1774
1774–1792	King	Louis XVI, grandson of Louis XV	b. 1754 guillotined 1793
1793–1795	Nominal King	Louis XVII, son of Louis XVI	b. 1785 d. 1795?

■ The First Republic

National Convention in 1792; Directory in 1795; Consulate in 1799

1799–1804	First consul	Napoleon Bonaparte	b. 1769 d. 1821

■ The First Empire

1804–1814	Emperor	Napoleon I	abdicated 1814
1815	Emperor	Napoleon I	

■ The Restoration

1814–1824	King	Louis XVIII, brother of Louis XVI		b. 1755 d. 1824
1824–1830	King	Charles X, brother of Louis XVIII	abdicated 1830	b. 1757 d. 1836
1830–1848	King	Louis-Philippe	abdicated 1848	b. 1773 d. 1850

■ The Second Republic

| 1848–1852 | President | Charles Louis Napoleon Bonaparte, nephew of Napoleon I | b. 1808 d. 1873 |

■ The Second Empire

| 1852–1871 | Emperor | Napoleon III (Charles Louis Napoleon) |

The Committee of Public Defense governed from 1870 to 1871.

■ The Third Republic

1871–1873	President	Louis Adolphe Thiers	b. 1797 d. 1877
1873–1879	President	Marie Edme Patrice Maurice de MacMahon	b. 1808 d. 1893
1879–1887	President	François Paul Jules Grévy	b. 1807 d. 1891
1887–1894	President	Marie-François Sadi-Carnot	b. 1837 d. 1894
1894–1895	President	Jean Paul Pierre Casimir-Périer	b. 1847 d. 1907
1895–1899	President	François Félix Faure	b. 1841 d. 1899
1899–1906	President	Émile Loubet	b. 1838 d. 1929
1906–1913	President	Clément Armand Falliéres	b. 1841 d. 1931
1913–1920	President	Raymond Poincaré	b. 1860 d. 1934
1920	President	Paul Deschanel	b. 1856 d. 1922
1920–1924	President	Alexandre Millerand	b. 1859 d. 1943
1924–1931	President	Gaston Doumergue	b. 1863 d. 1937
1931–1932	President	Paul Doumer	b. 185 assassinated 1932
1932–1940	President	Albert Lebrun	b. 1871 d. 1950

■ Vichy Government

| 1940–1944 | Chief of State | Henri Philippe Pétain | b. 1856 d. 1951 |
| 1942–1944 | Premier | Pierre Laval | b. 1883 executed 1945 |

■ Provisional Government

| 1944–1946 | Head of State | Charles André Joseph Marie de Gaulle | b. 1890 |
| 1946 | President | Felix Gouin | b. 1884 |

1946	President (provisional)	Georges Augustin Bidault	b. 1899
1946	President (provisional)	Léon Blum	b. 1872 d. 1950

■ The Fourth Republic

1947–1954	President	Vincent Auriol	b. 1884 d. 1966
1954–1959	President	René Coty	b. 1882 d. 1962

■ The Fifth Republic

1959–1969	President	Charles A. J. M. de Gaulle	b. 1890 d. 1970
1969–1974	President	Georges Pompidou	b. 1911 d. 1974
1974–1981	President	Valéry Giscard d'Estaing	b. 1926 d. 1996
1981–1995	President	François Mitterand	b. 1916 d. 1996
1995–	President	Jacques Chirac	b. 1932

■ Statesmen

1624–1642	First Minister	Richelieu, duc de (Armand Jean du Plessis)	b. 1585 d. 1642

Richelieu was one of France's most powerful statesmen. As Louis XIII's First Minister, he aimed to eliminate the Protestants as a political party, curtail the power of the nobles, and diminish the prestige of the Habsburgs. A patron of letters, he founded the French Academy.

1643–1661	First Minister	Jules Mazarin	b. 1602 d. 1661
1666–1691	Minister of War	Francois Michel Le Tellier, Marquis de Louvois	b. 1641
1665–1683	Treasurer	Jean Baptiste Colbert	b. 1619 d. 1683
1726–1743	First Minister	André Hercule de Fleury	b. 1653 d. 1743
1758–1761	Foreign Secretary	Étienne François de Choiseul	b. 1719 d. 1785
1766–1770	Minister of War	Étienne François de Choiseul	
1774–1776	Minister of Finance	Anne Robert Jacques Turgot	b. 1727 d. 1781
1776–1781	Minister of Finance	Jacques Necker	b. 1732 d. 1804
1783–1787	Minister of Finance	Charles Alexandre de Calonne	b. 1734 d. 1802
1788–1790	Minister of Finance	Jacques Necker	
1793–1794	Dictator	Maximilien Robespierre	b. 1758 guillotined 1794
1797–1807	Foreign Secretary	Charles Maurice de Talleyrand-Périgord	b. 1754 d. 1838
1814–1815	Prime Minister	Charles Maurice de Talleyrand-Périgord	
1830–1834	Minister of War	Nicolas Jean de Dieu Soult	b. 1769 d. 1851
1840–1848	Premier	François Pierre Guillaume Guizot	b. 1787 d. 1874

1880–1881	Premier	Jules Ferry	b. 1832 d. 1893
1881–1882	Premier	Léon Gambetta	b. 1838 d. 1882
1883–1885	Premier	Jules Ferry	
1906–1909	Premier	Georges Clemenceau	b. 1841 d. 1929

During WWI, Clemenceau, like Churchill in the WWII, embodied the policy of "Victory or Death." He was seventy-six years old when he became premier in 1917, a time when France's morale was low. Within weeks he restored the nation's confidence, and a year later the war ended in victory.

1909–1911	Premier	Aristide Briand	b. 1862 d. 1932
1912–1913	Premier	Raymond Poincaré	b. 1860 d. 1934
1913–1915	Premier	Aristide Briand	
1915–1917	Coalition head	Aristide Briand	
1917–1920	Premier	Georges Clemenceau	
1921–1922	Coalition head	Aristide Briand	
1922–1924	Premier	Raymond Poincaré	
1925–1926	Premier	Aristide Briand	
1926–1929	Premier	Raymond Poincaré	
1929	Premier	Aristide Briand	
1932	Premier	Aristide Briand	
1936–1937	Premier	Léon Blum	b. 1872 d. 1950
1938	Premier	Léon Blum	

■ Brittany

In the 10th century, Brittany threw off Frankish rule and maintained its identity. The marriages of the Duchess Anne to Charles VIII of France and then to Louis XII led to its union with France.

987–992	Duke	Conan I	d. 992
992–1008	Duke	Geoffroi I	d. 1008
1008–1040	Duke	Alain V	d. 1040
1040–1066	Duke	Conan II	d. 1066
1066–1084	Duke	Hoel V	d. 1084
1084–1112	Duke	Alain VI	d. 1112
1112–1148	Duke	Conan III	b. 1089 d. 1148
1148–1156	Duke	Eudes	d. 1156
1156–1171	Duke	Conan IV	d. 1171
1171–1186	Duke	Geoffroi II	b. 1158 d. 1186
1196–1203	Duke	Arthur I	b. 1187 d. 1203
1213–1237	Duke	Pierre I	d. 1250
1237–1286	Duke	Jean I	b. 1217 d. 1286

1286–1305	Duke	Jean II	b. 1239 d. 1305
1305–1312	Duke	Arthur II	b. 1262 d. 1312
1312–1341	Duke	Jean III	b. 1276 d. 1341
1341–1364	Duke	Charles	
1364–1399	Duke	Jean IV	
1399–1442	Duke	Jean V	
1442–1450	Duke	François I	b. 1414 d. 1450
1450–1457	Duke	Pierre II	
1457–1458	Duke	Arthur III	b. 1393 d. 1458
1458–1488	Duke	Francois II	
1488–1514	Duchess	Anne	b. 1477 d. 1514

■ Burgundy (Kingdom)

The Burgundian Kingdom was established in Gaul by Gundicar.

413–436	King	Gundicar	killed 436
436–473?	King	Gunderic	d. 473?
473–516	King	Gundobad, son of Gunderic	d. 516
516–523	King	Sigismund, son of Gundobad	d. 524
523–532	King	Gundimar, brother of Sigismund	killed 532
		Burgundy Incorporated into the Kingdom of the Franks in 532	
		Became an Independent Kingdom Again in 840	
840–855	Emperor	Louis I	b. 795? d. 855
855–863	King	Charles, son of Louis I	b. 823 d. 877
863–875	King	Louis II, son of Louis I (*See* Germany)	b. 806? d. 876
875–877	King	Charles the Bald, son of Louis I (*See* France)	b. 823 d. 877
877–879	King	Louis II the Stammerer, son of Charles the Bald	b. 846 d. 879

■ Provence (Lower Burgundy)

879–887	King	Boso of Vienne, brother-in-law of Charles the Bald	d. 887
887–924	King	Louis, son of Boso of Vienne	d. 928
924–933	King	Hugh of Arles (King of Italy)	d. 947

■ Upper (Transjurane) Burgundy

888–911	King	Rudolf I, son of Conrad, Count of Auxerre	d. 911
911–937	King	Rudolf II, son of Rudolf I	
		(of Upper and Lower Burgundy)	d. 937

■ Burgundy

937–993	King	Conrad, son of Rudolf II	
993–1032	King	Rudolf III, son of Conrad	d. 1032
		Burgundy United with Germany in 1034	
1034–1039	Emperor	Conrad II (King of Germany)	b. 990? d. 1039

■ Burgundy (Duchy)

956–965	Duke	Otto, brother of Hugh Capet	
965–1002	Duke	Henry, brother of Otto	d. 1002
1002–1017	Duke	Robert II (see France), son of Hugh Capet	
1017–1031	Duke	Henry (see France), son of Robert II	
1031–1075	Duke	Robert, son of King Robert of France	d. 1075
1075–1078	Duke	Hugh I, grandson of Robert	b. 1040? d. 1093
1078–1102	Duke	Odo (Eudes) I, brother of Hugh I	
1102–1142	Duke	Hugh II, nephew of Hugh I	
1162–1193	Duke	Hugh III, grandson of Hugh II	b. 1150? d. 1193
1193–1218	Duke	Odo (Eudes) III, son of Hugh III	
1218–1272	Duke	Hugh IV, grandson of Hugh III	b. 1212 d. 1272
1272–1309	Duke	Robert II	
1305–1315	Duke	Hugh V, grandson of Hugh IV	
1315–1350	Duke	Odo (Eudes) IV, son of Robert II	
1350–1361	Duke	Philippe de Rouvres	b. 1345 d. 1361
		Burgundy Returned to the French Crown in 1361	
1363–1404	Duke	Philip the Bold, son of John the Good, King of France	b. 1342 d. 1404
1404–1419	Duke	John the Fearless, son of Philip the Bold	b. 1371 murdered 1419
1419–1467	Duke	Philip II the Good, son of John the Fearless	b. 1396 d. 1467
1467–1477	Duke	Charles the Bold, son of Philip II the Good	b. 1433 killed 1477
1477–1482	Duchess	Mary (wife of Maximilian of Austria), daughter of Charles the Bold	b. 1457 d. 1482
1482–1506	Duke	Philip the Fair (King of Spain), son of Mary of Burgundy	b. 1478 d. 1506
1506–1529	Duke	Charles V (Holy Roman Emperor), son of Philip the Fair	b. 1500 d. 1558
		Duchy Incorporated into France in 1529	

■ Champagne

Champagne emerged as one of the most powerful vassal states of France during the Middle Ages.

864–866	Count	Robert	d. 866
1004–1037	Count	Eudes	d. 1037

1037–1047	Count	Etienne		d. 1047
1047–1089	Count	Thibaut I		d. 1089
1089–1125	Count	Hugues I		d. 1125
1148–1152	Count	Thibaut II		d. 1152
1152–1181	Count	Henri I		d. 1181
1181–1197	Count	Henri II	b. 1150	d. 1197
1197–1201	Count	Thibaut III		d. 1201
1201–1253	Count	Thibaut IV	b. 1201	d. 1253
1253–1270	Count	Henri III		d. 1274
1274–1304	Countess	Jeanne I	b. 1270	d. 1304
1304–1316	Count	Louis	b. 1289	d. 1316

From the mid-13th century, the Counts of Champagne were also Kings of Navarre. Jeanne I of Champagne, as Queen Juana of Navarre, married Philip IV of France. Their son, Louis X, inherited Champagne from his mother, and it subsequently was annexed to France.

■ Lorraine

The Duchy of Lorraine emerged in the 10th century as a fief of the Holy Roman Empire.

1312–1328	Duke	Frédéric IV	
1328–1346	Duke	Rodolphe	
1346–1391	Duke	Jean	
1391–1431	Duke	Charles I	
1431–1480	Duke	René I	
1480–1508	Duke	René II	
1508–1544	Duke	Antoine	
1544–1545	Duke	François	
1545–1608	Duke	Charles II	
1608–1624	Duke	Henri	
1624–1625	Duke	François II	d. 1632
1625–1634	Duke	Charles III (occupied by France)	d. 1675
1659–1669	Duke	Nicolas François (reoccupied by France)	d. 1670
1697–1729	Duke	Leopold	
1729–1735	Duke	François Etienne	d. 1765

François Etienne exchanged the throne of Lorraine for that of Tuscany in 1735. Lorraine was then given to Stanislaus I, the deposed King of Poland.

| 1735–1766 | King | Stanislaus | b. 1677 d. 1766 |

Lorraine was not raised to the rank of a kingdom, yet Stanislaus retained the title of King under the protection of his son-in-law, Louis XV of France. On the death of Stanislaus, Lorraine became part of France.

■ Normandy

Normandy was established by the Norsemen under Rollo.

| 911–927 | Viking Leader | Rollo | b. 860? d. 931 ? |

After invading northwest France, Rollo seized Rouen and the land surrounding it. Charles the Simple granted him part of Neustria. Rollo then embraced Christianity and became ruler of Normandy.

927–942	Duke	William I Longsword, son of Rollo	assassinated 942
942–996	Duke	Richard I the Fearless, son of William Longsword	d. 996
996–1027	Duke	Richard II the Good, son of Richard I	d. 1027
1027–1028	Duke	Richard III	
1028–1035	Duke	Robert the Devil, son of Richard II the Good	d. 1035
1035–1087	Duke	William I the Conqueror, son of Robert the Devil	b. 1027 d. 1087
1087–1106	Duke	Robert II, son of William the Conqueror	b. 1056 d. 1134
1106–1135	Duke	Henry I, son of William the Conqueror	b. 1068 d. 1135
1135–1167	Duchess	Matilda, daughter of Henry I	b. 1102 d. 1167
1135–1151	Duke	Stephen of Blois, nephew of Henry I	b. 1094? d. 1154
1151–1189	Duke	Henry II Plantagenet, grandson of Henry I	b. 1133 d. 1189
1189–1199	Duke	Richard I Coeur de Lion, son of Henry II	b. 1157 d. 1199
1199–1204	Duke	John Lackland, son of Henry II	b. 1167? d. 1216

Normandy Incorporated into France in 1204

Gabon (Gabonese Republic)

One of the earliest French settlements on the African coast, Gabon elected to remain an autonomous republic within the French Community in 1958. It has been fully independent since 1960.

| 1960–1967 | President | Léon M'ba |
| 1967– | President | Omar Bongo |

Gambia (The Republic of The Gambia)

In 1843 Gambia was established as a British colony. It became an independent state as a constitutional monarchy within the Commonwealth in 1965. In 1970 it became a republic.

1965–1966	Governor-General	Sir John Warburton Paul
1965–1994	Prime Minister	Sir Dauda Kairaba Jawara
1994–	President	Yahya A.J.J. Jammeh

Genoa *See* Italy

Georgia (Republic of Georgia)

Georgia corresponds to the ancient countries of Colchis and Iberia in the Caucasus. The history of the Christian kingdom of Georgia begins after the acceptance of Christianity by King Miriani of Iberia in the 4th century.

450–503	King	Vakhtang	
562–	King	Guaram	
c. 700		*Under Caliphate of the East*	
1089–1125	King	David II	
1008–1014	King	Bagrat IV	
1184–1212	Queen	Tamara	
1236–		*Under Rule of Mongols*	
1314–1346	King	Giorgi V	
1360–1393	King	Bagrat V	
1413–1443	King	Alexander	
		Georgia was divided into numerous kingdoms and principalities, some under Persian domination, others under Turkish.	
1744–1762	King of Kartlia	Taymurazi II	d. 1762
		Taymurazi II assumed the throne of Kartlia and placed his son on the throne of Kakhetia.	
1744–1762	King of Khaketia	Irakli II	d. 1798
1762–1798	King of Kartlia and Khaketia	Irakli II	
1798–1800	King of Kartlia and Khaketia	Giorgi XII	d. 1800
1801		*Russia annexed Kartlia and Khaketia and the remaining Georgian principalities between 1810 and 1867.*	

■ *Republic of Georgia*

The surrender of Russia to Germany in 1917 led to the short-lived Transcaucasian Republic, in which Georgia was linked with Armenia and Azerbaijan. An independent republic was declared in 1918.

1918–1921	President	Noe Jordania	b. 1869
	Premier	Akaki Chkhenkeli	
		In 1921 the Red Army entered Georgia, and it became a Soviet Socialist Republic. Although independence was regained in 1991, a modicum of stability was only achieved in 1995 in the wake of a period of considerable ethnic and civil strife.	
1995–2003	President	Eduard Shevardnadze	
2003–2004	President	Nino Burdzhanadze	
2004–	President	Mikheil Saakashvili	

Germany (Federal Republic of Germany)

English versions of the names of rulers of German-speaking states are:

Albert–Adalbert, Albrecht	Frederick–Friedrich	Louis–Ludwig
Charles–Karl	George–Georg	Maurice–Moritz
Ernest–Ernst	Henry–Heinrich	Philip–Philipp
Eugene–Eugen	Joseph–Josef	William–Wilhelm
Francis–Franz	John–Johann	

■ Emperors

Hohenzollern Dynasty

1871–1888	Emperor	William I (of Prussia)	b. 1797 d. 1888
1888	Emperor	Frederick III, son of William I	b. 1831 d. 1888
1888–1918	Emperor	William II, son of Frederick III	abdicated 1918 b. 1859 d. 1941

■ Republic

1919–1925	President	Friedrich Ebert	b. 1871 d. 1925
1925–1933	President	Paul von Hindenburg	b. 1847 d. 1934

■ National Socialist Regime

1934	President	Paul von Hindenburg	
1934–1945	Dictator	Adolf Hitler	b. 1889 d. 1945

Adolf Hitler's Nazi regime proved disastrous for his own nation, in addition to many others. When he committed suicide in April of 1945, Germany's cities were in ruins; millions of soldiers, civilians, and concentration camp prisoners were dead; and the entire country was occupied by British, French, American, and Russian troops.

1945–1949	*Allied Occupation*

■ Federal Republic

1949–1959	President	Theodor Heuss	b. 1884 d. 1959
1959–1969	President	Heinrich Lübke	b. 1894
1949–1963	Federal Chancellor	Konrad Adenauer	b. 1876 d. 1967
1963–1966	Chancellor	Ludwig Erhard	b. 1897 d. 1997
1966–1969	Chancellor	Kurt G. Kiesinger	b. 1904 d. 1988
1969–1974	Chancellor	Willy Brandt	b. 1913 d. 1992
1974–1982	Chancellor	Helmut Schmidt	b. 1918
1982–1998	Chancellor	Helmut Kohl	b. 1930
1998–	Chancellor	Gerhard Schroeder	b. 1944

■ Statesmen

1807–1808	First Minister (Prussia)	Karl von Stein	b. 1757 d. 1831
1813–1815		Karl von Stein	
1862–1871	Prime Minister (Prussia)	Otto Eduard Leopold, Prince von Bismarck	b. 1815 d. 1898
1871–1890	Chancellor	Otto Eduard Leopold, Prince von Bismarck	

Bismarck aimed to free the German states from foreign control and unite them under the crown of Prussia, which he accomplished at the expense of Austria and France. He restored the German Empire under a Hohenzollern king, with himself as chancellor.

1890–1894	Chancellor	Count Georg Leo von Caprivi	b. 1831 d. 1899
1894–1900	Chancellor	Prince Chlodwig Karl Viktor Hohenlohe-Schillingsfürst	b. 1819 d. 1901
1900–1909	Chancellor	Prince Bernhard von Bülow	b. 1849 d. 1929
1909–1917	Chancellor	Theobald von Bethmann-Hollweg	b. 1856 d. 1921
1917	Chancellor	Georg Michaelis	b. 1857 d. 1936
1917–1918	Chancellor	Count Georg von Hertling	b. 1843 d. 1919
1918	Chancellor	Maximilian (Prince Max of Baden)	b. 1867 d. 1929
1918–1919	Chancellor	Friedrich Ebert	b. 1871 d. 1925
1919	Prime Minister	Philipp Scheidemann	b. 1865 d. 1939
1919–1920	Prime Minister	Gustav Adolf Bauer	b. 1870 d. 1944
1920	Chancellor	Hermann Müller	b. 1876 d. 1931
1920–1921	Chancellor	Konstantin Fehrenbach	b. 1852 d. 1926
1921–1922	Chancellor	Karl Joseph Wirth	b. 1879 d. 1956
1922–1923	Chancellor	Wilhelm Cuno	b. 1876 d. 1933
1923	Chancellor	Gustav Stresemann	b. 1878 d. 1929
1923–1925	Chancellor	Wilhelm Marx	b. 1863 d. 1946
1925–1926	Chancellor	Hans Luther	b. 1879 d. 1962
1926–1928	Chancellor	Wilhelm Marx	
1928–1930	Chancellor	Hermann Müller	
1930–1932	Chancellor	Heinrich Brüning	
1932	Chancellor	Franz von Papen	
1932–1933	Chancellor	Kurt von Schleicher	b. 1882 d. 1934
1933–1945	Chancellor	Adolf Hitler	
1945	Chancellor	Karl Dönitz	

■ Democratic Republic (East Germany)

1949–1960	Chairman, Council of State	Wilhelm Pieck	d. 1960

1960–1973	Chairman, Council of State	Walter Ulbricht	b. 1893 d. 1973
1973	Chairman, Council of State	Friedrich Ebert	b. 1894 d. 1979
1973–1976	Chairman, Council of State	Willi Stoph	b. 1914 d. 1999
1976–1989	Chairman, Council of State	Erich Honecker	b. 1912 d. 1994
1989–1989	Chairman, Council of State	Egon Krenz	b. 1937

Baden developed from several petty states. It was formerly part of Swabia.

■ House of Baden-Durlach

1533–1552	Margrave	Ernst (abdicated)	b. 1482 d. 1553
1552–1577	Margrave	Karl II	b. 1529 d. 1577
1577–1604	Margrave	Ernst Friedrich	b. 1560 d. 1604
1604–1622	Margrave	Georg Friedrich (abdicated)	b. 1573 d. 1638
1622–1659	Margrave	Friedrich V	b. 1594 d. 1659
1659–1677	Margrave	Friedrich VI	b. 1617 d. 1677
1677–1688	Margrave	Friedrich VII	b. 1647 d. 1709
1688–1697	Margrave	(French intervention)	
1697–1709	Margrave	Friedrich VII (restored)	
1709–1738	Margrave	Karl III Wilhelm	b. 1679 d. 1738
1738–1803	Margrave	Karl Friedrich	b. 1728 d. 1811
1803–1806	Elector	Karl Friedrich	
1806–1811	Grand Duke	Karl Friedrich	
1811–1818	Grand Duke	Karl Ludwig Friedrich	
1818–1830	Grand Duke	Ludwig I	b. 1763 d. 1830
1830–1852	Grand Duke	Leopold I	b. 1790 d. 1852
1852–1907	Grand Duke	Friedrich I	b. 1826 d. 1907
1907–1918	Grand Duke	Friedrich II	b. 1857 d. 1928
1918		*The monarchy was abolished, and Baden became part of the German Republic.*	

■ Bavaria

912–937	Duke	Arnulf the Bad	
938–947	Duke	Berchtold, brother of Arnulf	d. 947
947–955	Duke	Henry I, brother of Otto the Great	d. 955

955–978	Duke	Henry II, son of Henry I	b. 915 d. 995
982–985	Duke	Henry III, son of Henry I	
985–995	Duke	Henry II	
995–1002	Duke	Henry IV, son of Henry II, Emperor 1002–1024	b. 973 d. 1024
1002–1026	Duke	Henry V of Lützelburg (Luxemburg)	d. 1026
1026–1042	Duke	Henry VI (Emperor Henry III)	
1042–1047	Duke	Henry VII	
1049–1053	Duke	Konrad I	
1053–1056	Duke	Henry VIII (Emperor Henry IV)	d. 1106
1056	Duke	Konrad II	
1056–1061	Duchess	Agnes	

■ Guelph (or Welf) Dynasty

1061–1070	Duke	Otto of Nordheim	d. 1083
1070–1101	Duke	Guelph I, son-in-law of Henry IV, Emperor	
1101–1120	Duke	Guelph II, son of Guelph I	
1120–1126	Duke	Henry IX, brother of Guelph II	d. 1126
1126–1139	Duke	Henry X the Proud, son of Henry IX	b. 1108? d. 1139
1139–1141	Duke	Leopold IV of Austria	d. 1141
1143–1156	Duke	Henry XI, brother of Leopold of Austria	
1156–1180	Duke	Henry XII the Lion, son of Henry X	deposed 1180 b. 1129 d. 1195

■ House of Wittelsbach

1180–1183	Duke	Otto I	b. 1120? d. 1183
1183–1231	Duke	Ludwig I, son of Otto I	b. 1174 assassinated 1231
1231–1253	Duke	Otto II the Illustrious, son of Ludwig I	d. 1253
1253–1294	Duke	Ludwig II the Stern, son of Otto II	b. 1229 d. 1294
1294–1317	Duke	Rudolph, son of Ludwig II	b. 1274
1314–1347	Co-ruler	Emperor Ludwig III, brother of Rudolph	b. 1283? d. 1347
		In 1329 the country was divided into Bavaria and the Palatinate.	
		Bavaria was divided after 1347 into several parts.	
1375–1397	Duke	John of Munich, grandson of Emperor Ludwig	abdicated 1397 d. 1413?
1397–1438	Duke	Ernst, son of John of Munich	d. 1438
1438–1460	Duke	Albert III the Pious, son of Ernst	d. 1460
1460–1467	Duke	Sigismund, son of Albert III	abdicated 1467 d. 1501
1460–1508	Duke	Albert IV, brother of Sigismund	d. 1508
1508–1550	Duke	William IV, son of Albert IV	d. 1550

1550–1579	Duke	Albert V, son of William IV	d. 1579
1579–1597	Duke	William V the Pious, son of Albert V	d. 1626
1597–1623	Duke	Maximilian I, son of William V	b. 1573 d. 1651
		Duchy Became an Electorate in 1623	
1623–1651	Elector	Maximilian I (The Great)	
1651–1679	Elector	Ferdinand Maria, son of Maximilian	b. 1636 d. 1679
1679–1706	Elector	Maximilian II Emanuel, son of Ferdinand Maria (Deposed after Blenheim, reinstated by Treaty of Utrecht)	b. 1662 d. 1726
1714–1726	Elector	Maximilian II Emanuel	
1726–1745	Elector	Charles Albert, son of Maximilian II Emanuel (Holy Roman Emperor, 1742–1745)	b. 1697 d. 1745
1745–1777	Elector	Maximilian III Joseph, son of Charles Albert	b. 1727 d. 1777
1777–1799	Elector	Charles Theodore of the Palatinate, son of John Christian Joseph	b. 1724 d. 1799
1799–1805	Elector	Maximilian IV Joseph	b. 1756 d. 1825
1806–1825	King	Maximilian I Joseph	
1825–1848	King	Ludwig I, son of Elector Maximilian	b. 1786 abdicated 1848 d. 1868
1848–1864	King	Maximilian II Joseph, son of Ludwig I	b. 1811 d. 1864
1864–1886	King	Ludwig II, son of Maximilian II	b. 1845 d. 1886
1886–1913	King	Otto, brother of Ludwig II deposed 1913	b. 1848 d. 1916
1886–1912	Regent	Luitpold, brother of Maximilian II	b. 1821 d. 1912
1912–1913	Regent	Ludwig III, son of Prince Regent Luitpold	b. 1845 d. 1921
1913–1918	King	Ludwig III	abdicated 1918

■ Brandenburg (Ascanian Dynasty)

1134–1170	Margrave	Albert I the Bear	b. 1100? d. 1170
1170–1184	Margrave	Otto I, son of Albert the Bear	b. 1130? d. 1184
1184–1205	Margrave	Otto II, son of Otto I	
1205–1220	Margrave	Albert II, brother of Otto II	b. 1174? d. 1220
1220–1266	Margrave	John I, son of Albert II	d. 1266
1220–1267	Margrave	Otto III, son of Albert II (ruled jointly with John I)	d. 1267
1266–1309	Margrave	Otto IV, son of John I	
1309–1319	Margrave	Waldemar the Great, nephew of Otto IV	b. 1281? d. 1319
1319–1320	Margrave	Henry the Child, cousin of Waldemar	d. 1320

■ Wittelsbach Dynasty

1322 1351	Margrave	Louis V, son of Emperor Louis III	b. 1315 d. 1361
1351–1365	Elector	Louis the Roman, brother of Louis V	b. 1330 d. 1365

1365–1373	Elector	Otto, brother of Louis	b. 1341 d. 1379
1373–1378	Emperor	Charles IV	b. 1316 d. 1378
1378–1417	Emperor	Sigismund of Hungary, son of Charles IV	b. 1368 d. 1437

■ Hohenzollern Dynasty

1417–1440	Elector	Frederick of Nuremberg	b. 1371 d. 1440
1440–1470	Elector	Frederick II, son of Frederick of Nuremberg	b. 1413 d. 1471
1470–1486	Elector	Albert III, brother of Frederick II	b. 1414 d. 1486
1486–1499	Elector	John Cicero, son of Albert III	b. 1455 d. 1499
1499–1535	Elector	Joachim I, son of John Cicero	b. 1484 d. 1535
1535–1571	Elector	Joachim II, son of Joachim I	b. 1513 d. 1571
1571–1598	Elector	John George, son of Joachim II	b. 1525 d. 1598
1598–1608	Elector	Joachim Frederick, son of John George	b. 1546 d. 1608
1608–1619	Elector	John Sigismund, son of Joachim Frederick	b. 1572 d. 1619
1619–1640	Elector	George William, son of John Sigismund	b. 1597 d. 1640
1640–1688	Elector	Frederick William, the "Great Elector," son of George William	b. 1620 d. 1688

After taking over a devastated country, Frederick William created a strong, standing army; rebuilt the war-damaged cities, including his capital, Berlin; founded the Prussian navy; and initiated colonial expansion in West Africa.

| 1688–1701 | Elector | Frederick III, son of Frederick William (*See* Prussia) | b. 1657 d. 1713 |

■ Brunswick (Wolfenbuttel Line)

Brunswick appeared as a separate state in the 16th century.

1568–1589	Duke	Julius	
1589–1613	Duke	Heinrich Julius	
1613–1634	Duke	Friedrich Ulrich	
1635–1666	Duke	August II	
1666–1704	Duke	Rudolf August	
1685–1714	Duke	Anton Ulrich (co-ruler)	
1714–1731	Duke	August Wilhelm	
1731–1735	Duke	Ludwig Rudolf	
1735	Duke	Ferdinand Albrecht	
1735–1780	Duke	Karl	b. 1713 d. 1780
1780–1806	Duke	Karl Wilhelm Ferdinand	b. 1735 d. 1806

*Brunswick Taken by the French in 1806
Annexed to the Kingdom of Westphalia in 1807
Duchy Restored in 1813*

1813–1815	Duke	Friedrich Wilhelm	b. 1771	d. 1815
1815–1830	Duke	Karl II (deposed)	b. 1804	d. 1873
1831–1884	Duke	Wilhelm	b. 1806	d. 1884

The line of the Dukes of Brunswick died with Wilhelm, and the country was governed by Prussian regents until 1913.

1913–1918	Duke	Ernest August	b. 1887	d. 1953

Brunswick Became Part of the German Republic in 1918

■ Cleves

? –1448	Duke	Adolf I	d. 1448
1448–1481	Duke	Johann I	
1481–1521	Duke	Johann II	
1521–1539	Duke	Johann III	
1539–1592	Duke	Wilhelm	
1592–1609	Duke	Johann Wilhelm	

The Dukedom of Cleves became extinct in 1609, and the Duchy was, after a long struggle, annexed to Brandenburg.

■ Hanover

Electorate of Hanover was created in 1692 from the Duchy of Brunswick-Lüneburg.

1692–1698	Elector	Ernest Augustus	b. 1629	d. 1698
1698–1727	Elector	George I	b. 1660	d. 1727

George I succeeded to the throne of Great Britain in 1714.

1727–1760	Elector	George II	b. 1683	d. 1760
1760–1807	Elector	George III	b. 1738	d. 1820
1807–1813		*Hanover Annexed to Westphalia by Napoleon*		
1813–1815	Elector	George III (restored)		

Hanover Raised to a Kingdom by the Congress of Vienna in 1815

1815–1820	King	George III		
1820–1830	King	George IV	b. 1762	d. 1830
1830–1837	King	William (William IV of England)	b. 1765	d. 1837

Since women were barred from the throne of Hanover, the personal union with Great Britain ended with the death of William IV and the ascension of Queen Victoria.

1837–1851	King	Ernest Augustus (son of George III)	b. 1771	d. 1851
1851–1866	King	George V	b. 1819	d. 1878

Hanover Annexed by Prussia in 1866

■ Hesse-Cassel (Ger. Hessen-Kassel)

1567–1592	Landgrave	Wilhelm IV	b. 1532 d. 1592
1592–1627	Landgrave	Moritz (abd.)	b. 1572 d. 1632
1627–1637	Landgrave	Wilhelm V	b. 1602 d. 1637
1637–1663	Landgrave	Wilhelm VI	b. 1629 d. 1663
1663–1670	Landgrave	Wilhelm VII	b. 1651 d. 1670
1670–1730	Landgrave	Karl	b. 1654 d. 1730
1730–1751	Landgrave	Friedrich I	b. 1676 d. 1751
1751–1760	Landgrave	Wilhelm VIII	b. 1682 d. 1760
1760–1785	Landgrave	Friedrich II	b. 1720 d. 1785
1785–1803	Landgrave	Wilhelm IX	b. 1743 d. 1821

The Landgrave of Hesse-Cassel assumed the title of Elector in 1803, with Wilhelm IX becoming the Elector Wilhelm I.

1803–1807	Elector	Wilhelm I	
1807–1815		*Hesse-Cassel Annexed to Kingdom of Westphalia*	

■ Hesse

Hesse emerged as a fief of the Holy Roman Empire in the 13th century.

1247–1308	Landgrave	Heinrich I	b. 1244 d. 1308
1308–1328	Landgrave	Otto	b. 1273 d. 1328
1328–1376	Landgrave	Heinrich II	b. 1297 d. 1376
1377–1413	Landgrave	Hermann I	b. 1340 d. 1413
1413–1458	Landgrave	Ludwig I	b. 1402 d. 1458
1458–1471	Landgrave	Ludwig II	b. 1438 d. 1471
1458–1483	Landgrave	Henrich III	b. 1440 d. 1483
1471–1493	Landgrave	Wilhelm I (abdicated)	b. 1466 d. 1515
1493–1509	Landgrave	Wilhelm II	b. 1468 d. 1509
1509–1567	Landgrave	Philipp	b. 1504 d. 1567

After the death of Philipp, Hesse was divided into several successor states, with Hesse-Cassel and Hesse-Darmstadt being the most important.

1815–1821	Elector	Wilhelm I (restored)	
1821–1847	Elector	Wilhelm II	b. 1777 d. 1847
1847–1866	Elector	Friedrich Wilhelm	b. 1802 d. 1875

Hesse-Cassel Annexed to Prussia in 1866

■ Hesse-Darmstadt

1567–1596	Landgrave	Georg I	b. 1547 d. 1596

1596–1626	Landgrave	Ludwig V	b. 1577 d. 1626
1626–1661	Landgrave	Georg II	b. 1605 d. 1661
1661–1678	Landgrave	Ludwig VI	b. 1630 d. 1678
1678	Landgrave	Ludwig VII	b. 1658 d. 1678
1678–1739	Landgrave	Ernst Ludwig	b. 1667 d. 1739
1739–1768	Landgrave	Ludwig VIII	b. 1691 d. 1768
1768–1790	Landgrave	Ludwig IX	b. 1719 d. 1790

In the course of the Napoleonic upheavals, Hesse-Darmstadt was raised to the rank of Grand Duchy.

1806–1830	Grand Duke	Ludwig I	b. 1753 d. 1830
1830–1848	Grand Duke	Ludwig II	b. 1777 d. 1848
1848–1877	Grand Duke	Ludwig III	b. 1806 d. 1877
1877–1892	Grand Duke	Ludwig IV	b. 1837 d. 1892
1892–1918	Grand Duke	Ernst Ludwig	b. 1868

In 1871 Hesse-Darmstadt entered the German Empire. In 1918 the Grand Duke was expelled, and the country became part of the new German Republic.

■ Palatinate

1294–1319	Count Palatine	Rudolph of Bavaria	
1319–1327	Count Palatine	Adolph the Simple, son of Rudolph	b. 1300 d. 1327
1327–1353	Count Palatine	Rudolph II, son of Rudolph I	b. 1306 d. 1353
1353–1390	Count Palatine	Rupert I, son of Rudolph I	b. 1309 d. 1390
1390–1398	Count Palatine	Rupert II, son of Adolph the Simple	b. 1335 d. 1398
1398–1410	Count Palatine	Rupert III, son of Rupert II (*See* Emperors of the Holy Roman Empire, 1400)	b. 1352 d. 1410
1410–1435	Count Palatine	Ludwig III, son of Rupert III	
1435–1449	Count Palatine	Ludwig IV, son of Ludwig III	b. 1424 d. 1449
1449–1476	Count Palatine	Frederick I the Victorious, son of Ludwig III	b. 1425 d. 1476
1476–1508	Count Palatine	Philip, son of Ludwig IV	b. 1448 d. 1508
1508–1544	Count Palatine	Ludwig V, son of Philip	b. 1478 d. 1544
1544–1556	Count Palatine	Frederick II the Wise, son of Philip	b. 1482 d. 1556
1556–1559	Count Palatine	Otto, grandson of Philip	b. 1502 d. 1559
1559–1576	Elector	Frederick III the Pious	b. 1515 d. 1576
1576–1583	Elector	Ludwig VI, son of Frederick III	b. 1539 d. 1583
1583–1592	Guardian of Frederick IV	John Casimir, son of Frederick III	b. 1543 d. 1592
1592–1610	Elector	Frederick IV the Upright, son of Ludwig VI	b. 1574 d. 1610
1610–1623	"The Winter King"	Frederick V, son of Frederick IV (*See* Czechoslovakia)	b. 1596 d. 1632

1623–1648		*Palatinate United with Bavaria*	
1648–1680	Elector	Charles Ludwig, son of Frederick V	b. 1617 d. 1680
1680–1685	Elector	Charles, son of Charles Ludwig	b. 1651 d. 1685
1685–1690	Elector	Philip William	b. 1615 d. 1690
1690–1716	Elector	John William, son of Philip William	b. 1658 d. 1716
1716–1742	Elector	Charles Philip, son of Philip William	b. 1661 d. 1742
1742–1799	Elector	Charles Theodore (*See* Bavaria)	b. 1724 d. 1799

Charles Theodore was a patron of art and literature. A dispute with his heir, Charles of Zweibrücken, resulted in the War of the Bavarian Succession. War was declared and peace concluded without any actual battles taking place.

■ Prussia (Hohenzollern Dynasty)

1701–1713	King	Frederick I, (Frederick III of Brandenburg)	b. 1657 d. 1713
1713–1740	King	Frederick William I, son of Frederick I	b. 1688 d. 1740
1740–1786	King	Frederick II the Great, son of Frederick William I	b. 1712 d. 1786

Frederick the Great enlarged the boundaries of Prussia and developed its resources. He had a taste for music and French literature, and corresponded with Voltaire, whom he invited to live at his court. He built the palace of Sans Souci at Potsdam.

1786–1797	King	Frederick William II, nephew of Frederick II	b. 1744 d. 1797
1797–1840	King	Frederick William III, son of Frederick William II	b. 1770 d. 1840
1840–1861	King	Frederick William IV, son of Frederick William III	b. 1795 d. 1888
1861–1871	King	William I, son of Frederick William IV	b. 1797 d. 1861

■ Saxony (Wettin Dynasty)

1381–1423	Duke	Frederick I the Warlike, son of Frederick of Meissen	b. 1369 d. 1428
1423–1428	Elector	Frederick I the Warlike	
1428–1464	Elector	Frederick II the Gentle, son of Frederick I	b. 1411? d. 1464
1464–1486	Elector	Ernest, son of Frederick II	b. 1441 d. 1486
1464–1500	Joint Ruler	Albert III, son of Frederick II	b. 1443 d. 1500
		Ernest and Albert Divided Saxony in 1485	
1486–1525	Elector	Frederick III the Wise, son of Ernest	b. 1463 d. 1525
1525–1532	Elector	John the Constant, son of Ernest	b. 1469 d. 1532
1532–1547	Elector	John Frederick the Magnanimous, son of John	b. 1503 d. 1554
1500–1539	Duke	George the Bearded, son of Albert	b. 1471 d. 1539
1539–1541	Duke	Henry the Pious, son of Albert	b. 1473 d. 1541
1541–1547	Duke	Maurice, son of Henry	b. 1521 d. 1553

1547–1553	Elector	Maurice, son of Henry		
1553–1586	Elector	Augustus I, brother of Maurice	b. 1526	d. 1586
1586–1591	Elector	Christian I, son of Augustus I	b. 1560	d. 1591
1591–1611	Elector	Christian II, son of Christian I	b. 1583	d. 1611
1611–1656	Elector	John George I, son of Christian I	b. 1585	d. 1656
1656–1680	Elector	John George II, son of John George I	b. 1613	d. 1680
1680–1691	Elector	John George III, son of John George II	b. 1647	d. 1691
1691–1694	Elector	John George IV, son of John George III	b. 1668	d. 1694
1694–1733	Elector	Frederick Augustus I, son of John George III (King of Poland from 1697)	b. 1670	d. 1733
1733–1763	Elector	Frederick Augustus II, son of Frederick Augustus I	b. 1696	d. 1763
1763	Elector	Frederick Christian, son of Frederick Augustus II	b. 1722	d. 1763
1763–1806	Elector	Frederick Augustus III, son of Frederick Christian	b. 1750	d. 1827
1806–1827	King	Frederick Augustus I the Just		

Frederick Augustus I refused the Polish crown in 1791.
At first an enemy of France and then an ally of Napoleon,
he was deprived of half of his kingdom by the Congress of Vienna.

1827–1836	King	Anthony, brother of Frederick Augustus I	b. 1755	d. 1836
1836 1854	King	Frederick Augustus II, nephew of Frederick Augustus I	b. 1797	d. 1854
1854–1873	King	John, brother of Frederick Augustus II	b. 1801	d. 1873
1873–1902	King	Albert, son of John	b. 1828	d. 1902
1902–1904	King	George, son of John	b. 1832	d. 1904
1904–1918	King	Frederick Augustus III, son of George	abdicated 1918 b. 1865	d. 1932

■ Swabia

Swabia was one of the principal states of the early Holy Roman Empire, corresponding roughly to Baden and Wurttemberg and adjacent territories.

916–926	Duke	Burchard I		d. 926
926–948	Duke	Hermann I		d. 948
948–957	Duke	Ludolf	b. 931	d. 957
957–973	Duke	Burchard II		d. 973
973–982	Duke	Otto I		d. 982
982–997	Duke	Conrad I		d. 997
997–1004	Duke	Hermann II		d. 1004
1004–1012	Duke	Hermann III		d. 1012
1012–1015	Duke	Ernst I	b. 970	d. 1015
1015–1030	Duke	Ernst II	b. 1007	d. 1030
1030–1039	Duke	Hermann IV		d. 1039

1039–1045	Duke	Heinrich	b. 1017 d. 1056
1045–1047	Duke	Otto II	d. 1047
1047–1057	Duke	Otto III	d. 1057
1057–1080	Duke	Rudolf	d. 1080
1080–1105	Duke	Friedrich I	d. 1105
1105–1147	Duke	Friedrich II	b. 1090 d. 1147
1147–1152	Duke	Friedrich III	b. 1122 d. 1190

Friedrich III assumed the throne of Germany in 1152 and was crowned Emperor in 1155. He is known to history as the Emperor Friedrich I Barbarossa.

1152–1167	Duke	Friedrich IV	b. 1144 d. 1167
1167–1191	Duke	Friedrich V	d. 1191
1191–1196	Duke	Conrad III	b. 1167 d. 1196
1196–1208	Duke	Philipp	b. 1176 d. 1208
1208–1219	Duke	Friedrich VI	b. 1194 d. 1250
1219–1235	Duke	Heinrich II (abdicated)	b. 1212 d. 1242
1235–1254	Duke	Conrad IV	b. 1228 d. 1254
1254–1268	Duke	Conrad V	b. 1252 d. 1268
1268		*The Duchy of Swabia broke up into many smaller successor states.*	

■ Westphalia

The kingdom of Westphalia existed from 807 to 1814.

1807–1813	King	Jerome, brother of Napoleon	abdicated 1813 b. 1784 d. 1860

■ Wurttemberg

1083–1105	Count	Conrad I	
1110	Count	Conrad II	
1134–1158	Count	Ludwig I	
1166–1181	Count	Ludwig II	
1201–1228	Count	Ludwig III	
1236–1241	Count	Eberhard I	
1241–1265	Count	Ulrich I	d. 1265
1265–1279	Count	Ulrich II	d. 1279
1279–1325	Count	Eberhard II	b. 1265 d. 1325
1325–1344	Count	Ulrich III	b. 1295 d. 1344
1344–1392	Count	Eberhard III	b. 1315 d. 1392
1344–1366	Count	Ulrich IV	d. 1366

1392–1417	Count	Eberhard IV	d. 1417
1417–1419	Count	Eberhard V	b. 1388 d. 1419
1419–1450	Count	Ludwig I	b. 1412 d. 1450
1450–1457	Count	Ludwig II	b. 1439 d. 1457
1457–1480	Count	Ulrich V	b. 1413 d. 1480
1480–1495	Count	Eberhard VI	b. 1445 d. 1496
1495–1496	Duke	Eberhard I	

Count Eberhard VI assumed the title of Duke in 1495 as Eberhard I.

1496–1498	Duke	Eberhard II	b. 1447 d. 1504
1498–1519	Duke	Heinrich	b. 1448 d. 1519
1498–1519	Duke	Ulrich VI	b. 1487 d. 1550

Interregnum

1534–1550	Duke	Ulrich VI (restored)	
1550–1568	Duke	Christopher	b. 1515 d. 1568
1568–1593	Duke	Ludwig III	b. 1554 d. 1593
1593–1608	Duke	Friedrich I	b. 1557 d. 1608
1608–1628	Duke	Johann Friedrich	b. 1585 d. 1628
1628–1674	Duke	Eberhard III	b. 1614 d. 1674
1674–1677	Duke	Wilhelm Ludwig	b. 1647 d. 1677
1677–1733	Duke	Eberhard IV	b. 1676 d. 1733
1733–1737	Duke	Karl Alexander	b. 1684 d. 1737
1737–1793	Duke	Karl Eugen	b. 1728 d. 1793
1793–1795	Duke	Ludwig Eugen	b. 1731 d. 1795
1795–1797	Duke	Friedrich Eugen	b. 1732 d. 1797
1797–1802	Duke	Friedrich II	b. 1754 d. 1816
1802–1806	Elector	Friedrich	

In 1802 Duke Friedrich II assumed the title of Elector, and in 1806 the title of King.

1806–1816	King	Friedrich	
1816–1864	King	Wilhelm I	b. 1781 d. 1864
1864–1891	King	Karl I	b. 1823 d. 1891
1891–1918	King	Wilhelm II	b. 1848 d. 1921

Wurttemberg joined the German Empire in 1871. It remained a Kingdom within the Empire until 1918, when the monarchy was overthrown and the country became part of the German Republic.

Ghana (Republic of Ghana)

Ghana was established in 1875 as a British colony of the Gold Coast. It has been an independent state and member of the British Commonwealth of Nations since 1957.

1957–1960	Prime Minister	Kwame Nkrumah
1960–1966	President	Kwame Nkrumah
1966–1969	Chair, National Liberation Council	A. J. Ankrah
1969–1969	Chair, National Liberation Council	Akwasi Amankwa Afrifa
1969–1970	Chair, Presidential Commission	Akwasi Amankwa Afrifa
1970–1970	Acting Chair, Presidential Com.	Nii Amaa Ollennu
1970–1972	Chair, Presidential Commission	Edward Akufo-Addo
1972–1979	Chair, National Redemption Council	Ignatius Kutu Acheamphong
1979–1981	President	Hilla Limann
1981–1993	Chair, Prov. Nat. Defense Council	Jerry John Rawlings
1993–2000	President	Jerry John Rawlings
2001–	President	John Agyekum Kufuor

Gold Coast *See* Ghana

Golden Horde *See* Mongolia

Great Britain *See* United Kingdom

Greece (Hellenic Republic)

While it is impossible to provide accurate lists of the rulers of all the provinces and republics of Ancient Greece, the best information available for the rulers of Athens, Sparta, and Syracusese are listed below.

Greece was ruled by Rome from 146 B.C. to A.D. 395. It became part of the Eastern Empire and was conquered by the Turks in 1460. Greece achieved independence from Turkey between 1821 and 1827.

■ *Modern Greece*

1828–1831	President	Giovanni Capo d'Istria	b. 1776 assassinated 1831

| 1831–1832 | President | Agostino Capo d'Istria, brother of Giovanni Capo d'Istria | b. 1778 d. 1857 |
| 1832–1862 | King | Otto I, son of Ludwig I of Bavaria | deposed 1862 b. 1815 d. 1867 |

Interregnum from 1862 to 1863

| 1863–1913 | King | George I, son of Christian IX of Denmark | b. 1845 assassinated 1913 |

Son of King Christian IX of Denmark, George I served in the Danish navy. After Otto I was deposed, George was elected King of the Hellenes by the Greek National Assembly in 1863. His wife, Grand Duchess Olga, was a niece of the Tsar of Russia.

1913–1917	King	Constantine I, son of George I	abdicated 1917 b. 1868 d. 1923
1917–1920	King	Alexander, son of Constantine I	b. 1893 d. 1920
1920–1922	King	Constantine I	
1922–1924	King	George II, son of Constantine I	abdicated 1924 b. 1890 d. 1947
1924–1935		*A Republic*	
1924–1926	President	Pavlos Konduriotis	b. 1857 d. 1935
1926	President	Theodoros Pangalos	b. 1878 d. 1952
1926–1929	President (provisional)	Pavlos Konduriotis	
1929–1935	President (provisional)	Alexandros Zaimis	b. 1856 d. 1936
1935	Regent	Georgios Kondylis	b. 1879 d. 1936
1935–1941	King	George II	
1941–1944		*German Occupation*	
1946–1947	King	George II	
1947–1964	King	Paul I, son of Constantine I	b. 1901 d. 1964
1964–1974	King	Constantine II, son of Paul I	b. 1941 deposed
		Monarchy Abolished by Referendum in 1973	
1974	President	Phaedon Gizikis	b. 1917 d. 1999
1974–1975	President	Michail Stasinopoulos	b. 1903 d. 2002
1975–1980	President	Constantine Tsatsos	b. 1899 d. 1987
1980–1985	President	Constantine Karamanlis	b. 1907 d. 1998
1985	President	Ioannis Alevras	b. 1912 d. 1995
1985–1990	President	Christos Sartzetakis	b. 1929
1990–1995	President	Constantine Karamanlis	b. 1907 d. 1998
1995–2005	President	Kostis Stephanopoulos	b. 1926
2005–	President	Karolos Papoulias	b. 1929

■ *Statesmen*

| 1910–1915 | Prime Minister | Eleutherios Venizelos | b. 1864 d. 1936 |

1917–1920	Prime Minister	Eleutherios Venizelos	
1924	Prime Minister	Eleutherios Venizelos	
1928–1932	Prime Minister	Eleutherios Venizelos	
1933	Prime Minister	Eleutherios Venizelos	

Venizelos strongly supported the Allied cause in the First World War but was opposed by the King, who was pro-German. After King Constantine was forced to abdicate, Venizelos brought Greece into the war. In 1935 he was condemned to death but received an amnesty upon George II's return.

1936–1941	Prime Minister	Ioannis Metaxas	b. 1871 d. 1941
1944–1945	Prime Minister	George Papandreou	b. 1888
1945	Prime Minister	Nicolas Plastiras	b. 1883 d. 1953
1945	Prime Minister	Petros Voulgaris	b. 1883 d. 1957
1945	Prime Minister	Archbishop Damaskinos	
1945	Prime Minister	Panaghiotis Canellopoulos	b. 1902
1945–1946	Prime Minister	Themistoclis Sophoulis	b. 1862 d. 1949
1946	Prime Minister	Panaghiotis Poulitsas	b. 1881
1946	Prime Minister	Constantine Tsaldaris	b. 1885
1946–1947	Prime Minister	Constantine Tsaldaris	
1947	Prime Minister	Demetrios Maximos	b. 1873 d. 1955
1947	Prime Minister	Constantine Tsaldaris	
1947–1948	Prime Minister	Themistocles Sophoulis	
1948–1949	Prime Minister	Themistocles Sophoulis	
1949	Prime Minister	Themistocles Sophoulis	
1949–1950	Prime Minister	Alexander Diomides	b. 1875 d. 1950
1950	Prime Minister	John Theotokis	b. 1880 d. 1963
1950	Prime Minister	Sophocles Venizelos	b. 1894 d. 1964
1950	Prime Minister	Nicolas Plastiras	
1950–1951	Prime Minister	Sophocles Venizelos	
1951–1952	Prime Minister	Nicholas Plastiras	
1952	Prime Minister	Demetrios Kioussopoulos	b. 1892
1952–1955	Prime Minister	Alexander Papagos	b. 1883 d. 1955
1955–1958	Prime Minister	Constantine Caramanlis	b. 1907
1958	Prime Minister	Constantine Georgacopoulos	b. 1890
1958–1961	Prime Minister	Constantine Caramanlis	
1961	Prime Minister	Constantine Dovas	b. 1898
1961–1963	Prime Minister	Constantine Caramanlis	
1963	Prime Minister	Panayiotis Pipinelis	b. 1899
1963	Prime Minister	Stylianos Mavromihalis	b. 1900

1963	Prime Minister	George Papandreou	
1963–1964	Prime Minister	John Paraskevopoulos	b. 1900
1964–1965	Prime Minister	George Papandreou	
1965	Prime Minister	George Athanassiadis-Novas	b. 1893
1965	Prime Minister	Elias Tsirimokos	b. 1907
1965–1966	Prime Minister	Stephanos Stephanopoulos	b. 1899
1966–1967	Prime Minister	Ioannis Paraskevopoulos	
1967	Prime Minister	Panayotis Kanellopoulos	b. 1902
1967	Prime Minister	Constantine Kollias	b. 1901 d. 1998
1967–1973	Prime Minister	George Papdopoulos	b. 1919 d. 1999
1973	Prime Minister	Spiros Markenisis	b. 1909 d. 2000
1973–1974	Prime Minister	Adamantios Androutsopoulos	b. 1919 d. 2000
1974–1980	Prime Minister	Constantine Karamanlis	b. 1907 d. 1998
1980–1981	Prime Minister	George Rallis	b. 1918
1981–1989	Prime Minister	Andreas Papandreou	b. 1919 d. 1996
1989	Prime Minister	Yiannis Grivas	b. 1923
1989–1990	Prime Minister	Xenophon Zolotas	b. 1904 d. 2004
1990–1993	Prime Minister	Constantine Mitsotakis	b. 1918
1993–1996	Prime Minister	Andreas Papandreou	
1996–2004	Prime Minister	Costas Dimitis	b. 1936
2004–	Prime Minister	Costas Karamanlis	b. 1956

■ Athens

Athens came into existence under a monarchy, which was replaced by hereditary nobility from 1000 to 683 B.C.

c. 621 B.C.	Lawgiver	Draco	
c. 594–570	Archon	Solon	b. 638? d. 559?
560–527	Tyrant	Pisistratus	d. 527
527–511	Tyrant	Hippias, son of Pisistratus	banished 511
527–514	Tyrant	Hipparchus, son of Pisistratus	assassinated 514
509–506	"Founder of Democracy"	Cleisthenes	
493–c. 470	General	Themistocles	b. 527? banished 470 d. 460?
		Persians Defeated at Marathon in 490 B.C.	
c. 470	General	Miltiades	b. 540? d. 489?
489–488	Chief Archon	Aristeides the Just, son of Lysimachus	b. 530? d. 468?
480–479	Strategos	Aristeides the Just	
		Athens Sacked by Xerxes in 480	
470–460	Leader	Cimon, son of Miltiades	b. 507? d. 449

c. 460–429	Leader	Pericles, son of Xanthippus	b. 495? d. 429
431–404		*Peloponnesian War*	
411–410		*Government of Four Hundred*	
404		*Oligarchy of "Thirty Tyrants"*	
404	General	Theramenes	
404	General	Theramenes	poisoned 404
404–403	General	Critias	killed 403
403	General	Thrasybulus	killed 389
338		*War with Philip of Macedon*	
334–323	Regent	Antipater	b. 398? d. 319
317–307	Governor	Demetrius Phalereus	b. 345? d. 283
306–300	King	Demetrius 1 Poliorcetes	b. 337? d. 283
295	Dictator	Lachares	
295–288	King	Demetrius 1 Poliorcetes	

The Chremonidean War lasted from 266 to 263 and was eventually subdued by the Romans in 146. Athens joined Mithridates in 88 and was then stormed by Sulla in 86.

■ Ancient Sparta (Laconia)

According to official legend, Sparta's constitution—known for its extreme militaristic values—was established by Lycurgus "The Lawgiver" in the 7th century B.C. The constitution provided for joint rule by two hereditary kings coming from different royal families.

	Joint Kings	Eurysthenes/Procles
	Joint Kings	Agis/Soüs
	Joint Kings	Echestratus/Eurypon
	Joint Kings	Labotas/Prytanis
	Joint Kings	Doryssus/[Eunomus]
	Joint Kings	Agesilaus/Polydectes
	Joint Kings	Archelaus/Charilaus
	Joint Kings	Teleclus, son of Archelaus/Nicander
	Joint Kings	Alcamenes, son of Teleclus/Theopompus
	King	Polydorus
	Joint Kings	Eurycrates/Zeuxidamus
	Joint Kings	Anaxander/Anaxidamus
	Joint Kings	Eurycratides/Archidamus I
	Joint Kings	Leon/Agesicles
	Joint Kings	Anaxandrides/Ariston
		Victory over Argos c. 545 B.C.
c. 519–491	Joint Kings	Cleomenes I (suicide c. 488)/Demaratus

		War with Athens in 505 B.C.	
490?–480	Joint Kings	Leonidas I (killed 480 B.C.)/Leotychides	
		Rebellion of Messenian Helots in 466 B.C.	
480	King	Pleistarchus	
458	Joint Kings	Pleistoanax/Archidamus II	
431–422	General	Brasidas	killed 422
		Peloponnesian War from 431 to 404 B.C.	
c. 426–399	Joint Kings	Pausanias/Agis II	
c. 400–360	Joint Kings	Agesipolis I/Agesilaus II (d. 360?)	
380–371	King	Cleombrotus I	killed 371
371	King	Agesipolis II	
370–309	Joint Kings	Cleomenes II/Archidamus III	
		Defeated by Philip of Macedon in 344 B.C.	
338–331	King	Agis III	killed 331
330	King	Eudamidas I	
309	Joint Kings	Areus I/Archidamus IV	
265	Joint Kings	Acrotatus/Eudamidas II	
264	King	Areus II	
244–241 ?	King	Agis IV	
285–236	Joint Kings	Leonidas II/Eurydamidas	
242–240	King	Cleombrotus II	
235–219	King	Cleomenes III, son of Leonidas (suicide 221)/Archidamus V	
		Captured by Antigonus Doson of Macedon in 221 B.C.	
219	Joint Kings	Agesipolis III/Lycurgus	
210	King	Machanidas	
207–192	Tyrant	Nabis	assassinated 192
		Conquered by Rome in 146 B.C.	

■ Ancient Syracuse

Syracuse was founded by Corinthian settlers around 733 B.C. No authentic information is available for the period before 485 B.C.

485–478 B.C.	Tyrant	Gelon (or Gelo)	d. 478
478–467	Tyrant	Hieron I, brother of Gelon	d. 467
466	Tyrant	Thrasybulus, brother of Gelon	
		Became Democratic Commonwealth in 466	
406–367	Tyrant	Dionysius the Elder	b. 430? d. 367

Dionysius the Elder reputedly feared attacks on his life and took extremely elaborate, protective precautions. Nontheless, he subdued the Sicilian cities warring against Carthage and extended his territory.

367–356	Tyrant	Dionysius II the Younger, son of Dionysius is the Elder	
355–354	Tyrant	Dion	b. 408? assassinated 354
347–344	Tyrant	Dionysius II	
343–337	Tyrant	Timoleon	d. 337?
		Oligarchy from 337 to 316	
316–289	Tyrant	Agathocles	b. 361 d. 289
288–279	Tyrant	Hicetas	
270?–215	Tyrant	Hieron II, relative of Archimedes	b. 308? d. 215
215	Tyrant	Hieronymus, grandson of Hieron II	assassinated 215
		Conquered by Rome in 212 B.C.	

Guatemala (Republic of Guatemala)

The Republic of Guatemala was established in 1839.

1838–1865	Dictator	Rafael Carrera	b. 1814 d. 1865
1865–1871	President	Vicente Cerna	
1871–1873	President (provisional)	Miguel Garcia Granados	
1873–1885	President	Justo Rufino Barrios	b. 1837? killed 1885
1885–1892	President	Manuel Lisandro Barillas	
1892–1898	President	José María Reyna Barrios, nephew of J. R. Barrios	b. 1853 assassinated 1898
1898–1920	Dictator	Manuel Estrada Cabrera	b. 1857 d. 1924
1920–1921	President	Carlos Herrera	
1921–1926	President	José María Orellana	b. 1872 d. 1926
1926–1930	President	Lázaro Chacón	b. 1873 d. 1931
1931	President (provisional)	José María Reyna Andrade	
1931–1944	Dictator	Jorge Ubico Castañeda	b. 1878 d. 1946
1944	President (provisional)	Federico Ponce Vaides	
1944–1945		*Revolutionary Junta*	
1945–1951	President	Juan José Arevalo	
1951–1954	President	Jacobo Arbenz Guzman	
1954–1957	President	Carlos Castillo Armas	
1958–1963	President	Miguel Ydigoras Fuentes	b. 1895
1963–1966	President	Enrique Peralta Azurdia	
1966–1970	President	Julio Cesar Mendez Montenegro	
1970–1974	President	Carlos Manuel Arana Osorio	
1974–1978	President	Kjell Eugenio Laugerud García	

1978–1982	President	Fernando Romeo Lucas García	
1982–1983	President	José Efraín Ríos Montt	
1983–1986	President	Oscar Humberto Mejía Víctores	
1986–1991	President	Marco Vinicio Cerezo Arévalo	
1991–1993	President	Jorge Serrano Elias	
1993–1996	President	Ramiro de León Carpio	
1996–2000	President	Alvaro Arzu	
2000–2004	President	Alfonso Portillo	
2004–	President	Oscar Berger Perdomo	

Guinea (Republic of Guinea)

Guinea was separated from Senegal and administered by France as a separate colony from 1891 to 1958.
It became an independent republic in 1958.

1958–1984	President	Ahmed Sékou Touré	d. 1984
1984–	Military Dictator/ President	Lansane Conte	

Guinea-Bissau (Republic of Guinea-Bissau)

An outpost of Portuguese colonialism since the 15th century, Guinea was a major source of slaves as recently as the 19th century. An armed rebellion for independence from Portugal began in 1961, but was only achieved in 1974, when the Portuguese regime changed and independence was granted voluntarily.

1974–1980	President	Luís Cabral
1980–1999	President	João Bernardo Vieira
2000–2003	President	Kumba Yala
2003–	President	Henrique Rosa

Guyana (Cooperative Republic of Guyana)

The former colony of British Guiana became independent in 1966.

1966–1980	Prime Minister	Linden Forbes Sampson Burnham
1980–1984	Prime Minister	Ptolemy Alexander Reid
1984–1985	Prime Minister	Hugh Desmond Hoyte
1985–1992	Prime Minister	Hamilton Green
1992–1997	Prime Minister	Samuel Archibald Anthony Hinds
1997	Prime Minister	Janet Rosenberg Jagan
1997–1999	Prime Minister	Samuel Archibald Anthony Hinds
1999	Prime Minister	Bharrat Jagdeo
1999–	Prime Minister	Samuel Archibald Anthony Hinds

Haiti (Republic of Haiti)

By winning its independence in 1792 by force of arms from France, Haiti became the second independent republic in the New World.

1794–1802	General-in-Chief	Pierre Dominique Toussaint l'Ouverture	b. 1743 d. 1803
		Independence Proclaimed in 1803	
1803	Governor	Jean Jacques Dessalines	b. 1758 assassinated l806
1804–1806	Emperor	Jacques I (Dessalines)	
1808–1810	President (of northern Haiti)	Henri Christophe	b. 1767 committed suicide 1820
1811–1820	Emperor	Henri Christophe (Henri I)	
1808–1818	President (of southern Haiti)	Alexandre Sabès Pétion	b. 1770 d. 1818
1818–1843	President (of southern Haiti)	Jean Pierre Boyer	b. 1776 d. 1850
1847–1849	President (of southern Haiti)	Faustin Elie Soulouque	b. 1785 d. 1867
1849–1858	Emperor	Faustin I (Soulouque)	
1859–1867	President	Nicholas Fabre Geffrard	b. 1806 d. 1879
1867–1868	President	Salnave	shot 1870
1870–1874	President	Nissage Saget	
1874–1876	President	Michel Domingue	
1876–1879	President	Boisrond Canal	
1879–1888	President	Louis Etienne Félicité Saloman	b. 1820 d. 1888
1889–1896	President	Florvil Hippolyte	
1896–1902	President	Tiresias Simon Sam	
1902	Provisional President	Boisrond Canal	
1902–1908	President	Nord Alexis	
1908–1911	President	Antoine Simon	
1911–1913	President	Simon Cincinnatus Leconte	
1913	President	Tancred Auguste	
1913–1914	President	Michel Oreste	
1914	President	Oreste Zamor	
1914	President	Davilmar Theodore	
1915	President	Vilbrun Guillaume Sam	massacred 1915
1915–1934		*Ruled by U.S.A.*	
1915–1922	President (under American supervision)	Philippe Sudre Dartiguenave	
1922–1930	President	Louis Borno	b. 1865 d. 1942
1930–1941	President	Sténio Joseph Vincent	b. 1874 d. 1959

1941–1946	President	Elie Lescot	b. 1883
1946–1950	President	Dumarsais Estimé	
1951–1956	President	Paul Magloire	
1957–1971	President	François Duvalier	b. 1907 d. 1971
1971–1986	President	Jean-Claude Duvalier	b. 1951
1991	President	Jean-Bertrand Aristide	
1991–1994		*Military Dictatorship*	
1994–1996	President	Jean-Bertrand Aristide	
1996–2001	President	René Préval	
2001–2004	President	Jean-Bertrand Aristide	
2004–	Interim President	Boniface Alexandre	

Hanover *See* Germany

Hawaii *See* United States of America

Hejaz *See* Saudi Arabia

Hesse *See* Germany

Hittite Empire

■ *Old Kingdom*

1740–1710 B.C.	King	Tudhaliyas I
1710–1680	King	Pu-sarrumas, son of Tudhaliyas I
1680–1650	King	Labarnas I, son of Pu-sarrumas
1650–1620	King	Labarnas II (Hattusilis I), son of Labarnas I
1620–1590	King	Mursilis I, adopted son of Labarnas II
1590–1560	King	Hantilis I, son-in-law of Mursilis I
1560–1550	King	Zidantas I, son-in-law (?) of Hantilis I
1550–1530	King	Ammunas, son of Zidantas I
1530–1525	King	Huzziyas I
1525–1500	King	Telipinus, brother-in-law of Huzziyas I
1500–1490	King	Alluwamnas, son (?) of Telipinus
1490–1480	King	Hantilis II (?)
1480–1470	King	Zidantas I (?)
1470–1460	King	Huzziyas II (?)

1460–1440	King	Tudhaliyas II
1440–1420	King	Arnuwandas I, son of Tudhaliyas II
1420–1400	King	Hattusilis II, brother of Arnuwandas I
1400–1385	King	Tudhaliyas III, son of Hattusilis II
1385–1375	King	Arnuwandas II, son of Tudhaliyas III
1375–1335	King	Suppiluliumas, brother of Arnuwandas II
1335–1334	King	Arnuwandus III, son of Suppiluliumas
1334–1306	King	Mursilis II, brother of Arnuwandas III
1306–1282	King	Muwatallis, son of Mursilis II
1282–1275	King	Urhi-Teshub, son of Muwatallis
1275–1250	King	Hattusilis III, uncle of Urhi-Teshub
1250–1220	King	Tudhaliyas IV, son of Hattusilis III
1220–1190	King	Arnuwandas IV, son of Tudhaliyas IV
	King	Suppiluliumas II (?), brother (?) of Arnuwandas IV

The Hittite Empire fell in about 1190 B.C. under attack by the Thracians, Phrygians, and Armenians.

Holland *See* Netherlands

Holy Roman Empire

The Holy Roman Empire constituted an attempt at reviving the Roman Empire in western Europe.

■ Frankish (Carolingian) Dynasty

800–814	Emperor of the West	Charlemagne, son of Pepin the Short	b. 742	d. 814

Originally King of the Franks, Charlemagne assumed the title of Emperor of the Romans and built an empire consisting of Gaul, Italy, and large areas of Germany and Spain. After being crowned in Rome on Christmas Day in 800, he enacted laws, patronized letters, and established schools.

814–840	Emperor of the West	Louis I the Pious, son of Charlemagne	b. 778	d. 840
840–855	Emperor	Lothair I, son of Louis I	b. 795?	d. 855
855–875	Emperor	Louis II, son of Lothair I	b. 825	d. 875
875–877	Emperor	Charles II the Bald, son of Louis I	b. 823	d. 877
877–881		*Imperial Throne Vacant*		
881–887	Emperor	Charles II the Fat, son of Louis II	b. 832	d. 888
887–899	Emperor	Arnulf of Carinthia, son of Carloman of Bavaria	b. 850?	d. 899
899–911	Emperor (not crowned)	Louis III the Child, son of Arnulf of Carinthia	b. 893	d. 911

911–918	Emperor (not crowned)	Conrad I, of Franconia	d. 918

■ Saxon Dynasty

919–936	Emperor (not crowned)	Henry I the Fowler	b. 876 d. 936
936–973	Emperor	Otto I the Great, son of Henry I	b. 912 d. 973
973–983	Emperor	Otto II, son of Otto I	b. 954 d. 983
983–1002	Emperor	Otto III, son of Otto II	b. 980 d. 1002
1002–1024	Emperor	Henry II the Saint, great-grandson of Otto I the Great	b. 973 d. 1024

■ Franconian (Salian) Dynasty

1024–1039	Emperor	Conrad II, descendant of Otto the Great	b. 990 d. 1039
1039–1056	Emperor	Henry III the Black, son of Conrad II	b. 1017 d. 1056
1056–1106	Emperor	Henry IV, son of Henry III	b. 1050 d. 1106
1106–1125	Emperor	Henry V, son of Henry IV	b. 1081 d. 1125
1125–1137	Emperor	Lothair II of Saxony	b. 1070 d. 1137

■ Hohenstaufen Dynasty

1138–1152	Emperor (not crowned)	Conrad III, grandson of Henry IV	b. 1093 d. 1152
1152–1190	Emperor	Frederick I (Barbarossa), nephew of Conrad III	b. 1123 d. 1190

Frederick "Redbeard" extended the Holy Roman Empire to Poland, Hungary, Burgundy, and Denmark, and ruled with an iron hand. On his way to join the Third Crusade against Saladin and the Saracens, he was drowned in Cilicia.

1190–1197	Emperor	Henry VI, son of Frederick I (Barbarossa)	b. 1165 d. 1197
1198–1208	Emperor (not crowned)	Philip of Swabia, brother of Henry VI	b. 1177 d. 1208
1198–1215	Emperor (rival)	Otto IV (of Brunswick), son of Henry the Lion	b. 1182 d. 1218
1215–1250	Emperor	Frederick II, son of Henry VI	b. 1194 d. 1250
1250–1254	Emperor (not crowned)	Conrad IV, son of Frederick II	b. 1228 d. 1254
1256–1271	King of the Romans	Richard, Earl of Cornwall, son of King John	b. 1209 d. 1272

The Great Interregnum from 1254 to 1273

■ Rulers of Various Houses

1273–1291	Emperor (not crowned)	Rudolf I of Habsburg, son of Albert IV	b. 1218 d. 1291

1292–1298	Emperor (not crowned)	Adolf of Nassau, son of Walfram II		b. 1255 killed 1298
1298–1308	Emperor (not crowned)	Albert I of Austria, son of Rudolf I		b. 1250 murdered 1308
1308–1313	Emperor	Henry VII of Luxemburg		b. 1269 d. 1313
1314–1325	Rival King	Frederick III of Austria, son of Albert I		b. 1286 d. 1330
1314–1347	Emperor	Ludwig IV of Bavaria		b. 1287 d. 1347
1347–1378	Emperor	Charles IV of Luxemburg, son of John of Luxemburg		b. 1316 d. 1378
1378–1400	Emperor	Wenceslaus of Bohemia, son of Charles IV		b. 1361 d. 1419
1400–1410	Emperor (not crowned)	Rupert of the Palatinate		b. 1352 d. 1410
1410–1411	Emperor	Jossus of Moravia, nephew of Charles IV		
1411–1437	Emperor	Sigismund of Hungary, brother of Wenceslaus		b. 1368 d. 1437

■ House of Habsburg

1438–1439	Emperor (not crowned)	Albert II of Habsburg		b. 1397 d. 1439
1440–1493	Emperor	Frederick III, great-great-grandson of Albert I		b. 1415 d. 1493
1493–1519	Emperor	Maximilian I, son of Frederick III		b. 1459 d. 1519
1519–1556	Emperor	Charles V, grandson of Maximilian I		b. 1500 d. 1558
1556–1564	Emperor	Ferdinand I, brother of Charles V	abdicated 1555	b. 1503 d. 1564
1564–1576	Emperor	Maximilian II, son of Ferdinand I		b. 1527 d. 1576
1576–1612	Emperor	Rudolf II, son of Maximilian II		b. 1552 d. 1612
1612–1619	Emperor	Matthias, son of Maximilian II		b. 1557 d. 1619
1619–1637	Emperor	Ferdinand II, nephew of Maximilian II		b. 1578 d. 1637
1637–1658	Emperor	Ferdinand III, son of Ferdinand II		b. 1608 d. 1658
1658–1705	Emperor	Leopold I, son of Ferdinand III		b. 1640 d. 1705
1705–1711	Emperor	Joseph I, son of Leopold I		b. 1678 d. 1711
1711–1740	Emperor	Charles VI, son of Leopold I		b. 1685 d. 1740
1740–1780	Empress	Maria Theresa, daughter of Charles VI		b. 1717 d. 1780
1742–1745	Emperor	Charles VII, son of Maximilian Emanuel, Elector of Bavaria		b. 1697 d. 1745

■ House of Habsburg-Lorraine

1745–1765	Emperor	Francis I, son of Leopold, Duke of Lorraine and Consort of Maria Theresa		b. 1708 d. 1765
1765–1790	Emperor	Joseph II, son of Francis I and Maria Theresa		b. 1741 d. 1790
1790–1792	Emperor	Leopold II, brother of Joseph II		b. 1747 d. 1792
1792–1806	Emperor	Francis II, son of Leopold II	abdicated 1806	b. 1768 d. 1835

The Holy Roman Empire was formally abolished under pressure from Napoleon in 1806, although Francis continued to reign as King of Austria, having acquired the title in 1804.

Holy See, The

While the existence of papal states under the secular authority of the Bishop of Rome extends back to the Middle Ages, the Vatican's current legal status as a sovereign state is based on the Lateran Pacts signed with Italy in 1929. The Holy See is a non-member state maintaining Permanent Observer status at the United Nations.

■ The First Bishops of Rome

41?–67?	Pope	St. Peter	d. 67?

Saint Peter was a disciple of John the Baptist and later of Jesus. He was imprisoned by Herod Agrippa I, but escaped and established the See of Antioch. According to tradition, he went to Rome and died a martyr during Nero's persecutions of the Christians.

67?–?79	Pope	St. Linus	d. 79?
79?–?91	Pope	St. Anacletus or Cletus	d. 91?
91–?100	Pope	St. Clement I (Clement of Rome)	d. 100?
100–?107	Pope	St. Evaristus	d. 107?
107–?116	Pope	St. Alexander I	d. 115
116–?125	Pope	St. Sixtus I	d. 125?
125–?136	Pope	St. Telesphorus	d. 136?
136–?140	Pope	St. Hyginus	d. 140 ?
140–?154	Pope	St. Pius I	d. 154?
154–?165	Pope	St. Anicetus	d. 165?
165–174	Pope	St. Soterus	d. 174?
174–189	Pope	St. Eleutherius	d. 189
189–198	Pope	St. Victor I	d. 198?
198–217	Pope	St. Zephyrinus	d. 217
217–222	Pope	St. Calixtus or Callistus I	d. 222
222–230	Pope	St. Urban I	d. 230
230–235	Pope	St. Pontian	
235–236	Pope	St. Anterus	d. 236
236–250	Pope	St. Fabian	
251–253	Pope	St. Cornelius	
251–?258	Pope	Novatianus (anti-pope*)	
253–254	Pope	St. Lucius I	d. 254
254–257	Pope	St. Stephen I	d. 257
257–258	Pope	St. Sixtus II	d. 258

* Pope set up in opposition to the canonically elected Pope.

258–268	Pope	St. Dionysius	d. 268
268–274	Pope	St. Felix I	d. 274
274–283	Pope	St. Eutychian	d. 283
282–296	Pope	St. Caius	d. 296
296–304	Pope	St. Marcellinus	d. 304
308–309	Pope	St. Marcellus I	d. 309
309?	Pope	St. Eusebius	
310?–314	Pope	St. Miltiades or Melchiades	d. 314
314–335	Pope	St. Sylvester I	d. 335
336	Pope	St. Mark	d. 336
337–352	Pope	St. Julius I (Rusticus)	d. 352
352–366	Pope	Liberius	d. 366
355–365	Pope	Felix II (anti-pope)	d. 365
366–367	Pope	Ursinus (anti-pope)	
366–384	Pope	St. Damasus I	b. 304? d. 384
384–399	Pope	St. Siricius	d. 399
399–401	Pope	St. Anastasius I	d. 401
401–417	Pope	St. Innocent I	d. 417
417–418	Pope	St. Zosimus	d. 418
418–419	Pope	Eulalius (anti-pope)	d. 423
418–422	Pope	St. Boniface I	d. 422
422–432	Pope	St. Celestine I	d. 432
432–440	Pope	St. Sixtus III	d. 440
440–461	Pope	St. Leo I the Great	b. 390? d. 461

Saint Leo the Great was renowned for his zeal against heretics.
He induced the Emperor to recognize the primacy of the Bishop of Rome,
persuaded Attila to spare the city, and prevented Genseric from destroying
Rome by making him moderate his troops' violence.

461–468	Pope	St. Hilary	d. 468
468–483	Pope	St. Simplicius	d. 483
483–492	Pope	St. Felix III (II)	d. 492
492–496	Pope	St. Gelasius I	d. 496
496–498	Pope	Anastasius II	d. 498
498–514	Pope	St. Symmachus	d. 514
498–505	Pope	Laurentius (anti-pope)	
514–523	Pope	St. Hormisdas	d. 523
523–526	Pope	St. John I	b. 470? d. 526
526–530	Pope	St. Felix IV (III)	d. 530

530–532	Pope	Boniface II	d. 532
530	Pope	Dioscorus (anti-pope)	
532–535	Pope	John II	d. 535
535–536	Pope	St. Agapetus I	d. 536
536–537	Pope	St. Silverius	d. 537
537?–555	Pope	Vigilius	d. 555
556–561	Pope	Pelagius I	d. 561
561–574	Pope	John III	d. 574
575–579	Pope	Benedict I	d. 579
579–590	Pope	Pelagius II	d. 590
590–604	Pope	St. Gregory I the Great	b. 540? d. 604

Saint Gregory I relinquished the office of Praetor of Rome to become a monk. When, after seeing some fair-haired youths in the slave market, he was told that they were Angels, he said they should be Angels, and immediately resolved on the conversion of their nation.

604–606	Pope	Sabinian	d. 606
607	Pope	Boniface III	d. 607
608–615	Pope	St. Boniface IV	d. 615
615–618	Pope	St. Deusdedit or Adeodatus I	d. 618
619–625	Pope	Boniface V	d. 625
625–638	Pope	Honorius I	d. 638
638–640	Pope	Severinus	d. 640
640–642	Pope	John IV	d. 642
642–649	Pope	Theodore I	d. 649
649–653	Pope	St. Martin I	d. 655
654–657	Pope	St. Eugene I	d. 657
657–672	Pope	St. Vitalian	d. 672
672–676	Pope	Adeodatus II	d. 676
676–678	Pope	Donus	d. 678
678–681	Pope	St. Agatho	d. 681
682–683	Pope	St. Leo II	d. 683
683–685	Pope	St. Benedict II	d. 685
685–686	Pope	John V	d. 686
686–687	Pope	Conon	d. 687
687–692	Pope	Paschal I	
687	Pope	Theodorus (anti-pope)	
687–701	Pope	St. Sergius I	d. 701
701–705	Pope	John VI	d. 705

705–707	Pope	John VII	d.	707
708	Pope	Sisinnius	d.	708
708–715	Pope	Constantine I	d.	715
715–731	Pope	St. Gregory II (Savelli)	d.	731
731–741	Pope	St. Gregory III	d.	741
741–752	Pope	St. Zachary	d.	752
752	Pope	Stephen II	d.	752
752–757	Pope	St. Stephen III	d.	757
757–767	Pope	St. Paul I	d.	767
767–768	Pope	Constantine (II) (anti-pope)	d.	769
768	Pope	Philippus		
768–772	Pope	Stephen IV	d.	772
772–795	Pope	Adrian I	d.	795
795–816	Pope	St. Leo III	d.	816
816–817	Pope	Stephen V	d.	817
817–824	Pope	St. Pascal I	d.	824
824–827	Pope	Eugene II	d.	827
827	Pope	Valentine	d.	827
827–844	Pope	Gregory IV	d.	844
844	Pope	John (anti-pope)		
844–847	Pope	Sergius II	d.	847
847–855	Pope	St. Leo IV	d.	855
855–858	Pope	Benedict III	d.	858
855	Pope	Anastasius (anti-pope)		
858–867	Pope	St. Nicholas I the Great	d.	867
867–872	Pope	Adrian II	d.	872
872–882	Pope	John VIII	d.	882
882–884	Pope	Marinus I (sometimes misnamed Martin II)	d.	884
884–885	Pope	St. Adrian III	d.	885
885–891	Pope	Stephen VI	d.	891
891–896	Pope	Formosus	d.	896
896	Pope	Boniface VI	d.	896
896–897	Pope	Stephen VII	d.	897
897	Pope	Romanus	d.	897
897	Pope	Theodore II	d.	897
898–900	Pope	John IX	d.	900
900–903	Pope	Benedict IV	d.	903

903	Pope	Leo V	d. 903
903–904	Pope	Christopher	d. 904
904–911	Pope	Sergius III	d. 911
911–913	Pope	Anastasius III	d. 913
913–914	Pope	Landus	d. 914
914–928	Pope	John X	d. 928
928	Pope	Leo VI	d. 928
929–931	Pope	Stephen VIII	d. 931
931–935	Pope	John XI	d. 935
936–939	Pope	Leo VII	d. 939
939–942	Pope	Stephen IX	d. 942
942–946	Pope	Marinus II (sometimes misnamed Martin III)	d. 946
946–955	Pope	Agapetus II	d. 955
955–964	Pope	John XII	b. 937? d. 964
964–965	Pope	Leo VIII	d. 965
964	Pope	Benedict V (anti-pope)	d. 966
965–972	Pope	John XIII	d. 972
973–974	Pope	Benedict VI	d. 974
974–983	Pope	Benedict VII	d. 983
983–984	Pope	John XIV	d. 984
984–985	Pope	Boniface VII (anti-pope)	
985–996	Pope	John XV	d. 996
996–999	Pope	Gregory V, nephew of Emperor Otto III	d. 999
997–998	Pope	John XVI (anti-pope)	d. 1013
999–1003	Pope	Sylvester II	d. 1003
1003	Pope	John XVII	d. 1003
1003–1009	Pope	John XVIII	d. 1009
1009–1012	Pope	Sergius IV	d. 1012
1012–1024	Pope	Benedict VIII	d. 1024
1012	Pope	Gregory (anti-pope)	
1024–1032	Pope	John XIX	d. 1032
1032–1044	Pope	Benedict IX	d. 1056

Pope Benedict IX, "the Boy Pope," had three terms as Pope. He appears to have been only eleven or twelve years old when first elected to the Papal See. In his third and last term, he was held to be the anti-pope to Clement II.

1044–1045	Pope	Sylvester III (anti-pope)	d. 1045
1045	Pope	Benedict IX	

1045–1046	Pope	Gregory VI		d. 1048
1046–1047	Pope	Clement II		d. 1047
1047–1048	Pope	Benedict IX (anti-pope)		
1048	Pope	Damasus II (Poppo)		d. 1048
1049–1054	Pope	St. Leo IX		d. 1054
1055–1057	Pope	Victor II		d. 1057
1057–1058	Pope	Stephen X		d. 1058
1058–1059	Pope	Benedict X (anti-pope)		
1058–1061	Pope	Nicholas II		d. 1061
1061–1073	Pope	Alexander II (di Badagio)		d. 1073
1061–1064	Pope	Honorius II (anti-pope)		d. 1072
1073–1085	Pope	St. Gregory VII (Hildebrand)	b. 1025?	d. 1085
1080–1100	Pope	Clement III (anti-pope)	b. 1030?	d. 1100
1087	Pope	Victor III		d. 1087
1088–1099	Pope	Urban II		d. 1099
1099–1118	Pope	Pascal II		d. 1118
1100	Pope	Theodoric (anti-pope)		
1102	Pope	Albertus (anti-pope)		
1105–1111	Pope	Sylvester IV (anti-pope)		
1118–1119	Pope	Gelasius II		d. 1119
1119–1124	Pope	Calixtus or Callistus II		d. 1124
1118–1121	Pope	Gregory VIII (anti-pope)		d. 1125
1124	Pope	Celestine (anti-pope)		
1124–1130	Pope	Honorius II		d. 1130
1130–1143	Pope	Innocent II		d. 1143
1130–1138	Pope	Anacletus II (anti-pope)		d. 1138
1138	Pope	Victor IV (anti-pope)		
1143–1144	Pope	Celestine II		d. 1144
1144–1145	Pope	Lucius II		d. 1145
1145–1153	Pope	Eugene III		d. 1153
1153–1154	Pope	Anastasius IV		d. 1154
1154–1159	Pope	Adrian IV (Breakspear)		d. 1159

Adrian IV, born Nicholas Breakspear of Langley, Hertfordshire, was the only Englishman to attain the Papal office. He upheld papal supremacy and granted Ireland to King Henry II.

1159–1181	Pope	Alexander III (Orlando)		d. 1181
1159–1164	Pope	Victor V (anti-pope)		
1164–1168	Pope	Pascal III (anti-pope)		d. 1168

1168–1178	Pope	Calixtus or Callistus III (anti-pope)	
1178–1180	Pope	Innocent III (anti-pope)	
1181–1185	Pope	Lucius III	d. 1185
1185–1187	Pope	Urban III	d. 1187
1187	Pope	Gregory VIII (Morra)	d. 1187
1187–1191	Pope	Clement III (Scolari)	d. 1191
1191–1198	Pope	Celestine III (Bobone)	b. 1106? d. 1198
1198–1216	Pope	Innocent III (Conti)	b. 1160 d. 1216
1216–1227	Pope	Honorius III (Savilli)	d. 1227
1227–1241	Pope	Gregory IX (Ugolino)	b. 1145? d. 1241
1241	Pope	Celestine lV	d. 1241
1243–1254	Pope	Innocent IV (Fieschi)	d. 1254
1254–1261	Pope	Alexander IV (Conti)	d. 1261
1261–1264	Pope	Urban IV (Pantaléon)	d. 1264
1265–1268	Pope	Clement IV (Foulques)	d. 1268
1271–1276	Pope	Gregory X (Visconti)	b. 1210 d. 1276
1276	Pope	Innocent V	d. 1276
1276	Pope	Adrian V	d. 1276
1276–1277	Pope	John XXI (Hispanus)	d. 1277
1277–1280	Pope	Nicholas III (Orsini)	b. 1216? d. 1280
1281–1285	Pope	Martin IV (Brie)	b. 1210? d. 1285
1285–1287	Pope	Honorius IV (Savelli)	b. 1210? d. 1287
1288–1292	Pope	Nicholas IV	d. 1292
1294	Pope	St. Celestine V (Murrone)	b. 1215 d. 1296
1294–1303	Pope	Boniface VIII (Caetani)	b. 1235? d. 1303
1303–1304	Pope	Benedict XI	d. 1304
		Papacy Removed to Avignon from Rome	
1305–1314	Pope	Clement V (de Gouth)	b. 1264 d. 1314
1316–1334	Pope	John XXII (d'Euse)	b. 1249 d. 1334
1328–1330	Pope	Nicholas V (anti-pope)	
1334–1342	Pope	Benedict XII	d. 1342
1342–1352	Pope	Clement VI (Roger)	b. 1291 d. 1352
1352–1362	Pope	Innocent VI (Aubert)	d. 1362
1362–1370	Pope	Urban V (Grimoard)	b. 1310 d. 1370
1370–1378	Pope	Gregory XI (de Beaufort)	b. 1331 d. 1378
		Gregory Returned to Rome in 1377	
1378–1394	Pope	Clement VII (anti-pope)	b. 1342? d. 1394
1378–1417		*Great Schism*	

1394–1423	Pope	Benedict XIII (de Luna) (anti-pope)	b. 1328? d. 1423?
		Papacy Returned to Rome	
1378–1389	Pope	Urban VI (Prignani)	b. 1318 d. 1389
1389–1404	Pope	Boniface IX (Tomacelli)	d. 1404
1404–1406	Pope	Innocent VII (Migliorati)	b. 1336? d. 1406
1406–1415	Pope	Gregory XII (Corrario)	b. 1327? d. 1417
		Papacy Removed to Pisa	
1409–1410	Pope	Alexander V (Philargos)	b. 1340? d. 1410
1410–1415	Pope	John XXIII (anti-pope)	b. 1370? d. 1419
		Papacy Returned to Rome	
1417–1431	Pope	Martin V (Colonna)	b. 1368 d. 1431
1424?–1429	Pope	Clement VIII (anti-pope)	b. 1380? d. 1446
1431–1447	Pope	Eugene IV (Condolmieri)	b. 1383 d. 1447
1439–1449	Pope	Felix V of Savoy (last anti-pope; resigned his claim in 1449)	d. 1451
1447–1455	Pope	Nicholas V (Parentucelli)	b. 1397 d. 1455
1455–1458	Pope	Calixtus or Callistus III (Borgia)	b. 1378 d. 1458
1458–1464	Pope	Pius II (Piccolomini)	b. 1405 d. 1464
1464–1471	Pope	Paul II (Barbo)	b. 1418 d. 1471
1471–1484	Pope	Sixtus IV (Rovere)	b. 1414 d. 1484
1484–1492	Pope	Innocent VIII (Cibò)	b. 1432 d. 1492
1492–1503	Pope	Alexander VI (Borgia)	b. 1430 d. 1503
1503	Pope	Pius III (Piccolomini)	b. 1439 d. 1503
1503–1513	Pope	Julius II (Rovere)	b. 1443 d. 1513
1513–1521	Pope	Leo X (Medici)	b. 1475 d. 1521
1522–1523	Pope	Adrian VI (Dedel)	b. 1459 d. 1523
1523–1534	Pope	Clement VII (Medici)	b. 1478? d. 1534
1534–1549	Pope	Paul III (Farnese)	b. 1468 d. 1549
1550–1555	Pope	Julius III (Monte)	b. 1487 d. 1555
1555	Pope	Marcellus II (Cervini)	b. 1501 d. 1555
1555–1559	Pope	Paul IV (Caraffa)	b. 1476 d. 1559
1559–1565	Pope	Pius IV (Medici)	b. 1499 d. 1565
1566–1572	Pope	St. Pius V (Ghislieri)	b. 1504 d. 1572
1572–1585	Pope	Gregory XIII (Buoncompagno)	b. 1502 d. 1585
1585–1590	Pope	Sixtus V (Peretti)	b. 1521 d. 1590
1590	Pope	Urban VII (Castagna)	b. 1521 d. 1590
1590–1591	Pope	Gregory XIV (Sfondrati)	b. 1535 d. 1591
1591	Pope	Innocent IX (Fachinetti)	b. 1519 d. 1591
1592–1605	Pope	Clement VIII (Aldobrandini)	b. 1536? d. 1605

1605	Pope	Leo XI (Medici)	b. 1535 d. 1605
1605–1621	Pope	Paul V (Borghese)	b. 1552 d. 1621
1621–1623	Pope	Gregory XV (Ludovisi)	b. 1554 d. 1623
1623–1644	Pope	Urban VIII (Barberini)	b. 1568 d. 1644
1644–1655	Pope	Innocent X (Pamfili)	b. 1574 d. 1655
1655–1667	Pope	Alexander VII (Chigi)	b. 1599 d. 1667
1667–1669	Pope	Clement IX (Rospigliosi)	b. 1600 d. 1669
1670–1676	Pope	Clement X (Altieri)	b. 1590 d. 1676
1676–1689	Pope	Innocent XI (Odescalchi)	b. 1611 d. 1689
1689–1691	Pope	Alexander VIII (Ottoboni)	b. 1610 d. 1691
1691–1700	Pope	Innocent XII (Pignatelli)	b. 1615 d. 1700
1700–1721	Pope	Clement XI (Albani)	b. 1649 d. 1721
1721–1724	Pope	Innocent XIII (Conti)	b. 1655 d. 1724
1724–1730	Pope	Benedict XIII (Orsini)	b. 1649 d. 1730
1730–1740	Pope	Clement XII (Corsini)	b. 1652 d. 1740
1740–1758	Pope	Benedict XIV (Lambertini)	b. 1675 d. 1758
1758–1769	Pope	Cement XIII (Rezzonico)	b. 1693 d. 1769
1769–1774	Pope	Clement XIV (Ganganelli)	b. 1705 d. 1774
1775–1799	Pope	Pius VI (Braschi)	b. 1717 d. 1799
1800–1823	Pope	Pius VII (Chiaramonti)	b. 1742 d. 1823
1823–1829	Pope	Leo XII (Della Genga)	b. 1760 d. 1829
1829–1830	Pope	Pius VIII (Castiglioni)	b. 1761 d. 1830
1831–1846	Pope	Gregory XVI (Cappellari)	b. 1765 d. 1846
1846–1878	Pope	Pius IX (Mastai-Ferretti)	b. 1792 d. 1878

Pius IX (Mastai-Ferretti) was Pope for more than thirty-one years. His reign was the longest of any Pope in history. After an insurrection in 1848, he was forced to flee temporarily. He convened the First Vatican Council, which promulgated the dogma of papal infallibility.

1878–1903	Pope	Leo XIII (Pecci)	b. 1810 d. 1903
1903–1914	Pope	St. Pius X (Sarto)	b. 1835 d. 1914
1914–1922	Pope	Benedict XV (della Chiesa)	b. 1854 d. 1922
1922–1939	Pope	Pius XI (Ratti)	b. 1857 d. 1939
1939–1958	Pope	Pius XII (Pacelli)	b. 1876 d. 1958
1958–1963	Pope	John XXIII (Roncalli)	b. 1881 d. 1963
1963–1978	Pope	Paul VI (Montini)	b. 1897 d. 1978
1978	Pope	John Paul (Luciani)	b. 1912 d. 1978
1978–2005	Pope	John Paul II (Wojtyla)	b. 1920 d. 2005
2005–	Pope	Benedict XVI (Ratzinger)	b.1927

Honduras (Republic of Honduras)

Honduras was proclaimed an independent sovereign state in 1838.

1864–1872	President	José M. Medina	
1872–1874	President	Celio Arias	
1874–1875	President	Marco Aurelio Soto	b. 1846 d. 1908
1875–1876	President	Ponciano Leiva	
1877–1883	President	Marco Aurelio Soto	
1883–1891	President	Luis Bográn	
1891–1894	President	Ponciano Leiva	
1894–1900	President	Policarpo Bonilla	b. 1858 d. 1926
1900–1903	President	Terencio Sierra	
1903–1907	President	Manuel Bonilla	b. 1849 d. 1913
1907–1911	President	Miguel R. Dávila	d. 1927
1911–1912	President (provisional)	Francisco Bertrand	d. 1927
1912–1913	President	Manuel Bonilla	
1913–1919	President	Francisco Bertrand	
1919–1924	President	Rafael López Gutiérrez	d. 1924
1924	*Civil War*		
1924–1925	President (provisional)	Vicente Tosta	d. 1928
1925–1929	President	Miguel Paz Baraona	d. 1931
1929–1933	President	Vicente Mejía Colindres	
1933–1948	President	Tiburcio Carías Andino	b. 1876 d. 1969
1949–1954	President	Juan Manuel Galvez	d. 1955
1954–1956	President	Juan Lozano Diaz	d. 1957
1957–1963	President	José Ramon Villeda Morales	d. 1971
1963–1971	President	Oswaldo López Arellano	b. 1921
1971–1972	President	Ramón Ernesto Cruz Uclés	d. 1985
1972–1975	President	Oswaldo López Arellano	
1975–1978	President	Juan Alberto Melgar Castro	d. 1987
1978–1982	President	Policarpo Paz García	
1982–1986	President	Roberto Suazo Córdova	
1986–1990	President	José Azcona Hoyo	
1990–1994	President	Rafael Leonardo Callejas Romero	
1994–1998	President	Carlos Roberto Reina Idiáquez	
1998–2002	President	Carlos Roberto Flores Facussé	
2002–	President	Ricardo Maduro Joest	

Hungary (Republic of Hungary)

No authentic information is available for the period before the arrival of the Magyars (Hunagars) under Arpád.

875–907		Arpád	d. 907
		Arpád Dynasty ruled Hungary until 1301.	
972–997	Duke	Geza	
997–1038	King	Stephen I (St. Stephen), son of Geza	b. 975? d. 1038
		Stephen I was known as "the Apostle of Hungary." He was crowned King with a crown sent by Pope Sylvester III. His title of "Apostolic King" was used by all subsequent Hungarian sovereigns. He suppressed the local religious practices, encouraged trade, and became the patron saint of Hungary, being canonized in 1087.	
1038–1041	King	Peter Orseolo, son-in-law of Stephen I	b. 1011? d. 1050?
1041–1044	King	Aba Samuel, brother-in-law of Stephen I	
1044–1046	King	Peter Orseolo	
1046–1060	King	Andrew I, cousin of Peter Orseolo	d. 1060
1060–1063	King	Bela I, brother of Andrew I	
1063–1074	King	Salomon, son of Andrew I	
1074–1077	King	Geza I, son of Bela I	
1077–1095	King	Ladislaus I, (St. Laszlo), son of Bela I	b. 1040 d. 1095
1095–1116	King	Salomon, nephew of Ladislaus I	b. 1070 d. 1116
1116–1131	King	Stephen II, son of Salomon abdicated 1131	b. 1100 d. 1131
1131–1141	King	Bela II, grandson of Bela I	
1141–1161	King	Geza II, son of Bela II	
1161–1162	King	Stephen III, son of Geza II	
1162–1163	King	Ladislaus II, son of Bela II	b. 1134 d. 1163
1163–1165	King	Stephen IV, son of Bela II	d. 1166
1165–1172	King	Stephen III	
1173–1196	King	Bela III, grandson of Bela II	d. 1196
1196–1204	King	Emeric, son of Bela III	
1204–1205	King	Ladislaus III, son of Emeric	b. 1179 d. 1205
1205–1235	King	Andrew II, son of Emeric	b. 1175 d. 1235
1235–1270	King	Bela IV, son of Andrew II	b. 1206 d. 1270
1270–1272	King	Stephen V, son of Bela IV	b. 1239 d. 1272
1272–1290	King	Ladislaus IV	b. 1262 murdered 1290
1290–1301	King	Andrew III, grandson of Andrew II	d. 1301
		End of Arpád Dynasty	
1301–1305	King	Wenceslaus of Bohemia	b. 1289 d. 1306
1305–1307	King	Otho of Bavaria	abdicated 1309 d. 1312

1308–1342	King	Charles I, grand-nephew of Ladislaus IV	b. 1288 d. 1342
1342–1382	King	Louis the Great, son of Charles I	b. 1326 d. 1382
		(See Poland*)*	
1382–1387	Queen	Mary, daughter of Louis the Great	b. 1370 d. 1395
1387–1437	King	Sigismund, husband of Mary	b. 1368 d. 1437
		(See Bohemia*)*	
1437–1439	King	Albert, son-in-law of Sigismund	b. 1397 d. 1439
1439–1440	Queen	Elizabeth, wife of Albert	d. 1443
1440–1444	King	Ladislaus of Poland, grandson of Mary	b. 1423? d. 1444
1444–1457	King	Ladislaus V, son of Albert	b. 1440 d. 1457
		(See Bohemia*)*	
1458–1490	King	Matthias Corvinus	b. 1440 d. 1490
1490–1516	King	Ladislaus of Bohemia, nephew of Ladislaus V	b. 1456 d. 1516
1516–1526	King	Louis II, son of Vladislav II of Bohemia	b. 1506 d. 1526

Hungary was divided after 1526 between Turkey and Austria.
(See Holy Roman Empire*)*

■ Voivodes of Transylvania

1526–1540	Prince (Governor)	John Zapolya	b. 1487 d. 1540
1540–1571	Prince (Governor)	John Sigismund, son of John Zapolya	b. 1540 d. 1571
1571–1572	Prince (Governor)	Gaspar Békesy	
1571–1576	Prince (Governor)	Stephen Bathory (King of Poland)	b. 1533 d. 1586
1576–1581	Prince (Governor)	Christopher, brother of Stephen Bathory	b. 1530 d. 1581
1581–1598	Prince (Governor)	Sigismund, son of Christopher	b. 1572 d. 1613
1599–1600	Prince (Governor)	Andrew, cousin of Sigismund	b. 1562
1600–1601	Prince (Governor)	Michael the Brave	
1602–1603	Prince (Governor)	Moyses Szekely	
1602–1605	Prince (Governor)	Rudolph II (Emperor)	
1605–1606	Prince (Governor)	Stephen Bocskai	b. 1557 d. 1606

Stephen Bocskai freed Transylvania from Habsburg domination.
With Turkish help, he overthrew northern Hungary. At the Treaty
of Vienna, he obtained political autonomy and religious liberty for
Hungarian Protestants. He is said to have been poisoned.

1607–1608	Prince (Governor)	Sigismund Rakoczi	b. 1544 d. 1608
1608–1613	Prince (Governor)	Gabriel Bathory, son of Stephen Bathory	b. 1589 murdered 1613
1613–1629	Prince (Governor)	Gabriel Bethlen	b. 1580
1630	Prince (Governor)	Stephen Bethlen	
1630–1648	Prince (Governor)	George Rakoczi, son of Sigismund	b. 1591 d. 1648

1648–1660	Prince (Governor)	George II, son of George Rakoczi	b. 1621 killed 1660
1658–1660	Prince (Governor)	Achatius Bocskai	
1661–1662	Prince (Governor)	Johann Kemeny	
1682–1699	Prince (Governor)	Emerich Tököli	
1662–1690	Governor (Turkish)	Michael Apafi	b. 1632 d. 1690
1690–1699	Governor (Turkish)	Michael II Apafi, son of Michael Apafi	abdicated 1699 b. 1680 d. 1713
		To Habsburg Hungary in 1699	
1704–1711	Prince	Francis Rakoczi	b. 1676 d. 1735
1711–1918		*Hungary under Austria*	
		Republic Proclaimed in 1919	
1919	President	Mihaly Karolyi	b. 1875 d. 1955
1919	Head of Bolshevik Government	Bela Kun	b. 1886 d. 1939
		Kingless Monarchy Established in 1919	
1919	Regent	Joseph of Austria	b. 1872
1920–1944	Regent	Admiral Miklos von Horthy of Nagybanya	b. 1868 d. 1957
1944–1945	Regent	Ferenc Szalasi	b. 1897 d. 1946
1944–1945	Regent (opposition government)	Bela Miklos	b. 1890 d. 1948
		Republic Proclaimed in 1946	
1946–1948	President	Zoltan Tildy	b. 1889
1948–1950	President	Arpad Szakasits	b. 1888
		Communist Regime Established in 1949	
1950–1952	President	Sandoe Ronai	b. 1892
1952–1967	President	Istvan Dobi	b. 1898 d. 1968
1967–1987	President	Pál Losonczi	b. 1919 d. 2005
1987–1988	President	Károly Németh	b. 1922
1988–1989	President	Brunó Ferenc Straub	b. 1914 d. 1996
1989–1990	President	Mátyás Szırös	b. 1933
1990–2000	President	Árpád Göncz	b. 1922
2000–2005	President	Ferenc Mádl	b. 1931
2005–	President	László Sólyom	b. 1942

■ Statesmen

1848–1849	Governor	Lajos Kossuth	b. 1802 d. 1884
1849	Commander-in-Chief of the Army	Arthur Gorgei	b. 1818 d. 1916
1867–1871	Prime Minister	Count Gyula Andrassy	b. 1823 d. 1890

1875–1890	Prime Minister	Koloman Tisza	b. 1830 d. 1902
1903–1905	Prime Minister	Istvan Tisza	b. 1861 d. 1918
1913–1917	Prime Minister	Istvan Tisza	
1892–1894	Prime Minister	Alexander Wekerle	b. 1848 d. 1921
1906–1910	Prime Minister	Alexander Wekerle	
1917–1918	Prime Minister	Alexander Wekerle	
1918–1919	Prime Minister	Mihaly Karolyi	
1919–1920	Prime Minister	Karoly Huszar	b. 1882
1920–1921	Prime Minister	Pal Teleki	b. 1879 d. 1941
1921–1931	Prime Minister	Count Istvan Bethlen	b. 1874
1932–1936	Prime Minister	Gyula Gombos	b. 1886 d. 1936
1936–1938	Prime Minister	Kalman Daranyi	b. 1886 d. 1939
1938–1939	Prime Minister	Bela Imredy	b. 1891 d. 1946
1939–1941	Prime Minister	Pal Teleki	
1942–1944	Prime Minister	Miklos Kallay	b. 1887
1945–1956	General Secretary	Matyas Rakosi	b. 1889
1956	General Secretary	Erno Gero	b. 1912
1956–1988	General Secretary	Janos Kadar	
1988–1989	General Secretary	Karoly Grosz	

Became a Mulitparty Parliamentary Democracy in 1989

1990–1993	Prime Minister	Jozsef Antall	
1993–1994	Prime Minister	Peter Boross	
1994–1998	Prime Minister	Gyula Horn	
1998–2002	Prime Minister	Viktor Orban	
2002–2004	Prime Minister	Peter Medgyessy	
2004–	Prime Minister	Ferenc Gyurscany	

Iceland (Republic of Iceland)

Iceland was ruled by Denmark from 1380. In 1918 it was recognized by Denmark as an independent sovereign state.

1918–1944	King	Christian X of Denmark	b. 1870 d. 1947

King Christian was responsible for the Act of Union between Denmark and Iceland. This made Iceland independent, except for its connection with Denmark through the person of a common sovereign.

1941–1944	Regent	Sveinn Björnsson	b. 1881 d. 1952

Became an Independent Republic in 1944

1944–1952	President	Sveinn Björnsson	
1952–1968	President	Ásgeir Ásgeirsson	b.1894 d. 1972
1968–1980	President	Kristján Eldjárn	b.1916 d. 1982

| 1980–1996 | President | Vigdís Finnbogadóttir | b.1930 |
| 1996– | President | Ólafur Ragnar Grímsson | b.1943 |

■ Statesmen

1918–1922	Prime Minister	Jon Magnusson	b. 1859 d. 1926
1922–1924	Prime Minister	Sigurdur Eggerz	b. 1875 d. 1945
1924–1926	Prime Minister	Jon Magnusson	
1926–1927	Prime Minister	Jon Thorlaksson	b. 1877 d. 1935
1927–1932	Prime Minister	Tryggvi Thorhallsson	b. 1889 d. 1935
1932–1934	Prime Minister	Asgeir Asgeirsson	
1934–1942	Prime Minister	Hermann Jonasson	b. 1896
1942	Prime Minister	Olafur Thors	b. 1892 d. 1964
1942–1944	Prime Minister	Björn Thordarson	b. 1879 d. 1963
1944–1947	Prime Minister	Olafur Thors	
1947–1949	Prime Minister	Stefan Joh. Stefansson	b. 1894
1949–1950	Prime Minister	Olafur Thors	
1950–1953	Prime Minister	Steingrimur Steinthorsson	b. 1893
1953–1956	Prime Minister	Olafur Thors	
1956–1958	Prime Minister	Hermann Jonasson	
1958–1959	Prime Minister	Emil Jonsson	b. 1902
1959–1963	Prime Minister	Olafur Thors	
1963–1970	Prime Minister	Bjarni Benediktsson	b. 1908
1970–1971	Prime Minister	Johan Hafstein	
1971–1974	Prime Minister	Olafur Johannesson	
1974–1978	Prime Minister	Geir Hallgrimsson	
1978–1979	Prime Minister	Olafur Johannesson	
1979–1980	Prime Minister	Benedikt Grondal	
1980–1983	Prime Minister	Gunnar Thoroddsen	
1983–1987	Prime Minister	Steingrimur Hermannsson	
1987–1988	Prime Minister	Porsteinn Palsson	
1988–1991	Prime Minister	Steingrimur Hermannsson	
1991–2004	Prime Minister	Davio Oddsson	
2004–	Prime Minister	Halldor Asgrimsson	

India (Republic of India)

Before the Mogul conquest, India largely consisted of many separate states.

| 320–298 B.C. | Emperor | Chandra Gupta Maurya | d. 286 B.C.? |
| 259–232 | Emperor | Asoka, grandson of Chandra Gupta | b. 273 d. 232 B.C. |

■ Mogul Emperors

A.D. 1526–1530	Emperor	Baber (Babar or Babur)	b. 1483 d. 1530
1530–1556	Emperor	Humayun, son of Baber	b. 1507 d. 1556
		Interregnum from 1544 to 1555 when Sher Shah ruled	
1556–1605	Emperor	Jalaluddin Mohammed Akbar, (Akbur the Great), son of Humayun	b. 1542 d. 1605

After assuming the reins of government at the age of eighteen, Akbar the Great won the empire back from the Hindus, conquering the Punjab, Gujarat, Bengal, Kashmir, and Sind. An able administrator, he was tolerant toward the many Indian religious faiths and established schools for Hindus, Muslims, and Parsees. He became known as "the Guardian of Mankind."

1605–1627	Emperor	Jahangir, son of Jalaluddin Mohammed Akbar	b. 1569 d. 1627
1628–1658	Emperor	Shah Jahan, son of Jahangir	deposed 1658 b. 1592 d. 1666
1658–1707	Emperor	Aurangzeb, son of Shah Jahan	b. 1618 d. 1707
		Persian Conquests from 1738	
1837–1857	Emperor (nominal)	Bahadur Shah II	deposed 1857 b. 1768? d. 1862
1857–1858		*Indian Mutiny*	

■ European Governors

1505–1509	Portuguese Viceroy	Francisco de Almeida	b. 1450? d. 1510
1509–1515	Portuguese Viceroy	Alfonso d'Albuquerque	b. 1453 d. 1515
1742–1754	French Governor-General	Joseph François Dupleix	b. 1697 d. 1763

■ English Governors-General

1758–1760	Governor-General	Robert Clive, Baron Clive of Plassey	b. 1725 d. 1774
1765–1767	Governor-General	Robert Clive, Baron Clive of Plassey	
1772–1785	Governor-General	Warren Hastings	b. 1732 d. 1818
1786–1793	Governor-General	Charles Cornwallis, Marquis Cornwallis	b. 1738 d. 1805
1793–1798	Governor-General	John Shore, Baron Teignmouth	b. 1751 d. 1834
1797–1805	Governor-General	Richard Colley Wellesley, Marquis Wellesley	b. 1760 d. 1842

1804–1805	Governor-General	Charles Cornwallis, Marquis Cornwallis		
1807–1813	Governor-General	Sir Gilbert Elliot-Murray-Kynynmound, Earl of Minto	b. 1751	d. 1814
1813–1823	Governor-General	Francis Rawdon-Hastings, Marquis of Hastings	b. 1754	d. 1826
1823–1828	Governor-General	William Pitt Amherst, Earl Amherst	b. 1773	d. 1857
1828–1835	Governor-General	Lord William Cavendish Bentinck	b. 1774	d. 1839
1836–1842	Governor-General	George Eden, Earl of Auckland	b. 1784	d. 1849
1842–1844	Governor-General	Edward Law, Earl of Ellenborough	b. 1790	d. 1871
1844–1848	Governor-General	Sir Henry Hardinge, Viscount Hardinge of Lahore	b. 1785	d. 1856
1848–1856	Governor-General	James Andrew Broun Ramsay, Earl and Marquis of Dalhousie	b. 1812	d. 1860
1856–1858	Governor-General	Charles John Canning, Earl Canning	b. 1812	d. 1862

*Government transferred from East India Company
to British Government in 1858*

■ Viceroys

1858–1862	Viceroy	Charles John Canning, Earl Canning		
1862–1863	Viceroy	James Bruce, Earl of Elgin	b. 1811	d. 1863
1864–1869	Viceroy	John Laird Mair, Baron Lawrence	b. 1811	d. 1879
1869–1872	Viceroy	Richard Southwell Bourke, Earl of Mayo	b. 1822	murdered 1872
1872–1876	Viceroy	Thomas George Baring, Earl of Northbrook	b. 1826	d. 1904
1876–1880	Viceroy	Edward Robert Bulwer Lytton, Earl of Lytton	b. 1831	d. 1891

Indian Empire Proclaimed in 1877

1880–1884	Viceroy	George Frederick Samuel Robinson, Marquis of Ripon	b. 1827	d. 1909
1884–1888	Viceroy	Frederick Temple Hamilton-Temple-Blackwood, Marquis of Dufferin and Ava	b. 1826	d. 1902
1888–1894	Viceroy	Henry Charles Keith Petty-Fitzmaurice, Marquis of Lansdowne	b. 1845	d. 1927
1894–1899	Viceroy	Victor Alexander Bruce, Earl of Elgin	b. 1849	d. 1917
1899–1905	Viceroy	George Nathaniel Curzon, Marquis of Kedleston	b. 1859	d. 1925
1905–1910	Viceroy	Gilbert John Elliot-Murray-Kynynmound, Earl of Minto	b. 1845	d. 1914
1910–1916	Viceroy	Charles Hardinge, Baron Hardinge of Penshurst	b. 1858	d. 1944
1916–1921	Viceroy	Frederick John Napier Thesiger, Viscount Chelmsford	b. 1868	d. 1933
1921–1926	Viceroy	Rufus Daniel Isaacs, Marquis of Reading	b. 1860	d. 1935
1926–1931	Viceroy	Edward Frederick Lindley Wood, Earl of Halifax	b. 1881	d. 1959
1931–1936	Viceroy	Freeman Freeman-Thomas, Marquis of Willingdon	b. 1866	d. 1941
1936–1943	Viceroy	Victor Alexander John Hope, Earl of Hopetoun and Marquis of Linlithgow	b. 1887	d. 1951
1943–1947	Viceroy	Archibald Percival Wavell, Earl Wavell	b. 1883	d. 1950

Dominion Established in 1947

| 1947–1948 | Viceroy | Louis Francis Albert Victor Nicholas Mountbatten, Earl Mountbatten of Burma | b. 1900 |
| 1948–1950 | Viceroy | Chakravarti Rajagopalachari | b. 1879 |

■ Republic

| 1947–1964 | Prime Minister | Pandit Jawaharlal Nehru | b. 1889 d. 1964 |

Pandit Nehru studied science and law at Harrow and Cambridge. As a Congress Party leader, he was frequently imprisoned. He played a leading part in the final negotiations for India's independence.

1964–1966	Prime Minister	Lal Bahadur Shastri	b. 1904 d. 1966
1966–1977	Prime Minister	Indira Gandhi, daughter of Jawaharlal Nehru	b. 1917
1977–1979	Prime Minister	Morarji Desai	
1979–1980	Prime Minister	Charan Singh	
1980–1984	Prime Minister	Indira Gandhi	b. 1917 assassinated 1984
1984–1989	Prime Minister	Rajiv Gandhi	
1989–1990	Prime Minister	V.P. Singh	
1990–1991	Prime Minister	Chandra Shekhar	
1991–1996	Prime Minister	P.V. Narasimha Rao	
1996	Prime Minister	Atal Bihari Vajpayee	
1996–1997	Prime Minister	H.D. Deve Gowda	
1997	Prime Minister	I.K. Gujral	
1998–2004	Prime Minister	Atal Bihari Vajpayee	
2004–	Prime Minister	Manmohan Singh	

■ National Leaders

Gopal Krishna Gokhale	b. 1866 d. 1915
Bal Gangadhar Tilak	b. 1856 d. 1920
Subhas Chandra Bose	b. 1897 d. 1945
Mohandas Karamchand Gandhi	b. 1869 assassinated 1948

Gandhi strove to bring about the cooperation of all Indians during the difficult situation that developed after the granting of independence to India. But on his way to a prayer meeting, this great teacher and exemplar of nonviolence was assassinated by a fanatic.

Indo-China *See* Cambodia; Laos; Vietnam

Indonesia (Republic of Indonesia)

As the Dutch East Indies, Indonesia was governed by the Netherlands from 1610 to 1945.

■ *Dutch East Indies*

1610–1614	Governor-General	Pieter Both
1614–1615	Governor-General	Gerrit Reijnst
1615–1619	Governor-General	Laurens Real
1619–1623	Governor-General	Jan Pietersz. Coen
1623–1627	Governor-General	Pieter Carpentier
1627–1629	Governor-General	Jan Pietersz. Coen
1629–1632	Governor-General	Jacques Specx
1632–1636	Governor-General	Hendrik Brouwer
1636–1645	Governor-General	Antonie van Diemen
1645–1650	Governor-General	Cornelis van der Lijn
1650–1653	Governor-General	Carel Reiniersz
1653–1678	Governor-General	Joan Maetsuyker
1678–1681	Governor-General	Rijklof van Goens
1681–1684	Governor-General	Cornelis Janszoon Speelman
1684–1694	Governor-General	Johannes Camphuys
1691–1704	Governor-General	Willem van Outhoorn
1704–1709	Governor-General	Joan van Hoorn
1709–1713	Governor-General	Abraham van Riebeeck
1713–1718	Governor-General	Christoffel van Swol
1718–1725	Governor-General	Hendrik Zwaardecroon
1725–1729	Governor-General	Mattheus de Haan
1729–1732	Governor-General	Diedrik Durven
1732–1735	Governor-General	Dirk van Cloon
1735–1737	Governor-General	Abraham Patras
1737–1741	Governor-General	Adriaan Valckenier
1714–1743	Governor-General	Joannes Thedens
1743–1750	Governor-General	Gustaaf Willem baron van Imhoff
1750–1761	Governor-General	Jacob Mossel
1761–1775	Governor-General	Petrus Albertus van des Parra
1775–1777	Governor-General	Jeremias van Riemsdijk
1777–1780	Governor-General	Reinier de Klerk

1780–1796	Governor-General	Willem Arnold Alting	
1796–1801	Governor-General	Pieter Gerardus van Overstraten	
1801–1804	Governor-General	Johannes Siberg	
1804–1808	Governor-General	Albertus Henricus Wiese	
1808–1811	Governor-General	Herman Willem Daendels	
1811	Governor-General	Jan Willem Janssens	
1811	English Governor	Sir Gilbert Elliot-Murray-Kynynmound, 1st Earl of Minto	b. 1751 d. 1814
1811–1816	English Governor	Sir Thomas Stamford Raffles	b. 1781 d. 1836
1816	English Governor	John Fendall	
1819–1826	Governor-General	Godert Alexander and Gerard Philip baron van der Capellen	
1826–1830	Governor-General	Hendrik Merkus baron de Kok	
1830–1833	Governor-General	Johannes graaf van der Bosch	
1833–1836	Governor-General (acting)	Jean Chrétien Baud	
1836–1840	Governor-General	Dominique Jacques de Eerens	
1840–1841	Governor-General (acting)	Carel Sirardus Willem van Hogendorp	
1841–1843	Governor-General (acting)	Pieter Merkus	
1843–1844	Governor-General	Pieter Merkus	
1844–1845	Governor-General (acting)	Joan Cornelis Reijnst	
1845–1851	Governor-General	Jan Jacob Rochussen	
1851–1856	Governor-General	Albertus Jacob Duymaer van Twist	
1856–1861	Governor-General	Charles Ferdinand Pahud	
1861	Governor-General (acting)	Arij Prins	
1861–1866	Governor-General	Ludolf Anne Jan Wilt baron Sloet van der Beele	
1866	Governor-General (acting)	Arij Prins	
1866–1872	Governor-General	Pieter Mijer	
1872–1875	Governor-General	James Loudon	
1875–1881	Governor-General	Johan Willem van Lansberge	
1881–1884	Governor-General	Frederiks' Jacob	
1884–1888	Governor-General	Otto van Rees	
1888–1893	Governor-General	Cornelis Pijnacker Hordijk	
1893–1899	Governor-General	Carel Herman Aart	
1899–1904	Governor-General	Willem Rooseboom	
1904–1909	Governor-General	Joannes Benedictus van Heutsz	

1909–1916	Governor-General	Alexander Willem Frederik Idenburg	
1916–1921	Governor-General	Johan Paul graaf van Limburg Stirum	
1921–1926	Governor-General	Dirk Fock	
1926–1931	Governor-General	Andries Cornelis Dirk de Graeff	
1931–1936	Governor-General	Bonifacius Cornelis de Jonge	
1936–1945	Governor-General	Alidius Warmoldus Lambertus Tjarda van Starkenborgh Stachouwer	
1945–1949		*Civil War*	

■ Republic of Indonesia

1950–1967	President	Mohammad Achmad Sukarno (or Soekarno)	b. 1901 d. 1970
1967–1998	President	Raden Suharto	
1998–1999	President	B.J. Habibie	
1999–2001	President	Abdurrahman Wahid	
2001–	President	Megawati Soekarnoputri	

Iran (Islamic Republic of Iran)

Traditionally known in the West as Persia, the ancient nation of Iran has retained a strong sense of cultural identity throughout its history.

■ Achaemenid Dynasty

550–529 B.C.	King	Cyrus the Great, son of Cambyses (I)	b. 600? killed 529
529–522	King	Cambyses II, son of Cyrus the Great	d. 522
522–521	Usurper	Pseudo-Smerdis (Gaumata)	killed 521
521–486	King	Darius I	b. 558? d. 486
486–465	King	Xerxes I, son of Darius I	b. 519? murdered 465
464–424	King	Artaxerxes I, son of Xerxes I	d. 424
424	King	Xerxes II, son of Artaxerxes I	murdered 424
423–404	King	Darius II, son of Artaxerxes I	d. 404
404–359	King	Artaxerxes II, son of Darius II	d. 359
359–338	King	Artaxerxes III, son of Artaxerxes II	murdered 338
338–336	King	Arses, son of Artaxerxes III	murdered 336
331–328	King	Artaxerxes IV	
331–323	Conqueror	Alexander the Great, son of Philip II of Macedon	b. 356 d. 323
323–312		*Internal Conflicts*	

■ Seleucid Dynasty 312–250

312–28	Ruler	Seleucus I (see Syria)	b. 358? assassinated 280
		The Seleucid Empire dissolved around 250 B.C.	

■ Arsacid Dynasty of Parthian Kings

c. 250–248 B.C.	King	Arsaces I	
248–214	King	Arsaces II Tiridates, brother of Arsaces I	
214–196	King	Arsaces III Artabanus, son of Arsaces II Tiridates	
196–181	King	Arsaces IV Priapatius	
181–174	King	Arsaces V Phraates, son of Arsaces IV Priapatius	
174–136	King	Arsaces IV Mithridates, son of Arsaces V Phraates	
136–127	King	Arsaces VII Phraates II, son of Arsaces VI Mithridates	
127–124	King	Arsaces VIII Artabanus II, uncle of Arsaces VII Phraates II	
124–87	King	Arsaces IX Mithridates II, son of Arsaces VIII Artabanus II	
87–77	King	Arsaces X Mnasciras	
76–69	King	Arsaces XI Sanatroices	
69–60	King	Arsaces XII Phraates III	
60–56	King	Arsaces XIII Mithridates III, son of Arsaces XII Phraates III	
56–37	King	Arsaces XIV Orodes I, son of Arsaces XII Phraates III	
37 ?–2	King	Arsaces XV Phraates IV	murdered? 2
37–27	Rival King	Tiridates II	
12–9	Rival King	Mithridates IV	
		Throne disputes from 2 B.C. to A.D. 10	
10 B.C.?–A.D. 40	King	Artabanus II d. 40	
51–91	King	Vologesus I	
107–130	King	Arsaces XXVI Osroes	
130–148	King	Arsaces XXVII Bolagases II	
148–190	King	Arsaces XXVIII Bolagases III, son of Arsaces XXVII Bolagases II	
190–208	King	Arsaces XXIX Bolagases IV	
208–222	King	Arsaces XXX Bolagases V, son of Arsaces XXX Bolagases V	
222–226	King	Arsaces XXXI Artabanus IV, brother of Arsaces XXX Bolagases V	

■ Sassanid Dynasty

226–241	King	Ardashir I (Artaxerxes), grandson of Sassan
241–272	King	Sapor I, (Shapur) son of Ardashir (Artaxerxes)
272–273	King	Hormisdas I (Hormuzd)
273–276	King	Baranes I, (Bahram) son of Sapor I
276–292	King	Baranes II, son of Baranes I
292–293	King	Baranes III, son of Baranes II
293–303	King	Narses (Narse)
301–309	King	Hormisdas II, (Hormuzd) son of Narses

309–379	King	Sapor II, (Shapur) son of Hormisdas II	
379–383	King	Ardashir II, brother of Sapor II	
383–388	King	Sapor III, (Shapur) son of Sapor II	
388–399	King	Baranes IV, (Bahram) son of Sapor II	
399–420	King	Yazdegerd I, grandson of Sapor II	
420–440	King	Baranes V, (Bahram) son of Yazdegerd I	
440–457	King	Yazdegerd II, son of Baranes V	
457–458	King	Hormisdas III, (Hormuzd) son of Yazdegerd II	
458–484	King	Peroz, (Firus) son of Yazdegerd II	
484–488	King	Balash, son of Yazdegerd II	
488–531	King	Kobad I, (Kavadh) son of Peroz	
531–578	King	Chosroes I, (Khustan) son of Kobad I	d. 579
578–590	King	Hormisdas IV, (Hormuzd) son of Chosroes I	assassinated 590
590–628	King	Chosroes II, son of Hormisdas IV	murdered 628
628	King	Kobad II, son of Chosroes II	
628–630	King	Ardashir III, grandson of Chosroes II	b. 621 murdered 630
		Anarchy from 630 to 632	
632–641	King	Yazdegerd III, grandson of Chosroes II	murdered 651

Persia was under the Caliphates from 641 to 1037; the Seljuks from 1037 to 1223; and the Mongols from 1223 to 1499.

■ Safawid Dynasty

1499–1524	Shah	Ismail I	b. 1486 d. 1524
1524–1576	Shah	Tahmasp I, son of Ismail I	b. 1514 d. 1576
1576–1577	Shah	Ismail II, son of Tahmasp I	b. 1551 d. 1577
1577–1586	Shah	Mohammed, son of Tahmasp I	
1586–1628	Shah	Abbas I (the Great), son of Shah Mohammed	b. 1557 d. 1628?
1628–1642	Shah	Safi I, grandson of Abbas I (the Great)	
1642–1667	Shah	Abbas II, son of Safi I	b. 1632 d. 1667
1668–1694	Shah	Safi II Suleiman, grandson of Safi I	
1694–1725	Shah	Husein, son of Safi II Suleiman	b. 1675? d. 1729
1725–1732	Shah	Tahmasp II, son of Husein	deposed 1732 d. 1739
1732–1736	Shah	Abbas III, son of Tahmasp II	deposed 1736
1736–1747	Shah	Nadir (Tahmasp Kuli Khan)	b. 1688 assassinated 1747
1747–1749	Shah	Ali Mardan	d. 1753
1748–1796	Counter-Regent	Ruch, grandson of Nadir	
1749–1760	Shah	Ismail III	

■ Zand Dynasty

1760–1779	Regent	Karim Khan	b. 1699? d. 1779
1785–1795	Shah	Luft Ali Khan, son of Karim Khan	murdered 1795

■ Kajar Dynasty

1795–1797	Shah	Agha Mohammed Khan	b. 1720 murdered 1797
1797–1834	Shah	Fath Ali, nephew of Agha Mohammed Khan	b. 1762? d. 1834
1834–1848	Shah	Mohammed, grandson of Fath Ali	d. 1848
1848–1896	Shah	Nasir-ad-Din, son of Mohammed	b. 1831 assassinated 1896
1896–1907	Shah	Muzaffar-ad-Din, son of Nasir-ad-Din	b. 1853 d. 1907
1907–1909	Shah	Mohammed Ali, son of Muzaffar-ad-Din	b. 1872 d. 1930
1909–1925	Shah	Ahmed Mirza, son of Mohammed Ali	b. 1898 d. 1930

■ Pahlevi Dynasty

1923–1941	Prime Minister/Shah	Riza Pahlevi	b. 1878 d. 1944
1941–1979	Prime Minister/Shah	Mohammed Riza Pahlevi	b. 1919 d. 1980
		In 1979 the westernizing Pahlevi Dynasty was overthrown by an Islamic revolution whose spiritual and political leader was the Ayatollah Ruholla Khomeini.	
1980–1981	President	Abolhassan Bani-Sadr	
1981		*Provisional Presidential Council*	
1981	President	Mohammad Ali Raja'i	
1981		*Provisional Presidential Council*	
1981–1989	President	Sayyed Mohammed Ali Khamenei	
1989–1997	President	Hojatolislam Ali Akbar Hashemi Rafsanjani	
1997–	President	Mohammad Khatami-Ardakani	

Iraq (Republic of Iraq) (*See also* Assyria; Babylonia)

Known to the Greeks and Romans as Mesopotamia, Iraq corresponds to ancient Assyria and Babylonia. It was under Turkish rule until 1919 and under a British Mandate from 1919 to 1921.

1921–1933	King	Faisal I, son of Husein ibn-Ali of Hejaz	b. 1885 d. 1933
1933–1939	King	Ghazi, son of Faisal I	b. 1912 d. 1939
1939–1958	King	Faisal II, son of Ghazi	b. 1935 assassinated 1958
1939–1953	Regent	Abdullah, uncle of Faisal II	assassinated 1958
1958		*Became Military Republic*	
1963–1966	President	Abdul Salam Mohammed Aref	b. 1921 d. 1966
1966–1968	President	Abdul Razhman Arif	

1968–1979	President	Ahmad Hasan al-Bakr	
1979–2003	President	Saddam Hussein	
		U.S.-led Coalition Provisional Authority from 2003 to 2004	
2004–2005	Transition Prime Minister	Iyad Allawi	
2005–	Prime Minister	Ibrahim al-Jaafari	b. 1947

Ireland (Official U.N. Name)

Conn Céd-cathach founded the Middle Kingdom (Meath) and began the High Kingship of Tara in 200.

377–405	High King	Niall of the Nine Hostages	d. 405
		Owen (Eoghan) and Conall founded the Kingdom of Aileach in 400.	
–432	High King	Loeguire, son of Niall	
		St. Patrick began his mission in Ireland in 432. Norse Invasions from 795 to 1014	
900–908	King of Cashel	Cormac MacCullenan	
–919	High King	Niall Glundubh	d. 919
–1002	King	Malachy II	
1002–1014	King	Brian Boru	b. 926 killed 1014
		Interregnum from 1022 to 1072	
1014–1064	King of Munster	Donnchad, son of Brian	
1064–1086	King of Munster	Turlough (Toirdelbach) nephew of Donnchad	b. 1009 d. 1086
1086–1119	King of Munster	Muirchertach O'Brien, son of Turlough (Toirdelbach)	d. 1119
		Before the Anglo-Norman invasions began in the 12th century, Ireland was a loose organization of four or five kings under an elective overlord.	
1119–1153	High King	Turlough (Toirdelbach) More O'Connor	d. 1153
1134–1171	King of Leinster	Dermot MacMurrough	b. 1110? d. 1171
1153–1166	King	Muirchertach MacLochlainn	
1166–1175	High King	Roderic *or* Rory O'Connor, son of Turlough (Toirdelbach)	b. 1116? d. 1198
		Roderic was the last native king of Ireland. The Pope granted Ireland to King Henry II of England in 1172.	
1177	Dominus Hiberniae	John, son of Henry II	b. 1167? d. 1216
1235	Ruler of Connaught	Richard de Burgo	
1376–1417	King of Leinster	Art MacMurrough	
1477–1513	King of Leinster	Gerald Fitzgerald, Earl of Kildare	d. 1513
1487	King	Edward VI (Lambert Simnel)	b. 1477? d. 1525
		Lambert Simnel was an English imposter to the throne who was groomed to impersonate the son of the Duke of Clarence.	

He was taken to Ireland and crowned King Edward VI in Dublin's cathedral. Pardoned for his role in the plot, he became a royal falconer.

1513–1534	Deputy Governor	Gerald Fitzgerald, Earl of Kildare	b. 1487	d. 1534
1541	King of Ireland	Henry VIII of England	b. 1491	d. 1547
1547–1553	King of Ireland	Edward VI, son of Henry VIII	b. 1537	d. 1553

Plantation of Leix and Offaly in 1556; Plantation of Munster in 1586; Tyrone War from 1594 to 1603; foundation of British Colony in Ulste from 1608 to 1610

1599	Lord Lieutenant of Ireland	Robert Devereux, 2nd Earl of Essex	b. 1566	d. 1601
1632–1638	Lord Deputy	Sir Thomas Wentworth, Earl of Strafford	b. 1593	beheaded 1641
1640	Lord Lieutenant	Sir Thomas Wentworth, Earl of Strafford		
1644–1649	Lord Lieutenant	James Butler, Earl, Marquis and Duke of Ormonde	b. 1610	d. 1688
1649–1650	Lord Lieutenant	Oliver Cromwell	b. 1599	d. 1658
1653–1658	Lord Protector	Oliver Cromwell		
1660–1685	King	Charles II	b. 1630	d. 1685
1661–1669	Lord Lieutenant	James Butler, Earl, Marquis and Duke of Ormonde		
1670–1672	Lord Lieutenant	John Berkeley, Baron Berkeley		d. 1678
1672–1677	Lord Lieutenant	Arthur Capel, Earl of Essex	b. 1631	d. 1683
1677–1685	Lord Lieutenant	James Butler, Earl, Marquis and Duke of Ormonde		
1687–1691	Lord Deputy	Richard Talbot, Earl of Tyrconnell	b. 1630	d. 1691
1703–1705	Lord Lieutenant	James Butler, Earl, Marquis and Duke of Ormonde	b. 1665	d. 1745
1710–1711	Lord Lieutenant	James Butler, Earl, Marquis and Duke of Ormonde		
1713	Lord Lieutenant	Charles Talbot, Earl and Duke of Shrewsbury	b. 1660	d. 1718
1722–1730	Lord Lieutenant	John Carteret, Earl Granville	b. 1690	d. 1763
1767–1774	Lord Lieutenant	George Townshend, Viscount and Marquis Townshend	b. 1724	d. 1807
1795	Lord Lieutenant	William Wentworth, Earl Fitzwilliam	b. 1748	d. 1833
1795–1798	Lord Lieutenant	Sir John Jeffreys Pratt, Earl and Marquis of Camden	b. 1759	d. 1840
1798–1801	Lord Lieutenant	Charles Cornwallis, Marquis Cornwallis	b. 1738	d. 1805

Rebellion 1798

United with England in 1801

1801–1806	Lord Lieutenant	Earl of Hardwicke	b. 1757	d. 1834
1806–1807	Lord Lieutenant	Duke of Bedford	b. 1792	d. 1839
1807–1813	Lord Lieutenant	Duke of Richmond	b. 1764	d. 1819
1813–1817	Lord Lieutenant	Earl Whitworth	b. 1752	d. 1825
1817–1821	Lord Lieutenant	Earl Talbot	b. 1777	d. 1849
1821–1828	Lord Lieutenant	Marquis of Wellesley	b. 1760	d. 1842
1828–1829	Lord Lieutenant	Marquis of Anglesey	b. 1768	d. 1854
1829–1830	Lord Lieutenant	Duke of Northumberland	b. 1785	d. 1847

1830–1833	Lord Lieutenant	Marquis of Anglesey		
1833–1834	Lord Lieutenant	Marquis of Wellesley		
1834–1835	Lord Lieutenant	Earl of Haddington	b. 1780	d. 1858
1835–1839	Lord Lieutenant	Marquis of Normanby	b. 1797	d. 1863
1839–1841	Lord Lieutenant	Viscount Ebrington (afterwards Earl Fortescue)	b. 1783	d. 1861
1841–1844	Lord Lieutenant	Earl de Grey	b. 1781	d. 1859
1844–1846	Lord Lieutenant	Lord Heytesbury	b. 1779	d. 1860
1846–1847	Lord Lieutenant	Earl of Bessborough	b. 1781	d. 1847
1847–1852	Lord Lieutenant	Earl of Clarendon	b. 1800	d. 1870
1852–1853	Lord Lieutenant	Earl of Eglinton	b. 1812	d. 1861
1853–1855	Lord Lieutenant	Earl of St. Germans	b. 1798	d. 1877
1855–1858	Lord Lieutenant	Earl of Carlisle	b. 1802	d. 1864
1858–1859	Lord Lieutenant	Earl of Eglinton		
1859–1864	Lord Lieutenant	Earl of Carlisle		
1864–1866	Lord Lieutenant	Lord Wodehouse (afterwards Earl of Kimberley)	b. 1826	d. 1902
1866–1868	Lord Lieutenant	Marquis of Abercorn	b. 1811	d. 1885
1868–1874	Lord Lieutenant	Earl Spencer	b. 1835	d. 1910
1874–1876	Lord Lieutenant	Duke of Abercorn		
1876–1880	Lord Lieutenant	Duke of Marlborough	b. 1822	d. 1883
1880–1882	Lord Lieutenant	Earl Cowper	b. 1834	d. 1905
1882–1885	Lord Lieutenant	Earl Spencer	b. 1835	d. 1910
1885–1886	Lord Lieutenant	Earl of Carnarvon	b. 1831	d. 1890
1886	Lord Lieutenant	Earl of Aberdeen	b. 1847	d. 1934
1886–1889	Lord Lieutenant	Marquis of Londonderry	b. 1852	d. 1915
1889–1892	Lord Lieutenant	Earl of Zetland	b. 1844	d. 1929
1892–1895	Lord Lieutenant	Lord Houghton	b. 1858	d. 1945
1895–1902	Lord Lieutenant	Earl Cadogan	b. 1840	d. 1915
1902–1905	Lord Lieutenant	Earl of Dudley	b. 1867	d. 1932
1905–1915	Lord Lieutenant	Earl of Aberdeen	b. 1847	d. 1934
1915–1918	Lord Lieutenant	Baron Wimborne	b. 1873	d. 1939
1918–1921	Lord Lieutenant	Viscount French	b. 1852	d. 1925
1921–1922	Lord Lieutenant	Viscount Fitzallen of Derwent	b. 1855	d. 1947
1875–1891	Nationalist leader	Charles Stewart Parnell	b. 1846	d. 1891
1916–1921	Nationalist leader	Eamon de Valera	b. 1882	

*Born in New York of a Spanish father and an Irish mother,
Valera was sentenced in 1916 by the British to life imprisonment
for his part in the Easter Week Rebellion. He was amnestied in 1917,
rearrested in 1918, and escaped from prison in 1919. Subsequently,*

he became president of the League of Nations Assembly as well as premier and president of the Irish Republic.

■ Irish Free State

1922	President	Arthur Griffith	b. 1872 d. 1922
1922	Head of Provisional Government	Michael Collins	b. 1890 killed 1922
1922–1932	President of Executive Council	William Thomas Cosgrave	
1932–1937	President of Executive Council	Eamon de Valera	
1921–1927	Governor-General of Free State	Timothy Michael Healy	b. 1855 d. 1931
1928–1932	Governor-General	James McNeill	b. 1869 d. 1938
1932–1937	Governor-General	Donal Buckley	

■ Republic of Ireland

Presidents

1938–1945	President	Douglas Hyde	b. 1860
1945–1959	President	Sean Thomas O'Kelly (O Ceallaigh)	b. 1883 d. 1966
1959–1973	President	Eamon de Valera	b. 1882 d. 1975
1973–1974	President	Erskine Childers	b. 1905 d.1974
1974–1976	President	Cearbhall Ó Dálaigh	b. 1911 d. 1978
1976–1990	President	Dr. Patrick Hillery	
1990–1997	President	Mary Robinson	
1997–	President	Mary McAleese	

Prime Ministers

1937–1948	Prime Minister	Eamon de Valera
1948–1951	Prime Minister	John Aloysius Costello
1951–1954	Prime Minister	Eamon de Valera
1954–1957	Prime Minister	John A. Costello
1957–1959	Prime Minister	Eamon de Valera
1959–1966	Prime Minister	Seán F. Lemass
1966–1973	Prime Minister	John Lynch
1973–1977	Prime Minister	Liam Cosgrave
1977–1979	Prime Minister	John Lynch
1979–1981	Prime Minister	Charles Haughey

1981–1982	Prime Minister	Garret FitzGerald
1982	Prime Minister	Charles Haughey
1982–1987	Prime Minister	Garret FitzGerald
1987–1992	Prime Minister	Charles Haughey
1992–1994	Prime Minister	Albert Reynolds
1994–1997	Prime Minister	John Bruton
1997–	Prime Minister	Bertie Ahern

■ Northern Ireland

Northern Ireland's separate government was established in 1920.

1922–1945	Governor	James Albert Edward Hamilton, Duke of Abercorn	b. 1869 d. 1953
1945–1952	Governor	William Spencer Leveson Gower, Earl Granville	b. 1880 d. 1953
1952–1964	Governor	John De Vere Loder, Baron Wakehurst	b. 1895
1964–	Governor	Lord Erskine of Rerrick	b. 1893
1921–1940	Prime Minister	James Craig, Viscount Craigavon	b. 1871 d. 1940

Viscount Craigavon resigned from the position of Financial Secretary to the British Admiralty in 1920 to become the first Prime Minister of Northern Ireland—a post he held until his death. He was a firm opponent of Home Rule.

1940–1943	Prime Minister	John Miller Andrews	b. 1871 d. 1956
1943–1963	Prime Minister	Basil Stanlake Brooke, Viscount Brookeborough	b. 1888 d. 1963
1963–1969	Prime Minister	Terence Marne O'Neill	b. 1914
1969–1971	Prime Minister	James Dawson Chichester-Clark	b. 1923
1971–1972	Prime Minister	Brian Arthur Deane Faulkner	b. 1921

In 1972, after three years of sectarian violence that resulted in more than 400 dead and thousands injured, Britain suspended the Ulster Parliament. Efforts to establish a stable system of semiautonomous government for Northern Ireland had not been fully successful as late as 2004.

Israel (State of Israel)

BIBLICAL TIMES

■ Period of United Monarchy

1050–1011 B.C.	King	Saul	killed 1011 B.C.
1011–971	King	David	d. 971 B.C.?
971–931	King	Solomon, son of David	d. 931 B.C.?

■ Period of Divided Monarchy
Northern Kingdom of Israel

931–910 B.C.	King	Jeroboam I	d. 910?
910–909	King	Nadab, son of Jeroboam I	assassinated 909
909–886	King	Baasha	d. 886?
886–885	King	Elah, son of Baasha	assassinated 885
885–884	King	Zimri	
885–880	King	Tibni	
885–874	King	Omri	d. 874?
874–853	King	Ahab, son of Omri	d. 853?
853–852	King	Ahaziah, son of Ahab	d. 852?
852–841	King	Jehoram, brother of Ahaziah	d. 841?
841–814	King	Jehu ben-Nimshi	d. 814?
814–798	King	Jehoahaz, son of Jehu	d. 798?
798–782	King	Joash, son of Jehoahaz	d. 782?
793–792	Co-Regent	Jeroboam	d. 753?
782–753	King	Jeroboam II, son of Joash	
753–752	King	Zachariah, son of Jeroboam II	assassinated 752
752	King	Shallum	killed 752
752–742	King	Menahem	d. 742?
742–740	King	Pekahiah, son of Menahem	assassinated 741
740–732	King	Pekah	killed 732
732–723	King	Hoshea	d. 723?
		End of Kingdom of Israel	

Southern Kingdom of Judah

931–913 B.C.	King	Rehoboam, son of Solomon	
913–911	King	Abijah (or Abijam), son of Rehoboam	
911–870	King	Asa, son of Abijah	d. 870?
873–872	Co-regent	Jehoshaphat	
870–848	King	Jehoshaphat, son of Asa	d. 848?
848–841	King	Jehoram, son of Jehoshaphat	d. 841?
843–842	King	Ahaziah, son of Jehoram	killed 842?
842–837	Queen	Athaliah, mother of Ahaziah	killed 837
835–791	King	Joash, son of Ahaziah	assassinated 791
791	King	Amaziah, son of Joash	assassinated 791
791–740	King	Uzziah, son of Amaziah	

750–	Co-regent	Jotham, son of Uzziah	d. 732?
740–732	King	Jotham	
740–732	King	Ahaz, son of Jotham	d. 716?
744–743	Co-regent	Ahaz	
732–716	Co-regent	Ahaz	
716–687	King	Hezekiah, son of Ahaz (Co-regent 729)	b. 740? d. 687?
696–695	Co-regent	Manasseh, son of Hezekiah	d. 642?
687–642	King	Manasseh	
642–640	King	Amon, son of Manasseh	assassinated 640
640–609	King	Josiah, son of Amon	b. 638? d. 608?
609	King	Jehoahaz, son of Josiah	
609–597	King	Jehoiakim, son of Josiah	d. 597?
597	King	Jehoiachin (Coniah), son of Jehoiakim	b. 615? d. 560?
597–587	King	Zedekiah (Mattaniah), son of Josiah (Zedekiah was the last King of Judah)	

Judah was conquered by the Babylonians. Thereafter, the Jews in Palestine were under foreign rule until the revolt of the Maccabees against the successors of Alexander the Great of Macedonia.

■ Maccabees

168–167 B.C.		Mattathias	d. 166?
166–161		Judas Maccabaeus, son of Mattathias	d. 160
161–143	High Priest	Jonathan, son of Mattathias	
143–135	High Priest	Simon, son of Mattathias	
135–105	High Priest	John Hyrcanus, son of Simon	
104–103	King	Judah (Aristobulus I), son of John Hyrcanus	b. 140? d. 103
103–76	King	Alexander Jannaeus, son of John Hyrcanus	
76–67	King	Alexandra, wife of Alexander Jannaeus	d. 67
67–63	King	Hyrcanus II, son of Alexandra	d. 30
67–63	Rival King	Aristobulus II	d. 48

Maccabean State under Roman Rule

■ Tetrarchs

63–40 B.C.	Ethnarch	Hyrcanus II	
40–37	Rival King	Antigonus II, son of Aristobulus II	b. 80? d.37
41–4	Ethnarch	Herod the Great	b. 73? d. 4
4 B.C.–A.D. 6	Ethnarch	Herod Archelaus, son of Herod the Great	d. A.D. 18?
4 B.C.–A.D. 38	Ethnarch	Herod Antipas, son of Herod the Great	d. A.D. 40?

| 4 B.C.–A.D. 34 | Ethnarch | Philip, son of Herod the Great | d. A.D. 34 |
| 40–44 | Ethnarch | Herod Agrippa I, grandson of Herod the Great | b. 10? B.C d. A.D. 44 |

Palestine governed by proconsuls from A.D. 44; Jerusalem destroyed in 70; Persian dominion from 614 to 629; Arab dominion from 636 to 1099; Crusaders established Kingdom of Jerusalem

■ Kings of Jerusalem

1099–1100	Protector of the Holy Sepulchre	Godfrey of Bouillon	b. 1060 d. 1100
1100–1118	King	Baldwin I, brother of Godfrey of Bouillon	b. 1058 d. 1118
1118–1131	King	Baldwin II, nephew of Baldwin I	d. 1131
1131–1143	King	Fulk of Anjou, son-in-law of Baldwin II	b. 1092 d. 1143
1143–1162	King	Baldwin III, son of Fulk of Anjou	b. 1130 d. 1162
1162–1174	King	Amalric I, brother of Baldwin III	b. 1135 d. 1174
1174–1185	King	Baldwin IV, son of Amalric I	b. 1161 d. 1185
1185–1186	King	Baldwin V, nephew of Baldwin IV	b. 1178 d. 1186
1186–1192	King	Guy of Lusignan	b. 1140 d. 1194

Saladin Captured Jerusalem in 1187

Third Crusade from 1189 to 1192

1190–1192	Rival Regent	Conrad of Montferrat, son-in-law of Amalric	assassinated 1192
1192–1197	King	Henry of Champagne	
1197–1205	King	Amalric II of Cyprus, brother of Guy of Lusignan	b. 1144 d. 1205
1205–1229	King	John of Brienne	b. 1148 d. 1237
1229–1244	King	Frederick II (German Emperor), son-in-law of John of Brienne	b. 1148 d. 1250

Jerusalem conquered by the Sultan of Egypt in 1244; Palestine under Turkish rule from 1518 to 1918; conquered by Britain from 1917 to 1918; League of Nations mandate in 1923; divided into Israel and Jordan under United Nations auspices in 1948

MODERN STATE OF ISRAEL

■ Presidents

1948–1952	President	Chaim Weizmann	b. 1874 d. 1952
1952–1963	President	Itzhak Ben-Zvi	b. 1884 d. 1963
1963–1973	President	Zalman Shazar	b. 1889 d.1974
1973–1978	President	Ephraim Katzir	b. 1916
1978–1983	President	Yitzhak Navon	b. 1921
1983–1993	President	Chaim Herzoq	b. 1918 d. 1997
1993–2000	President	Ezer Weizman	b. 1924 d. 2005

2000–	President	Moshe Katsav	b. 1945

■ Prime Ministers

1948–1953	Prime Minister	David Ben-Gurion	b. 1886
1953–1955	Prime Minister	Moshe Sharett	b. 1894
1955–1963	Prime Minister	David Ben-Gurion	
1963–1969	Prime Minister	Levi Eshkol	b. 1895
1969–1974	Prime Minister	Golda Meir	
1974–1977	Prime Minister	Yitzhak Rabin	
1977–1983	Prime Minister	Menachem Begin	
1983–1984	Prime Minister	Yitzhak Shamir	
1984–1986	Prime Minister	Shimon Peres	
1986–1992	Prime Minister	Yitzhak Shamir	
1992–1995	Prime Minister	Yitzhak Rabin	assassinated in office
1995–1996	Prime Minister	Shimon Peres	
1996–1999	Prime Minister	Benjamin Netanyahu	
1999–2001	Prime Minister	Ehud Barak	
2001–	Prime Minister	Ariel Sharon	

Italy (Italian Republic)

Romulus Augustulus, the last ruler of the Western Roman Empire, was deposed by the Scirian, Odoacer, in A.D. 476.

■ Scirians

476–493	King	Odoacer	b. 434? murdered 493

■ Ostrogoths

493–526	King	Theodoric the Great, son of Theodemir	b. 454? d. 526

Theodoric was a hostage at the Byzantine Court at Constantinople for ten years as a youth. After succeeding his chieftain father, he became the most powerful Gothic King, invading and conquering Italy and murdering Odoacer with his own hands. He appears in the Nibelungenlied *as "Dietrich von Bern."*

526–534	King	Athalaric, grandson of Theodoric	b. 516 d. 534
534–536	King	Theodat	assassinated 536
536–540	King	Vitiges, brother-in-law of Athalaric	
540	King	Theodebald (Hildibald)	assassinated 540
540–541	King	Eraric	
541–552	King	Totila, nephew of Theodebald	killed 552

552–553	King	Teias	
553–568		*Italy under Byzantine Empire*	

■ Lombards

568–573	King	Alboin	d. 573
573–575	King	Cleph	
575–584		*Interregnum*	
584–590	King	Autharis, husband of Theodelinda, son of Cleph	d. 590
590	Queen	Theodelinda, wife of Autharis	
590–615	King	Agilulf, Theodelinda's consort	
615–625	King	Adaloald, son of Agilulf	
625–636	King	Arioald, son-in-law of Agilulf	
636–652	King	Rotharis, son-in-law of Agilulf	d. 652
652–661	King	Aribert I	
662–671	King	Grimoald, son-in-law of Aribert	
671–674	King	Garibald, son of Grimoald	
674–688	King	Bertharit, son of Aribert	
688–700	King	Cunibert, son of Bertharit	
701–712	King	Aribert II	
712–744	King	Liutprand (Luitprand)	b. 690? d. 744
744–749	King	Rachis of Friuli	
749–756	King	Aistulf, brother of Rachis of Friuli	d. 756
756–774	King	Desiderius	deposed 774

■ Carolingian Dynasty

774–814	King	Charlemagne, son-in-law of Desiderius	b. 742 d. 814
814–818	King	Bernard, grandson of Charlemagne	
818–855	King	Lothair I, grandson of Charlemagne	b. 796? d. 855
		(See Germany *and* France*)*	
855–875	King	Louis II, son of Louis I	b. 804? d. 876
875–877	King	Charles the Bald, son of Louis I	b. 823 d. 877
		(See France*)*	
877–880	King	Carloman, nephew of Lothair I	b. 828 d. 880
		(See Germany*)*	
880–887	King	Charles the Fat, brother of Carloman	b. 839 d. 888

■ Other Kings

888–894	King	Guy of Spoleto	d. 894
894–898	King	Lambert, son of Guy of Spoleto	
899–905	King	Louis III of Burgundy, grandson of Louis II	b. 880 d. 928?
888–923	King (rival)	Berengarius of Friuli, great-grandson of Charlemagne	d. 924
923–933	King	Rudolph II of Burgundy, son of Rudolph I	d. 937
933–947	King	Hugh of Arles	d. 947
		(See Burgundy)	
947–950	King	Lothair II, son of Hugh of Arles	d. 950
950–961	King	Berengarius II of Ivrea, grandson of Berengarius of Friuli	d. 966
961–973	King	Otto the Great, son of Henry I the Fowler	b. 912 d. 973
		(See Germany)	

The Italian peninsula was subject to the Holy Roman Empire from 961 to 1254 and was divided into many small states until reunification in 1861.

English versions of the names of rulers of Italian-speaking states are:

Alexander–Alessandro	Henry–Enrico	Maximilian–Massimiliano
Caesar–Cesare	Humbert–Umberto	Peter–Pier, Piero, Pietro
Charles–Carlo	Joanna–Giovanna	Philip–Filippo
Conrad–Corrado	John–Giovanni	Roger–Ruggiero
Francis–Francesco	Joseph–Giuseppe	Victor–Vittorio
Frederick–Federigo	Louis–Lodovico, Luigi	

■ Kingdom of Italy

1861–1878	King	Vittorio Emanuele II	
1878–1900	King	Umberto I, son of Vittorio Emanuele II	b. 1844 assassinated 1900
1900–1946	King	Vittorio Emanuele III, son of Umberto I	b. 1869 d. 1947

Vittorio Emanuele III was King of Italy for nearly half a century. Although he was declared "Emperor of Ethiopia" in 1936 and "King of Albania" in 1939, his real power and authority declined under the Fascist regime.

1946	King	Umberto II, son of Vittorio Emanuele III	b. 1904

Republic Declared in 1946

■ Premiers of Italy

1852–1859	Premier	Count Camillo Cavour	b. 1810 d. 1861
1860–1861	Premier	Count Camillo Cavour	

Hero of the Risorgimento, Cavour devoted himself to the liberation and unification of Italy, which he accomplished through his

extraordinary diplomatic skills with Prince Louis Napoleon,
Vittorio Emmanuele, and Garibaldi.

1876–1879	Premier	Agostino Depretis	b. 1813 d. 1887
1881–1887	Premier	Agostino Depretis	
1878	Premier	Benedetto Cairoli	b. 1825 d. 1889
1879–1881	Premier	Benedetto Cairoli	
1887–1891	Premier	Francesco Crispi	b. 1819 d. 1901
1892–1893	Premier	Giovanni Giolitti	b. 1842 d. 1928
1893–1896	Premier	Francesco Crispi	
1903–1905	Premier	Giovanni Giolitti	
1906–1909	Premier	Giovanni Giolitti	
1911–1914	Premier	Giovanni Giolitti	
1920–1921	Premier	Giovanni Giolitti	
1922–1943	Premier	Benito Mussolini	b. 1883 murdered 1945

Mussolini gradually transferred the government into a
dictatorship according to the principles of fascism.

1944–1945	Premier	Ivanoe Bonomi	b. 1873
1945	Premier	Ferruccio Parri	b. 1890
1945–1953	Premier	Alcide De Gasperi	b. 1881 d. 1954
1953–1954	Premier	Giuseppe Pella	b. 1902
1954	Premier	Amintore Fanfani	b. 1908
1954–1955	Premier	Mario Scelba	b. 1901
1955–1957	Premier	Antonio Segni	b. 1895
1957–1958	Premier	Adone Zoli	b. 1887
1958–1959	Premier	Amintore Fanfani	
1959–1960	Premier	Antonio Segni	
1960	Premier	Fernando Tambroni	b. 1901
1960–1963	Premier	Amintore Fanfani	
1963	Premier	Giovanni Leone	b. 1908
1963–1968	Premier	Aldo Moro	b. 1916
1968	Premier	Giovanni Leone	
1968–1970	Premier	Mariano Rumor	
1970–1972	Premier	Emilio Colombo	
1972–1973	Premier	Giulio Andreotti	
1973–1974	Premier	Mariano Rumor	
1974–1976	Premier	Aldo Moro	
1976–1979	Premier	Giulio Andreotti	
1979–1980	Premier	Francesco Cossiga	

1980–1981	Premier	Arnaldo Forlani	
1981–1982	Premier	Giovanni Spadolini	
1982–1983	Premier	Amintore Fanfani	
1987	Premier	Bettino Craxi	
1987–1988	Premier	Giovani Goria	
1988–1989	Premier	Ciriaco de Mita	
1989–1992	Premier	Giulio Andreotti	
1992–1993	Premier	Giuliano Amato	
1993–1994	Premier	Carlo Aseglio Ciampi	
1994	Premier	Silvio Berlusconi	
1995–1996	Premier	Lamberto Dini	
1996–1998	Premier	Romano Prodi	
1998–2000	Premier	Massimo D'Alema	
2000–2001	Premier	Giuliano Amato	
2001–	Premier	Silvio Berlusconi	

Governors of Regions Later Incorporated into Italy

■ Apulia and Calabria

1057–1059	Count	Robert Guiscard, brother of Roger Guiscard	b. 1015? d. 1085
1059–1085	Duke	Robert Guiscard (see Sicily)	
1085–1111	Duke	Roger Bursa, son of Robert Guiscard	
1111–1127	Duke	Guillaume, son of Roger Bursa	
1127		*Apulia United with Sicily*	

■ Genoa

The city-state of Genoa developed into a maritime power of the first rank by the 13th century. It was first ruled by consuls of the republic and then by doges from 1339.

1339–1363	Doge	Simone Boccanera	b. 1300? d. 1363
1528–1560	Dictator (Censor)	Andrea Doria	b. 1466 d. 1560
		Fell to the French in 1797, becoming the Ligurian Republic. Annexed to the Kingdom of Sardinia in 1815	

■ Milan

House of Visconti

1277–1295	Duke	Ottone V	b. 1207? d. 1295
1295–1302	Duke	Matteo, grandnephew of Ottone V	b. 1255 d. 1322
1311–1322	Duke	Matteo	

1322–1328	Duke	Galeazzo I, son of Matteo	b. 1277? d. 1328
1328–1339	Duke	Azzo, son of Galeazzo I	b. 1302 d. 1339
1339–1349	Duke	Lucchino, son of Matteo	b. 1287? murdered 1349
1349–1354	Duke	Giovanni, brother of Lucchino	b. 1290? d. 1354
1354–1355	Duke	Matteo II, nephew of Giovanni	assassinated 1355
1355–1378	Duke	Galeazzo II, nephew of Giovanni	b. 1320 d. 1378
1354–1385	Duke	Bernabo, nephew of Giovanni	murdered 1385
1378–1402	Duke	Giovanni Galeazzo, son of Galeazzo II	b. 1351 d. 1402

Giovanni Galeazzo became ruler of central and northern Italy and attempted to have Milan recognized as a Duchy of the Holy Roman Empire. He bought the city of Pisa and was responsible for building Milan's grand cathedral. A patron of art and literature, he died of the plague.

1402–1412	Duke	Gianmaria, son of Giovanni Galeazzo	b. 1389 assassinated 1412
1412–1447	Duke	Filippo Maria, son of Giovanni Galeazzo	b. 1392 d. 1447
1447–1450		*Ambrosian Republic*	

House of Sforza

1450–1466	Duke	Francesco Sforza, son-in-law of Filippo Maria	b. 1401 d. 1466
1466–1476	Duke	Galeazzo Maria, son of Francesco Sforza	b. 1444 assassinated 1476
1476–1481	Duke	Giovanni Galeazzo, son of Galeazzo Maria	b. 1469 d. 1494
1481–1499	Duke	Lodovico (il Moro), son of Francesco Sforza	b. 1451 d. 1508
1499–1512		*Milan under France*	
1512–1515	Duke	Massimiliano, son of Lodovico il Moro	b. 1491 d. 1530
1515–1522		*Milan under France*	
1522–1535	Duke	Francesco II, son of Lodovico il Moro	b. 1492 d. 1535

Milan was under Spain from 1535 to 1714; under Austria from 1714 to 1797; under France from 1797 to 1814; under Austria again from 1814 to 1859; and united with Sardinia in 1859.

■ Modena

House of Este

1452–1471	Duke	Borso d'Este	b. 1413 d. 1471
1471–1505	Duke	Ercole I, brother of Borso d'Este	b. 1431 d. 1505
1505–1534	Duke	Alfonso I, son of Ercole I	b. 1486 d. 1534
1534–1559	Duke	Ercole II, son of Alfonso I	b. 1508 d. 1559
1559–1597	Duke	Alfonso II, son of Ercole II	b. 1533 d. 1597
1597–1628	Duke	Cesare, grandson of Alfonso I	b. 1533 d. 1628
1628–1629	Duke	Alfonso III, son of Cesare	d. 1644

1629–1658	Duke	Francesco I, brother of Alfonso III	b. 1610	d. 1658
1658–1662	Duke	Alfonso IV, son of Francesco I	b. 1634	d. 1662

Alfonso IV was father of the Catholic princess Mary Beatrice, who became the second wife of King James II of England. She bore him seven children, among them James Francis Edward, "The Old Pretender."

1662–1694	Duke	Francesco II, son of Alfonso IV	b. 1660	d. 1694
1694–1737	Duke	Raynold Rinaldo	b. 1655	d. 1737
1737–1745	Duke	Francesco III, son of Raynold Rinaldo	b. 1698	d. 1780
1748–1780	Duke	Francesco III		
1780–1796	Duke	Ercole III Rinaldo, son of Francesco III	b. 1727	d. 1803
1796–1814		*Under France*		
1814–1846	Duke	Francesco IV, son of Ercole III Rinaldo	b. 1779	d. 1846
1846–1859	Duke	Francesco V, son of Francesco IV	b. 1819	d. 1875

Modena Incorporated into the Kingdom of Italy in 1860

■ Naples

The Kingdom of Naples was united with Sicily from 1130 to 1282; 1435 to 1458; 1503 to 1713; 1720 to 1806; and 1815 to 1860.

House of Anjou

1266–1285	King	Charles I, brother of Louis IX	b. 1226	d. 1285
1285–1309	King	Charles II, son of Charles I	b. 1246	d. 1309
1309–1343	King	Robert the Good, son of Charles II		d. 1343
1343–1381	Queen	Joanna I, granddaughter of Robert the Good	b. 1327?	murdered 1382
1381–1386	King	Charles III of Durazzo, great-grandson of Charles II	b. 1345	d. 1386
1386–1414	King	Ladislas, son of Charles III of Durazzo	b. 1379?	d. 1414
1414–1435	Queen	Joanna II, sister of Ladislas	b. 1371	d. 1435
1435–1442	Titular King	René I, son of Louis of Anjou	b. 1409	d. 1480

House of Aragon

1435–1458	King	Alfonso I, son of Ferdinand I of Aragon	b. 1385	d. 1458
1458–1494	King	Ferdinand (Ferrante) I, son of Alfonso I	b. 1423	d. 1494
1494–1495	King	Alfonso II, son of Ferrante I abdicated 1495	b. 1448	d. 1495
1495–1496	King	Ferrante II, son of Alfonso II	b. 1469	d. 1496
1496–1501	King	Federigo, uncle of Ferrante II	b. 1452	d. 1504

Naples was united with France from 1501 to 1503; with Spain from 1503 to 1707; with Austria from 1707 to 1734; with Spain again from 1734 to 1759; and was part of the Kingdom of the Two Sicilies from 1759 to 1860.

Bourbon Dynasty

1735–1759	King	Carlo III, son of Philip V of Spain abdicated 1759	b. 1716 d. 1788
1759–1806	King	Ferrante IV, son of Carlo III	b. 1751 d. 1825
1806–1808	King	Joseph Bonaparte abdicated 1808	b. 1768 d. 1844
1808–1815	King	Joachim I Napoleon (Murat)	b. 1767 shot 1815
1815–1816	King	Ferrante IV	

Kingdom of the Two Sicilies

1816–1825	King	Ferrante I (Ferrante IV of Naples)	
1825–1830	King	Francesco I, son of Ferrante I	b. 1777 d. 1830
1830–1859	King	Ferrante II, son of Francesco I	b. 1810 d. 1859
1859–1860	King	Francesco II, son of Ferrante II	b. 1846 d. 1894
1860	Dictator	Giuseppe Garibaldi	b. 1807 d. 1882

Garibaldi organized the expedition of "The Thousand Heroes," the famous Redshirts, and invaded Sicily, landing under the protection of British naval vessels. Four months later, he expelled Francesco II from Naples, defeating the Kingdom of the Two Sicilies.

Naples Incorporated into the Kingdom of Italy in 1860

■ Parma
Farnese Dynasty

1545–1547	Duke	Pier Luigi, son of Alessandro Farnese (Pope Paul III)	b. 1503 assassinated 1547
1547–1586	Duke	Ottavio, son of Pier Luigi	b. 1520 d. 1586
1586–1592	Duke	Alessandro, son of Ottavio	b. 1545 d. 1592
1592–1622	Duke	Ranuccio I, son of Alessandro	b. 1569 d. 1622
1622–1646	Duke	Odoardo, son of Ranuccio I	b. 1612 d. 1646
1646–1694	Duke	Ranuccio II, son of Odoardo	b. 1630 d. 1694
1694–1727	Duke	Francesco, son of Ranuccio II	b. 1678 d. 1727
1727–1731	Duke	Antonio, brother of Francesco	b. 1679 d. 1731

Bourbon Dynasty

1731–1735	Duke	Carlo I (Charles III, King of Spain)	b. 1716 d. 1788
		Parma under Austrian Rule from 1735 to 1748	
1748–1765	Duke	Philip I, son of Philip V, King of Spain	b. 1720 d. 1765
1765–1802	Duke	Ferdinand (Ferrante) I, son of Philip I	d. 1802
1803–1807	Duke	Carlo II (Charles Louis), son of Louis I, King of Etruria	b. 1799 d. 1883
		Parma under France from 1802 to 1815	

1815–1847	French Empress	Marie Louise, second wife of Napoleon I	b. 1791 d. 1847
1847–1849	Duke	Carlo II, abdicated 1849	
1849–1854	Duke	Carlo III, son of Carlo II	b. 1823 assassinated 1854
1854–1859	Duke	Roberto I, son of Carlo III	b. 1848 d. 1907
1854–1859	Duchess-regent	Louise Marie, mother of Roberto	b. 1819 d. 1864

Parma Incorporated into the Kingdom of Italy in 1860

■ Sardinia

Sardinia was acquired by the Dukes of Savoy in 1720.

1720–1730	King	Vittorio Amedeo II, of Savoy	abdicated 1730
1730–1773	King	Carlo Emanuele I, son of Vittorio Amedeo	b. 1701 d. 1773
1773–1796	King	Vittorio Amedeo II, son of Carlo Emanuele I	b. 1726 d. 1796
1796–1802	King	Carlo Emanuele II, son of Vittorio Amedeo III abdicated 1802	b. 1751 d. 1819
1805–1814	Viceroy	Eugene de Beauharnais, stepson of Napoleon	b. 1781 d. 1824
1802–1821	King	Vittorio Emanuele I, son of Vittorio Amedeo III	abdicated 1821 b. 1759 d. 1824
1821–1831	King	Carlo Felice, son of Vittorio Amedeo III	b. 1756 d. 1831
1831–1849	King	Carlo Alberto, son of Carlo Emanuele	abdicated 1849 b. 1798 d. 1849
1849–1861	King	Vittorio Emanuele II, son of Carlo Alberto	b. 1820 d. 1878

Sardinia Incorporated into the Kingdom of Italy in 1861

■ Savoy

Savoy was given to Umberto in 1048 by Conrad, Emperor of Germany.

1048–1050	Count	Umberto I (Umberto Biancamano)	b. 970? d. 1050?
1050–1056	Count	Amedeo I, son of Umberto	d. 1056
1056–1060	Count	Oddone, son of Umberto	d. 1060
1060–1080	Count	Amedeo II, son of Oddone	d. 1080
1080–1103	Count	Umberto II, son of Amedeo II	d. 1103
1103–1149	Count	Amedeo III, son of Umberto II	d. 1149
1149–1189	Count	Umberto III, son of Amedeo III	d. 1189
1189–1222	Count	Tommaso I	d. 1222
1233–1253	Count	Amedeo IV, son of Tommaso I	d. 1253
1253–1263	Count	Boniface, son of Amedeo IV	d. 1263
1263–1268	Count	Pietro II, brother of Amedeo IV	d. 1268
1268–1285	Count	Filippo I, brother of Amedeo IV	b. 1207 d. 1285
1285–1323	Count	Amedeo V, brother of Filippo I	b. 1249 d. 1323
1323–1329	Count	Eduardo, son of Amedeo V	d. 1329
1329–1343	Count	Aimone, son of Amedeo V	d. 1343

1343–1383	Count	Amedeo VI, son of Aimone	b. 1334 d. 1383
1383–1391	Count	Amedeo VII, son of Amedeo VI	b. 1360 d. 1391
1391–1416	Count	Amedeo VIII, son of Amedeo VII	b. 1383 d. 1451
1416–1434	Count	Amedeo VIII	
1434–1465	Count	Louis, son of Amedeo VIII	d. 1465
1465–1471	Count	Amedeo IX, son of Louis	b. 1435 d. 1472
1472–1482	Count	Philibert I, son of Amedeo IX	b. 1464 d. 1482
1482–1489	Count	Carlo I, son of Philibert I	b. 1468 d. 1490
1489–1496	Count	Carlo II, son of Carlo I	d. 1496
1496–1497	Count	Filippo II, son of Louis	d. 1497
1497–1504	Count	Philibert II, son of Filippo II	d. 1504
1504–1553	Count	Carlo III, brother of Philibert II	d. 1553
1553–1580	Count	Emanuele Philibert, son of Carlo III	b. 1528 d. 1580
1580–1630	Duke	Carlo Emanuele I, son of Emanuele Philibert	b. 1562 d. 1630
1630–1637	Duke	Vittorio Amedeo I, son of Carlo Emanuele	b. 1587 d. 1637
1637–1638	Duke	Francesco, son of Vittorio Amedeo I	d. 1638
1638–1675	Duke	Carlo Emanuele II, son of Vittorio Amedeo I	b. 1634 d. 1675
1675–1713	Duke	Vittorio Amedeo II, son of Carlo Emanuele II	b. 1666 d. 1732

(See Sardinia)

■ Sicily

Norman Rulers

1072–1101	Count	Roger I, brother of Robert Guiscard	b. 1031 d. 1101
1101–1105	Count	Simon, son of Roger I	
1105–1130	Count	Roger II, son of Roger I	b. 1093 d. 1154
1130–1154	King	Roger II	
1154–1166	King	Guillaume I the Bad, son of Roger II	d. 1166
1166–1189	King	Guillaume II the Good, son of Guillaume I	d. 1189
1189–1194	King	Tancred, grandson of Roger II	d. 1194

Hohenstaufen Dynasty

1194–1197	Emperor	Henry VI, son of Frederick I	b. 1165 d. 1197

Henry VI kept the crusader King Richard I a prisoner for two years before ransoming him at a heavy price. Henry died as he was about to set off on a crusade of his own to the Holy Land.

1197–1250	Emperor	Frederick II, son of Henry VI	b. 1194 d. 1250
1250–1254	King	Conrad IV, son of Frederick II	b. 1228 d. 1254
1258–1266	King	Manfred, son of Frederick II	b. 1232? killed 1266
1266–1268	King	Conradin, son of Conrad IV	b. 1252 beheaded 1268

1268–1282	King	Charles I of Anjou, son of Louis VIII	b. 1226 d. 1285
		(See Naples*)*	

House of Aragon

1282–1285	King	Pedro III, son-in-law of Manfred	b. 1236 d. 1285
		(See Aragon*)*	
1285–1295	King	James II, son of Pedro III	b. 1260? d. 1327
1296–1337	King	Frederick II, son of Pedro III	b. 1272 d. 1337
1337–1342	King	Pedro II, son of Frederick II	
1342–1355	King	Louis, son of Pedro II	
1355–1377	King	Frederick III, son of Pedro II	b. 1341 d. 1377
1377–1402	Queen	Maria, daughter of Frederick III	
1402–1409	King	Martin I, son-in-law of Frederick III	
1409–1410	King	Martin II	
1410–1416	King	Ferdinand I	
1416–1458	King	Alphonso I	
		King of Naples and Sicily from 1435 to 1458	
1458–1479	King	John	
1479–1516	King	Ferdinand II (of United Spain)	

Sicily was under Spain from 1479 to 1707; under Austria from 1707 to 1713; under Savoy from 1713 to 1720; under Austria again from 1720 to 1734; under Spain again from 1734 to 1759; and was part of the Kingdom of the Two Sicilies from 1759 to 1860.

■ Tuscany

House of Medici of Florence

1434–1464	Ruler	Cosimo the Elder	b. 1389 d. 1464
1464–1469	Ruler	Piero, son of Cosimo	b. 1414 d. 1469
1469–1491	Ruler	Lorenzo I the Magnificent, son of Piero	b. 1449 d. 1492

Lorenzo the Magnificent was a tyrannical ruler but made Florence rich and prosperous. He was largely responsible for causing the Tuscan dialect to become the standard speech in Italy. He was a distinguished writer, poet, and patron of the arts.

1492–1494	Ruler	Pietro, son of Lorenzo I	b. 1471 d. 1503
1494–1498	Ruler	Girolamo Savonarola	b. 1452 executed 1498
		Medici Banished from Florence	
1498–1502		Period of disorder	
1502–1512	Ruler	Piero Soderini	b. 1448 d. 1552
		Medici Restored	
1512–1514	Ruler	Giuliano	b. 1479 d. 1516

1513–1519	Duke	Lorenzo II, son of Pietro	b. 1492 d. 1519
1519–1523	Duke	Giulio (Pope Clement VII)	b. *c.* 1475 d. *c.* 1534
1524–1527	Duke	Ippolito, grandson of Pietro	b. 1511 d. 1535
1531–1537	Duke	Alessandro, son of Lorenzo	b. 1510 assassinated 1537
1537–1569	Duke	Cosimo I, son of Giovanni	b. 1519 d. 1574
1569–1574	Grand Duke	Cosimo I	
1574–1587	Grand Duke	Francesco, son of Cosimo I	b. 1541 d. 1587
1587–1609	Grand Duke	Ferrante I, son of Cosimo I	b. 1549 d. 1609
1609–1621	Grand Duke	Cosimo II, son of Ferrante I	b. 1590 d. 1621
1621–1670	Grand Duke	Ferrante II, son of Cosimo II	b. 1610 d. 1670
1670–1723	Grand Duke	Cosimo III, son of Ferrante II	b. 1642 d. 1723
1723–1737	Grand Duke	Giovanni, son of Cosimo III	b. 1671 d. 1737

House of Lorraine

1737–1765	Grand Duke	Francis I (Franz Stefan)	b. 1708 d. 1765
		Francis became the Emperor of Holy Roman Empire in 1745.	
1765–1790	Grand Duke	Leopold I, son of Francis I	b. 1747 d. 1792
1790–1801	Grand Duke	Ferrante III, son of Leopold I	b. 1769 d. 1824
1801–1814		*Tuscany Became a French Protectorate*	

■ Etruria

Etruria was the Napoleonic revival of the Latin name for Tuscany.

1801–1803	King	Louis I of Parma (see Parma)	b. 1773 d. 1803
1803–1807	King	Charles Louis, son of Louis I of Parma	b. 1799 d. 1883
1807–1809		*Etruria Became a French Department*	

■ Tuscany

| 1809–1814 | Grand Duchess | Elise Bonaparte, sister of Napoleon | b. 1777 d. 1820 |
| | | *Elise was made Princess of Piombino and Lucca in 1805.* | |

House of Lorraine (restored)

1814–1824	Grand Duke	Ferrante III (restored)	
1824–1859	King	Leopold II, son of Ferrante III	abdicated 1859 b. 1797 d. 1870
1859–1860	King	Ferrante IV, son of Leopold II	b. 1835 d. 1908
		Tuscany Incorporated into the Kingdom of Italy in 1861	

■ Venice

Venice emerged as an independent city-state in 697. It was ruled by an elected duke or "doge," and acquired control over much of the eastern Mediterranean coast. The later doges are listed below.

1423–1457	Doge	Francesco Foscari	d. 1457
1457–1462	Doge	Pasquale Malipiero	
1462–1471	Doge	Cristoforo Moro	
1471–1473	Doge	Nicolo Trono	
1473–1474	Doge	Nicolo Marcello	
1474–1476	Doge	Pietro Mocenigo	
1476–1478	Doge	Andrea Vendramin	
1478–1485	Doge	Giovanni Mocenigo	
1485–1486	Doge	Marco Barbarigo	
1486–1501	Doge	Agostino Barbarigo	
1501–1521	Doge	Leonardo Loredano	
1521–1523	Doge	Antonio Grimani	b. 1436 d. 1523
1523–1539	Doge	Andrea Gritti	
1539–1545	Doge	Pietro Lando	
1545–1553	Doge	Francesco Donato	
1553–1554	Doge	Marcantonio Trevisano	
1554–1556	Doge	Francesco Venier	
1556–1559	Doge	Lorenzo Priuli	
1559–1567	Doge	Girolamo Priuli	
1567–1570	Doge	Pietro Loredano	
1570–1577	Doge	Alviso I Mocenigo	
1577–1578	Doge	Sebastiano Venier	
1578–1585	Doge	Nicolo da Ponte	
1585–1595	Doge	Pasquale Cicogna	
1595–1606	Doge	Marino Grimani	
1607–1612	Doge	Leonardo Donato	
1612–1615	Doge	Marcantonio Memo	
1615–1618	Doge	Giovanni Bembo	
1618	Doge	Nicolo Dona	
1618–1623	Doge	Antonio Priuli	
1623–1625	Doge	Francesco Centurioni	
1625–1630	Doge	Giovanni I Cornari	
1630–1631	Doge	Nicolo Centurioni	
1631–1646	Doge	Francesco Erizzo	
1646–1655	Doge	Francesco Molin	

1655–1656	Doge	Carlo Contarini	
1656–1658	Doge	Bertuccio Valier	
1658–1659	Doge	Giovanni Pesaro	
1659–1675	Doge	Domenico Contarini	
1675–1676	Doge	Nicolo Sagredo	
1676–1683	Doge	Alviso Contarini	
1683–1688	Doge	Marcantonio Giustiniani	
1688–1694	Doge	Francesco Morosini	b. 1618 d. 1694
1694–1700	Doge	Silvestro Valier	
1700–1709	Doge	Alviso II Mocenigo	
1709–1722	Doge	Giovanni II Cornari	
1722–1732	Doge	Alviso III Mocenigo	
1733–1734	Doge	Carlo Ruzzini	
1734–1741	Doge	Alviso Pisani	
1741–1752	Doge	Pietro Grimani	
1752–1762	Doge	Francesco Loredano	
1762–1763	Doge	Marco Foscarini	b. 1696 d. 1763
1763–1779	Doge	Alviso IV Mocenigo	
1779–1789	Doge	Paolo Renier	
1789–1797	Doge	Lodovico Manin	

Napoleon conquered Venice in 1797 and ceded it to Austria. It was ceded to the Napoleonic Kingdom of Italy in 1805, regained by Austria in 1814, and fell to the new Kingdom of Italy under the House of Savoy in 1866.

Ivory Coast *See* Côte d'Ivoire

Jamaica (Official U.N. Name)

Jamaica was discovered by Christopher Columbus in 1494. It was under Spanish rule to 1655 and then British rule from 1670. It has been an independent state and a member of the British Commonwealth since 1962.

1962–1972	Governor-General	Clifford Clarence Campbell	
1962–1967	Prime Minister	William Alexander Bustamante	b. 1884 d. 1977
1967	Prime Minister	Donald Burns Sangster	b. 1911 d. 1967
1967–1972	Prime Minister	Hugh Lawson Shearer	
1972–1980	Prime Minister	Michael Manley	
1980–1989	Prime Minister	Edward Seaga	
1989–1992	Prime Minister	Michael Manley	
1992–	Prime Minister	Percival J. "P.J." Patterson	

Japan (Official U.N. Name)

According to legend, the Japanese state was founded in 660 B.C. However, authentic dates are not available for the periods prior to the A.D. 6th century.

592–628	Empress	Suiko Tenno
592–622	Regent	Prince Shotoku
628– ?	Emperor	Jomei
? –645	Empress	Kogyoku
645–661	Heads of State	Nakatomi Kamatari and Naka-no-oe
661–671	Emperor	Tenchi
672–686	Emperor	Temmu
686–697	Empress	Jito
697–703	Emperor	Mommu
703–724?	Empress	Gemmyo
724–749	Emperor	Shomu
749–758	Empress	Koken (abdicated)
758–764	Emperor	Junnin
764–770	Empress	Shotoku (Koken restored, assumed new name)
770–781	Emperor	Konin
781–806	Emperor	Kammu

Following the reign of Kammu, power passed to noble families, notably the Fujiwaras, while emperors became mere figureheads.

1017–1067	Regent	Fujiwara Yorimichi
1068–1072	Emperor	Gosanjo
1072–1129	Emperor	Shirakawa
1129–1156	Emperor	Toba
1156–1158	Emperor	Goshirakawa
1160–1181	Regent	Taira Kiyomori
1180–1185	Emperor	Antoku
1185–1199	Shogun	Minamoto Yoritomo
1199–1203	Shogun	Minamoto Yorii
1203–1219	Shogun	Minamoto Sanetomo
1224–1242	Shogunal Regent	Hojo Yasutoki
1318–1339	Emperor	Godaigo
1338–1573		*Period of Feudal Disorder*

■ *Edo Shogunate*

1603–1605	Shogun	Iyeyasu Tokugawa	b. 1542 d. 1616

1605–1623	Shogun	Hidetada, son of Iyeyasu	b. 1579 d. 1633
1623–1651	Shogun	Iyemitsu, son of Hidetada	b. 1604 d. 1651
1651–1680	Shogun	Iyetsuna	b. 1641 d. 1680
1680–1709	Shogun	Tsunayoshi	b. 1646 d. 1709
1709–1712	Shogun	Iyenobu	b. 1662 d. 1712
1713–1716	Shogun	Iyetsugu	b. 1709 d. 1716
1716–1745	Shogun	Yoshimune	b. 1684 d. 1751
1754–1760	Shogun	Iyeshize	b. 1711 d. 1761
1760–1786	Shogun	Iyeharu	b. 1736 d. 1786
1787–1837	Shogun	Iyenari	b. 1773 d. 1841
1837–1853	Shogun	Iyeoshi, son of Iyenari	b. 1793 d. 1853
1853–1858	Shogun	Iyesada, brother of Iyeoshi	b. 1853 d. 1858
1858–1866	Shogun	Iyemochi	b. 1846 d. 1866
1866–1867	Shogun	Yoshinobu (Hitotsubashi)	b. 1837 d. 1913
		Meiji Restoration	
1867–1912	Emperor	Meiji (Mutsuhito), son of Komei	b. 1852 d. 1912
1912–1926	Emperor	Taisho (Yoshihito), son of Mutsuhito	b. 1879 d. 1926
1926–1989	Emperor	Hirohito, son of Yoshihito	b. 1901 d. 1989
1989–	Emperor	Akihito	b. 1933

■ Statesmen

1886–1901	Prime Minister	Hirobumi Ito	b. 1841 d. 1909
1913–1914	Prime Minister	Gombei Yamamoto	b. 1852 d. 1933
1923–1924	Prime Minister	Gombei Yamamoto	
1936–1937	Prime Minister	Koki Hirota	b. 1878 d. 1948
1937–1939	Prime Minister	Fumimaro Konoye	b. 1891 d. 1945
1940–1941	Prime Minister	Fumimaro Konoye	
1945	Prime Minister	Prince Higashikuni	
1945–1946	Prime Minister	Kijuro Shidehara	b. 1872 d. 1951
1946–1947	Prime Minister	Shigeru Yoshida	b. 1878
1947–1948	Prime Minister	Tetsu Katayama	b. 1887
1948	Prime Minister	Hitoshi Ashida	
1948–1954	Prime Minister	Shigeru Yoshida	
		American Occupation from 1945 to 1952	
1945–1951	Allied C in C	Douglas MacArthur	b. 1878 d. 1964
1951–1952	Allied C in C	Matthew B. Ridgway	b. 1895
1952		*Japan Regains Status as Sovereign State*	

1954–1956	Prime Minister	Ichiro Hatoyama	
1956–1957	Prime Minister	Tanzan Ishibashi	
1957–1960	Prime Minister	Nobusuke Kishi	
1960–1964	Prime Minister	Hayato Ikeda	b. 1899
1964–1972	Prime Minister	Eisaku Sato	b. 1901
1972–1974	Prime Minister	Kakuei Tanaka	
1994–1976	Prime Minister	Miki Takeo	
1976–1978	Prime Minister	Takeo Fukuda	
1978–1980	Prime Minister	Masayoshi Ohira	
1980–1982	Prime Minister	Zenko Suzuki	
1982–1987	Prime Minister	Yasuhiro Nakasone	
1987–1989	Prime Minister	Noboru Takeshita	
1989	Prime Minister	Sosuke Uno	
1989–1991	Prime Minister	Toshiki Kaifu	
1991–1993	Prime Minister	Kiichi Miyazawa	
1993–1994	Prime Minister	Morihiro Hosokawa	
1994	Prime Minister	Tsutomu Hata	
1994–1996	Prime Minister	Tomiichi Murayama	
1996–1998	Prime Minister	Ryutaro Hashimoto	
1998–2000	Prime Minister	Keizo Obuchi	
2000–2001	Prime Minister	Yoshiro Mori	
2001–	Prime Minister	Junichiro Koizumi	

Jerusalem *See* Israel

Jordan (Hashemite Kingdom of Jordan)

Transjordanian Palestine was previously under Turkish rule and British mandate. Jordan declared independence in 1923.

1921–1946	Amir	Abdullah Ben Al-Hussein	b. 1882 assassinated 1951

Name changed to the Hashemite Kingdom of the Jordan in 1946.

1946–1951	King	Abdullah Ben Al-Hussein	
1951–1952	King	Talal Ben Abdullah	b. 1909 abdicated 1952
1953–1999	King	Hussein Ben Tala	b. 1935
1999–	King	Abdullah bin al-Hussein II	

Judah *See* Israel

Kazakhstan (Republic of Kazakhstan)

Kazakhstan declared independence from the Soviet Union on December 16, 1991.

| 1991– | President | Nursultan Nazarbayev | b. 1940 |

Kenya (Republic of Kenya)

Formerly a British colony, Kenya became an independent state as a member of the Commonwealth in 1963. It became a republic in 1964.

1964–1978	President	Jomo Kenyatta	b. 1892? d. 1978
1978–2002	President	Daniel Toroitich arap Moi	b. 1924
2002–	President	Emilio Mwai Kibaki	b. 1931

Kiribati (Republic of Kiribati)

Comprised of a number of coral atolls in the Pacific, including Christmas Island, the Kiribati nation gained its independence from the United Kingdom in 1979.

1979–1991	President	Ieremia Tabai	
1991–1994	President	Teatao Teannaki	
1994–2003	President	Teburoro Tito	
2003–	President	Anote Tong	

Korea *See* North Korea; South Korea

Kuwait (State of Kuwait)

Kuwait had a special relationship with Britain from 1899 to 1961, and became completely independent in 1961.

1950–1965	Amir	Shaikh Abdullah as-Salim as-Sabah	b. 1890
1965–1977	Amir	Shaikh Sabah al-Salim al-Sabah	b. 1913
1977–	Amir	Jaber Al-Ahmad Al-Jaber Al-Sabah	b. 1928

Kyrgyzstan (Kyrgyz Republic)

This nation, with a population of about 5 million in 2004, gained its independence from the Soviet Union in 1991. Askar Akayev, the president of the Kyrgyz Academy of Sciences, has been the president of the nation ever since.

Laos (Lao People's Democratic Republic)

Laos was a French Protectorate from 1893 and became an independent sovereign state within the French Union in 1949.

| 1949–1959 | King | Sisavang Vong | b. 1885 d. 1959 |
| 1959–1975 | King | Savang Vatthana | b. 1907 |

A Communist revolution by Lao People's Revolutionary Party,
led by President Khamtay Siphandone, took place in 1975.

Latvia (Republic of Latvia)

Formerly a province of the Russian Empire, Latvia was an independent state from 1918 to 1940.
It was occupied by Germany from 1941 to 1944 and then made a Soviet republic from 1944 to 1991.

1918–1920	Chairman of Council	Jan Chakste	
1920–1922	President of Assembly	Jan Chakste	
1922–1925	President	Jan Chakste	
1925–1927	President	Jan Chakste	d. 1927
1927–1929	President	Gustav Zemgals	
1930–1933	President	Albert Kviesis	
1933–1936	President	Albert Kviesis	
1936–1940	President	Karlis Ulmanis	

Latvia's status as a Soviet Republic was never officially recognized
by the United States. De facto *independence was achieved in 1991.*

1990–1993	President (acting)	Anatolijis Gorbunovs
1993–1999	President	Guntis Ulmanis
1999–	President	Vaira Vike-Freiberga

Lebanon (Lebanese Republic)

Lebanon corresponds roughly to ancient Phoenicia, which was later under Macedonian, Roman,
Byzantine, and Ottoman rule.

Part of Ottoman Empire in 1861

1873–1883	Governor	Rustem Pasha	
1883–1892	Governor	Wassa Pasha	d. 1892
1892–1902	Governor	Naoum Pasha	

French Mandate from 1921 to 1941
Became Independent State in 1941
Evacuation of Last Foreign Troops in 1946

1943–1952	President	Sheikh Bishara el Khoury
1952–1958	President	Camille Chamoun
1958–1964	President	Fuad Chehab
1964–1970	President	Charles Helou
1970–1976	President	Suleiman Franjieh
1976–1982	President	Elias Sarkis
1982–1988	President	Amine Gemayel

1988–1989	Acting President	Selim al-Hoss	
1989	President	Rene Moawad	assassinated 1989
1989–1998	President	Elias Hrawi	
1988–	President	Emile Lahoud	

Under the constitution, Emile Lahoud's term was only intended to be six years. However, in 2004, under military pressure from the Syrian government, the parliament voted to extend his term for an additional three years.

Leon *See* Spain

Lesotho (Kingdom of Lesotho)

Formerly the British Protectorate of Basutoland, Lesotho became an independent monarchy in 1966.

1966–1987	King	Motlotlehi Moshoeshoe II	Exiled
1987–1995	King	Letsie III	
1995–1996	King	Motlotlehi Moshoeshoe II, reinstated	d. 1996
1996–	King	Letsie III (reascended)	
1966–1986	Prime Minister	Chief Joseph Leabua Jonathan	b. 1914
1993–1998	Prime Minister	Ntsu Mokhehle	
1998		*Interim Political Authority*	
1998	Prime Minister	Pakalitha Mosisili	b. 1945

Liberia (Republic of Liberia)

Founded by the American Colonization Society in 1822, Liberia was recognized as an independent black republic in 1847.

1848–1856	President	Joseph. Jenkins Roberts
1856–1864	President	Steven Allen Benson
1864–1868	President	Daniel B. Warner
1868–1870	President	James S. Payne
1870–1871	President	Edwin .J. Roye
1871–1872	President	J.S. Smith
1872–1876	President	J.J. Roberts
1876–1878	President	J.S. Payne (2nd term)
1878–1883	President	A.W. Gardener
1883–1884	President	A.F. Russell
1884–1892	President	H.R. Johnson
1892–1898	President	J.J. Cheeseman
1898–1902	President	W.D. Coleman

1902 1904	President	G.W. Gibson	
1904–1912	President	A. Barclay	
1912–1920	President	Daniel Howard	
1920–1930	President	Charles Dunbar Burgess King	
1930–1944	President	Edwin J. Barclay	
1944–1971	President	William Tubman	
1971–1980	President	William R. Tolbert	
1980–1990	President	Samuel K. Doe	
1990–1993	President	Amos Sawyer	
1993	President	Bismarck Kuyon	
1993–1994	President	Philip Banks	
1994–1995	President	David Kpormakor	
1995–1996	President	Wilton Sankawulo	
1996–1997	President	Ruth Perry	
1997–2004	President	Charles Ghankay Taylor	
2003	President	Moses Blah	
2003–	President	Charles Gyude Bryant	

Libya (Great Socialist People's Libyan Arab Jamahariya)

Throughout most of history, the peoples of Libya have been subjected to varying degrees of foreign control. Under the Ottoman Empire, the region constituted the territories of Tripolitania and Cyrenaica, which were occupied by Italy from 1911 to 1939. When Libya declared its independence in 1951, it was the first country to gain independence through the newly formed United Nations.

1951–1969	King	Idris I	Exiled 1969
1969–	Dictator	Muammar Gaddafi	b. 1942

Liechtenstein (Principality of Liechtenstein)

Liechtenstein was a principality of Vaduz that was formed in 1342. It was constituted as the Principality of Liechtenstein in 1719 and became an independent state in 1866.

1938–1989	Prince	Franz Josef II	b. 1906
1989–	Prince	Hans Adam II	

Lithuania (Republic of Lithuania)

Lithuania was an independent Grand Duchy until 1385, when it was united with Poland. From 1795 it was a province of the Russian Empire; an independent republic from 1918 to 1940; and under German occupation from 1941 to 1944.

1919–1921	Provisional President	Antanas Smetona	b. 1874 d. 1944
1922–1926	President	Antanas Stulgenskis	

1926	President	V. Grinius (overthrown)	
1926–1940	President	Antanas Smetona	

In 1944 Lithuania was occupied by Russian troops and made a Soviet Republic. Although independence was once again declared in 1990, Soviet troops were only withdrawn in 1993.

1990–1992	President	Vytautas Landsbergis	
1992–1998	President	Algirdas Mykolas Brazauskas	
1998–2003	President	Valdas Adamkus	
2003–2004	President	Rolandas Paksas	
2004	Acting President	Arturas Paulauskas	
2004–		Valdas Adamkus	

Luxembourg (Grand Duchy of Luxembourg)

Luxembourg was a county until Wenceslaus I, the first Duke of Luxembourg, came to power. It was a duchy until 1815, when it became a Grand Duchy.

■ House of Ardennes

963–998	Count	Sigefroi	
998–1026	Count	Henry I	
1026–1047	Count	Henry II	
1047–1059	Count	Giselbert	
1059–1086	Count	Conrad I	d. 1086
1086–1096	Count	Henry III	
1096–1129	Count	William	
1129–1136	Count	Conrad II	

■ House of Namur

1136–1196	Count	Henry IV the Blind	d. 1196
1196–1247	Countess	Ermesinde	d. 1247

■ House of Limbourg

1247–1281	Count	Henry V	b. 1217 d. 1281
1281–1288	Count	Henry VI	
1288–1310	Count	Henry VII (German emperor 1308–1313)	b. 1275? d. 1313
1310–1346	Count	John the Blind of Bohemia, son of Henry VII	b. 1296 d. 1346
1346–1353	Count	Charles I, son of John (Emperor Charles IV)	b. 1316 d. 1378
1353–1383	Duke	Wenceslaus I, son of John the Blind	b. 1337 d. 1383

		Became Duchy in 1354		
1383–1388	Duke	Wenceslaus II (Emperor), son of Charles	b. 1361	d. 1419
1388–1411	Duke	Jobst of Moravia		
1411–1412	Duke	Wenceslaus II		
1412–1415	Duke	Anton of Brabant and Elizabeth of Görlitz (pretenders)		
1415–1419	Duchess	Elizabeth (alone)		
1419–1425	Duke	Johann of Bavaria		
1425–1444	Duchess	Elizabeth (alone)		
		Joined Burgundy in 1444		

■ House of Burgundy

1443–1467	Duke	Philip III the Good, son of John the Fearless	b. 1396	d. 1467
1467–1477	Duke	Charles the Bold, son of Philip the Good	b. 1433	d. 1477
1477–1482	Duchess	Mary of Burgundy, daughter of Charles the Bold	b. 1456	d. 1482
1482–1506	Duke	Philip I the Handsome, son of Mary	b. 1478	d. 1506
1506–1555	Emperor	Charles V, son of Philip I	b. 1500	d. 1558

■ Spanish Rule

1555–1598	King	Philip II, son of Charles V	b. 1527	d. 1598
1598–1621	Archduke	Albert	b. 1559	d. 1621
1621–1665	King	Philip IV, son of Philip III	b. 1605	d. 1665
1665–1684	King	Charles II, son of Philip IV	b. 1661	d. 1700

■ French Rule

1684–1697	King	Louis XIV, son of Louis XIII	b. 1638	d. 1715

■ Spanish Rule

1697–1700	King	Charles II	b. 1661	d. 1700
1700–1711	King	Philip of Anjou, grandson of Louis XIV	b. 1683	d. 1746
1711–1714	Elector	Maximilian II Emanuel of Bavaria	b. 1662	d. 1726

■ Austrian Rule

1714–1740	Emperor	Charles VI, son of Leopold I	b. 1685	d. 1740
1740–1780	Empress	Maria Theresa, daughter of Charles VI	b. 1717	d. 1780
1780–1790	Emperor	Joseph II, son of Maria Theresa	b. 1741	d. 1790
1790–1792	Emperor	Leopold II, brother of Joseph II	b. 1747	d. 1792

| 1792–1795 | Emperor | Francis II | b. 1768 d. 1835 |

■ French Rule

1795–1799		*The Directory*
1799–1814		*Consulate and Empire*
1814–1815		*Grand Duchy Created by Congress of Vienna*

■ House of Orange

The Grand Duchy was linked by personal union with the crown of Holland.

| 1815–1840 | Grand Duke | William I, King of the Netherlands, son of William V, Prince of Orange | b. 1772 d. 1843 |

In 1806 William VI of Nassau lost his lands because he refused to join the Confederation of the Rhine. When he became King of the Netherlands (as William I) in 1815, he was granted the title of Grand Duke of Luxembourg.

| 1840–1849 | Grand Duke | William II, son of William I | b. 1792 d. 1849 |
| 1849–1890 | Grand Duke | William III, son of William II | b. 1817 d. 1890 |

■ House of Nassau

1890–1905	Grand Duke	Adolphus, Duke of Nassau	b. 1817 d. 1905
1905–1912	Grand Duke	William IV, son of Adolphus	b. 1852 d. 1912
1912–1919	Grand Duchess	Marie-Adélaïde, daughter of William IV	abdicated 1919 b. 1894 d. 1924
1919–1964	Grand Duchess	Charlotte, sister of Marie-Adélaïde	b. 1896
1964–1999	Grand Duke	Jean, son of Charlotte	abdicated b. 1921
1999–	Grand Duke	Henri, son of Jean	b. 1955

Lydia

Lydia was situated on the Aegean coast of Asia Minor.

c. 700 B.C.	King	Gyges
617–560	King	Alyattes
560–546	King	Croesus

Lydia was conquered by Cyrus the Great of Persia in 546 B.C. Thereafter, it was a dependency of Persia, Macedonia, Syria, and eventually a province of Rome.

Macedonia (Republic of Macedonia)

■ Ancient Kingdom

729 B.C.	King	Perdiccas I	
700	King	Philip I	
500	King	Amyntas I	d. 498
498–454	King	Alexander I	
454–413	King	Perdiccas II, son of Alexander I	d. 413?
413–399	King	Archelaus, son of Perdiccas II	murdered 399
394–370	King	Amyntas II, nephew of Perdiccas II	
369–368	King	Alexander II	
368–360	King	Perdiccas III, brother of Philip II	d. 359
360–359	King	Amyntas III, grandson of Amyntas II	executed 336
359–335	King	Philip II, brother of Perdiccas III	b. 382 assassinated 336
336–323	King	Alexander III the Great, son of Philip II	b. 356 d. 323

At the age of sixteen, Alexander the Great quelled a rising of Macedonian hill tribes. Appointed Captain-General of the Hellenes, he crossed into Asia in 334 B.C. Within twelve years, he destroyed the Persian Empire and conquered Syria, Phoenicia, Egypt, Persia, Bactria, Bokhara, and the Punjab. Alexander took the Macedonian army as far eastward as the Hyphasis (Beas) in India.

323	King	Philip III (Aridaeus), son of Philip II	murdered 317
323–310	King	Alexander IV, son of Alexander the Great	murdered 310
316–297	King	Cassander, son of Antipater	b. 350? d. 297
306–301	King	Antigonus I	b. 382 d. 301

Antigonus Cyclops, one of Alexander the Great's generals, tried to make himself master of Asia. He briefly secured control of Asia Minor and Syria after a war with Seleucus, Lysimachus, and Cassander. His invasion of Ptolemy's Egypt was unsuccessful. Later, at the age of eighty-one, he was killed in battle with his three old enemies.

297–294	King	Alexander V, son of Cassander	murdered 294
294–283	King	Demetrius I Poliorcetes, son of Antigonus	b. 337? d. 283
283–273	King	Antigonus II Gonatas, grandson of Antigonus I	b. 319?
273	King	Pyrrhus of Epirus	b. 318? killed 272
272–239	King	Antigonus II Gonatus	
239–232	King	Demetrius II, son of Antigonus Gonatus	d. 230
232	King	Philip	
229–221	King	Antigonus III Doson, nephew of Antigonus Gonatas	d. 221
220–179	King	Philip V, son of Demetrius II	b. 237 d. 179

179–168	King	Perseus, son of Philip V	d. 165?
		Became Roman Province in 168	

■ Modern Macedonia

In 1991 Macedonia declared its independence from Yugoslavia.

1991–1999	President	Kiro Gligorov
1999–	President	Boris Trajkovski

Madagascar (Republic of Madagascar)

Discovered by the Portuguese in 1506, Madagascar remained independent under a native dynasty until it was annexed by France in the late 19th century. Most of the recent sovereigns are listed below.

1810–1828	King	Radama I	
1828–1861	Queen	Ranavalona I	
1861–1863	King	Radama II (assassinated)	d. 1863
1863–1868	Queen	Rasoaherina	
1868–1883	Queen	Ranavalona II	
1883–1896	Queen	Ranavalona III (deposed)	b. 1861 d. 1916
		Monarchy Abolished under French Rule	
		Madagascar became independent in 1960 as the Malagasy Republic.	
1960–1972	President	Philibert Tsiranana	b. 1912
1972–1975	President	Gabriel Ramanantsoa	
1975	President	Richard Ratsimandrava	assassinated
1975–1993	President	Didier Ratsiraka	
1993–1996	President	Albert Zafy	
1996–1997	President	Norbert Ratsirahonana	
1997–2001	President	Didier Ratsiraka	
2001–2005		*Disputed Presidency*	
2005–	President	Marc Ravalomanana	

Malawi (Republic of Malawi)

Formerly the British Protectorate of Nyasaland, Malawi became an independent state and member of the British Commonwealth in 1964.

1964–1966	Governor-General	Sir Glyn Smallwood Jones	b. 1908
1964–1966	Prime Minister	Hastings Kamuzu Banda	b. 1905
		Republic Proclaimed in 1966	
1966–1994	President	Hastings Kamuzu Banda	
1994–2004	President	Bakili Muluzi	
2004–	President	Bingu wa Mutharika	

Malaysia (Official U.N. Name)

The Federation of Malaysia came into being in 1963, uniting the Federation of Malaya with the former British Possessions of Singapore, Sabah (British North Borneo), and Sarawak. Singapore seceded from the Federation in 1965. Malaysia is a constitutional monarchy in which the nominal head of state is a king who is elected for a five-year term among the nine sultans of the peninsular Malaysian states.

1965–1970	Prime Minister	Tunku Abdul Rahman	b. 1903
1970–1976	Prime Minister	Tun Abdul Razak	b. 1922
1976–1981	Prime Minister	Tun Hussein Onn	b. 1922
1981–2003	Prime Minister	Mahathir bin Mohomad	b. 1925
2003–	Prime Minister	Abdullah Ahmad Badawi	b. 1939

Maldives (Republic of Maldives)

Now a republic, the Maldives were governed as an independent Islamic sultanate for most of the last millennium. The sultanate was abolished three years after its independence from Britain in 1965.

1964–1968	Sultan	Al Amir S'r Mohamed Farid Didi
1964–1978	Prime Minister/ President	Ibrahim Nasir
1978–	President	Maumoon Abdul Gayoom

Mali (Republic of Mali) *See also* Senegal

Formerly the French Overseas Territory of Soudan, Mali was an autonomous republic within the French Community from 1958 to 1960. Under the name of the Sudanese Republic, it became jointly independent with Senegal in 1960 as the Mali Federation. After Senegal withdrew from the Federation in the same year, the Sudanese Republic retained the name Mali.

1960–1968	President	Modibo Keita
1968–1992	President	Moussa Traore
1992–2002	President	Alpha Oumar Konare
2002–	President	Amadou Toumani Toure

Malta (Republic of Malta)

Malta was under Roman rule from 216 B.C. to A.D. 870; under the Arabs from 870 to1090; under the Normans from 1090; under the Knights of St. John from 1530 to 1798; under the protection of Britain from 1802 to 1814; and was annexed to Britain from 1814 to 1964. It became an independent state within the British Commonwealth in 1964.

1964–1971	Prime Minister	George Borg Olivier
1971–1984	Prime Minister	Dominic Mintoff
1984–1987	Prime Minister	Carmelo Mifsud Bonnici
1987–1996	Prime Minister	Edward Fenech Adami
1996–1998	Prime Minister	Alfred Sant
1998–2004	Prime Minister	Edward Fenech Adami
2004–	Prime Minister	Lawrence Gonzi

Marshall Islands (Republic of the Marshall Islands)

The Marshall Islands have been a parliamentary democracy in free association with the United States since 1986. The Head of State in 2005 was President Kessai H. Note.

Mauritania (Islamic Republic of Mauritania)

Mauritania was an autonomous republic within the French Community from 1958 to 1960, and has been fully independent since 1960. The modern republic of Mauritania does not correspond territorially to the ancient North African Kingdom with the same name.

1960	Prime Minister	Moktar Ould Daddah	b. 1924
1961–1978	President and Prime Minister	Moktar Ould Daddah	
1978–1979	Military leader	Mustapha Ould Salek	
1980–1984	Military leader	Mohamed Khouna Ould Haidalla	
1984–	Prime Minister	Maaouiya Sid'Ahmed Taya	

Mauritius (Republic of Mauritius)

Mauritius was settled by the Dutch in 1638; was under the French from 1721 to 1810; was a British colony from 1810 to 1967; and became independent in 1968.

1968–1982	Prime Minister	Sir Seewoosagur Ramgoola
1982–1995	Prime Minister	Sir Anerood Jugnauth
1995–2000	Prime Minister	Navinchandra Ramgoolam
2000–2003	Prime Minister	Sir Anerood Jugnauth
2003–	Prime Minister	Paul Raymond Berenger

Mesopotamia *See* Assyria; Babylonia; Iraq

Mexico (United Mexican States)

Prior to the Spanish conquest of Mexico, many civilizations rose and declined, including the Olmecs, Mayas, and Toltecs. The Aztecs were descended from barbarian tribes who had conquered earlier people of a higher culture and assumed their ways.

■ Aztec Civilization
c. A.D. 1200–1524

	King	Huitzilihuitl	sacrificed

City-state of Tlatelolco (Tlatelolca)

Tlatelolco was founded between 1325 and 1338.

1375–	King	Cuacuauhpitzahuac

−1428	King	Tlacateotl	executed 1428
c. 1429–1440	King	Nezahualcoyotl	
−1473	King	Moquiuix	

City-state of Tenochitlan (Tenochca)

Tenochitlan was founded around 1325.

1375–	*Huetlatoani* (Emperor)	Acamapicktli	
−1428	*Huetlatoani* (Emperor)	Chimalpopoca	executed 1428
1428–1436	*Huetlatoani* (Emperor)	Itzcoatl	b. 1360? d. 1440?
1440–1469	*Huetlatoani* (Emperor)	Mocteczuma Ilhuicamira (Montezuma I)	c. 1390–1464
1469–1481	*Huetlatoani* (Emperor)	Axayacatl	d. 1477
1486–1502	*Huetlatoani* (Emperor)	Ahuitzotl	
1502–1520	*Huetlatoani* (Emperor)	Mocteczuma Xocoyotzin (Montezuma II)	b. 1480 d. 1520
1520–1525	*Huetlatoani* (Emperor)	Cuauhtémoc	d. 1525

■ Tepanec Empire (1347–1427)

−1427	*Huetlatoani* (Emperor)	Tezozomoc	d. 1427

■ Tarascan Civilization (c. 1400–1522)

c. 1370	King	Tariacuri	
	King	Tzitzie Pandacuare	
−1522	King	Tagoxoan Zincicha	

■ Spanish Conquest and Colonization

1517	Discoverer	Francisco Fernandez de Córdoba	d. 1518
1518	Discoverer	Juan de Grijalva	d. 1527?
1519	Discoverer	Hernán Cortés	b. 1485 d. 1547
		Colony organized by Cortés in 1520	
1522–1524	Governor, Capt.-General	Hernán Cortés	

1524–1526		*Government disintegrated in absence of Cortés.*	
1527–1528	Governor, Capt.-General	Hernán Cortés	
1528–1530		Ruled by first audencia, composed of Beltrán Nuño de Guzmán, Pres.; Alonso Parada; Francisco Maldonado; Juan Ortíz de Matienzo; and Diego Delgadillo	
		Cortés Returned as Captain-general in 1530	
1531		Second audencia, composed of Sebastian Ramírez de Fuenleal, Bishop of Santo Domingo; Juan Salmerón; Francisco Ceynos; Vasco de Quiroga; and Alonso Maldonado	
1535–1550	Viceroy	Antonio Mendoza	b. 1490? d. 1552
1550–1564	Viceroy	Luis de Velasco	d. 1564
1590–1595	Viceroy	Luis de Velasco	
1607–1611	Viceroy	Luis de Velasco	b. 1534 d. 1617
1673–1680	Viceroy	Fray Payo Enríque de Rivera	
1711–1716	Viceroy	Fernando de Alencastre Noroña y Silva	
1722–1734	Viceroy	Juan de Acuña	b. 1658 d. 1734
1746–1755	Viceroy	Juan Francisco de Güemes y Horcasitas, Count of Revillagigedo	b. 1682? d. 1766
1766–1771	Viceroy	Carlos Francisco de Croix, Marqués de Crois	b. 1702 d. 1786
1771–1779	Viceroy	Antonio María Bucareli y Ursúas	b. 1717 d. 1779
1789–1794	Viceroy	Juan Vicente de Güemes Pacheco y Padillo, Count of Revillagigedo	b. 1740 d. 1799
1803–1808	Viceroy	José de Iturrigaray	b. 1742 d. 1814
	Viceroy	Pedro de Garibay	
	Viceroy	Archbishop Francisco Javier de Lizana	
1810–1813	Viceroy	Francisco Javier Venegas	
1813–1816	Viceroy	Félix María Calleja del Rey	b. 1750 d. 1828
1816–1821	Viceroy	Juan Ruiz de Apodeca	b. 1754 d. 1835

■ Independent Mexico

1822–1823	Emperor	Agustin de Iturbide	b. 1783 shot 1824
		Proclaimed Emperor Agustin I in 1821 after establishing Mexican independence, Iturbide led a conservative liberal state. Forced into exile in 1823 and later executed, conservatives think of him as the father of Mexican independence.	
		Republic Established from 1823 to 1824	
1824–1829	President	Guadalupe Victoria	b. 1789 d. 1843
1829	President	Vicente Guerrero	b. 1783? shot 1831
1829	President (acting)	José María de Bocanegra	

1829–1832	President	Anastasio Bustamante	b. 1780	d. 1853
1832	President (acting)	Melchor Múzquiz		
1832–1833	President	Manuel Gómez Pedraza	b. 1788?	d. 1851
1833–1835	President	Antonio López de Santa Anna	b. 1795?	d. 1876

General Santa Anna was an acclaimed hero after many victories over the Spanish during Mexico's fight for independence. Due to his experience, he was sent to Texas to crush the revolution and subsequently became commander at the Battle of the Alamo and Goliad before his defeat by Sam Houston.

1835–1836	President	Miguel Barragán		
1836–1837	President	José Justo Corro		
1837–1841	President	Anastasio Bustamante		
1841	President (acting)	Javier Echeverría		
1841–1842	President	Antonio López de Santa Anna		
1842–1843	President	Nicolás Bravo	b. 1787?	d. 1854
1843	President (provisional)	Antonio López de Santa Anna		
1843–1844	President	Valentín Canalizo	b. 1797?	d. 1847?
1844	President	Antonio López de Santa Anna		
1844	President (acting)	José Joaquin Herrera	b. 1792	d. 1854
1844	President (acting)	Valentín Canalizo		
1844–1845	President	José Joaquín Herrera		
1846	President	Mariano Paredes y Arrillaga		
1846	President	Nicolás Bravo		
1846	President (acting)	José Mariano Salas		

War with the United States from 1846 to 1848

1846–1847	President (acting)	Valentín Gómes Farías		
1847	President	Antonio López de Santa Anna		
1847	President	Pedro María Anaya		
1847	President	Antonio López de Santa Anna		
1847	President (provisional)	Manuel de la Peña y Peña	b. 1789	d. 1850
1847–1848	President (acting)	Pedro María Anaya		
1848	President	Manuel de la Peña y Peña		
1848–1851	President	José Joaquín Herrera		
1851–1853	President	Mariano Arista	b. 1802	d. 1855
1853	President (acting)	Juan Bautista Ceballos		
1853	President (acting)	Manuel M. Lombardine		
1853–1855	Dictator	Antonio López de Santa Anna		

1855	President (acting)	Martín Carrera	
1855	President (acting)	Juan Álvarez	b. 1790? d. 1867
1855–1857	President	Ignacio Comonfort	b. 1812 killed 1863
1857–1861	President (provisional)	Benito Pablo Juárez	b. 1806 d. 1872

A full-blooded native and Mexico's most revered political hero, Benito Juárez was the first leader to enact truly liberal policies. He opposed the privileges of the clergy and military, and attempted to transfer political power from the rich to the masses.

French Intervention from 1861 to 1867

1864–1867	Emperor	Maximilian	b. 1832 executed 1867

Sent by Napoleon to be Emperor of Mexico because France was unable to collect Mexico's unpaid debts, Maximilian of Austria was opposed by nationalist liberals and was later deserted by Napoleon, who had been influenced by the United States. He was executed by Juárez after a short, ill-fated reign.

1872–1876	President	Sebastián Lerdo de Tejada	
1876	President (provisional)	Porfirio Díaz	b. 1830 d. 1915
1876–1877	President (acting)	Juan N. Méndez	
1877	President (provisional)	Porfirio Diáz	
1877–1880	President	Porfirio Diáz	
1880–1884	President	Manuel González	b. 1833 d. 1893
1884–1911	President	Porfirio Diáz	
1911	President (provisional)	Francisco León De la Barra	b. 1863 d. 1939
1911–1931	President	Francisco Indalecio Madero	b. 1873 shot 1913
1913	President (provisional)	Pedro Lascurain	
1913–1914	President (provisional)	Victoriano Huerta	b. 1854 d. 1916
1914	President (provisional)	Francisco Carbajal	
1914	President	Venustiano Carranza	b. 1859 murdered 1920
1914–1915	President	Eulalio Martín Gutiérrez	
1915	President (provisional)	Roque González Garza	
1915	President (provisional)	Francisco Lagos Cházaro	
1915–1917	President (provisional)	Venustiano Carranza	

1917–1920	President	Venustiano Carranza	

In 1917 Carranza drafted Mexico's Constitution, which was still the basis of its government in 2005. It provided freedom of worship, divided large-landed estates, declared the nation owner of all natural resources, and confiscated all church property.

1920	President (provisional)	Adolfo de la Huerta	d. 1955
1920–1924	President	Alvaro Obregón	b. 1880 assassinated 1928
1924–1928	President	Plutarco Elías Calles	b. 1877 d. 1945
1928–1930	President (provisional)	Emilio Portes Gil	
1930–1932	President	Pascual Ortiz Rubio	
1932–1934	President (provisional)	Abelardo L. Rodríguez	b. 1889
1934–1940	President	Lázaro Cárdenas	b. 1895
1940–1946	President	Manuel Ávila Camacho	b. 1897 d. 1955
1946–1952	President	Miguel Alemán Valdés	
1952–1958	President	Adolfo Ruiz Cortines	
1958–1964	President	Adolfo López Mateos	
1964–1970	President	Gustavo Diaz Ordaz	
1970–1976	President	Luis Echeverría Álvarez	
1976–1982	President	José López Portillo	
1982–1988	President	Miguel de la Madrid Hurtado	
1988–1994	President	Carlos Salinas de Gortari	
1994–200	President	Ernesto Zedillo P. de León	
2000–	President	Vicente Fox Quesada	

■ National Leaders

1810–1815	Revolutionary leader	José María Morélos y Pavon	b. 1765 executed 1815
1810–1811	Revolutionary leader	Miguel Hidalgo y Castillo	b. 1753 executed 1811

Micronesia (Federated States of Micronesia)

Consisting of six hundred and seven islands, Micronesia's system of government since 1986 has been a constitutional confederation in free association with the United States. The president in 2005 was Joseph J. Urusemal.

Moldova (Republic of Moldova)

Admitted to the United Nations in 1992 after the breakdown of the Soviet Union, Moldova rejected efforts of reunification with Romania.

1992	President	Mircea Snegur	

1992–1996	Prime Minister	Andrei Sangheli
1997–2001	President	Petru Lucinschi
2001–	President	Vladimir Voronin

Monaco (Principality of Monaco)

English versions of the names of rulers of French-speaking states are:

Baldwin–Baudouin	John–Jean	Philip–Philippe
Francis–François	James–Jacques	Rudolph–Rodolphe
Henry–Henri	Odo–Eudes	Stephen–Etienne
Hugh–Hugues	Peter–Pierre	Theobald–Thibaut
		William–Guillaume

c. 1100	Ruler	Otto Canella	b. 1070 d. 1143
	Ruler	Grimaldo	
	Ruler	Oberto	
	Ruler	Grimaldi	
	Ruler	Lanfranco	
1310	Seigneur of Cagnes	Rainier I Grimaldi	b. 1267 d. 1314
	Seigneur	Charles I	d. 1357
1407	Seigneur	Rainier II, son of Charles I	b. 1350 d. 1407
		Ambroise/John I/Antoine, sons of Rainier II	
1427–1454	Sole seigneur	John I	b. 1382 d. 1454
1454–1457	Seigneur	Catalan, son of John I	d. 1457
1457	Sovereign	Claudine, daughter of Catalan	b. 1451 d. 1514
1465	Seigneur	Lambert, husband of Claudine	b. 1420 d. 1494
1494–1505	Seigneur	John II, son of Claudine and Lambert	d. 1505
1505–1523	Seigneur	Lucien, brother of John	d. 1523
1523–1532	Seigneur	Augustin, brother of John	d. 1532
1532–1581	Seigneur	Honoré I, son of Lucien	b. 1522 d. 1581
1581–1589	Seigneur	Charles II, son of Honoré I	b. 1555 d. 1589
1589–1604	Seigneur	Hercules I, brother of Charles II	b. 1562 d. 1604
1604–1612	Seigneur	Honoré II, son of Hercules I	b. 1597 d. 1662
1612–1662	Prince	Honoré II	
1662–1701	Prince	Louis I, grandson of Honoré II	b. 1642 d. 1701
1701–1731	Prince	Antoine I, son of Louis I	b. 1661 d. 1731
1731	Princess	Louise-Hippolyte, daughter of Antoine I	b. 1697 d. 1731
1731–1733	Prince	James I, husband of Louise-Hippolyte	abdicated 1733
1733–1795	Prince	Honoré III, son of Louise-Hippolyte, and James I	b. 1720 d. 1795

Monaco was annexed to France in 1793 and restored

to the Grimaldis in 1814.

1795–1819	Prince	Honoré IV, son of Honoré III	b. 1758 d. 1819
1819–1841	Prince	Honoré V, son of Honoré IV	b. 1778 d. 1841
1841–1856	Prince	Florestan I, brother of Honoré V	b. 1785 d. 1856
1856–1889	Prince	Charles III, son of Florestan I	b. 1818 d. 1889
1889–1922	Prince	Albert I, son of Charles III	b. 1848 d. 1922
1922–1949	Prince	Louis II, son of Albert I	b. 1870 d. 1949
1949–2005	Prince	Rainier III, grandson of Louis II	b. 1923 d. 2005
2005–	Prince	Albert II, son of Rainier III	

Albert is the son of Prince Rainier III and the famous American actress, Grace Kelly.

Mongolia (Official U.N. Name)

As Outer Mongolia, Mongolia was tributary to China prior to 1924, when the Republic of Mongolia was established under Russian protection. Inner Mongolia remained under Chinese rule.

| ? –1924 | Khan | Bogdo Gegen Khan | |

In 1924 the Khan was deposed and the Republic was declared.

Although the modern state of Mongolia was admitted to the United Nations in 1961, a government truly independent of the Soviet Union was only established in 1990.

| 1990–1997 | President | Punsalmaagiyn Ochirbat | b. 1942 |
| 1997– | President | Natsagiyn Bagabandi | b. 1950 |

■ Mongol Empire

| 1206–1227 | Khan | Genghis Khan (Temujin) | b. 1162 d. 1227 |

Genghis Khan, the "Very Mighty Ruler," succeeded his father as chief of their tribe at the age of thirteen. A military genius, he became Khan of all the Mongols. He invaded China, Korea, India, Persia, and Russia. At his death, his kingdom stretched from the Pacific to the Volga, and from Siberia to the Persian Gulf.

1227–1232	Khan	Tului (Tule), son of Genghis Khan	
1227–1229	Khan	Jagatai (Chagatai), son of Genghis Khan	d. 1242
1229–1241	Khan	Ogadai, son of Genghis Khan	b. 1185 d. 1241
	Khan	Juji (Juchi), son of Genghis Khan	
1241–1255	Khan	Batu Khan, son of Juji (see Golden Horde)	d. 1255
1246–1248	Khan	Kuyuk, son of Ogadai	d. 1248
1248	Khan	Kaidu, grandson of Ogadai	d. 1301
1251–1259	Khan	Mangu Khan, son of Tului	b. 1207? d. 1259
1259–1294	Khan	Kublai Khan, son of Tului	b. 1216 d. 1294

| 1260–1265 | Khan | Hulagu, son of Tului | b. 1217 d. 1265 |
| | | *(See* China*)* | |

■ Golden Horde

The Golden Horde was an offshoot of the Mongols who briefly ruled over Russia and Eastern Europe. Their Empire fell to Tamerlane in 1395.

1223–1256	Khan	Batu Khan, grandson of Genghis Khan	d. 1256
1257–1267	Khan	Birkai, brother of Batu Khan	d. 1267
1267–1280	Khan	Mangu	
1290–1312	Khan	Toktai	
1313–1340	Khan	Uzbek	d. 1340
1340–1357	Khan	Janibeg Khan, son of Uzbek	murdered 1357
1357	Khan	Berdibek, son of Janibeg Khan	murdered 1370
1370–1381	Khan	Mamai	
1381–1395	Khan	Toktamish (of Eastern Kipchaks)	
1395–1405	Khan	Timur Lenk (Tamerlane), descendant of Ghengis Khan	b. 1336? d. 1405

Montenegro *See* Serbia; Montenegro

Morocco (Kingdom of Morroco)

Morocco corresponds in part to ancient Mauretania. It was under the Romans from the 1st to 5th centuries. It fell to the Vandals in the 5th century and to the Arabs in 682. It was under the Almoravide dynasty from 1061 to 1149; the Almohade dynasty from 1149 to 1269; the Marinide dynastry from 1269 to 1471; the Wattasi dynasty from 1471 to 1548; the Sa'adi (Sherifian) dynasty from 550 to 1668; and the Filali (Alaouite) dynasty from 1668. The recent rulers are below.

1822–1859	Sultan	Abd ur-Rahman II	b. 1778 d. 1859
1859–1873	Sultan	Mohammed XVII	b. 1803 d. 1873
1873–1894	Sultan	Al-Hasan	
1894–1908	Sultan	Abd-ul-Aziz IV (deposed)	b. 1881? d. 1943
1908–1912	Sultan	Mulai Hafid	b. 1875? d. 1937
1912–1927	Sultan	Mulai Yusef	
		French Protectorate from 1912 to 1956	
		Independent Sovereign State since 1956	
1927–1957	Sultan	Sidi Mohammed ben Yusef	b. 1911 d. 1961

(Title changed from Sultan to King)

1957–1961	King	Mohammed V (Sidi Mohammed ben Yusef)	
1961–1999	King	Hassan II, son of Mohammed V	b. 1930 d. 1999
1999-	King	Mohammed VI, son of Hassan II	

Moyen-Congo *See* Congo (Brazzaville)

Mozambique (Republic of Mozambique)

1975–1986	President	Samora Machel
1986–2004	President	Joaquim Chissano
2004–	President	Armando Guebuza

Myanmar *See* Burma

Namibia (Republic of Namibia)

Known as South West Africa while under South African control, Namibia gained independence through a combination of armed rebellion and international pressure.

1990–2004	President	Sam Nujoma
2004–	President	Hifikepunye Pohamba

Nauru (Republic of Nauru)

Admitted to the United Nations in 1999, Nauru is a small oval-shaped island in the western Pacific Ocean.

1998–1999	President	Bernard Dowiyogo
1999–2000	President	Rene Harris
2000–2001	President	Bernard Dowiyogo
2001–2003	President	Rene Harris
2003	President	Bernard Dowiyogo
2003	President	Derog Gioura
2003	President	Ludwig Scotty
2003–2004	President	Rene Harris
2004–	President	Ludwig Scotty

Nepal (Kingdom of Nepal)

Although a kingdom, Nepal was actually ruled from 1848 to 1951 by hereditary prime ministers, the Ranas, who kept the kings in protective custody. In 1951 the king was restored to real power. Subsequent experiments with democratization have met with limited success. In 2001 the king and most of the royal family were killed by the heir-apparent, Dipendra, and the throne passed to the deceased king's brother.

1911–1955	King	Tribhubana	b. 1906	d. 1955
1955–1972	King	Mahendra	b. 1920	d. 1972
1972–2001	King	Birenda	b. 1945	d. 2001
2001–	King	Gyanendra	b. 1947	

Netherlands (Kingdom of the Netherlands)

Inhabited in early times by the Batavi, Frisii, and Saxons, the Netherlands split into many small, independent states after 843. It was attached to Burgundy in the 15th century and was ruled by the Habsburgs from 1477.

1482–1506	Count	Philip the Handsome, son of Maximilian I and Mary of Burgundy	b. 1478 d. 1506
1506–1555	Count	Charles V, son of Philip the Handsome	b. 1500 d. 1558
1555–1581	Count	Philip II, son of Charles V	b. 1527 d. 1598
		Revolt Against Spain from 1572 to 1609	

■ Governors

1507–1530	Governor	Margaret of Savoy, daughter of Mary of Burgundy	b. 1480 d. 1530
1531–1555	Governor	Mary of Hungary, daughter of Philip the Handsome	b. 1505 d. 1558
1555–1559	Governor	Emmanuel Philibert of Savoy, nephew of Margaret	b. 1528 d. 1580
1559–1567	Governor	Margaret of Parma, daughter of Charles V	b. 1522 d. 1586
1567–1573	Governor	Fernando Alvarez de Toledo, Duke of Alba	b. 1508 d. 1582?
1573–1576	Governor	Luis de Zuñigay y Requesens	d. 1576
1576–1578	Governor	Don John of Austria, son of Charles V	b. 1547 d. 1578
1578–1592	Governor	Alessandro Farnese, son of Margaret of Parma *(See* Parma*)*	b. 1545 killed 1592

■ Dutch Republic

1579–1584	Stadtholder	William I, the Silent, Prince of Orange	b. 1533 assassinated 1584

William the Silent became a page to Emperor Charles V in 1548. He led the "War of Liberation" against the Spanish armies of the Duke of Alba. After the provinces of Holland declared their independence from Spain, he became a hereditary stadtholder.

1584–1625	Stadtholder	Maurice, son of William, Prince of Orange	b. 1567 d. 1625

War with Spain from 1621 to 1648

1625–1647	Stadtholder	Frederick Henry, half-brother of Maurice	b. 1584 d. 1647
1647–1650	Stadtholder	William II, son of Frederick Henry	b. 1626 d. 1650
1650–1672		*Stadtholdership Suspended*	
1672–1702	Stadtholder	William III of Orange, son of William II	b. 1650 d. 1702

*Succeeded to the English Throne in 1688
Republic from 1702 to 1747*

1747–1751	Hereditary Stadtholder of all provinces	William IV Friso, son of John William Friso	b. 1711 d. 1751
1751–1795	Stadtholder	William V, son of William IV Friso	b. 1748 d. 1806

■ Bonapartes

The Batavian Republic was established by France from 1795 to 1806.

1806–1810	King	Louis Bonaparte, nephew of Napoleon	abdicated 1810 b. 1778 d. 1846
1810–1813		*Holland Incorporated into France*	

■ Kingdom of the Netherlands

Belgium was annexed to the Netherlands in 1815.

1815–1840	King	William I, son of William V	abdicated 1840 b. 1772 d. 1843
		Belgian Provinces Seceded in 1830	
1840–1849	King	William II, son of William I	b. 1792 d. 1849
1849–1890	King	William III, son of William II	b. 1817 d. 1890
1890–1948	Queen	Wilhelmina, daughter of William III	abdicated 1948 b. 1880 d. 1962
1948–1980	Queen	Juliana, daughter of Wilhelmina	b. 1909 d. 2004

Queen Juliana married a German prince, Bernhard of Lippe-Biesterfeld, in 1937, which caused controversy at the time. Interestingly, the marriages of Juliana's daughters to Spanish and German husbands nearly thirty years later were also strongly criticized on religious and political grounds.

1980–	Queen	Beatrix, daughter of Juliana	b. 1938

■ Statesmen

1572–1585	Grand Pensionary	Paulus Buys	b. 1531 d. 1594
1586–1619	Grand Pensionary	Johan van Olden Barnevelt	b. 1547 executed 1619
1621–1629	Grand Pensionary	Anthonis Duyck	b. 1560 d. 1629
1631–1636	Grand Pensionary	Adriaan Pauw	b. 1585 d. 1653
1636–1651	Grand Pensionary	Jacob Cats	b. 1577 d. 1660
1651–1653	Grand Pensionary	Adriaan Pauw	
1653–1672	Grand Pensionary	Johan de Witt	b. 1625 murdered 1672
1672–1689	Grand Pensionary	Gaspar Fagel	b. 1629 d. 1689
1689–1720	Grand Pensionary	Anthonie Heinsius	b. 1641 d. 1720
1720–1727	Grand Pensionary	Isaac van Hoornbeek	b. 1665 d. 1727
1727–1736	Grand Pensionary	Simon van Slingelandt	b. 1664 d. 1736
1736–1746	Grand Pensionary	Anthony van der Heim	b. 1693 d. 1746
1746–1749	Grand Pensionary	Jacob Gilles	b. 1691 d. 1765
1749–1772	Grand Pensionary	Pieter Steyn	b. 1706 d. 1772
1772–1787	Grand Pensionary	Pieter van Bleiswijk	b. 1724 d. 1790
1787–1795	Grand Pensionary	Laurens Pieter van de Spiegel	b. 1737 d. 1800
1945	Prime Minister	Pieter Sjoerd Gerbrandy	b. 1885 d. 1961

1945–1946	Prime Minister	Willem Schermerhorn	b. 1894
1946–1948	Prime Minister	Louis Joseph Maria Beel	b. 1902
1948–1951	Prime Minister	Willem Drees	b. 1886
1951–1952	Prime Minister	Willem Drees	
1952–1956	Prime Minister	Willem Drees	
1956–1958	Prime Minister	Willem Drees	
1958–1959	Prime Minister	Louis Joseph Maria Beel	
1959–1963	Prime Minister	Jan Eduard de Quay	b. 1901
1963–1965	Prime Minister	Victor Gerard Marie Marijnen	b. 1917
1965–1967	Prime Minister	Joseph Maria Laurens Theo Cals	b. 1914
1967–1971	Prime Minister	Piet de Jong	b. 1915
1971–1973	Prime Minister	Barend Biesheuvel	b. 1920 d. 2001
1973–1977	Prime Minister	Joop den Uyl	b. 1919 d. 1987
1977–1982	Prime Minister	Dries van Agt	b. 1931
1982–1994	Prime Minister	Ruud Lubbers	b. 1939
1994–2002	Prime Minister	Wim Kok	b. 1938
2002–	Prime Minister	Jan Peter Balkenende	b. 1956

New Zealand (Official U.N. Name)

Prior to British settlement in 1840, New Zealand was under the rule of chieftains of the Maori race, the Polynesian inhabitants of the country.

1840–1842	Governor	William Hobson	d. 1842
1842–1843	Administrator	Willoughby Shortland	
1843–1845	Governor	Robert R. FitzRoy, natural descendant of King Charles II	b. 1805 d. 1865
1845–1853	Governor	Sir George Grey	b. 1812 d. 1898
1854–1855	Administrator	Robert Henry Wynyard	
1855–1861	Governor	Thomas Gore Browne	
1861–1868	Governor	Sir George Grey	
1868–1873	Governor	Sir George Ferguson Bowen	b. 1821 d. 1899
1873	Administrator	Sir George Alfred Arney	
1873–1874	Governor	Sir James Fergusson	b. 1832 d. 1907
1874–1879	Governor	The Marquess of Normanby	b. 1819 d. 1890
1879	Administrator	Sir James Prendergast	
1879–1880	Governor	Sir Hercules George Robert Robinson, Baron Rosmead	b. 1824 d. 1897
1880	Administrator	Sir James Prendergast	
1880–1882	Governor	Sir Arthur Charles Hamilton Gordon, Baron Stanmore	b. 1829 d. 1912
1882–1883	Administrator	Sir James Prendergast	
1883–1889	Governor	Sir William Francis Drummond Jervois	

1889	Administrator	Sir James Prendergast	
1889–1892	Governor	William Hillier, Earl of Onslow	b. 1853 d. 1911
1892	Administrator	Sir James Prendergast	
1892–1897	Governor	The Earl of Glasgow	b. 1833 d. 1915
1897	Administrator	Sir James Prendergast	
1897–1904	Governor	Uchter John Mark, Earl of Ranfurly	b. 1856 d. 1933
1904–1910	Governor	William Lee, Baron Plunket	b. 1864 d. 1920
1910	Administrator	Sir Robert Stout	
1910–1912	Governor	John Poynder Dickson-Poynder, Baron Islington	
1912–	Administrator	Sir Robert Stout	
1912–1917	Governor	Arthur William de Brito Savile Foljambe, Earl of Liverpool	b. 1870 d. 1941
1917–1920	Governor-General	Arthur William de Brito Savile Foljambe, Earl of Liverpool	
1920	Administrator	Sir Robert Stout	
1920–1924	Governor-General	John Rushworth, Viscount Jellicoe of Scapa	b. 1859 d. 1935
1924	Administrator	Sir Robert Stout	
1924–1930	Governor-General	Sir Charles Fergusson, son of Sir James Fergusson	b. 1865 d. 1951
1930	Administrator	Sir Michael Myers	
1930–1935	Governor-General	Sir Charles Bathurst, Viscount Bledisloe	b. 1867
1935–1941	Governor-General	George Vere Arundell Monckton-Arundell, Viscount Galway	b. 1882 d. 1943
1941–1946	Governor-General	Cyril Louis Norton, Baron Newall	b. 1886 d. 1964
1946–1952	Governor-General	Bernard Cyril, Baron Freyberg	b. 1890
1952–1957	Governor-General	Charles Willoughby Moke, Baron Norrie	b. 1893
1957–1962	Governor-General	Charles John Lyttelton, Viscount Cobham	b. 1909
1962–1967	Governor-General	Sir Bernard Edward Fergusson, son of Sir Charles Fergusson	b. 1911
1967–1972	Governor-General	Sir Arthur Porritt	b. 1900
1972–1977	Governor-General	Sir Denis Blundell	
1977–1980	Governor-General	Sir Keith Holyoake	
1980–1985	Governor-General	The Hon. Sir David Beattie	
1985–1990	Governor-General	The Rt. Rev. Paul Reeves	
1990–1996	Governor-General	Dame Catherine Tizard	
1996–2001	Governor-General	The Rt. Hon. Sir Michael Hardie Boys	
2001–	Governor-General	Dame Silvia Cartwright	

■ Prime Ministers

1856	Prime Minister	Henry Sewell	b. 1807 d. 1879
1856	Prime Minister	Sir William Fox	b. 1812 d. 1893
1856–1861	Prime Minister	Edward William Stafford	b. 1819 d. 1901

1861–1862	Prime Minister	Sir William Fox	
1862–1863	Prime Minister	Alfred Domett	b. 1811 d. 1887
1863–1864	Prime Minister	Sir Frederick Whitaker	b. 1812 d. 1891
1864–1865	Prime Minister	Frederick Aloysius Weld	b. 1823 d. 1891
1865–1869	Prime Minister	Edward William Stafford	
1869–1872	Prime Minister	Sir William Fox	
1872	Prime Minister	Edward William Stafford	
1872–1873	Prime Minister	George Marsden Waterhouse	b. 1824 d. 1906
1873	Prime Minister	Sir William Fox	
1873–1875	Prime Minister	Sir Julius Vogel	b. 1835 d. 1899
1875–1876	Prime Minister	Daniel Pollen	b. 1813 d. 1896
1876	Prime Minister	Sir Julius Vogel	
1876–1877	Prime Minister	Sir Harry Albert Atkinson	b. 1831 d. 1892
1877–1879	Prime Minister	Sir George Grey	b. 1812 d. 1898
1879–1882	Prime Minister	Sir John Hall	b. 1824 d. 1906
1882–1883	Prime Minister	Frederick Whitaker	
1883–1884	Prime Minister	Sir Harry Albert Atkinson	
1884	Prime Minister	Robert Stout	b. 1844 d. 1930
1884	Prime Minister	Sir Harry Albert Atkinson	
1884–1887	Prime Minister	Sir Robert Stout	
1887–1891	Prime Minister	Sir Harry Albert Atkinson	
1891–1893	Prime Minister	John Balance	b. 1839 d. 1893
1893–1906	Prime Minister	Richard John Seddon	b. 1845 d. 1906
1906	Prime Minister	William Hall-Jones	b. 1851 d. 1936
1906–1912	Prime Minister	Sir Joseph George Ward	b. 1856 d. 1930
1912	Prime Minister	Thomas Mackenzie	b. 1854 d. 1930
1912–1925	Prime Minister	William Ferguson Massey	b. 1856 d. 1925
1925	Prime Minister	Sir Francis Henry Dillon Bell	b. 1821 d. 1898
1925–1928	Prime Minister	Joseph Gordon Coates	b. 1878 d. 1943
1928–1930	Prime Minister	Sir Joseph George Ward	b. 1856 d. 1930
1930–1935	Prime Minister	George William Forbes	b. 1869 d. 1947
1935–1940	Prime Minister	Michael Joseph Savage	b. 1872 d. 1940
1940–1949	Prime Minister	Peter Fraser	b. 1884 d. 1950
1949–1957	Prime Minister	Sir Sidney George Holland	b. 1893 d. 1961
1957	Prime Minister	Keith Jacka Holyoake	b. 1904
1957–1960	Prime Minister	Walter Nash	b. 1882
1960–1972	Prime Minister	Keith Jacka Holyoake	
1972	Prime Minister	John Ross Marshall	

1972–1974	Prime Minister	Norman Eric Kirk
1974–1975	Prime Minister	Wallace Rowling
1975–1984	Prime Minister	Sir Robert Muldoon
1984–1989	Prime Minister	David Lange
1989–1990	Prime Minister	Sir Geoffrey Palmer
1990	Prime Minister	Michael Moore
1990–1997	Prime Minister	James Bolger
1997–1999	Prime Minister	Jenny Shipley
1999–	Prime Minister	Helen Clark

Nicaragua (Republic of Nicaragua)

Nicaragua was ruled by Spain from 1524 to 1821 and was briefly part of the Mexican Empire of Iturbide before joining the Central American Confederation in 1825. It has been an independent republic since 1838.

1853–1854	President	Frutos Chamorro	
1855	President	José Maria Estrada	
1859–1867	President	Tomás Martínez	b. 1812 d. 1873
1867–1871	President	Fernando Guzmán	
1871–1875	President	Vicente Cuadra	
1875–1879	President	Pedro Joaquin Chamorro	
1879–1883	President	Joaquin Zavala	
1883–1887	President	Adan Cárdenas	
1887–1889	President	Evaristo Carazo	d. 1889
1889–1893	President	Roberto Sacasa	b. 1853 d. 1919
1893–1909	President	José Santos Zelaya	
1909–1910	President (provisional)	José Madriz	
1911	President	Juan J. Estrada	
1911–1916	President	Adolfo Díaz	b. 1874
1917–1920	President	Emiliano Chamorro Vargas	b. 1871
1921–1923	President	Diego Manuel Chamorro, nephew of Emiliano Chamorro Vargas	d. 1923
1923–1924	President (provisional)	Bartolome Martinez	
1925–1926	President	Carlos Solorzano	
1926	President	Emiliano Chamorro Vargas	
1926–1928	President	Adolfo Diaz	
1929–1932	President	José Maria Moncada	d. 1945
1933–1936	President	Juan Bautista Sacasa	b. 1874 d. 1946

1936	President (provisional)	Carlos Brenes Jarquin	
1937–1947	President	Anastasio Somoza	b. 1896 assassinated 1956
1947	President	Leonardo Arguello	
1947	President	Benjamin Lacayo-Sacasa	
1947–1950	President	Victor M. Roman y Reyes	
1951–1956	President	Anastasio Somoza	
1957–1963	President	Luis A. Somoza Debayle, son of Anastasio Somoza	b. 1922
1963–1966	President	Rene Schick Guiterrez	b. 1909
1966	President	Lorenzo Guerrero	b. 1900
1967–1972	President	Anastasio Somoza Debayle	
		Junta Rule from 1972 to 1974	
1979	Presdident	Francisco Urcuyo Malianos	
		Government Junta of National Reconstruction from 1979 to 1984	
1984–1990	President	Daniel Ortega Saavedra	
1990–1997	President	Violeta Barrios del Chamorro	
1997–2002	President	Arnaldo Aleman Lacayo	
2002–	President	Enrique Bolanos Geyer	

Niger (Republic of Niger)

1960–1974	President	Hamani Diori	
1974–1987	President	Seyni Kountche	d. 1987
1987–1993	President	Ali Saibou	
1993–1996	President	Mahamane Ousmane	
1996–1999	President	Ibrahim Baré Maïnassara	
1999	(Transitional government)	Daouda Mallam Wanke	
1999–	President	Tandja Mamadou	

Nigeria (Federal Republic of Nigeria)

Formerly a British colony, Nigeria became independent as a member of the Commonwealth in 1960, assuming a republic form of government in 1963.

1960–1963	Governor-General	Nnamdi Azikiwe	b. 1904
1963–1966	President	Nnamdi Azikiwe	
1966–1966	Head of Military Council	Johnson Aguiyi-Ironsi	b. 1924
1966–1975	Head of Military Council	Yokubu Gowon	

1975–1976	Head of Military Council	Murtala Mohammed	b. 1938 d. 1976
1976–1979	Head of Military Council	Olusegsun Obasanjo	b. 1937
1979–1983	President	Shehu Shagari	b. 1925
1983–1985	Chair, Supreme Military Council	Muhammadu Buhari	b. 1942
1985–1993	President, Military Council	Ibrahim Babaginda	b. 1941
1993	Interim President	Ernest Shonekan	b. 1936
1993–1998	Chair, Prov. Ruling Council	Sani Abacha	b. 1943 d. 1998
1998–1999	Chair, Prov. Ruling Council	Abdulsalami Abubakar	b. 1942
1999–	President	Olusegun Obasano	

Northern Ireland *See* Ireland

North Korea (Democratic People's Republic of Korea)
See also South Korea

Since Korea was divided following World War II, the northern partition has remained a highly centralized communist state. The current absolute ruler assumed his office upon the death of his father.

1948–1994	Dictator	Kim Il Sung	b. 1912	d. 1994
1994–	Dictator	Kim Jong Il	b. 1942	

Norway (Kingdom of Norway)

872–930	King	Harald Fairhair (Harald I)	b. 850?	d. 933

After conquering and deposing other Norwegian earls, Harald compelled them to leave Norway. They settled in the Orkneys, Hebrides, Shetlands, and, most importantly, in Normandy, where their descendants became dukes, kings, and crusaders.

930–934	King	Erik Bloodaxe (Eric I), son of Harald		d. 954?
934–961	King	Haakon the Good (Haakon I), son of Harald	b. 914?	killed 961
961–970	King	Harald Graypelt (Harald II) son of Erik	b. 930?	killed 970
970–995	Ruler	Earl Haakon	b. 937?	d. 995
995–1000	King	Olaf Tryggvason (Olaf I)	b. 969	killed 1000
1000–1016	Rulers	Earls Erik and Svein, sons of Earl Haakon		d. 1024?
1016–1030	King	Olaf II Haraldson (St. Olaf)	b. 995?	killed 1030

Following his own conversion, St. Olaf attempted to forcibly convert

all of Norway to Christianity. The various petty rulers reacted
by successfully appealing for help from Canute the Great of Denmark.
Olaf fled to Sweden. In attempting to reconquer Norway, he
was defeated and killed. He was canonized in 1164.

1030–1035	King	Canute the Great, son of Sweyn Forkbeard	b. 1000	d. 1035
1035–1047	King	Magnus the Good (Magnus I), son of St. Olaf		d. 1047
1047–1066	King	Harald Hardrade (Harald III) descendant of Harald I	b. 1015	d. 1066
1066–1093	King	Olaf the Peaceful (Olaf III), son of Harald III		d. 1093
1093–1103	King	Magnus Barefoot (Magnus II), son of Olaf III	b. 1073	d. 1103
1103–1122	King	Eystein I, son of Magnus	b. 1089	d. 1122
1103–1130	King	Sigurd the Crusader (Sigurd I), son of Magnus	b. 1089?	d. 1130
1130–1135	King	Magnus the Blind (Magnus III), son of Sigurd	b. 1115?	killed 1139
1130–1136	Rival King	Harald Gilchrist (Harald IV)	b. 1103?	killed 1136
		Civil War from 1134 to 1135		
1136–1161	Joint	Inge I, son of Harald		killed 1161
	Kings	Sigurd II Mund, son of Harald	b. 1134	killed 1155
1142–1157	King	Eystein II, son of Harald		assassinated 1157
1161–1162	King	Haakon (Haakon II), son of Sigurd	b. 1147	killed 1162
1163–1184	King	Magnus (Magnus IV), son of Erling Skakke	b. 1156	killed 1184
1184–1202	King	Sverre,? son of Sigurd Mund	b. 1152?	d. 1202
1202–1204	King	Haakon Sverreson (Haakon III)		d. 1204
1204–1217	King	Inge Baardson		
1217–1263	King	Haakon (Haakon IV), ? son of Haakon III	b. 1204	d. 1263
1263–1280	King	Magnus the Lawmender (Magnus VI), son of Haakon	b. 1238	d. 1280
1280–1299	King	Erik (Erik II), son of Magnus	b. 1268	d. 1299
1299–1319	King	Haakon (Haakon V), son of Magnus	b. 1270	d. 1319
1319–1355	King	Magnus (Magnus VII), grandson of Haakon	b. 1316	d. 1374
1355–1380	King	Haakon (Haakon VI), son of Magnus	b. 1339	d. 1380

■ Kings of Denmark and Norway 1380–1814

1380–1387	King	Olav (Olav IV), son of Haakon	b. 1370	d. 1387
1387–1412	Queen	Margaret, mother of Olav	b. 1353	d. 1412
1389–1442	King	Erik of Pomerania (Erik III), grandnephew of Margaret	b. 1382	d. 1459
		Union of Kalmar in 1397		
1442–1448	King	Christopher III of Bavaria, nephew of Eric	b. 1418	d. 1448
1448–1481	King	Christian I, son of Theodoric, Count of Oldenburg	b. 1426	d. 1481
1481–1513	King	John I, son of Christian I	b. 1455	d. 1513
1513–1523	King	Christian II, son of John of Saxony	b. 1481	d. 1559

1523–1533	King	Frederik I, son of Christian I	b. 1471? d. 1533
1534–1559	King	Christian III, son of Frederik I	b. 1503 d. 1559
1559–1588	King	Frederik II, son of Christian III	b. 1534 d. 1588
1588–1648	King	Christian IV, son of Frederik II	b. 1577 d. 1648
1648–1670	King	Frederik III, son of Christian IV	b. 1609 d. 1670
1670–1699	King	Christian V, son of Frederik III	b. 1646 d. 1699
1699–1730	King	Frederik IV, son of Christian V	b. 1671 d. 1730
1730–1746	King	Christian VI, son of Frederik IV	b. 1699 d. 1746
1746–1766	King	Frederik V, son of Christian VI	b. 1723 d. 1766
1766–1808	King	Christian VII, son of Frederik V	b. 1749 d. 1808
1808–1814	King	Frederik VI, son of Christian VII	b. 1768 d. 1839
1814	Danish Governor	Christian Frederik	

■ Kings of Sweden and Norway 1814–1905

1814–1818	King	Carl XIII, son of Adolphus Frederik	b. 1748 d. 1818
1818–1844	King	Carl XIV Johan (Marshal Bernadotte)	b. 1763? d. 1844
1844–1859	King	Oscar I, son of Carl Johan	b. 1799 d. 1859
1859–1872	King	Carl XV, son of Oscar I	b. 1826 d. 1872
1872–1905	King	Oscar II, son of Oscar I	abdicated 1905 b. 1829 d. 1907
		Independent Kingdom from 1905	

■ Kings of Norway Since 1905

1905–1957	King	Haakon VII, son of Frederik VIII of Denmark	b. 1872 d. 1957
		German Occupation from 1940 to 1945	
1957–1991	King	Olav V, son of Haakon VII	b. 1903 d. 1991
1991–	King	Harald V, son of Olaf V	b. 1937

■ Statesmen

1858–1861	Head of Government	Chr. Birch-Reichenwald	b. 1814 d. 1891
1861–1880	Prime Minister	Frederik Stang	b. 1808 d. 1884
1880–1884	Prime Minister	Chr. Aug. Selmer	b. 1816 d. 1889
1884	Prime Minister	Chr. Schweigaard	b. 1838 d. 1899
1884–1889	Prime Minister	Johan Sverdrup	b. 1816 d. 1892
1889–1891	Prime Minister	Emil Stang	b. 1834 d. 1912
1891–1893	Prime Minister	Johannes Steen	b. 1853 d. 1921
1893–1895	Prime Minister	Emil Stang	

1895–1898	Prime Minister	Georg Francis Hagerup	b. 1853 d. 1921
1898–1902	Prime Minister	Johannes Steen	
1902–1903	Prime Minister	Otto Blehr	b. 1847 d. 1927
1903–1905	Prime Minister	Georg Francis Hagerup	
1905–1907	Prime Minister	Christian Michelsen	b. 1857 d. 1925
1907–1908	Prime Minister	J. Lövland	b. 1857 d. 1925
1908–1910	Prime Minister	Gunnar Knudsen	b. 1848 d. 1928
1910–1912	Prime Minister	Wollert Konow	b. 1848 d. 1928
1912–1913	Prime Minister	Jens Bratlie	b. 1856 d. 1939
1913–1920	Prime Minister	Gunnar Knudsen	b. 1848 d. 1928
1920–1921	Prime Minister	Otto B. Halvorsen	b. 1872 d. 1923
1921–1923	Prime Minister	Otto Blehr	
1923	Prime Minister	Otto B. Halvorsen	
1923–1924	Prime Minister	Abraham Berge	b. 1851 d. 1936
1924–1926	Prime Minister	Johan Ludwig Mowinckel	b. 1870 d. 1943
1926–1928	Prime Minister	Ivar Lykke	b. 1872 d. 1949
1928	Prime Minister	Christopher Hornsrud	b. 1859 d. 1960
1928–1931	Prime Minister	Johan Ludwig Mowinckel	
1931–1932	Prime Minister	Peder Kilstad	b. 1878 d. 1932
1932–1933	Prime Minister	Jens Hundseid	b. 1883 d. 1965
1933–1935	Prime Minister	Johan Ludwig Mowinckel	
1935–1945	Prime Minister	Johan Nygaardsvold	b. 1879 d. 1952
1945–1951	Prime Minister	Einar Gerhardsen	b. 1897 d. 1987
1951–1955	Prime Minister	Oscar Torp	b. 1893 d. 1958
1955–1963	Prime Minister	Einar Gerhardsen	
1963	Prime Minister	John Lyng	b. 1905 d. 1978
1963–1965	Prime Minister	Einar Gerhardsen	
1965–1971	Prime Minister	Per Borthen	
1971–1972	Prime Minister	Trygve Bratteli	b. 1910 d. 1984
1972–1973	Prime Minister	Lars Korvald	
1973–1976	Prime Minister	Trygve Bratteli	
1976–1981	Prime Minister	Odvar Nordli	
1981–1981	Prime Minister	Gro Harlem Brundtland	
1981–1986	Prime Minister	Kare Willoch	
1986–1989	Prime Minister	Gro Harlem Brundtland	
1989–1990	Prime Minister	Jan P. Syse	b. 1930 d. 1997
1990–1996	Prime Minister	Gro Harlem Brundtland	
1996–1997	Prime Minister	Thorbjorn Jagland	b. 1950

1997–2000	Prime Minister	Kjell Magne Bondevik	b. 1947
2000–2001	Prime Minister	Jens Stoltenberg	b. 1959
2001–	Prime Minister	Kjell Magne Bondevik	

■ Statesmen

| 1946–1953 | Secretary-General of the United Nations | Trygve Lie | |

Numidia

Numidia was a kingdom of North Africa corresponding roughly to modern-day Algeria.

c. 200 B.C.	King	Narva	
	King	Gala	
	King	Desalces	
	King	Capusa	
	King	Lacumaces	
201–148	King	Masinissa	b. c. 238 d. 148
148–118	King	Micipsa	d. 118
	King	Gulussa	
	King	Atherbal	
112–104	King	Jugurtha (deposed)	d. 104
	King	Hiempsal I	
	King	Hierta	
	King	Hiempsal II	
? –46	King	Juba I	d. 46
30–25	King	Juba II	d. A.D. 19
	King	Ptolemy	d. A.D. 40

Most of Numidia was annexed to Rome after 46 B.C. Juba II and Ptolemy actually ruled the adjacent territory of Mauretania.

Nyasaland *See* Malawi

Oman (Sultanate of Oman)

The Sultanate of Muscat and Oman was under Portuguese rule from 1508, and fell under Persian influence after 1648. Now it is independent under British protection. The present dynasty dates from 1741.

| 1932–1970 | Sultan | Said bin Taimur | b. 1910 d. 1972 |
| 1970– | | Qaboos bin Sa'id | b. 1940 |

Pakistan (Islamic Republic of Pakistan) *See also* India

Separated from India and established as a British Dominion in 1947, Pakistan continues to be a member of the Commonwealth of Nations.

1947–1948	Governor-General	Mohammed Ali Jinnah	b. 1876	d. 1948

A Muslim lawyer in India and president of the All-India Moslem League, Mohammed Ali Jinnah was the "Father of Pakistan."

1948–1951	Governor-General	Khwaja Nazimuddin		
1951–1955	Governor-General	Ghulam Mohammed	b. 1895	d. 1956
1955–1958	Governor-General	Iskander Mirza		
		(and later President)		
1958–	President	Mohammed Ayub Khan		

Islamic Republic Proclaimed in 1956

1947–1951	Prime Minister	Liaquat Ali Khan	b. 1895	d. 1951
1951–1953	Prime Minister	Khwaja Nazimuddin		
1953–1955	Prime Minister	Mohammed Ali	b. 1909	d. 1963
1955–1956	Prime Minister	Chaudhri Mohammed Ali		
1956–1958	Prime Minister	H. S. Suhrawardy	b. 1893	d. 1963
1958–1969	Military Dictator/ President	Mohammad Ayub Khan	b. 1907	d. 1974
1969–1970	President	Agha Mohammed Yahya Khan		
1970–1977	President	Zulfikar Ali Bhutto		
1977–1985	Military Dictator	Muhammad Zia ul-Haq		d. 1988
1985–1988	Prime Minister	Muhammad Khan Junejo		
1988–1990	Prime Minister	Benazir Bhutto,		
1990–1990	Prime Minister	Ghulam Mustafa Jatoi		
1990–1993	Prime Minister	Muhammad Nawaz Sharif		
1993–1993	Prime Minister	Balakh Sher Mazari		
1993–1993	Prime Minister	Muhammad Nawaz Sharif		
1993–1993	Prime Minister	Moin Qureshi		
1993–1996	Prime Minister	Benazir Bhutto		
1996–1997	Prime Minister	Miraj Khalid		
1997–1999	Prime Minister	Muhammad Nawaz Sharif		
1999–2002	Military Dictator/ President	Pervez Musharraf		
2002–2004	Prime Minister	Zafrullah Khan Jamali		
2004–2004	Prime Minister	Chaudhry Shyjaat Hussain		
2004–	Prime Minister	Shaukat Aziz		

Palau (Republic of Palau)

A constitutional republic in free association with the United States, Palau consists of eight principal islands and more than two hundred and fifty smaller islands lying roughly 500 miles southeast of the Philippines. Full independence was gained in 1994.

Palestinian Authority *See also* Israel; Jordan

In 1993, as a result of the Oslo Accords between Israel and the Palestine Liberation Organization, a new structure of government was established as a step toward the creation of an independent state for Palestinians.

1994–2004	President/Chair	Yasser Arafat	b. 1929 d. 2004
2004–2005	Acting Chair	Rauhi Fattouh	
2005–	President/Chair	Mahmoud Abbas	

Panama (Republic of Panama)

Panama was a department of the United States of Colombia until 1903.

1904–1908	President	Manuel Amador Guerrero	b. 1833 d.1909
1908–1910	President	José Domingo de Obaldía	
1910	President (acting)	Carlos Antonio Mendoza	
1910–1912	President (acting)	Pablo Aroscmena	
1912–1916	President	Belisario Porras	b. 1856 d. 1942
1916–1918	President	Ramón Valdez	
1918	President (acting)	Ciro Luis Urriola	
1918–1920	President (acting)	Belisario Porras	
1920	President	Ernesto Lefevre	
1920–1924	President	Belisario Porras	
1924–1928	President	Rodolfo Chiari	
1928–1931	President	Florencio Harmodio Arosemena	b. 1873 d. 1945
1931	President (provisional)	Harmodio Arias	
1931–1932	President	Ricardo J. Alfaro	
1932–1936	President	Harmodio Arias	
1936–1939	President	Juan Demóstenes Arosemena, brother of Florencio Harmodio Arosemena	b. 1879 d. 1939
1939–1940	President (acting)	Augusto Samuel Boyd	b. 1879 d. 1957
1940–1941	President	Arnulfo Arias	
1941–1945	President	Ricardo Adolfo de la Guardia	
1945–1948	President	Enrique Adolfo Jimenez	
1948–1949	President	Domingo Díaz Arosemena	
1949–1951	President	Arnulfo Arias	

1951–1952	President	Alcibíades Arosemena	
1952–1955	President	José Antonio Remon Cantesa	assassinated 1955
1955–1956	President	José Arias Espinosa	
1956–1960	President	Ernesto de la Guardia	
1960–1964	President	Roberto F. Chiari	
1964–1968	President	Marco Aurelio Robles	
1968–1968	President	Arnulfo Arias Madrid	
1968–1969	Junta Chair	José María Pinilla Fábrega	
1969–1978	President	Demetrio Lakas Bahas	
1978–1982	President	Aristides Royo	
1982–1984	President	Ricardo de la Espriella	
1984–1984	President	Jorge Illueca	
1984–1985	President	Nicolás Ardito Barletta Vallarino	
1985–1988	President	Eric Arturo Delvalle	
1988–1989	Acting Pres.	Manuel Solís Palma	
1989	Prov. Pres.	Francisco Rodirguez	
1989–1994	President	Guillermo Endara Galimany	
1994–1999	President	Ernesto Pérez Balladares	
1999–2004	President	Mireya Moscoso	
2004–	President	Martín Torrijos	

Papacy *See* Holy See, The

Papua New Guinea (Independent State of Papua New Guinea)

A constitutional monarchy in the Commonwealth of Nations, Papua New Guinea was formerly administered by Australia.

1977–1980	Prime Minister	Michael Somare
1980–1982	Prime Minister	Julius Chan
1982–1985	Prime Minister	Michael Somare
1985–1988	Prime Minister	Paias Wingti
1988–1992	Prime Minister	Rabbie Namaliu
1992–1994	Prime Minister	Paias Wingti
1994–1997	Prime Minister	Julius Chan
1997–1999	Prime Minister	Bill Skate
1999–2002	Prime Minister	Mekere Morauta
2002–	Prime Minister	Michael Somare

Paraguay (Republic of Paraguay)

Paraguay gained independence from Spain in 1811.

1811–1840	Dictator	José Gaspar Rodríguez Francia	d. 1840
1842–1862	Dictator	Carlos Antonio López, nephew of José Gaspar Rodríguez Francia	b. 1790 d. 1862
1862–1870	Dictator	Francisco Solano López, son of Carlos Antonio López	b. 1827 killed 1870
1870–1871	President	Cirilo Rivarola	d. 1871
1871–1874	President	Salvador Jovellanos	
1874	President	Juan Bautista Gil	assassinated 1874
1877–1878	President (acting)	Higinio Uriarte	
1878–1880	President	Cándido Barreiro	d. 1880
1880–1885	President	Bernardino Caballero	b. 1831 d. 1885
1886–1890	President	Patricio Escobar	
1890–1894	President	Juan González	
1894–1898	President	Juan Bautista Egusquiza	
1898–1902	President	Emilio Aceval	
1902	President	Hector Carvallo	
1902–1904	President	Juan B. Escurra	
1904–1905	President (provisional)	Juan Gaona	
1906	President	Cecilio Báez	b. 1862 d. 1941
1906–1908	President	Benigno Ferreira	
1908–1910	President	Emiliano González Navero	b. 1861 d. 1938
1910–1911	President	Manuel Gondra	
1911	President (provisional)	Albino Jara	
1911–1912	President (provisional)	Liberato Marcial Rojas	
1912	President (provisional)	Pedro Peña	
1912	President (provisional)	Emiliano González Navero	
1912–1916	President	Eduardo Schaerer	
1916–1919	President	Manuel Franco	d. 1919
1919–1920	President (acting)	José Montero	
1920–1921	President	Manuel Gondra	
1921	President (acting)	Félix Paiva	
1921–1923	President (provisional)	Eusebio Ayala	b. 1875 d. 1942

1923–1924	President (provisional)	Eligio Ayala	
1924	President (provisional)	Luis Riart	
1924–1928	President	Eligio Ayala	
1928–1931	President	José Patricio Guggiari	b.1884 d. 1957
1931–1932	President (provisional)	Emiliano González Navero	
1932	President	José Patricio Guggiari	
1932–1936	President	Eusebio Ayala	
1936–1937	President (provisional)	Rafael Franco	
1937–1938	President (provisional)	Félix Paiva	
1938–1939	President (provisional)	Félix Paiva	
1939–1940	President	José Félix Estigarribia	b. 1888 d. 1940
1940–1948	President	Higinio Morínigo	b. 1887
1948	President (provisional)	Juan Manuel Frutos	
1948–1949	President	J. Natalicio Gonzalez	
1949	President (provisional)	Raimundo Rolón	
1949–1950	President	Felipe Molas Lopez	
1950–1954	President	Federico Chávez	
1954	President	Tomas Romero Pereira	
1954–1989	President/Dictator	Alfredo Stroessner	b. 1912
1989–1993	President	Andres Rodriguez	
1993–1998	President	Juan Carlos Wasmosy	
1998–1999	President	Raul Cubas Grau	
1999–2003	President	Luis Gonzalez Macchi	
2003–	President	Nicanor Duarte Frutos	

Pergamum

263–241 B.C.	Ruler	Eumenes I	d. 241 B.C.
241–197	King	Attalus I Soter, nephew of Eumenes I	b. 269 d. 197
197–158?	King	Eumenes II, son of Attalus I	d. 158?
158?–138	King	Attalus II Philadelphus, son of Attalus I	b. 220 d. 138
138–133	King	Attalus III Philometor, nephew of Attalus II	b. 171 d. 133

King Attalus III bequeathed the Kingdom to Rome in 33 B.C.

Persia *See* Iran

Peru (Republic of Peru)

Before the Spanish conquest, Peru was the heart of a large empire ruled by the Incas. The Incan emperors were overthrown, and Peru was ruled by Spanish viceroys until the establishment of the republic in 1821.

1821–1822	Protector	José de San Martín	b. 1778 d. 1850

San Martín began the liberation of Peru. After numerous successes, he established himself as "protector" of Peru. In the meantime, Simón Bolívar landed at Guayaquil. As San Martín wanted no rivalry for power, the two generals agreed to meet. Details of the meeting are one of the best-kept secrets in history. To this day, no one knows why San Martín, a selfless, social-minded patriot, resigned and retired to Europe, leaving the total conquest of Peru to Bolívar.

1823	President	José de la Riva Agüero	b. 1783 d. 1858
1823	President	José Bernardo Tagle	
1823–1827	Dictator	Simón Bolívar (see Venezuela)	b. 1783 d. 1830
1827–1829	President	José de la Mar	
1829–1833	President	Agustín Gamarra	b. 1785 killed 1841
1833–1834	President (acting)	Luis José de Orbegoso	
1834–1835	President	Manuel Salazar y Baquíjano	
1835–1836	President	Felipe Santiago Salaverry	b. 1806 shot 1836
1836–1839	President	Andrés Santa Cruz	b. 1792? d. 1865
1839–1841	President	Agustín Gamarra	
1841–1845	President (acting)	Manuel Menéndez	b. 1790? d. 1845?
1845–1851	President	Ramón Castilla	b. 1797 d. 1867
1851–1855	President	José Rufino Echenique	
1855–1862	President	Ramón Castilla	
1862–1863	President	Miguel de San Román	
1863–1865	President (acting)	Juan Antonio Pezet	
1865–1868	Dictator	Mariano Ignacio Prado	b. 1826 d. 1901
1868–1872	President	José Balta	b. 1816 murdered 1872
1872–1876	President	Manuel Pardo	b. 1834 assassinated 1878
1876–1879	President	Mariano Ignacio Prado	
1879–1881	President	Nicolás de Piérola	b. 1839 d. 1913
1881	President (acting)	Francisco García Calderón	b. 1832 d. 1905
1881–1883	President	Lizardo Montero	
1883–1885	President	Miguel Iglesias	b. 1822 d. 1901
1885–1886	President	Antonio Arenas	

1886–1890	President	Andrés Avelino Cáceres	b. 1836? d. 1923
1890–1894	President	Remigio Morales Bermúdez	b. 1836 d. 1894
1894	President	Justiniano Borgoño	
1894–1895	President	Andrés Avelino Cáceres	
1895–1899	President	Nicolás de Piérola	
1899–1903	President	Eduardo López de Romaña	
1903–1904	President	Manuel Candamo	b. 1842 d. 1904
1904	President	Serapio Calderón	
1904–1908	President	José Pardo, son of Manuel Pardo	b. 1864 d. 1947
1908–1912	President	Augusto Bernadino Leguía	b. 1863 d. 1932

Although Leguía modernized and developed Peru during his administrations and promulgated the Constitution of 1920, he was roundly condemned for his compromises during the Tacna-Arica Controversy Settlement. A ruthless dictator, he was overthrown and imprisoned in 1929, accused of misappropriating government funds.

1912–1914	President	Guillermo Enrique Billinghurst	b. 1851 d. 1915
1914	President (provisional)	Óscar Raimundo Benavides	b. 1876 d. 1945
1915–1919	President	José Pardo	
1919	President (provisional)	Augusto Bernadino Leguía	
1919–1924	President	Augusto Bernadino Leguía	
1924–1929	President	Augusto Bernadino Leguía	
1930–1931		*Junta*	
1931	President (provisional)	Ricardo Leonicio Elías	
1931	President (provisional)	Gustavo A. Jiménez	
1931	President (provisional)	David Samamez Ocampo	
1931–1933	President	Luis M. Sánchez Cerro	b. 1889 assassinated 1933
1933–1939	President	Óscar Raimundo Benavides	b. 1876 d. 1945
1939–1945	President	Manuel Prado Ugarteche	
1945–1948	President	José Luis Bustamante y Rivero	
1948–1950	President	Manuel A. Odría	
		Military Junta	
1950–1956	President (Constitutional)		Manuel A. Odría
1956–1962	President	Manuel Prado Ugarteche	
1962	Statesman	Victor Raul Hoya de la Torre	b. 1895 d. 1979

Founder of APRA (Peru's radical reform but anti-Communist party) and defender of Indian rights, Victor became an influential political figure throughout Latin American. Championing the nationalist revolutionary cause, he suffered years of exile. When in 1962 he won the presidency by a narrow plurality, a military junta invalidated the elections and seized power.

1962–1963	President	Ricardo Pérez Godoy	
		Military Junta	
1963–1968	President	Fernando Belaunde Terry	
1968–1975	President	Juan Velasco Alvarado	
1975–1980	President	Francisco Morales Bermudez	
1980–1985	President	Fernando Belaunde Terry	
1985–1990	President	Alan García Pérez	
1990–2000	President	Alberto Kenyo Fujimori	
2000–2001	President	Valentín Paniagua Corazo	
2001–	President	Alejandro Toledo Manrique	

Philippines, The (Republic of the Philippines)

The Philippines were ruled by Spain from 1565 to 1897 and by the United States from 1898 to 1946.

1898–1901	President	Emilio Aguinaldo	b. 1870? d. 1964
1900	U.S. Military Governor	Wesley Merritt	b. 1834 d. 1910
1901–1904	U.S. Civil Governor	William Howard Taft	b. 1857 d. 1930
1904–1906	U.S. Civil Governor	Luke Edward Wright	b. 1846 d. 1922
1906	U.S. Civil Governor	Henry Clay Ide	b. 1844 d. 1921
1906–1909	U.S. Civil Governor	James Francis Smith	b. 1859 d. 1928
1909–1913	U.S. Civil Governor	William Cameron Forbes	b. 1870 d. 1959
1913–1921	U.S. Civil Governor	Francis Burton Harrison	b. 1873 d. 1957
1921–1927	U.S. Civil Governor	Leonard Wood	b. 1860 d. 1927
1927–1929	U.S. Civil Governor	Henry Lewis Stimson	b. 1867 d. 1950
1929–1932	U.S. Civil Governor	Dwight Filley Davis	b. 1879 d. 1945
1932–1933	U.S. Civil Governor	Theodore Roosevelt, Jr., son of President Theodore Roosevelt	b. 1887 d. 1944
1933–1934	U.S. Civil Governor	Frank Murphy	b. 1890 d. 1949
1935–1937	U.S. High Commissioner	Frank Murphy	
1937–1939	U.S. High Commissioner	Paul Vories McNutt	b. 1891 d. 1955
1939–1942	U.S. High Commissioner	Francis Bowes Sayre, son-in-law of President Wilson	b. 1885
		Commonwealth Government Inaugurated in 1935	

1935–1944	President	Manuel Luis Quezon y Molina	b. 1878 d. 1944
1942–1945		*Japanese Occupation*	
1943–1945	President	José P. Laurel	
1944–1946	President	Sergio Osmeña	b. 1878 d. 1961
		Republic Inaugurated in 1946	
1946–1948	President	Manuel Roxas y Acuña	b. 1892 d. 1948
1948–1953	President	Elpidio Quirino	
1954–1957	President	Ramón Magsaysay	d. 1957
1957–1961	President	Carlos P. García	
1961–1965	President	Diosdado Macapagal	
1965–1986	Pres./Dictator	Ferdinand E. Marcos	b. 1917
1986–1992	President	Corazón Aquino	
1992–1998	President	Fidel Ramos	
1998–2001	President	Joseph Ejercito Estrada	
2001–	President	Gloria Macapagal-Arroyo	

Poland (Republic of Poland)

■ Piast Dynasty

No authentic information is available for the period before the Kingdom of the Piasts.

962–992	King	Mieszko I	b. 922 d. 992
992–1025	King	Boleslaus I, son of Mieszko I	b. 967 d. 1025
1025–1034	King	Mieszko II, son of Boleslaus I	b. 990 d. 1034
1034–1058	King	Casimir I, son of Mieszko II	b. 1016 d. 1058
1058–1079	King	Boleslaus II, son of Casimir I	b. 1039 d. 1081
1079–1102	King	Ladislaus I, son of Casimir I	b. 1043 d. 1102
1102–1138	King	Boleslaus III, son of Ladislaus I	b. 1085 d. 1138
1138–1146	King	Ladislaus II, son of Boleslaus III	b. 1105 d. 1159
1146–1173	King	Boleslaus IV, son of Boleslaus III	b. 1120 d. 1173
1173–1177	King	Mieszko III, son of Boleslaus III	b. 1126 d. 1202
1177–1194	King	Casimir II, son of Boleslaus III	b. 1138 d. 1197
1194–1227	King	Leszek the White, son of Casimir II	b. 1186 d. 1227
1232–1238	King	Henry I, son of Boleslaus of Silesia	b. 1163 d. 1238
1238–1241	King	Henry II, son of Henry I	b. 1191 d. 1241
1241–1243	King	Konrad I, son of Casimir II	b. 1181 d. 1247
1241–1279	King	Boleslaus V, the Chaste	b. 1226 d. 1279
1279–1288	King	Leszek the Black, son of Casimir I of Cuyavia	b. 1240 d. 1288
1288–1290	King	Henry IV Probus, son of Henry III of Silesia	b. 1257 d. 1290

1295–1296	King	Przemyslav II, son of Przemyslav I	b. 1257 d. 1296
1300–1305	King	Wenceslaus II of Bohemia, son of Ottokar of Bohemia	b. 1271 d. 1305
1306–1333	King	Ladislaus I, son of Casimir I of Cuyavia (King from 1320)	b. 1261 d. 1333
1333–1370	King	Casimir III, son of Ladislaus I	b. 1310 d. 1370

Casimir the Great was a born ruler. He gave his country effective government for nearly forty years, befriended the peasants, and codified the laws.

1370–1382	King	Louis of Hungary, nephew of Casimir III	b. 1326 d. 1382
1382–1384		*Civil Wars*	

■ House of Jagello

1384–1399	Queen	Hedwig, wife of Jagello, daughter of Louis of Hungary	b. 1374 d. 1399
1386–1434	King	Ladislaus II Jagello, consort of Hedwig	b. 1348 d. 1434
1434–1444	King	Ladislaus III, son of Ladislaus II Jagello	b. 1424 d. 1444
1447–1492	King	Casimir IV, son of Ladislaus II Jagello	b. 1427 d. 1492
1492–1501	King	John I, son of Casimir IV	b. 1459 d. 1501
1501–1506	King	Alexander, son of Casimir IV	b. 1461 d. 1506
1506–1548	King	Sigismund I, son of Casimir IV	b. 1467 d. 1548
1548–1572	King	Sigismund II, son of Sigismund I	b. 1520 d. 1572

■ Elective Kings

1573–1574	King	Henry III of Anjou	b. 1551 d. 1589
1576–1586	King	Stephen Batory, son-in-law of Sigismund I	b. 1533 d. 1586
1587 1632	King	Sigismund III, grandson of Sigismund I	b. 1566 d. 1632
1632–1648	King	Ladislaus IV, son of Sigismund III	b. 1595 d. 1648
1648–1668	King	John II Casimir, son of Sigismund III	abdicated 1668 b. 1609 d. 1672
1669–1673	King	Michael Wiśniowiecki	b. 1640 d. 1673
1674–1696	King	John III Sobieski	b. 1629 d. 1696

With 20,000 Polish troops, John III Sobieski relieved the Turkish siege of Vienna in 1683, drove the Turks back to the Raab, and freed Hungary. Sobieski led the decisive charge of Polish cavalry that brought victory. For this act, he was acclaimed the hero of Christendom.

1697–1704	King	Augustus II of Saxony, son of John George of Saxony	b. 1670 d. 1733
1704–1709	King	Stanislaus Leszczynski	b. 1677 d. 1766
1709–1733	King	Augustus II of Saxony	
1733–1763	King	Augustus III, son of Augustus II	b. 1696 d. 1763
1764 1795	King	Stanislaus Augustus Poniatowski	abdicated 1795 b. 1732 d. 1798

Partitioned by Russia, Austria, and Prussia in 1772, 1793, and 1795

*Central Poland created Grand Duchy of Warsaw by Napoleon with
Frederick Augustus I of Saxony as ruler from 1807 to 1814.*

Regained Independence in 1918

■ Republic

1918–1922	Head of State	Joseph Pilsudski	b. 1867	d. 1935

*Pilsudski organized a private Polish army. On the outbreak of
war in 1914, he fought with his army under the Austrians against
the Russians. He refused to join the Central Powers, and after
they collapsed he went to Warsaw. From 1920 he was a virtual
dictator of Poland.*

1922	President	Gabriel Narutowicz	b. 1865	d. 1922
1922–1926	President	Stanislaw Wojciechowski	b. 1869	d. 1953
1926–1939	President	Ignacy Moscicki	b. 1867	d. 1946
1939–1945		*German Occupation*		
1939–1945	London Government	Wladyslaw Raczkiewicz	b. 1885	d. 1947
1945–1947	Chairman of the National Council of the People	Boleslaw Bierut	b. 1892	d. 1956

Communist Regime Established in 1947

1947–1952	Chairman	Józef Cyrankiewicz
1954–1970	Chairman	Józef Cyrankiewicz
1970–1980	Chairman	Piotr Jaroszewicz
1980–1981	Chairman	Józef Pinkowski
1981–1985	Chairman	Wojciech Jaruzelski
1985–1990	President	Wojciech Jaruzelski
1990–1995	President	Lech Walesa

*The legalization of the solidarity movement and the election
of Walesa marked the beginning of pluralistic democracy in Poland.*

1995–	President	Aleksander Kwasniewski

■ Danzig

The city of Danzig and its environs were detached from Germany after World War I and were made a free city.

1920–1930	President of Senate	Dr. Heinrich Sahm
1931–1933	President of Senate	Dr. E. Ziehm
1933–1934	President of Senate	Dr. Herman Rauschning
1934–1937	President of Senate	Arthur Greiser

*By 1938 Danzig was in the hands of the local Nazi Party and was
virtually administered as a German possession. Formal German
control took place after the outbreak of World War II. After the war,
the territory was assigned to Poland.*

Pontus

Pontus corresponded to what is modern-day northeastern Turkey.

486–479 B.C.	King	Artabazes	d. 479
479– ?	King	?	
? –401	King	Rhodobates	
401–363	King	Mithridates I	
363–337	King	Ariobarzanes	
337–302	King	Mithridates II	
302–266	King	Mithridates III	
266–214	King	Mithridates IV	
214–157	King	Pharnaces	
157–122	King	Mithridates V	d. 122
122–63	King	Mithridates VI the Great	b. 132 d. 63

Mithridates VI was defeated and deposed by the Romans, after which Pontus was partitioned into states tributary to the Roman Empire.

Portugal (Portuguese Republic)

Portugal in ancient times was called Lusitania. It was under Roman and Moorish rule before emerging as an independent state—arguably the first modern nation-state in history.

English versions of the names of rulers of Portuguese-speaking states are:

Charles Carlos	Ferdinand–Fernando	John–João
Denis–Diniz	Henry–Enrique	Michael–Miguel
Edward–Duarte	James–Diego	Peter–Pedro

■ House of Burgundy

1094–1112	Count	Henry of Burgundy, grandson of Robert I of Burgundy	b. 1057 d. 1112
1112–1128	Regent	Teresa of Castile, consort of Henry of Burgundy	
1128–1140	Count	Alfonso I, son of Henry of Burgundy	b. 1094? d. 1185
1140–1185	King	Alfonso I	
		Declared an Independent Monarchy in 1140	
1185–1211	King	Sancho I, son of Alfonso I	b. 1154 d. 1211
1211–1223	King	Alfonso II (the Fat), son of Sancho 1	b. 1186 d. 1223
1223–1245	King	Sancho II, son of Alfonso II	b. 1210? d. 1248
1245–1279	King	Alfonso III, son of Alfonso II	b. 1210? d. 1279
1279–1325	King	Diniz, son of Alfonso III	b. 1261 d. 1325
1325–1357	King	Alfonso IV, son of Diniz	b. 1291 d. 1357
1357–1367	King	Pedro I, son of Alfonso IV	b. 1320 d. 1367
1367–1383	King	Ferdinand I, son of Pedro I	b. 1345 d. 1383
1383–1385		*Internal Conflicts*	

■ House of Aviz

1385–1433	King	John I, son of Peter of Burgundy	b. 1358 d. 1433
1433–1438	King	Edward I, son of John 1	b. 1391 d. 1438
1438–1481	King	Alfonso V (Africano), son of Edward I	b. 1432 d. 1481
1481–1495	King	John II, son of Alfonso V	b. 1455 d. 1495

John II was known as "the Perfect," yet in the course of his struggles with the feudal nobles, he executed the Duke of Braganza and murdered the Duke of Viseu. It was during his reign that Bartholomeu Diaz discovered the Cape of Good Hope and opened the way to the East.

1495–1521	King	Emanuel I, grandson of Alfonso V	b. 1469 d. 1521

The reign of Emanuel I is significant for remarkable sea voyages by Portuguese seamen, such as the opening of an all-sea route to India by Vasco da Gama, Cabral's landing in Brazil, and Corte-Real's voyage to Labrador.

1521–1557	King	John III, son of Emanuel I	b. 1502 d. 1557
1557–1578	King	Sebastian, grandson of John III	b. 1554 killed 1578
1578–1580	King	Henry, brother of John III	b. 1512 d. 1580
1580	King	Antonio, nephew of Henry	b. 1531 d. 1595
1580–1640		*Ruled by Spain*	

■ House of Braganza

1640–1656	King	John IV, descendant of John I	b. 1604 d. 1656
1656–1667	King	Alfonso VI, son of John IV	b. 1643 d. 1683
1667–1683	Regent	Pedro II, son of John IV	b. 1648 d. 1706
1683–1706	King	Pedro II	
1706–1750	King	John V, son of Pedro II	b. 1689 d. 1750
1750–1777	King	Joseph Emanuel, son of John V	b. 1714 d. 1777
1777–1816	Queen	Maria I, daughter of Joseph Emanuel	b. 1734 d. 1816
1777–1786	Joint ruler	Pedro III, son of John V, husband of Maria I	b. 1717 d. 1786
1799–1816	Regent	John, son of Maria	b. 1767 d. 1826
1816–1826	King	John VI	
1826	King	Pedro IV, son of John VI	abdicated 1826 b. 1798 d. 1834
1826–1828	Queen	Maria II, daughter of Pedro	b. 1819 d. 1853
1828–1834	King (usurper)	Miguel, uncle of Maria II	abdicated 1834 b. 1802 d. 1866
1834–1853	Queen	Maria II	
1853–1861	King	Pedro V, son of Maria II	b. 1837 d. 1861
1861–1889	King	Louis I, son of Maria II	b. 1838 d. 1889
1889–1908	King	Carlos I, son of Louis I	b. 1863 assassinated 1908
1908–1910	King	Emanuel II, son of Carlos I	abdicated 1910 b. 1888 d. 1932

■ Republic

Portugal was proclaimed a republic in 1910.

1910–1911	President (provisional)	Teófilo Braga	b. 1843	d. 1919
1911–1915	President	Manoel José de Arriaga	b. 1840	d. 1917
1915	President	Teófilo Braga		
1915–1917	President	Bernardino Luiz Machado Guimaraes	b. 1851	d. 1944
1918–1918	President	Sidônio Bernadino Cardoso de Silva Paes	b. 1872	d. 1918
1918–1919	President (provisional)	João de Canto e Castro Silva Antunes	b. 1862	d. 1934
1919–1923	President	António José de Almeida	b. 1866	d. 1929
1923–1925	President	Manoel Teixeira Gomes	b. 1860	d. 1914
1925–1926	President	Bernardino Luiz Machado Guimaraes		
1926–1951	President	Antonio Oscar de Fragoso Carmona	b. 1869	d. 1951
1932–1968	Dictator	Antonio de Oliveira Salazar	b. 1889	d. 1970
1968–1974	Premier	Marcelo Caetano	b. 1906	d. 1980
1974	Mil. President	Antonio de Spínola		
1974–1976	Mil. President	Fransisco da Costa Gomes		
1976–1986	President	António Ramalho Eanes	b. 1935	
1986–1996	President	Mário Soares		
1996–	President	Jorge Sampaio		

Puerto Rico

A self-governing Commonwealth in association with the United States of America, Puerto Rico was visited by Christopher Columbus in 1493.

1510	Spanish Governor	Juan Ponce de Léon	b. 1460?	d. 1521
1511	Spanish Governor	Juan Cerón		
1512–1513	Spanish Governor	Rodrigo de Moscoso		
1513–1515	Spanish Governor	Cristóbal de Mendoza		
1515–1517	Spanish Governor	Juan Ponce de Léon		
1519–1521	Spanish Governor	Antonio de la Gama		
1521–1523	Spanish Governor	Pedro Moreno		
1523–1524	Spanish Governor	Alonso Manso		
1524–1529	Spanish Governor	Pedro Moreno and Antonio de la Gama		
1530–1536	Spanish Governor	Francisco Manuel de Lando		
1536–1537	Spanish Governor	Vasco de Tiedra		
1537–1544	Spanish Governor	Dos Alcaldes Ordinarios		
1544–1545	Spanish Governor	Gerónimo Lebrón		

1545–1546	Spanish Governor	Iñigo López Cervantes de Loaisa
1546–1548	Spanish Governor	Diego de Caraza
1548–1550	Spanish Governor	Dos Alcaldes Ordinarios
1550–1555	Spanish Governor	Luis de Vallejo
1555	Spanish Governor	Licenciado Esteves
1555–1561	Spanish Governor	Diego de Caraza
1561–1564	Spanish Governor	Antonio de la Llama Vallejo
1564–1568	Spanish Governor	Francisco Bahamonde de Lugo
1568–1574	Spanish Governor	Francisco de Solís
1575–1579	Spanish Governor	Francisco de Obando y Mexia
1580	Spanish Governor	Gerónimo de Aguero Campuzano
1580–1581	Spanish Governor	Juan de Céspedes
1581–1582	Spanish Governor	Juan López Melgarejo
1582–1593	Spanish Governor	Diego Menéndez de Valdés
1593–1597	Spanish Governor	Pedro Suarez
1597–1598	Spanish Governor	Antonio de Mosquera
1598–1599	Spanish Governor	Alonso de Mercado
1602–1608	Spanish Governor	Sancho Ochoa de Castro
1608–1614	Spanish Governor	Gabriel de Roxas
1613–1620	Spanish Governor	Felipe de Beaumont y Navarra
1620–1625	Spanish Governor	Juan de Vargas
1625–1630	Spanish Governor	Juan de Haro
1631–1635	Spanish Governor	Enrique Enriquez de Sotomayor
1635–1641	Spanish Governor	Iñigo de la Mota Sarmiento
1640–1641	Spanish Governor	Agustín de Silva y Figueroa
1641–1642	Spanish Governor	Juan de Bolaños
1642–1648	Spanish Governor	Fernando de la Riva Aguero
1649–1655	Spanish Governor	Diego de Aguilera y Gamboa
1655–1660	Spanish Governor	José Novoa y Moscoso
1660–1664	Spanish Governor	Juan Pérez de Guzmán
1664–1670	Spanish Governor	Gerónimo de Velasco
1670–1674	Spanish Governor	Gaspar de Arteaga
1674	Spanish Governor	Diego Robladillo
1675–1678	Spanish Governor	Alonso de Campos
1678–1683	Spanish Governor	Juan de Robles Lorenzana
1683–1685	Spanish Governor	Gaspar Martínez de Andino
1685–1690	Spanish Governor	Juan Francisco de Medina

1690–1695	Spanish Governor	Gaspar de Arredondo
1695–1697	Spanish Governor	Juan Francisco Medina
1697–1698	Spanish Governor	Tomás Franco
1698–1699	Spanish Governor	Antonio Robles
1700–1703	Spanish Governor	Gabriel Gutiérrez de Rivas
1703	Spanish Governor	Diego Villarán
1703	Spanish Governor	Francisco Sánchez
1704–1705	Spanish Governor	Pedro de Arroyo y Guerrero
1706	Spanish Governor	Juan Francisco Morla
1706–1708	Spanish Governor	Francisco Granados
1709–1714	Spanish Governor	Juan de Ribera
1716	Spanish Governor	José Carreño
1716–1720	Spanish Governor	Alonso Bertodano
1720–1724	Spanish Governor	Francisco Danio Granados
1724–1730	Spanish Governor	José Antonio de Mendizábal
1731–1743	Spanish Governor	Matías de Abadía
1743–1744	Spanish Governor	Domingo Pérez de Nandares
1744–1750	Spanish Governor	Juan José Colomo
1750–1751	Spanish Governor	Agustín de Parejas
1751–1753	Spanish Governor	Esteban Bravo de Rivero
1753–1757	Spanish Governor	Felipe Ramírez de Estenós
1757–1759	Spanish Governor	Esteban Bravo de Rivero
1759–1760	Spanish Governor	Mateo de Guazo Calderón
1760–1761	Spanish Governor	Esteban Bravo de Rivero
1761–1766	Spanish Governor	Ambrosio de Benavides
1766	Spanish Governor	Marcos de Vergara
1766–1770	Spanish Governor	José Trentor
1770–1776	Spanish Governor	Miguel de Muesas
1776–1783	Spanish Governor	José Dufresne
1783–1789	Spanish Governor	Juan Dabán
1789	Spanish Governor	Francisco Torralbo
1789–1792	Spanish Governor	Miguel Antonio de Ustariz
1792–1794	Spanish Governor	Francisco Torralbo
1794–1795	Spanish Governor	Enrique Grimarest
1795–1804	Spanish Governor	Ramón de Castro y Gutiérrez
1804–1809	Spanish Governor	Toribio de Montes
1809–1820	Spanish Governor	Salvador Meléndez y Ruíz

1820	Spanish Governor	Juan Vasco y Pascual
1820–1822	Spanish Governor	Gonzalo de Arostegui y Herrera
1822	Spanish Governor	José Navarro
1822	Spanish Governor	Francisco González de Linares
1822–1837	Spanish Governor	Miguel de la Torre
1837–1838	Spanish Governor	Francisco Moreda y Prieto
1838–1841	Spanish Governor	Miguel López de Baños
1841–1844	Spanish Governor	Santiago Méndez de Vigo
1844–1847	Spanish Governor	Rafael de Aristegui y Vélez
1847–1848	Spanish Governor	Juan Prim
1848–1851	Spanish Governor	Juan de la Pezuela Cevallos
1851–1852	Spanish Governor	Enrique de España y Taberner
1852–1855	Spanish Governor	Fernando de Norzagaray y Escudero
1855	Spanish Governor	Andrés Garcia Camba
1855–1857	Spanish Governor	José Lemery
1860	Spanish Governor	Fernando Cotoner y Chacón
1860–1862	Spanish Governor	Rafael Echague
1862–1863	Spanish Governor	Rafael Izquierdo
1862–1865	Spanish Governor	Félix María de Messina
1865–1867	Spanish Governor	José María Marchesi
1867–1868	Spanish Governor	Julión Juan Pavía
1868–1870	Spanish Governor	José Laureano Sanz y Posse
1870–1873	Spanish Governor	Gabriel Baldrich y Palau
1872	Spanish Governor	Ramón Gómez Pulido
1872	Spanish Governor	Simón de la Torre
1872–1873	Spanish Governor	Joaquín Eurile
1873	Spanish Governor	Juan Martínez Plowes
1873–1874	Spanish Governor	Rafael Primo de Rivera y Sobremonte
1874–1875	Spanish Governor	José Laureano Sanz y Posse
1875–1877	Spanish Governor	Segundo de la Portilla
1877–1878	Spanish Governor	Manuel de la Serna y Pinzón
1878–1881	Spanish Governor	Eulogio Despujols y Dussay
1881–1883	Spanish Governor	Segundo de la Portilla
1883–1884	Spanish Governor	Miguel de la Vega Inclán
1884	Spanish Governor	Ramón Fajardo
1884–1887	Spanish Governor	Luis Dabán y Ramírez de Arellano
1887	Spanish Governor	Romualdo Palacios

1887–1888	Spanish Governor	Juan Contreras	
1888–1890	Spanish Governor	Pedro Ruíz Dana	
1890	Spanish Governor	José Pascual Bonanza	
1890–1893	Spanish Governor	José Lasso y Pérez	
1893–1895	Spanish Governor	Antonio Dabán y Ramírez de Arellano	
1895–1896	Spanish Governor	José Gamir	
1896	Spanish Governor	Emilio March	
1896–1898	Spanish Governor	Sabás Marín	
1898	Spanish Governor	Ricardo Ortega	
1898	Spanish Governor	Andrés González Muñoz	
1898	Spanish Governor	Rocardo Ortega	
1898	Spanish Governor	Manuel Macías Casado	
1898	Spanish Governor	Ricardo Ortega	
		Ceded to the U.S.A. in 1898	
1898	Military Governor	John Rutter Brooke	b. 1838 d. 1926
1898–1899	Military Governor	Guy V. Henry	
1899–1900	Military Governor	George Whitefield Davis	b. 1839 d. 1918
1900–1902	Civil Governor	Charles Herbert Allen	b. 1848 d. 1934
1902–1904	Civil Governor	William H. Hunt	
1904–1907	Civil Governor	Beekman Winthrop	
1907–1909	Civil Governor	Regis II. Post	
1909–1913	Civil Governor	George R. Colton	
1913–1921	Civil Governor	Arthur Yater	
1921–1923	Civil Governor	E. Montgomery Reilly	
1923–1929	Civil Governor	Horace Mann Towner	
1929–1932	Civil Governor	Theodore Roosevelt, Jr.	b. 1887 d. 1944
1932–1933	Civil Governor	James R. Beverly	
1933–1934	Civil Governor	Robert H. Gore	
1934–1939	Civil Governor	Blanton Winship	
1939–1940	Civil Governor	William Daniel Leahy	b. 1875 d. 1959
1941	Civil Governor	Guy J. Swope	
1941–1946	Civil Governor	Rexford G. Tugwell	
1946–1949	Civil Governor	Jesús T. Piñero	
1949–1964	Civil Governor	Luis Muñoz Marín	
1964–1969	Civil Governor	Roberto Sanchez Vilella	
1969–1973	Civil Governor	Luis A. Ferré	
1973–1977	Civil Governor	Rafael Hernández Colón	

1977–1985	Civil Governor	Carlos Romero Barceló
1985–1993	Civil Governor	Rafael Hernández Colón
1993–2001	Civil Governor	Pedro Rosselló González
2001–2005	Civil Governor	Sila M. Calderón
2005–	Civil Governor	Aníbal Acevedo Vilá

Qatar (State of Qatar)

Formerly a sheikhdom under British protection, Qatar became independent in 1971 when efforts for it to be a part of the United Arab Emirates failed.

–1960	Sheikh	Ali bin Abdullah Al-Thani
1960–1972	Sheikh	Ahmed bin Ali bin Abdullah Al-Thani
1972–1995	Sheikh	Khalifa Bin Hamad Al Thani
1995–	Sheikh	Hamad bin Khalifa Al-Thani

Roman Empire, The

The traditional date of Rome's foundation is April 21, 753 B.C.

753–716 B.C.	Legendary King	Romulus, son of Rhea Silvia	
716–672	Legendary King	Numa Pompilius	
672–640	Legendary King	Tullus Hostilius	
640–616	Legendary King	Ancus Marcius, grandson of Numa Pompilius	
616–578	Legendary King	Lucius Tarquinius Priscus	
578–534	Legendary King	Servius Tullius, son-in-law of Tarquinius Priscus	
534–509	Legendary King	Lucius Tarquinius Superbus, son of Tarquinius Priscus	
509–31		A *Republic*	
60	First Triumvirate	Caesar, Pompey and Crassus	
43–28	Second Triumvirate	Octavian, Antony and Lepidus Gaius Julius Caesar	b. 100 B.C. assassinated 44 B.C.

Captured by pirates, Caesar threatened to crucify them—a promise he carried out faithfully as soon as possible after he was ransomed. Few dispute Caesar's military genius, but his role and achievements as statesman are still a subject of controversy, as they were more than 2,000 years ago.

Gnaeus Pompeius Magnus	b. 106 B.C. murdered 48 B.C.
Marcus Licinius Crassus	b. 115 B.C.? executed 53 B.C.
Octavian (Augustus), grand-nephew and adopted son of Julius Caesar	b. 63 B.C. d. A.D. 14
Antony (Marcus Antonius)	b. 83 B.C.? d. 30 B.C.
Marcus Aemilius Lepidus	d. 13 B.C.

■ Claudian Dynasty

27 B.C.–A.D. 14	Emperor	Augustus (Octavian)	

First of the Roman emperors, Gaius Julius Caesar Octavianus was given the title of Augustus by the Roman senate in recognition for his outstanding services to the state. Despite his early crimes and cruelties, Augustus carried through reforms which united the Empire and secured peace. He ranks as one of the greatest statesmen of all time.

14–37	Emperor	Tiberius, stepson of Augustus	b. 42 B.C. d. A.D. 37
37–41	Emperor	Caligula (Gaius Caesar), grand-nephew of Tiberius	b. 12 assassinated 41
41–54	Emperor	Claudius I, nephew of Tiberius	b. 10 B.C. poisoned A.D. 54
54–68	Emperor	Nero, stepson of Claudius	b. 37 committed suicide 68

There can be little doubt that Nero was mad. He seized the throne, excluding the rightful heir, Britannicus, and then killed him; killed his own mother and wife; executed Seneca; and also killed his second wife Poppaea. In addition, he persecuted the Christians on a trumped-up charge of burning Rome.

68–69	Emperor	Galba	b. 3 B.C. assassinated A.D. 69
69	Emperor	Otho	b. 32 committed suicide 69
69	Emperor	Vitellius	b. 15 murdered 69

■ Flavian Dynasty

69–79	Emperor	Vespasian	b. 9 d. 79
79–81	Emperor	Titus, son of Vespasian	b. 41? d. 81
81–96	Emperor	Domitian, son of Vespasian	b. 51 assassinated 96

■ Antonine Dynasty

96–98	Emperor	Nerva	b. 35? d. 98
98–117	Emperor	Trajan	b. 53? d. 117
117–138	Emperor	Hadrian, nephew of Trajan	b. 6 d. 138

Hadrian visited Britain and was responsible for building a line of fortifications, Hadrian's Wall, from the Solway Firth to Wallsend on the mouth of the River Tyne. The line was intended to be a barrier against the Picts and Scots.

138–161	Emperor	Antoninus Pius	b. 86 d. 161
161–180	Emperor	Marcus Aurelius, son-in-law of Antoninus Pius	b. 121 d. 180
161–169	Co-regent	Lucius Aurelius Verus, adopted brother of Marcus Aurelius	b. 130 d. 169
180–192	Emperor	Commodus, son of Marcus Aurelius	b. 161 murdered 192

■ African and Syrian Emperors

193	Emperor	Pertinax	b. 126 assassinated 193
193–211	Emperor	Septimius Severus	b. 146 d. 211
193	Emperor (rival)	Didius Julianus	b. 133 murdered 193
193–194	Emperor (rival)	Pescennius Niger	
193–197	Emperor (rival)	Albinus	beheaded 197
211–217	Emperor (rival)	Caracalla, son of Septimius Severus	b. 188 assassinated 217
211–212	Co-Regent	Geta, son of Septimius Severus	b. 189 murdered 212
217–218	Emperor	Macrinus	b. 164 killed 218
218–222	Emperor	Heliogabalus (Elagabalus)	b. 204 assassinated 222
222–235	Emperor	Alexander Severus, cousin of Heliogabalus	b. 208? murdered 235
235–238	Emperor	Maximinus Thrax	b. 173 murdered 238
238	Emperor (rival)	Gordianus I (Africanus)	b. 158 committed suicide 238
238	Co-Regent	Gordianus II, son of Gordianus I	b. 192 killed 238
238	Emperor	Pupienus Maximus	murdered 238
238	Co-Regent	Balbinus	murdered 238
238–244	Emperor	Gordianus III, grandson of Gordianus I	b. 224? murdered 244
244–249	Emperor	Philip the Arabian	killed 249
249–251	Emperor	Decius	b. 201 killed 251
251–253	Emperor	Gallus	b. 205? murdered 253?
253	Emperor	Aemilianus	b. 206? d. 253
253–260	Emperor	Valerian	d. 269?
260–268	Emperor	Gallienus, son of Valerian	assassinated 268

■ Illyrian Emperors

268–270	Emperor	Caudius II (Gothicus)	b. 214 d. 270
270–275	Emperor	Aurelian	b. 212 assassinated 275
275–276	Emperor	Tacitus	b. 200? murdered 276
276	Emperor	Florian, brother of Tacitus	killed 276
276–282	Emperor	Probus	murdered 282
282–283	Emperor	Carus	b. 223? killed 283
283–285	Emperor	Carinus, son of Carus	murdered 285

■ Later Emperors

Before the formal division of the Empire into East and West, many emperors ruled simultaneously.

284–305	Emperor	Diocletian	b. 245 d. 313

Diocletian is the Roman emperor most strongly associated with the persecution of the Christians. In 303 he issued an edict against them. Though he abdicated in 305 and retired to Dalmatia, the fierce persecutions lasted for 10 years.

285–305	Emperor	Maximian	committed suicide 310
305–306	Emperor	Constantius I (Chlorus)	b. 250 d. 306
306–311	Emperor	Galerius	d. 311
306–307	Emperor	Severus	d. 307
307–313	Emperor	Maximinus, nephew of Galerius	d. 313
307–337	Emperor	Constantine I the Great, son of Constantius I	b. 288 d. 337
306–312	Emperor	Maxentius, son of Maximian	drowned 312
311–324	Emperor	Licinius, adopted son of Galerius	b. 270? executed 324
337–340	Emperor	Constantine II, son of Constantine I	b. 316? killed 340
337–350	Emperor	Constans I, son of Constantine I	b. 320 assassinated 350
337–361	Emperor	Constantius II, son of Constantine I	b. 317 d. 361
361–363	Emperor	Julian the Apostate, cousin of Constantius II	b. 331 killed 363
363–364	Emperor	Jovian	b. 331 d. 364
364		*Division of the Empire*	
364–375	Emperor (West)	Valentinian I	b. 321 d. 375
364–378	Emperor (East)	Valens, brother of Valentinian I	b. 328? killed 378
375–383	Emperor (West)	Gratian, son of Valentinian I	b. 359 assassinated 383
375–392	Emperor (West)	Valentinian II, son of Valentinian I	b. 371 d. 392
379–394	Emperor (East)	Theodosius I	b. 346 d. 395
383–388	Emperor (West)	Maximus	executed 388
392–394	Emperor (West)	Eugenius	killed 394
394–395	Emperor (West)	Theodosius	

The Divided Roman Empire

Western Roman Empire

395–423	Emperor	Honorius, son of Theodosius I	b. 384 d. 423
425–455	Emperor	Valentinian III, nephew of Honorius	b. 419 murdered 455
455	Emperor	Petronius Maximus	killed 455
455–456	Emperor	Avitus	d. 456
457–461	Emperor	Majorian	d. 461
461–465	Emperor	Livius Severus	d. 465
467–472	Emperor	Anthemius, son-in-law of Marcian	killed 472
472	Emperor	Olybrius, son-in-law of Valentinian III	
473–474	Emperor	Glycerius	
474–475	Emperor	Julius Nepos	assassinated 480?

| 475–476 | Emperor | Romulus Augustulus, son of Orestes | b. 461? |

The Western Roman Empire ended in 476 A.D. when Augustulus was defeated by Odoacer.

Eastern Roman (Byzantine) Empire

■ Theodosian Dynasty

| 395–408 | Emperor | Arcadius, son of Theodosius I | b. 378? d. 408 |
| 408–450 | Emperor | Theodosius II, son of Arcadius | b. 401 d. 450 |

■ Thracian Dynasty

450–457	Emperor	Marcianus, brother-in-law of Theodosius II	b. 392 d. 457
457–474	Emperor	Leo I the Great	b. 400? d. 474
474	Emperor	Leo II, grandson of Leo I the Great	d. 474
474–491	Emperor	Zeno, father of Leo II	b. 426 d. 491
491–518	Emperor	Anastasius I, son-in-law of Leo II	b. 430 d. 518

■ Justinian Dynasty

| 518–527 | Emperor | Justin I | b. 450 d. 527 |

With his code of Roman Law, the Emperor Justinian improved the conditions of slaves, codified and reformed the laws, and laid the foundations of the civil law of many modern nations.

527–565	Emperor	Justinian I, nephew of Justin I	b. 483 d. 565
565–578	Emperor	Justin II, nephew of Justinian I	d. 578
578–582	Emperor	Tiberius II Constantinus	d. 582
582–602	Emperor	Maurice, son-in-law of Tiberius II	b. 540 assassinated 602
602–610	Emperor	Phocas	beheaded 610

■ Heraclian Dynasty

610–641	Emperor	Heraclius	b. 575? d. 641
641	Emperor	Constantine III, son of Heraclius	b. 612? d. 641
641	Co-Regent	Heracleonas, son of Heraclius	b. 614?
641–668	Emperor	Constans II, son of Constantine III	b. 630 murdered 668
668–685	Emperor	Constantine IV, son of Constans II	b. 648 d. 685
685–695	Emperor	Justinian II, son of Constantine IV	b. 669 assassinated 711
695–698	Emperor	Leontius	killed 705
698–705	Emperor	Tiberius III Apsimar	beheaded 705
705–711	Emperor	Justinian II	

711–713	Emperor	Philippicus	
713–716	Emperor	Anastasius II	executed 721
716–717	Emperor	Theodosius III	d. 718?

■ Isaurian Dynasty

717–741	Emperor	Leo III the Isaurian	b. 680? d. 741
741–775	Emperor	Constantine V, son of Leo III	b. 718 d. 775
775–780	Emperor	Leo IV, son of Constantine V	b. 750? d. 780
780–790	Empress (regent)	Irene, wife of Leo IV	b. 752 d. 803
780–797	Emperor	Constantine VI, son of Irene	b. 770 murdered 797?
797–802	Empress	Irene	
802–811	Emperor	Nicephorus I	killed 811
811	Emperor	Stauracius	
811–813	Emperor	Michael I, son-in-law of Nicephorus I	d. 845
813–820	Emperor	Leo V the Armenian	assassinated 820

■ Amorian Dynasty

820–829	Emperor	Michael II	d. 829
829–842	Emperor	Theophilus, son of Michael II	d. 842
842–857	Empress (regent)	Theodora, mother of Michael III	d. 867?
842–867	Emperor	Michael III, son of Theophilus	assassinated 867

■ Macedonian Dynasty

867–886	Emperor	Basil I the Macedonian	b. 813? d. 886
886–912	Emperor	Leo VI, son of Michael III	b. 866 d. 912
913–919	Emperor	Constantine VII, son of Leo VI	b. 905 d. 959
919–944	Emperor (regent)	Romanus I, stepfather of Constantine VII	d. 948
944–959	Emperor	Constantine VII	
959–963	Emperor	Romanus II, son of Constantine VII	b. 939 d. 963
963–969	Emperor	Nicephorus II	b. 912? murdered 969
969–976	Emperor	John I Zimisces	b. 925 d. 976
976–1025	Emperor	Basil II, son of Romanus II	b. 958? d. 1025
1025–1028	Emperor	Constantine VIII, son of Romanus II	b. 960? d. 1028
1028–1034	Emperor	Romanus III, son-in-law of Constantine VIII	b. 968? d. 1034
1034–1041	Emperor	Michael IV, son-in-law of Constantine VIII	d. 1041
1041–1042	Emperor	Michael V, nephew of Michael IV	
1042–1055	Emperor	Constantine IX, son-in-law of Constantine VIII	b. 1000? d. 1055

1055–1056	Empress	Theodora, daughter of Constantine VIII	b. 980 d. 1056
1056–1057	Emperor	Michael VI	
1057–1059	Emperor	Isaac I Comnenus	d. 1061

■ Ducas Dynasty

1059–1067	Emperor	Constantine X Ducas	b. 1007? d. 1067
1067–1071	Emperor	Romanus IV	murdered 1071
1071–1078	Emperor	Michael VII, son of Constantine X	
1078–1081	Emperor	Nicephorus III Botaniates	d. 1081

■ Comnenus Dynasty

1081–1118	Emperor	Alexius I Comnenus, nephew of Isaac I	b. 1048 d. 1118
1118–1143	Emperor	John II Comnenus, son of Alexius I Comnenus	b. 1088 d. 1143
1143–1180	Emperor	Manuel I Comnenus, son of John II Comnenus	b. 1120 d. 1180
1180–1183	Emperor	Alexius II, son of Manuel I Comnenus	b. 1168? murdered 1183
1183–1185	Emperor	Andronicus I, grandson of Alexius I Comnenus	b. 1110? murdered 1185

■ Angelus Dynasty

1185–1195	Emperor	Isaac II Angelus	executed 1204
1195–1203	Emperor	Alexius III, brother of Isaac II	d. 1210
1203–1204	Emperor	Alexius IV, son of Isaac II	executed 1204
1204	Emperor	Alexius V	executed 1204

■ Latin Dynasty

1204–1205	Emperor	Baldwin I, son of Baldwin V, Count of Hainault	b. 1171 killed 1205?

A leader of the Fourth Crusade, Baldwin I was elected the first Latin emperor by the crusaders following their capture of Constantinople. The following year he was beaten, captured, and killed by the Greeks and Bulgarians.

1205–1216	Emperor	Henry, brother of Baldwin I	b. 1174? d. 1216
1216–1217	Emperor	Peter, brother-in-law of Baldwin I	d. 1217
1217–1219	Empress (regent)	Yolande, wife of Peter	d. 1220?
1219–1228	Emperor	Robert, son of Peter	d. 1228
1228–1261	Emperor	Baldwin II, brother of Robert	b. 1217 d. 1273

■ Lascaris Dynasty (Empire of Nicaea)

1206–1222	Emperor	Theodore I Lascaris, son-in-law of Alexius III	d. 1222

1222–1254	Emperor	John III Ducas, son-in-law of Theodore Lascaris	b. 1193 d. 1254
1254–1258	Emperor	Theodore II Lascaris, son of John III Ducas	b. 1221 d. 1258
1258–1261	Emperor	John IV Lascaris, son of Theodore II Lascaris	b. 1250 d. 1269
1259–1261	Regent	Michael Palaeologus	b. 1234 d. 1282

■ Palaeologogus Dynasty

1261–1282	Emperor	Michael VIII Palaeologus	
1282–1328	Emperor	Andronicus II, son of Michael VIII	b. 1260 d. 1332
1328–1341	Emperor	Andronicus III, grandson of Andronicus II	b. 1296 d. 1341
1341–1347	Emperor	John V Palaeologus, son of Andronicus III	b. 1332 d. 1391
1347–1355	Emperor	John VI Cantacuzene	b. 1292 d. 1383
1376–1379	Emperor (rival)	Andronicus IV, son of John V Palaeologus	d. 1385
1379–1391	Emperor	John V	
1391–1425	Emperor	Manuel II Palaeologus, son of John V Palaeologus	b. 1350 d. 1425
1391–1412	Emperor Co-Regent	John VII, son of Andronicus IV	b. 1360 d. 1412
1425–1448	Emperor	John VIII, son of Manuel II Palaeologus	b. 1390 d. 1448
1448–1453	Emperor	Constantine XI, son of Manuel II Palaeologus	b. 1403 killed 1453

Last Emperor of the Eastern Empire, Constantine XI fought bravely against the Turkish armies, but was killed in the last stages of the battle for Constantinople at one of the gates of the city.

The Eastern Empire ended with the capture of Constantinople by the Turks in 1453.

Romania (Official U.N. Name)

Part of the Roman Empire in ancient times, Romania was overrun by barbarian tribes from the 6th to the 12th centuries. Wallachia was founded around 1290, and Moldavia was founded around 1340. Both Wallachia and Moldavia were united in 1859.

1859–1866	Prince	Alexander John (Alexandru Ioan) I (Cuza) of Moldavia	b. 1820 d. 1873
1866–1881	Prince	Karl Eitel Friedrich of Hohenzollern-Sigmaringen	b. 1839 d. 1914

Karl was elected ruler of Romania by the assemblies of Moldavia and Wallachia. He was invested in Constantinople by the Sultan, who granted him the right to maintain an army of 30,000 men. The German prince's position was difficult during the Franco-German War, due to the Romanian people's strong pro-French sympathies.

1881		*Recognized as a Kingdom*	
1881–1914	King	Carol I (Karl)	
1914–1927	King	Ferdinand I, nephew of Carol I	b. 1865 d. 1927
1927–1930	King	Michael (Mihai), grandson of Ferdinand I	b. 1921
1930–1940	King	Carol II, son of Ferdinand and father of Michael	b. 1893 d. 1953

> *King of Romania from 1930 to 1940, Carol II was married to the daughter of King Constantine of the Hellenes, but it was his association with Madame Lupescu that attracted the world's attention during most of his life.*

1940–1947	King	Michael

■ People's Republic (Communist Regime Established in 1948)

1948–1952	President	Constantin I. Parhon	b. 1874
1952–1958	President	Petru Groza	b. 1884 d. 1958
1958–1961	Head of State	Ion Gheorghe Maurer	b. 1902
1961–1965	Chairman of State Council	Gheorghe Gheorghiu-Dej	b. 1901 d. 1965
1965–	President	Chivu Stoica	b. 1908
1952–1955	President	Gheorghe Gheorghiu-Dej	
1961–1974	Chairman of Council of Ministers	Ion Gheorghe Maurer	
1967–1989	Dictator	Nicolae Ceausescu	
1990–1996	President	Ion Iliescu	
1996–2001	President	Emil Constantinescu	
2001–	President	Ion Iliescu	

Russia (Russian Federation)

Norsemen, under Rurik, settled at Kiev in the 9th century. Under Rurik's descendants, Russia was divided into numerous independent principalities—said to number sixty-four between the 11th and 13th centuries.

■ Grand Dukes of Kiev

862–879	Grand Duke	Rurik of Novgorod	d. 879
879–912	Grand Duke	Oleg (Helgi)	
912–945	Grand Duke	Igor, son of Rurik of Novgorod	
945–955	Regent	St. Olga, wife of Igor	d. 969
955–972	Grand Duke	Sviatoslav, son of Igor	
972–977	Grand Duke	Yaropolk, son of Sviatoslav	
977–1015	Grand Duke	St. Vladimir, son of Sviatoslav	b. 956? d. 1015
1015–1019	Grand Duke	Sviatopolk, son of St. Vladimir	
1019–1054	Grand Duke	Yaroslav, son of St. Vladimir	d. 1054
1054–1073	Grand Duke	Izhaslav (Isiaslav), son of Yaroslav	d. 1078
1073–1076	Grand Duke	Sviatoslav, son of Yaroslav	
1078–1093	Grand Duke	Vsevolod, son of Yaroslav	
1093–1113	Grand Duke	Sviatopolk, son of Izhaslav	

1113–1125	Grand Duke	Vladimir Monomachus, son of Vsevolod	b. 1053 d. 1125
1125–1132	Grand Duke	Mstislav, son of Vladimir Monomachus	
1132–1139	Grand Duke	Yaropolk, brother of Mstislav	
1139–1146	Grand Duke	Vsevolod, great-grandson of Yaroslav	
1146–1154	Grand Duke	Izhaslav II, son of Mstislav	

The title of Grand Duke passed from Kiev to Vladimir after 1154.

■ Grand Dukes of Vladimir

1154–1157	Grand Duke	Yuri (George) Dolgoruki, son of Vladimir Monomachus	
1157–1175	Grand Duke	Andrey Bogolyubski, son of Yuri Dolgoruki	
1176–1212	Grand Duke	Vsevolod, son of Yuri Dolgoruki	
1212–1218	Grand Duke	Konstantin, son of Vsevolod	
1218–1238	Grand Duke	Yuri II, son of Vsevolod	

Invasion of Golden Horde in 1223

1238–1246	Grand Duke	Yaroslav II, son of Vsevolod	
1246–1253	Grand Duke	Andrey, son of Yaroslav II	
1253–1263	Grand Duke	Aleksandr Nevsky, son of Yaroslav II	b. 1220? d. 1263
1263–1272	Grand Duke	Yaroslav of Tver, son of Yaroslav II	
1272–1276	Grand Duke	Basil, son of Yaroslav II	
1276–1293	Grand Duke	Demetrius, son of Aleksandr Nevsky	
1293–1304	Grand Duke	Andrey, son of Aleksandr Nevsky	
1304–1318	Grand Duke	Michael of Tver	
1318–1326	Grand Duke	Yuri Danilovich of Moscow, grandson of Yaroslav II	
1326–1328	Grand Duke	Alexander of Tver, son of Michael of Tver	

■ Grand Dukes of Moscow

1328–1341	Grand Duke	Ivan I (Kalita), brother of Yuri Danilovich of Moscow	d. 1341
1341–1353	Grand Duke	Simeon, son of Ivan I	
1353–1359	Grand Duke	Ivan II, son of Ivan I	b. 1326 d. 1359
1359–1389	Grand Duke	Demetrius Donskoi, son of Ivan II	b. 1350 d. 1389
1389–1425	Grand Duke	Basil I, son of Demetrius Donskoi	b. 1371 d. 1425
1425–1462	Grand Duke	Basil II, son of Basil I	b. 1415 d. 1462
1462–1505	Grand Duke	Ivan III the Great, son of Basil II	b. 1440 d. 1505
1505–1533	Grand Duke	Basil III, son of Ivan the Great	b. 1479 d. 1533
1533–1584	"Tsar of all Russia" (from 1547)	Ivan IV the Terrible, son of Basil III	b. 1530 d. 1584

Ivan the Terrible was the first Russian ruler to use the title

1584–1598	Tsar	Fedor I, son of Ivan IV	b. 1557 d. 1598
1598–1605	Tsar	Boris Godunov, brother-in-law of Fedor I	b. 1552 d. 1605
1605	Tsar	Fedor II, son of Boris Godunov	b. 1589 murdered 1605
1605–1606	Usurper	Dmitri (Demetrius I)	murdered 1606
1606–1610	Ruler	Basil IV Shuiski	b. 1552 d. 1612
1607–1610	Usurper	Demetrius II	killed 1610
1610–1612	Ruler	Ladislaus IV of Poland, son of Sigismund III	b. 1595 d. 1648

■ Tsars (Emperors) (House of Romanov)

1613–1645	Emperor	Michael I	b. 1596 d. 1645
1645–1676	Emperor	Aleksei (Alexis), son of Michael	b. 1629 d. 1676
1676–1682	Emperor	Fedor III, son of Aleksei	b. 1656 d. 1682
1682–1689	Emperor	Ivan V, son of Aleksei	deposed 1689 b. 1666 d. 1696
1682–1689	Regent	Sophia, daughter of Aleksei	b. 1657 d. 1704
1682–1725	Emperor	Peter I the Great, son of Aleksei	b. 1672 d. 1725
1725–1727	Empress	Catherine I, consort of Peter I the Great	b. 1684 d. 1727
1727–1730	Emperor	Peter II, grandson of Peter I the Great	b. 1715 d. 1730
1730–1740	Empress	Anna (Duchess of Courland), daughter of Ivan V	b. 1693 d. 1740
1740–1741	Emperor	Ivan VI, grand-nephew of Anna	b. 1740 murdered 1764
1741–1762	Empress	Elizabeth Petrovna, daughter of Peter I the Great	b. 1709 d. 1762
1762	Emperor	Peter III, nephew of Elizabeth	b. 1728 murdered 1762
1762–1796	Empress	Catherine II the Great, consort of Peter III	b. 1729 d. 1796

1796–1801	Emperor	Paul I, son of Peter III	b. 1754 murdered 1801
1801–1825	Emperor	Alexander I, son of Paul I	b. 1777 d. 1825
1825–1855	Emperor	Nicholas I, son of Paul I	b. 1796 d. 1855
1855–1881	Emperor	Alexander II, son of Nicholas I	b. 1818 assassinated 1881
1881–1894	Emperor	Alexander III, son of Alexander II	b. 1845 d. 1894
1894–1917	Emperor	Nicholas II, son of Alexander III	abdicated 1917 b. 1868 murdered 1918

■ Statesmen

1696–1727	Leading Minister	Prince Aleksandr Danilovich Menshikov	b. 1672 d. 1729
1730–1740	Leading Minister	Ernst Johann Biron, Duke of Kurland	b. 1690 d. 1772
1721–1741	Foreign Minister	Heinrich J. F. Ostermann	d. 1747
1732–1741	Field Marshal	Burkhard Christoph von Münnich	b. 1683 d. 1767
1762–1767	Field Marshal	Burkhard Christoph von Münnich	
1762–1781	Leading Minister	Nikita Ivanovich Panin	b. 1718 d. 1783
1774–1791	Leading Minister	Grigori Aleksandrovich Potemkin	b. 1739 d. 1791
1809–1812	Leading Minister	Mikhail Mikhailovich Speranski	b. 1772 d. 1839
1806–1825	Minister of War	Aleksei Andreevich Arakcheyev	b. 1769 d. 1834
1880–1881	Minister of Interior	Mikhail Tarielovich Loris-Melikov	b. 1825? d. 1888
1880–1905	Procurator of the Holy Synod	Konstantin Petrovich Pobedonostsev	b. 1827 d. 1907
1856–1882	Foreign Minister	Prince Aleksandr Mikhailovich Gorchakov	b. 1798 d. 1883
1882–1895	Foreign Minister	Nikolai Karlovich de Giers	b. 1820 d. 1895
1895–1896	Foreign Minister	Prince Aleksei Borisovich Lobanov-Rostovski	b. 1824 d. 1896
1897–1900	Foreign Minister	Mikhail Nikolaevich Muraviev	b. 1845 d. 1900
1900–1906	Foreign Minister	Vladimir Nikolaevich Lamsdorf	b. 1845 d. 1907
1906–1909	Foreign Minister	Aleksandr Petrovich Izvolski	b. 1856 d. 1919
1892–1903	Minister of Finance	Sergei Yulievich Witte	b. 1849 d. 1915
1906–1911	Premier	Petr Arkadevich Stolypin	b. 1863 assassinated 1911
1917	Premier	Prince Georgi Evgenievich Lvov	b. 1861 d. 1925
1917	Premier	Aleksandr Feodorovich Kerenski	

Revolutionary Period from 1917 to 1922

U.S.S.R. (Union of Soviet Socialist Republics)
■ Chairmen of the Presidium of the Supreme Soviet

1923–1946	President	Mikhail Ivanovich Kalinin	b. 1875 d. 1946
1946–1953	President	Nikolai Mikhailovich Shvernik	
1953–1960	President	Klimentiy Efremovich Voroshilov	
1960–1964	President	Leonid Ilyich Brezhnev	
1964–1966	President	Anastas Ivanovich Mikoyan	
1966–	President	Nicolai Victorovich Podgotny	

■ Chairmen of the Council of People's Commissars (Ministers)

1917–1924	Premier	Nikolai Lenin (Vladimir Ilich Ulyanov)	b. 1870 d. 1924

When Lenin was twenty years old, his older brother was

executed for a plot against the life of the tsar. As soon as news of revolutionary disturbances in Russia reached him in Switzerland in 1917, he sought to return to Russia and was allowed by the Germans to cross Germany in a sealed train. In Russia he took over leadership of the revolutionary movement. His embalmed body is still on public exhibition in a tomb in Red Square, Moscow.

1924–1930	Premier	Aleksei Ivanovich Rykov	b. 1881 executed 1938
1930–1941	Premier	Vyacheslav Mikhailovich Molotov (Skryabin)	b. 1890
1941–1953	Premier	Joseph Stalin	

Stalin ruled the Soviet Union with an iron hand for nearly thirty years. He expelled his rival, Trotsky, from the party and secured his banishment in 1929. During his 1936–1937 purges of the Communist party and Soviet army, millions of Russians perished. In the Second World War he directed Russian military operations against Germany.

1953–1955	Premier	Georgi Maximilianovich Malenkov	b. 1901
1955–1958	Premier	Nikolai Aleksandrovich Bulganin	b. 1895
1958–1964	Premier	Nikita Sergeyevich Khrushchev	b. 1894
1964–1982	Premier	Leonid Ilyich Brezhnev	
1982–1984	Premier	Yuriy Vladimirovich Andropov	
1984–1985	Premier	Konstantin Ustinovich Chernenko	
1985–1991	Premier	Mikhail Sergeyevich Gorbachev	

With the dissolution of the Soviet Union in the waning days of 1991, the Russian Federation became its formal successor.

■ *Russian Federation*

1991–1999	President	Boris Yeltsin
1999–	President	Vladimir Putin

Rwanda (Republic of Rwanda)

Under German rule until World War I and under Belgian administration thereafter, this republic, formerly known as Ruanda, became independent in 1962. In 1994 as many as 800,000 Rwandans were killed in what has been described as a genocide of unprecedented swiftness.

1961–1973	President	Grogoire Kayibanda	b. 1925
1973–1994	President	Juvenal Habyarimana	killed in plane crash 1994
		Genocide and Chaos	
2003–	President	Paul Kagame	

Saint Kitts and Nevis (Federation of Saint Kitts and Nevis)

Having previously formed part of a federation with the island of Anguilla, which opted to remain a British dependency, Saint Kitts and Nevis became a fully independent state in 1983.

1967–1978	Prime Minister	Robert L. Bradshaw
1978–1979	Prime Minister	Paul Southwell
1979–1980	Prime Minister	Lee Moore
1980–1995	Prime Minister	Kennedy A. Simonds
1995–	Prime Minister	Denzil Douglas

Saint Vincent and the Grenadines (Official U.N. Name)

Covering thirty-two islands, some of which are privately owned, St. Vincent and the Grenadines has been an independent state within the Commonwealth of Nations since 1979.

1974–1984	Prime Minister	Milton Cato
1984–2000	Prime Minister	James Fitz-Allen Mitchell
2000–2001	Prime Minister	Arnhim Eustace
2001–	Prime Minister	Ralph Gonsalves

Samoa (Independent State of Samoa)

Formerly known as Western Samoa, in contradistinction with the easterly American Somoa, this nation has the largest population of Polynesian people aside from the Maori of New Zealand. As the first Polynesian state to regain independence in 1962, Samoa's constitution is a mix of parliamentary democracy and constitutional monarchy.

1959–1970	Prime Minister	Mata'afa Mulinu'u II
1970–1973	Prime Minister	Tupua Tamasese Lealofi IV
1973–1975	Prime Minister	Mata'afa Mulinu'u II
1975–1976	Prime Minister	Tupua Tamasese Lealofi IV
1976–1982	Prime Minister	Tupuola Taisi Tufuga Efi
1982	Prime Minister	Va'ai Kolone
1982	Prime Minister	Tupuola Taisi Tufuga Efi
1982–1985	Prime Minister	Tofilau Eti Alesana
1985–1988	Prime Minister	Va'ai Kolone
1988–1998	Prime Minister	Tofilau Eti Alesana
1998–	Prime Minister	Tuilaepa Sailclc Malielegaoi

San Marino (Republic of San Marino)

San Marino is a republic governed by a Great and General Council of sixty members, which in turn selects two Captains Regent to act as co-heads of state for six-month terms.

São Tomé and Príncipe (Democratic Republic of São Tomé and Príncipe)

This tiny nation-state, whose name in Portuguese means "Saint Thomas and Prince," consists of two volcanic islands in the Gulf of Guinea on the Atlantic coast of Africa.

1975–1991	President	Manuel Pinto da Costa
1991	President	Miguel dos Anjos da Cunha Lisboa Trovoada
1995	President	Manuel Quintas de Almeida
1995–2001	President	Miguel dos Anjos da Cunha Lisboa Trovoada
2001–2003	President	Fradique Melo Bandeira de Menezes
2003–2003	President	Fernando Pereira
2003–	President	Fradique Melo Bandeira de Menezes

Saudi Arabia (Kingdom of Saudi Arabia)

■ Wahhabi Dynasty

1753–1766	Chief	Mohammed Ibn-Saud	
1766–1803	Chief	Abd-al-Azis, son of Mohammed Ibn-Saud	
1803–1814	Chief	Saud, son of Abd-al-Azis	
		Turks Captured Mecca and Medina in 1812	
1814–1818	Chief	Abd-allah, son of Saud	
1901	Sultan of Nejd	Abd-al-Rahman, descendant of Mohammed Ibn-Saud	d. 1901
1901–1926	Sultan of Nejd	Ibn Saud (Abd-al-Azis III)	b. 1880 d. 1953
1926	King of the Hejaz and Nejd	Ibn Saud (Abd-al-Azis III)	
1932–1953	King of Saudi Arabia	Ibn Saud	
1953–1964	King of Saudi Arabia	Ibn Saud (Abd-al-Azis IV) son of Ibn Saud	
1964–1975	King of Saudi Arabia	Faisal, brother of Ibn Saud	
1975–1982	King of Saudi Arabia	Khalid, half-brother of Faisal	
1982–2005	King of Saudi Arabia	Fahd, half-brother of Khalid	
2005–	King of Saudi Arabia	Abdullah, half-brother of Fahd	

■ The Hejaz

Proclaimed an independent kingdom in 1916

1916–1924	King	Husein ibn-Ali	b. 1856 d. 1931
1924–1925	King	Ali ibn-Husein, son of Husein ibn-Ali	b. 1878 d. 1935
1925–1926		*Conquered by the Kingdom of Saudi Arabia*	

Senegal (Republic of Senegal)

A former French Overseas Territory, Senegal became jointly independent with the former French Sudan in 1960 in the Mali Federation. The Federation was dissolved in the same year, with Senegal retaining its own name and the Sudanese Republic adopting the name of Mali.

1960–1980	President	Léopold Sédar Senghor	b. 1907 d. 2001
1981–2000	President	Abdou Diouf	b. 1935
2000–	President	Abdoulaye Wade	b. 1926

Serbia and Montenegro (Official U.N. Name) *See also* Yugoslavia

This present nation-state is a weak federal republic that came into being under a constitutional charter adopted in 2003. It is the successor-state to the Federal Republic of Yugoslavia, an original member of the United Nations. However, as a distinct geographic entity, Serbia and Montenegro emerged from the chaotic breakup of the former Yugoslavia in 1997.

1997–2000	President	Slobodan Milosovich
2000–2003	President	Vojislav Kostunika
2003–	President	Svetozar Marovic

■ Serbia

Established in the 7th century by emigrants from the Carpathian Mountains, Serbia was ruled by Turkey from 1459 to 1829.

1804–1813	National Leader	Karageorge (George Petrović)	b. 1766? d. 1817
		Karageorge, "Black George," was the founder of Serbian independence. Supplanted as the Serbian national leader by Milos Obrenovic I, Karageorge was murdered in his sleep, and his head was sent to Constantinople. This act led to a long feud between the two rival dynasties.	
1817–1839	Prince	Miloš Obrenović	b. 1780 d. 1860
1839	Prince	Milan, son of Miloš Obrenović	b. 1819 d. 1839
1839–1842	Prince	Michael, son of Miloš Obrenović	b. 1823 assassinated 1868
1842–1858	Prince	Alexander Karadjordjević, son of Karageorge	b. 1806 d. 1885
1858–1860	Prince	Miloš Obrenović	
1860–1868	Prince	Michael, son of Miloš Obrenović	
1868–1882	Prince	Milan, grand-nephew of Miloš Obrenović	b. 1854 d. 1901
1882		*Prince Milan Assumed the Title of King*	
1882–1889	King	Milan I	abdicated 1889
1889–1903	King	Alexander I, son of Milan I	b. 1876 assassinated 1903
1903–1921	King	Peter I Karadjordjević, son of Alexander	b. 1844 d. 1921
		Occupied by Austria from 1915 to 1918	
		Part of Yugoslavia since 1918	

■ Montenegro

Montenegro was independent since the 14th Century.

1697–1737	Prince-Bishop	Danilo Petrović	b. 1677 d. 1737
1737–?	Prince-Bishop	Sava	d. 1782
? –1766	Prince-Bishop	Vasili	d. 1766
1766–1774	Prince-Bishop	Stephen the Little	murdered 1774
1774–1782	Prince-Bishop	Sava	
1782–1830	Prince-Bishop	Peter I, nephew of Sava	b. 1760? d. 1830
1830–1851	Prince-Bishop	Peter II, nephew of Peter I	b. 1812 d. 1851
1851–1860	Lord	Danilo II	b. 1826 assassinated 1860
1860–1910	Prince	Nicholas I, nephew of Danilo II	b. 1841 d. 1921
1910–1918	King	Nicholas I	abdicated 1918

*Nicholas I obtained recognition for Montenegro's independence
from the European powers in 1878—an independence his
country had defended since 1389. When Austria-Hungary
attacked Serbia in 1914, he immediately went to Serbia's aid.*

*Occupied by Austria from 1916 to 1918
Incorporated with Yugoslavia from 1918
Communist Republican Regime Installed in 1945*

Seychelles (Republic of Seychelles)

A sovereign republic since 1976, when it ceased to be a British colony, this nation experienced a seven-fold increase in per capita income in less than thirty years of independence.

1976–1977	President	James Mancham
1977–2004	President	France Albert Rene
2004–	President	James Michel

Siam *See* Thailand

Sierra Leone (Republic of Sierra Leone)

A former British possession, Sierra Leone became independent within the Commonwealth in 1961.

1962–1967	Governor-General	Sir Henry J.L. Boston	
1961–1967	Prime Minister	Sir Albert Michael Margai	b. 1910
1967–1968	Head of Military Junta	Lt.-Col. Andrew Juxon-Smith	
1968–1985	Prime Minister	Siaka Stevens	
1985–1992	Prime Minister	Joseph Saidu Momoh	
1992–1996	Provisional Military Head	Valentine Strasser	

1996	Provisional Military Head	Julius Maada Bio
1996–1997	President	Ahmad Tejan Kabbah
1997–1998	Revolutionary Military Head	Johnny Paul Koroma
1998–	President	Ahmad Tejan Kabbah

Singapore (Republic of Singapore) *See also* Malaysia

Part of the Federation of Malaysia from 1963 to 1965, Singapore became independent in 1965.

1965–1970	President	Yusof bin Ishak
1970–1971	President	Yeoh Ghim Seng
1971–1981	President	Benjamin Henry Sheares
1981	President	Yeoh Ghim Seng
1981–1985	President	Chengara Veetil Devan Nair
1985	President	Wee Chong Jin
1985	President	Yeoh Ghim Seng
1985–1993	President	Wee Kim Wee
1993–1999	President	Ong Teng Cheong
1999–	President	Sellapan Ramanathan

Slovakia (Slovak Republic)

Slovakia was part of Czechoslovakia from 1918 until 1938, when it enjoyed a period of questionable autonomy as a puppet-state of Nazi Germany.

1939–1945	President	Josef Tiso	b. 1887 hanged 1947

From the end of World War II until the breakup of the Soviet Union, Slovakia, as part of Czechoslovakia, was subject to external domination. However, in 1993, through a peaceful process, Slovakia once again gained its autonomy.

1992–1998	Prime Minister	Vladimir Meciar
1998–	Prime Minister	Mikulas Dzurinda

Slovenia (Republic of Slovenia)

The Slovenian people demonstrated a strong commitment to the principles of democracy and national autonomy in the years leading up to the achievement of independence from Yugoslavia in 1990. Thus, the military efforts of the Belgrade government to keep Slovenia under its authority were quickly recognized as futile, and the Yugsoslav forces were withdrawn after a ten-day, nearly bloodless civil war.

1990–1992	Prime Minister	Lojze Peterle
1992–2000	Prime Minister	Janez Drnovsek

2000	Prime Minister	Andrej Bajuk
2000–2002	Prime Minister	Janez Drnovsek
2002–2004	Prime Minister	Anton "Tone" Rop
2004–	Prime Minister	Janez Jansa

Solomon Islands (Official U.N. Name)

The Solomon Islands declared independence from Great Britain on July 7, 1978.

1978–1981	Prime Minister	Peter Kenilorea
1981–1984	Prime Minister	Solomon Mamaloni
1984–1986	Prime Minister	Peter Kenilorea
1986–1989	Prime Minister	Ezekiel Alebua
1989–1993	Prime Minister	Solomon Mamaloni
1993–1994	Prime Minister	Francis Billy Hilly
1994–1997	Prime Minister	Solomon Mamaloni
1997–2000	Prime Minister	Bartholomew Ulufa'alu
2000–2001	Prime Minister	Manasseh Sogavare
2001–	Prime Minister	Allan Kemakeza

Somalia (Official U.N. Name)

The Republic of Somalia came into being in 1960, through the union of the former British colony of Somaliland and the Italian trusteeship of Somalia.

1961–1967	President	Aden Abdulla Osman Daar	b. 1908
1967–1969	President	Abdirashid Ali Shermarke	
1969	President	Moktar Muhammad Husayn	
1969–1991	President	Muhammad Siad Barre	

According to the U.S. State Department in 2005, Somalia has been without a central government since 1991.

South Africa (Republic of South Africa)

■ Cape Colony

Cape Colony was settled by the Dutch in the mid-17th century and was seized by Britain in 1795.

1797–1803	Governor	George Macartney, Earl Macartney	b. 1737 d. 1806
		British Military Administration from 1806 to 1814	
1814–1826	Governor	Lord Charles Somerset	
1828–1833	Governor	Sir Galbraith Lowry Cale	b. 1772 d. 1842
1834–1838	Governor	Sir Benjamin D'Urban	b. 1777 d. 1849
1838–1843	Governor	Sir George Thomas Napier	b. 1784 d. 1855

1843–1844	Governor	Sir Peregrine Maitland	b. 1777 d. 1854
1846–1847	Governor	Sir Henry Pottinger	b. 1789 d. 1856
1847–1852	Governor	Sir Harry Smith	b. 1787 d. 1860
1852–1854	Governor	Sir George Cathcart	b. 1794 killed 1854
1854–1861	Governor	Sir George Grey	b. 1812 d. 1898
1861–1869	Governor	Sir Philip Edmond Wodehouse	
1870–1877	Governor	Sir Henry Barkly	b. 1815 d. 1898
1877–1880	Governor	Sir Henry Bartle Edward Frere	b. 1815 d. 1884
1880–1889	Governor	Sir Hercules George Robert Robinson, Baron Rosmead	b. 1824 d. 1897
1889–1895	Governor	Henry Brougham Loch, Baron Loch of Drylaw	b. 1827 d. 1900
1895–1897	Governor	Sir Hercules George Robert Robinson, Baron Rosmead	
1897–1905	High Commissioner	Alfred Milner, Viscount Milner	
1905–1910	High Commissioner	William Waldegrave Palmer, Viscount Wolmer	
1872–1878	Prime Minister	John Charles Molteno	b. 1814 d. 1886
1878–1881	Prime Minister	Sir John Gordon Sprigg	b. 1830 d. 1913
1881–1882	Prime Minister	John Charles Molteno	
1886–1890	Prime Minister	Sir John Gordon Sprigg	
1890–1896	Prime Minister	Cecil John Rhodes	b. 1853 d. 1902

Rhodes made a fortune from the Kimberley diamond fields; obtained land north of Bechuanaland by cession from Lobengula, King of the Matabele; and tried to establish a South African British dominion. Following the failure of the Jameson Raid, he was forced to resign as premier and devoted his energies to developing Rhodesia.

1896–1898	Prime Minister	Sir John Gordon Sprigg	
1900–1904	Prime Minister	Sir John Gordon Sprigg	
1904–1908	Prime Minister	Leander Starr Jameson	b. 1853 d. 1917
1908–1910	Prime Minister	John Xavier Merriman	b. 1841 d. 1926

■ Transvaal Republic

The Transvaal Republic was recognized by Britain as independent in 1852.

1852–1853	Head of State	Andries Wilhelmus Jacobus Pretorius	b. 1799 d. 1853
1855–1871	President	Marthinus Wessels Pretorius	b. 1819 d. 1901
1872–1877	President	Thomas Francois Burgers	b. 1834 d. 1881
1877–1880		*Transvaal Annexed by England*	
1883–1902	President	Stefanus Johannes Paulus Kruger	b. 1825 d. 1904

As a boy, "Oom Paul" accompanied his family in the Great Trek of 1836 to 1840. Afterwards, he became a founder of the Transvaal state. A leader of the Boer rebellion of 1880, he tried in vain to obtain intervention of various European powers in the Boer War.

| 1902–1905 | Governor | Alfred Milner, Viscount Milner | |
| 1905–1910 | Governor | William Waldegrave Palmer, Viscount Wolmer | |

■ Orange Free State

The Orange Free state was recognized by Britain as independent in 1854.

1854–1855	President	Josias Philippus Hoffman	b. 1807 d. 1879
1855–1859	President	Jacobus Nicolaas Boshoff	b. 1808 d. 1881
1859–1863	President	Marthinus Wessel Pretorius	b. 1819 d. 1901
1864–1888	President	Johannes Hendricus Brand	b. 1823 d. 1888
1888–1896	President	Francis William Reitz	b. 1844 d. 1934
1896–1902	President	Marthinus Theunis Steyn	b. 1857 d. 1916
1902–1905	Governor	Alfred Milner, Viscount Milner	b. 1854 d. 1925
1905–1910	Governor	William Waldegrave Palmer, Viscount Wolmer	b. 1859 d. 1942

Became a Province of the Union in 1910

■ Natal

Natal was settled by the British in 1824.

1845–1849	Lieutenant-Governor	Martin Thomas West	d. 1849
1850–1855	Lieutenant-Governor	Benjamin Chilley Campbell Pine	b. 1813 d. 1891
1856–1864		Sir John Scott	b. 1814 d. 1898

Constituted a Distinct British Colony in 1856

1864–1865	Lieutenant-Governor	John Maclean	b. 1810 d. 1878
1867–1872	Lieutenant-Governor	Robert William Keate	b. 1814 d. 1873
1872–1873	Lieutenant-Governor	Anthony Musgrave	b. 1828 d. 1888
1873–1875	Lieutenant-Governor	Sir Benjamin Chilley Campbell Pine	
1875–1880	Lieutenant-Governor	Sir Henry Ernest Gascoigne Bulwer	b. 1836 d. 1914
1879–1880	Governor and High Commissioner for South East Africa	Sir Garnet Joseph Wolseley	b. 1833 d. 1913
1880–1881	Governor and High Commissioner for South East Africa	Sir George Pomeroy-Colley	b. 1835 killed 1881
1882–1885	Governor	Sir Henry Ernest Gascoigne Bulwer	
1886–1889	Governor	Sir Arthur Elibank Havelock	b. 1844 d. 1908
1889–1893	Governor	Sir Charles Bullen Hugh Mitchell	b. 1836 d. 1899

Achieved Self-government in 1893

| 1893–1901 | Governor | Sir Walter Francis Hely-Hutchinson | b. 1849 d. 1913 |

1901–1907	Governor	Sir Henry Edward McCallum	b. 1852 d. ?
1907–1909	Governor	Sir Matthew Nathan	b. 1862 d. 1939
1910	Governor	Paul Sanford Methuen, Baron Methuen	b. 1845 d. 1932

After fighting in the Ashanti, Egyptian, and Boer Wars, and acting as a colonial governor, Baron Methuen ended a life of public service as Governor and Constable of the Tower of London.

1893–1897	Premier	Sir John Robinson	b. 1839 d. 1903
1897	Premier	Sir Harry Escombe	b. 1838 d. 1899
1897–1899	Premier	Sir Henry Binns	b. 1837 d. 1899
1899–1903	Premier	Sir Albert Henry Hime	b. 1842 d. 1919
1903–1905	Premier	Sir George Morris Sutton	b. 1834 d. 1913
1905–1906	Premier	Charles John Smythe	b. 1852 d. 1918
1906–1910	Premier	Frederick Robert Moor	b. 1853 d. 1927

The self-governing colonies of the Cape of Good Hope, Natal, the Transvaal, and the Orange River Colony united on May 31, 1910.

■ Union of South Africa

1910–1914	Governor-General	Herbert John Gladstone, Viscount Gladstone	b. 1854 d. 1930
1914–1920	Governor-General	Sydney Charles Buxton, Earl Buxton	b. 1853 d. 1934
1920–1924	Governor-General	Prince Arthur Frederick Patrick Albert of Connaught	b. 1883 d. 1938
1924–1931	Governor-General	Alexander Augustus Frederick William Alfred George, Earl of Athlone	b. 1874 d. 1957
1931–1937	Governor-General	George Herbert Hyde Villiers, Earl of Clarendon	b. 1877 d. 1955
1937–1943	Governor-General	Sir Patrick Duncan	b. 1870 d. 1943
1943–1945	Governor-General (acting)	Nicolas Jacobus De Wet	b. 1873 d. 1960
1946–1950	Governor-General	Gideon Brand van Zyl	b. 1873 d. 1956
1951–1959	Governor-General	Ernest George Jansen	b. 1881 d. 1959
1959–1961	Governor-General	Charles Robberts Swart	b. 1894
1910–1919	Prime Minister	Louis Botha	b. 1862 d. 1919
1919–1924	Prime Minister	Jan Christiaan Smuts	b. 1870 d. 1950
1924–1939	Prime Minister	James Barry Munnik Hertzog	b. 1866 d. 1942
1939–1948	Prime Minister	Jan Christiaan Smuts	

As a formal, legal system, the notorious policy of racial segregation termed apartheid ("separateness") may be traced to the ascendancy in 1948 of the National Party through a whites-only electoral process.

1948–1954	Prime Minister	Daniel Francois Malan	b. 1874 d. 1959
1954–1958	Prime Minister	Johannes Gerhardus Strijdom	b. 1873 d. 1958

| 1958–1961 | Prime Minister | Hendrik Frensch Verwoerd | b. 1901 assassinated 1966 |

Under pressure from the Commonwealth because of its racist policies, South Africa relinquished its status as a British Dominion and became a republic.

■ Republic of South Africa

1961	State President	Charles Robberts Swart
1961–1966	Prime Minister	Hendrik Frensch Verwoerd
1966–1978	Prime Minister	Balthazar John Vorster
1978–1984	Prime Minister	Pieter Willem Botha
1984–1989	President	Pieter Willem Botha
1989–1994	President	Frederik Willem de Klerk

■ Presidents under the Post-apartheid Regime

| 1994–1999 | President | Nelson Rolihlahla Mandela |
| 1999– | President | Thabo Mvuyelwa Mbeki |

South Korea (Republic of Korea)

The history of Korea can be traced back to 668 when the Silla Dynasty began. The Chosun Dynasty ruled from 1392 until 1910, when the Japanese began a period of colonial rule that ended with Japan's defeat in the Second World War.

1948–1960	President	Syngman Rhee	b. 1875 d. 1965
1960–1961	President	Yun Bo-seon
1961–1979	President	Park Chung Hee
1979–1980	President	Choi Kyu-ha
1980–1988	President	Chun Doo-hwan
1988–1993	President	Roh Tae-woo
1988–1993	President	Pak Chung Hi
1993 1998	President	Kim Young-sam
1998–2003	President	Kim Dae-jung
2003–	President	Roh Moo-hyun

South Vietnam *See* Vietnam

Soviet Union *See* Russia

Spain (Kingdom of Spain)

Spain was under Roman rule until it was conquered by the Visigoths.

English versions of the names of rulers of Spanish-speaking states are:

Catherine–Catalina	Louis–Luis
Charles–Carlos	Peter–Pedro
Francis–Francisco	Philip–Felipe
James–Jaime, Diego	Raymond–Ramon
Joanna–Juana	Theobald–Teobaldo
John–Juan	

■ Visigothic Spains

412–415	King	Ataulfo (Ataulphus)	assassinated 415
419–451	King	Teodoredo (Theodoric)	
466–484	King	Eurico (Euric)	
484–507	King	Alarico (Alaric)	
507–532	King	Amalarico (Amalaric)	
554–567	King	Atanagildo (Athanagild)	
572–586	King	Leovigildo (Leovigild)	
586–601	King	Recaredo (Reccared)	
612–621	King	Sisebuto (Sisebut)	
621–631	King	Suintila (Swintilla)	
642–649	King	Chindavinto (Chindaswinth)	
649–672	King	Recesvinto (Recceswinth)	
672–680	King	Wamba	
680–687	King	Ervigio (Euric)	
709–711	King	Don Rodrigo (Roderic)	?killed 711

■ First Moorish Emirate

711–714	Emir	Tarik and Muza
714–717	Emir	Abdelaziz
718–719	Emir	Alhor
730–732	Emir	Abderraman el Gafeki

■ Second Moorish Emirate

756–788	Emir	Abd-er-Rahman I (Abderraman el Gafeki)	b. 731 d. 788
788–796	Emir	Hisham (Hixen) I, son of Abd-er-Rahman I	b. 757 d. 796
796–822	Emir	Hakam (Alhaken) I, son of Hisham I	d. 822
822–852	Emir	Abd-er-Rahman II, son of Hakam	b. 788 d. 852

852–886	Emir	Mohammed, son of Abd-er-Rahman II	
886–888	Emir	Mundhir, son of Mohammed	
888–912	Emir	Abdallah, son of Mohammed	
912–929	Emir	Abd-er-Rahman III, grandson of Abdallah	b. 891 d. 961

■ Omayad Caliphate of Cordova

929–961	Caliph	Abd-er-Rahman III	

Abd-er-Rahman III was the greatest prince of the Spanish Omayad dynasty. He subdued the Arab aristocrats, repulsed the North African Fatimites, and proclaimed himself caliph.

961–976	Caliph	Hakam (Alhaken) II, son of Abd-er-Rahman III	b. 913? d. 976
976–1009	Caliph	Hisham (Hixen) II, son of Hakam II	d. 1016?
1010–1016	Caliph	Hisham II	

Internal Conflicts and Division after 1009

1027–1031	Caliph	Hisham (Hixen) III	d. 1031

From 1031 to 1492, Moorish Spain was divided into numerous kingdoms, known as taifas. *The most important of these were Cordova, Toledo, Seville, Granada, Jaen, Murcia, Valencia, and Zaragoza. The last independent Moorish Kingdom was Granada, whose last king was Boabdil (1492).*

■ Kingdom of Asturias

718–737	King	Pelayo	
739–757	King	Alfonso I "the Catholic," son-in-law of Pelayo	
757–791	King	Fruela I	
	King	Aurelio	
	King	Silo	
	King	Mauregato	
	King	Bermudo I "the Deacon"	

The above kings were known as "reyes holgazanes" or "Lazy Kings" of Asturias.

791–842	King	Alfonso II "the Chaste"	d. 842
842–850	King	Ramiro I, son of Bermudo I	
850–866	King	Ordoño I, son of Ramiro	
866–909	King	Alfonso III "the Great"	b. 848 d. 912

■ Kingdom of Leon

914–924	King	Ordoño II, son of Alfonso III	

931–951	King	Ramiro II
951–956	King	Ordoño III, son of Ramiro II
956–966	King	Sancho I "the Fat," brother of Ordoño III
966–982	King	Ramiro III, son of Sancho
	King	Bermudo II, son of Ordoño III
999–1027	King	Alfonso V "the Noble"
1027–1037	King	Bermudo III

■ County (Condado) of Castile

860 ?	Count	Rodrigo
	Count	Diego Rodriguez
	Count	The Judges Nuño Rasura and Lain Calvo
923 ?–970?	Count	Fernan Gonzalez
970 ?–995	Count	Garci Fernández, son of Fernan Gonzalez
995–1021	Count	Sancho García
1021–1028	Count	García Sánchez

■ Kingdoms of Leon and Castile United

1035–1065	King	Fernando I, son of Sancho III of Navarre, married to Doña Sancha de León, sister of Bermudo III of León	d. 1065
1065–1072	King	Sancho II, son of Fernando	assassinated 1072
1072–1109	King	Alfonso VI, brother of Sancho II	d. 1109

Alfonso VI is the hero in many Spanish legends. The truth of some of these stories is perhaps questionable, but there is no doubt that he was a strong and astute leader, protector of his Muslim subjects, and much respected by his Arab enemies.

1109–1126	Queen	Doña Urraca, daughter of Alfonso VI	b. 1081 d. 1126
1126–1157	King	Alfonso VII "the Emperor," son of Urraca	d. 1157

■ Kingdom of Castile

1157–1158	King	Sancho III, son of Alfonso VII	d. 1158
1158–1214	King	Alfonso VIII, son of Sancho III	b. 1155 d. 1214
1214–1217	King	Enrique I, son of Alfonso	b. 1203? d. 1217

■ Kingdom of Leon

1157–1188	King	Fernando II, son of Alfonso VII
1188–1230	King	Alfonso IX, son of Fernando II

■ Kingdoms of Castile and Leon United

| 1217–1252 | King | Fernando III "the Saint," son of Alfonso IX of Leon | b. 1199 d. 1252 |
| 1252–1284 | King | Alfonso X "the Wise," son of Fernando III | b. 1226? d. 1284 |

Alfonso X encouraged the study of astronomy and attempted to put the laws of his kingdoms in order. He tried to unite Spain in a crusade, but was opposed by his second son Sancho, who also opposed him when he made an ally of Morocco.

1284–1295	King	Sancho IV, son of Alfonso X	b. 1258 d. 1295
1295–1312	King	Fernando IV, son of Sancho IV	b. 1285 d. 1312
1312–1350	King	Alfonso XI, son of Fernando IV	b. 1310 d. 1350
1350–1369	King	Pedro I "the Cruel," son of Alfonso XI	b. 1334 killed 1369
1369–1379	King	Enrique II, brother of Pedro	b. 1333 d. 1379
1379–1390	King	Juan I, son of Enrique II	b. 1358 d. 1390
1390–1406	King	Enrique III, son of Juan	b. 1379 d. 1406
1406–1454	King	Juan II, son of Enrique III	b. 1405 d. 1454
1454–1474	King	Enrique IV, son of Juan II	b. 1425 d. 1474
1474–1504	Queen	Isabel I, daughter of Juan II ("The Catholic" who married Fernando II of Aragon, thus uniting the Kingdoms of Castile and Aragon in 1479)	d. 1504
1504–1506	King	Felipe I, son-in-law of Isabel (Last separate Sovereign of Castile)	b. 1478 d. 1506

■ Kingdom of Navarre

840–850?	King	Iñigo Arista
905–925	King	Sancho Garcés
925–970	King	García Sánchez
1000–1035	King	Sancho "the Great"
1035–1054	King	García I
1054–1076	King	Sancho IV

■ Kingdom of Aragon

| 1035–1063 | King | Ramiro I |
| 1063–1094 | King | Sancho Ramirez |

■ Kingdoms of Navarre and Aragon United

1076–1094	King	Sancho Ramirez
1094–1104	King	Pedro I
1104–1134	King	Alfonso I "the Fighter"

■ Kingdom of Navarre

1134–1150	King	García Ramirez	
1150–1194	King	Sancho VI "the Wise"	
1194–1234	King	Sancho VII "the Strong"	
1234–1253	King	Teobaldo I	
1253–1270	King	Teobaldo II	
1270–1274	King	Enrique I	
1274–1307	Queen	Juana I	
		Navarre belonged to France from 1284 to 1328.	
1328–1349	Queen	Juana II	
1349–1387	King	Carlos II "the Bad"	
1387–1425	King	Carlos III "the Noble"	
1425–1441	Queen	Doña Blanca	
1441–1446	King	Don Carlos de Viana	
1461–1479	King	Juan II of Aragon	
1479–1481	King	Francisco Febo	
1481–1512	Queen	Catalina de Albret	
		Joined to Castile and Aragon in 1512	

■ Kingdom of Aragon

1134–1137	King	Ramiro II "the Monk," brother of Alfonso I "the Fighter"

■ Majorca

Majorca was detached from Aragon in 1276 and was established as a separate kingdom.

1276–1311	King	Jaime I	b. 1243	d. 1311
1311–1324	King	Sancho		d. 1324
1324–1343	King	Jaime II	b. 1315	d. 1349
		Majorca Reunited with Aragon in 1343.		

■ County (Condado) of Catalonia

874–898	Count	Wifredo "the Hairy"
1035–1076	Count	Ramón Berenguer I
1096–1131	Count	Ramón Berenguer III
1131–1162	Count	Ramón Berenguer IV

■ Kingdom of Aragon United to Catalonia

1162–1196	King	Alfonso II, son of Ramón Berenguer IV
1196–1213	King	Pedro II, son of Alfonso II
1213–1276	King	Jaime I "the Conqueror," son of Pedro II
1276–1285	King	Pedro III "the Great," son of Jaime I
1285–1291	King	Alfonso III, son of Pedro III
		Alfonso III of Aragon was surnamed "the Great" because he succeeded in uniting his kingdom at the expense of the Moorish Omayad princes.
1291–1327	King	Jaime II, brother of Alfonso III
1327–1336	King	Alfonso IV
1336–1387	King	Pedro IV "the Ceremonious," son of Alfonso IV
1387–1395	King	Juan I, son of Pedro IV
1395–1410	King	Martin I "the Humane," brother of Juan I
1410–1412		*The throne was vacant when the Agreement of Caspe was held.*
1412–1416	King	Fernando I, brother of Juan II of Castile
1416–1458	King	Alfonso V "the Magnanimous," son of Fernando
1479–(1516)	King	Fernando II "the Catholic" (Married Isabel of Castile, uniting the Kingdoms of Aragon and Castile) b. 1452 d. 1516

■ Kingdom of Spain

1479–1504	"The Catholic Monarchs"	Isabel I and Fernando V (II of Aragon)
		Spanish expansion into the New World was initiated under the auspices of Isabel with the first voyage of Columbus in 1492.
1505–1506	Regent	Fernando V
1506	Regent	Felipe "the Handsome," husband of "Mad Joan," daughter of Isabel and Fernando b. 1478 d. 1506
1507–1516	Regent	Fernando V
1516–1517	Regent	Cardinal Cisneros
1516–1556	King	Carlos I (or V of Holy Roman Empire) b. 1500 d. 1558
1556–1598	King	Felipe II, son of Carlos b. 1527 d. 1598
1598–1621	King	Felipe III, son of Felipe II b. 1578 d. 1621
1621–1665	King	Felipe IV, son of Felipe III b. 1605 d. 1665
1665–1700	King	Carlos II, son of Felipe IV b. 1661 d. 1700
1700–1724	King	Felipe V of Bourbon, great-grandson of Felipe IV abdicated 1724 b. 1683 d. 1746
1724	King	Luis I, son of Felipe V d. 1724
1724–1746	King	Felipe V

1746–1759	King	Fernando VI, son of Felipe V	b. 1713 d. 1759
1759–1788	King	Carlos III, son of Felipe V	b. 1716 d. 1788
1788–1808	King	Carlos IV, son of Carlos III	abdicated b. 1748 d. 1819
1808–1813	King	Joseph Bonaparte (imposed by Napoleon)	b. 1768 d. 1844
1808–1833	King	Fernando VII, son of Carlos IV	b. 1784 d. 1833
1833–1840	Regent	María Cristina, widow of Fernando VII	b. 1806 d. 1878
1840–1843	Regent	Don Baldomero Espartero	b. 1792 d. 1879
1833–1868	Queen	Isabel II, daughter of Fernando VII	
		dethroned 1868 abdicated 1870	b. 1830 d. 1904
1868–1870	Regent	Francisco Serrano	b. 1810 d. 1885
1870–1873	King	Amadeo of Savoy (abdicated)	b. 1845 d. 1890

■ 1st Republic

1873–1874	President	Estanislao Figueras, José Pi y Margall, Nicolas Salmerón and Emilio Castelar	
1874	Head of Provisional Government	Francisco Serran	
1874–1885	King	Alfonso XII, son of Isabel II	b. 1857 d. 1885
1885–1902	Regent	María Cristina, widow of Alfonso XII	b. 1858 d. 1929
1886–1931	King	Alfonso XIII, son of Alfonso XII (dethroned)	b. 1886 d. 1941

Alfonso XIII was born a king, being proclaimed a sovereign at birth. On the day of his marriage in 1906 to a granddaughter of Queen Victoria, a bomb was thrown at his carriage, but he escaped injury. Outlawed by the Republicans, he fled the country and never returned to Spain. He was, however, reinstated as a citizen by Franco.

■ 2nd Republic

1931–1936	President	Niceto Alcalá Zamora	b. 1877 d. 1949
1936	President	Manuel Azaña	b. 1880 d. 1940
1936–1939		*Civil War*	
1936–1975	Chief of State	Francisco Franco	b. 1892 d. 1975
		Since 1947, Spain has officially been a Kingdom.	
1975–	King	Juan Carlos de Borbón y Borbón	b. 1938

■ Statesmen

1621–1643	First Minister	Gaspar de Guzman, Count of Olivares	b. 1587 d. 1645
1715–1719	First Minister	Giulio Alberoni	b. 1664 d. 1752
1765–1773	First Minister	Pedro Pablo Abarca y Bolea, Count of Aranda	b. 1718 d. 1799
1777–1792	First Minister	José Moñino y Redondo, Count of Floridablanca	b. 1728 d. 1808

1792–1808	First Minister	Manuel de Godoy	b. 1767 d. 1851
1844–1868	First Minister	Ramón María Narváez, Duke of Valencia	b. 1800 d. 1868
1923–1930	Dictator	Miguel Primo de Rivera y Orbaneja	b. 1870 d. 1930
1976–1982	Prime Minister	Adolfo Suarez	
1982–1996	Prime Minister	Felipe Gonzalez	
1996–2004	Prime Minister	José María Aznar	
2004–	Prime Minister	José Luis Zapatero	

Sri Lanka (Democratic Socialist Republic of Sri Lanka) (Ceylon)

The ancient chronicles of the nation then known as Ceylon trace the country's rulers back to the 6th century B.C. Except for Devanampiya Tissa, who ruled from 250 to 210 B.C., the names prior to the mid-2nd century B.C. have not been authenticated.

161–137 B.C.	King	Dutthagamani
137–119	King	Saddhatissa
119	King	Thulatthana
119–109	King	Lanjatissa
109–103	King	Khallata Naga
103–102	King	Vattagamani
102–89		*Under rule of Tamils from South India*
89–77	King	Vattagamani (restored)
76–62	King	Mahaculi Mahatissa
62–50	King	Coronaga
50–47	King	Tissa
47	King	Siva
47	King	Vatuka
47	King	Darubhatika Tissa
47	King	Niliya
47–42	Queen	Anula
41–19	King	Kutakanna Tissa
19 B.C.–A.D.9	King	Bhatika Abhaya
9–21	King	Mahadathika Mahanaga
22–31	King	Amanda-gamani Abhaya
31–34	King	Kanirajanu Tissa
34–35	King	Culabhaya
35	Queen	Sivali
35–44	King	Ilanaga
44–52	King	Candamukha Siva
52–59	King	Yasalalaka Tissa

59–65	King	Sabha
65–109	King	Vasabha
109–112	King	Vankanasika Tissa
112–134	King	Gajabahu I
134–140	King	Mahallaka Naga
140–164	King	Bhatika Tissa
164–192	King	Kanittha Tissa
192–194	King	Khujjanaga
194–195	King	Kuncanaga
195–214	King	Sirinaga I
214–236	King	Voharika Tissa
236–244	King	Abhayanaga
244–246	King	Sirinaga II
246–247	King	Vijaya-kumara
247–251	King	Samghatissa I
251–253	King	Sirisamghabodhi
253–266	King	Gothabhaya
266–276	King	Jetthatissa I
276–303	King	Mahasena
303–331	King	Sirimeghavanna
331–340	King	Jetthatissa II
340–368	King	Buddhadasa
368–410	King	Upatissa I
410–432	King	Mahanama
432	King	Chattagahaka Jantu
432–433	King	Mittasena
433–459		*Under rule of Tamils from South India*
459–477	King	Dhatusena
477–495	King	Kasyapa I
495–512	King	Moggallana I
512–520	King	Kurnara-Dhatusena
520–521	King	Kittisena
521	King	Siva
522	King	Upatissa II
522–535	King	Silakala
535	King	Dathapabhuti
535–555	King	Moggallana II
555–573	King	Kittisirimegha

573–575	King	Mahanaga
575–608	King	Aggabodhi I
608–618	King	Aggabodhi II
618	King	Samghatissa II
618–623	King	Moggallana III
623–632	King	Silameghavanna
632	King	Aggabodhi III
632	King	Jetthatissa III
633–643	King	Aggabodhi III (restored)
643–650	King	Dathopatissa I
650–659	King	Kassapa II
659	King	Dappula I
659–667	King	Hatthadatha I
667–683	King	Aggabodhi IV
683–684	King	Datta
684	King	Hatthadatha II
684–718	King	Manavamma
718–724	King	Aggabodhi V
724–730	King	Kassapa III
730–733	King	Mahinda I
733–772	King	Aggabodhi VI
772–777	King	Aggabodhi VII
777–797	King	Mahinda II
797–801	King	Udaya I
801–804	King	Mahinda III
804–815	King	Aggabodhi VIII
815–831	King	Dappula II
831–833	King	Aggabodhi IX
833–853	King	Sena I
853–887	King	Sena II
887–898	King	Udaya II
898–914	King	Kassapa IV
914–923	King	Kassapa V
923–924	King	Dappula III
924–935	King	Dappula IV
935–938	King	Udaya III
938–946	King	Sena III
946–954	King	Udaya IV

954–956	King	Sena IV
956–972	King	Mahinda IV
972–982	King	Sena V
982–1029	King	Mahinda V
1029–1040	King	Kassapa VI
1040–1042	King	Mahalana-Kitti
1042–1043	King	Vikkama-Pandu
1043–1046	King	Jagatipala
1046–1048	King	Parakkama-Pandu
1048–1054	King	Loka
1054–1055	King	Kassapa VII
1055–1110	King	Vijayabahu I
1110–1111	King	Jayabahu I
1111–1132	King	Vikramabahu I
1132–1153	King	Gajabahu II
1153–1186	King	Parakramabahu I
1186–1187	King	Vijayabahu II
1187–1196	King	Nissamkamalla
1196	King	Vikramabahu II
1196–1197	King	Codaganga
1197–1200	Queen	Lilavati
1200–1202	King	Sahassamalla
1202–1208	Queen	Kalyanavati
1208	King	Dharmasoka
1209	King	Anikanga
1209–1210	Queen	Lilavati (restored)
1210–1211	King	Lokesvara
1211–1212	Queen	Lilavati (restored)
1212–1215	King	Parakrama Pandu
1215–1232	King	Magha
1232–1236	King	Vijayabahu III
1236–1270	King	Parakramabahu II
1270–1272	King	Vijayabahu IV
1272–1284	King	Bhuvanaikabahu I
1285–1286		*Interregnum*
1287–1293	King	Parakramabahu III
1293–1302	King	Bhuvanaikabahu II
1302–1326	King	Parakramabahu IV

1326– ?	King	Bhuvanaikabahu III	
? –1341	King	Vijayabahu V	
1341–1351	King	Bhuvanaikabahu IV	
1344–1357	King	Parakramabahu V (joint sovereign with preceding)	
1357–1374	King	Vikramabahu III	
1372–1408	King	Bhuvanaikabahu V (began reign as co-sovereign)	
1408–1467	King	Parakramabahu VI	
1467–1469	King	Jayabahu II	
1470–1478	King	Bhuvanaikabahu VI	
1478–1484	King	Parakramabahu VII	
1484–1508	King	Parakramabahu VIII	
		Invaded by the Portuguese in 1505	
		Captured by the Dutch in 1656	
		Captured from the Dutch by the English in 1795	
1798–1805	Governor	Frederick North	b. 1766 d. 1827
		Constituted a British Crown Colony in 1802	
1805–1812	Governor	Sir Thomas Maitland	b. 1759 d. 1824
1812–1822	Governor	Sir Robert Brownrigg	b. 1759 d. 1833
1822–1824	Governor	Sir Edward Paget	b. 1775 d. 1849
1824–1831	Governor	Sir Edward Barnes	b. 1776 d. 1838
1831–1837	Governor	Sir Robert Wilmot Horton	b. 1784 d. 1841
1837–1841	Governor	J. A. Stewart Mackenzie	b. 1776 d. 1845
1841–1847	Governor	Sir Colin Campbell	b. 1792 d. 1863
1847–1850	Governor	Lord Torrington	b. 1812 d. 1884
1850–1855	Governor	Sir George Anderson	b. 1791 d. 1857
1855–1860	Governor	Sir Henry Ward	b. 1797 d. 1860
1860–1865	Governor	Sir Charles MacCarthy	b. 1820 d. 1864
1865–1872	Governor	Sir Hercules Robinson (1st Baron Rosmead)	b. 1824 d. 1897
1872–1877	Governor	Sir William Gregory	b. 181/ d. 1892
1877–1883	Governor	Sir James Longden	b. 1827 d. 1891
1883–1890	Governor	Sir Arthur Hamilton Gordon	b. 1829 d. 1912
1890–1895	Governor	Sir Arthur Havelock	b. 1844 d. 1908
1895–1903	Governor	Sir Joseph West Ridgeway	b. 1844 d. 1930
1903–1907	Governor	Sir Henry Blake	b. 1840 d. 1918
1907–1913	Governor	Sir Henry McCallum	b. 1852 d. 1919
1913–1916	Governor	Sir Robert Chalmers	b. 1853 d. 1938
1916–1918	Governor	Sir John Anderson	b. 1858 d. 1918
1918–1925	Governor	Sir William Manning	b. 1863 d. 1932

1925–1927	Governor	Sir Hugh Clifford	b. 1866 d. 1941
1927–1931	Governor	Sir Herbert Stanley	b. 1872 d. 1955
1931–1933	Governor	Sir Graeme Thomson	b. 1875 d. 1933
1933–1937	Governor	Sir Reginald Edward Stubbs	b. 1876 d. 1947
1937–1944	Governor	Sir Andrew Caldecott	b. 1884 d. 1951

Self-government within the British Commonwealth in 1948

1944–1949	Governor	Sir Henry Monck-Mason Moore
1949–1954	Governor-General	Viscount Soulbury
1954–1962	Governor-General	Sir Oliver Ernest Goonetilleke
1962–1972	Governor-General	William Gopallawa
1972–1978	President	William Gopallawa
1978–1989	President	Junius Richard Jayawardene
1989–1993	President	Ranasinghe Premadasa
1993–1994	President	Dingiri Banda Wijetunge
1994–	President	Chandrika Kumaratunga

■ Statesmen

1960–1965	Prime Minister	Sirimavo Bandaranaike
1965–1970	Prime Minister	Dudley Senanayake
1970–1977	Prime Minister	Sirimavo Bandaranaike
1977–1978	Prime Minister	Junius R. Jayawardena
1978–1989	Prime Minister	Ranasinghe Premadasa
1989–1993	Prime Minister	Dingiri Banda Wijetunge
1993–1994	Prime Minister	Ranil Wickremesinghe
1994	Prime Minister	Chandrika Bandaranaike Kamaratunga
1994–2000	Prime Minister	Sirimavo Bandaranaike
2000–2001	Prime Minister	Ratnasiri Wickremanayake
2001–2004	Prime Minister	Ranil Wickremesinghe
2004–	Prime Minister	Mahinda Rajapakse

Sudan (Republic of the Sudan)

Administered by a Governor-General on behalf of Great Britain and Egypt from 1899 to 1956, Sudan became an independent republic in 1956.

1956–1958	Prime Minister	Abdullah Khalil
1958–1964	President	Ibrahim Abboud
1964–1967	Chairman of	Ismail al-Azhari
	Supreme Council of State	

1965–1966	Prime Minister	Muhammad Ahmed Mahgoub
		Political Instability from 1966 to 1969
1969–1985	Prime Minister	Gaafar Muhammad Nimeiri,
1985–1986	Junta Chair	Suwar al-Dahab
1986–1991	Prime Minster	Sadiq al-Mahdi
1991–	President	Omar Hassan al-Bashir

Suriname (Republic of Suriname)

The former Dutch colony of Guyana, Suriname began to acquire increasing autonomy from the Netherlands during the 1950s, culminating with independence in 1975.

1975–1980	President	Johan H. E. Ferrier
1980–1988	Military Leader	Dési Delano Bouterse
1988–1990	President	Ramsewak Shankar
1990	President	Iwan Graanoogst
1990–1991	President	Johannes Petrus Kraag
1991–1996	President	Ronald Venetiaan
1996–2000	President	Jules Albert Wijdenbosch
2000–	President	Ronald Venetiaan

Swaziland (Kingdom of Swaziland)

A neighbor of South Africa, Swaziland was guided to independence as a separate state rather than being incorporated into a larger nation because of its British colonial overlord's opposition to apartheid. It has been independent since 1968.

1982	King	Sobhuza II
1982–1984	Queen-Regent	Dzeliw
1984–1986	Queen-Regent	Ntombi. Ntombi
1986–	King	Mswati III

Sweden (Kingdom of Sweden)

No authentic information is available for the period prior to the 6th century, in which many petty kingdoms existed.

500	King	Egil
	King	Ottar, son of Egil
	King	Adils, son of Ottar
600	King	Osten, son of Adils
	King	Ingvar, son of Osten
	King	Anund, son of Ingvar
	King	Ingjald Illråde, son of Anund
	King	Olof Tratalja, son of Ingjald Illråde

800	King	Sigurd Ring	
	King	Ragnar Lodbrok	
	King	Bjorn Ironside, son of Ragnar Lodbrok	
850–882	King	Eric VI, son of Ragnar Lodbrok	
	King	Bjorn, son of Eric VI	
	King	Olof, son of Bjorn	
	King	Emund Eriksson, son of Eric VI	
	King	Eric VII, son of Bjorn d. 994	
		Swedish Kingdom Established by Eric VII	
994–1022	King	Olof Sköttkonung, son of Eric VI	d. 1022
1022–1050	King	Anund Jakob, son of Olof Sköttkonung	d. 1050
1050–1060	King	Emund the Old, brother of Anund Jakob	d. 1060
1060–1066	King	Steinkel, son-in-law of Emund the Old	d. 1066
		Internal Wars from 1066 to 1080	
1080–1110	King	Halstan, son of Steinkel	
1080–1112	Co-Regent	Inge, son of Steinkel	
1112–1118	King	Philip, son of Halstan	
1112–1125	Co Regent	Inge, brother of Philip	

■ Sverker and Eric Dynasties

1133–1156	King	Sverker	d. 1156
1150–1160	Rival king	Eric IX (St. Eric)	beheaded 1160
1160–1161	King	Magnus Henriksson, great-grandson of Inge	
1161–1167	King	Charles VII, son of Sverker	assassinated 1167
1167–1195	King	Knut Eriksson, son of Eric IX	
1195–1208	King	Sverker Karlsson, son of Charles VII	d. 1210
1208–1216	King	Eric X, son of Knut Eriksson	d. 1216
1216–1222	King	John I Sverkersson, son of Sverker Karlsson	b. 1201? d. 1222
1222–1250	King	Eric XI, son of Eric X	b. 1216 d. 1250
1229–1234	Rival king	Knut Lange, great-grandson of Eric IX	
1248–1266	Regent	Earl Birger, father of Waldemar I	d. 1266

■ Folkung Dynasty

1250–1275	King	Waldemar I, nephew of Eric XI	b. 1238? d. 1302?
1275–1290	King	Magnus I Ladulås, brother of Waldemar	b. 1240 d. 1290
1290–1318	King	Birger II, son of Magnus Ladulås	b. 1280 d. 1321
		Union of Kalmar between Sweden and Norway in 1319	

1319–1365	King	Magnus Eriksson II, grandson of Magnus Ladulås	b. 1316 d. 1374
1356–1359	Co-Regent	Eric XII, son of Magnus Eriksson	b. 1339 d. 1359
1365–1389	King	Albert of Mecklenburg, nephew of Magnus	b. 1340?d. 1412
1389–1412	Regent	Margaret, consort of Hakan	b. 1353 d. 1412
1396–1439	King	Eric XIII of Pomerania (Eric VII of Denmark), grandnephew of Margaret	b. 1382 d. 1459
		Union of Kalmar between Sweden, Norway, and Denmark in 1397	
1435–1436	Regent	Engelbrekt Engelbrektsson	murdered 1436
1438–1440	Regent	Karl Knutsson	b. 1409 d. 1470
1440–1448	King	Christopher of Bavaria, nephew of Eric	b. 1418 d. 1448
1448–1457	King	Charles VIII (Karl Knutsson)	
1457–1464	King	Christian I of Denmark	b. 1426 d. 1481
1464–1465	King	Charles VIII (Karl Knutsson)	
1465–1466	Regent	Jons Bengtsson Oxenstierna	d. 1467
1466–1467	Regent	Erik Axelsson Tott	d. 1481
1467–1470	King	Charles VIII (Karl Knutsson)	
1470–1497	Regent	Sten Sture the Elder, nephew of Charles VIII	b. 1440?d. 1503
1497–1501	King	John (Hans) II of Denmark	b. 1455 d. 1513
1501–1503	Regent	Sten Sture	
1503–1512	Regent	Svante Nilsson Sture	d. 1512
1512–1520	Regent	Sten Sture the Younger, son of Svante Nilsson Sture	b. 1492?d. 1520
1520–1521	King	Christian II, son of John II of Denmark	b. 1481 d. 1559

■ House of Vasa

1521–1523	Regent	Gustavus Eriksson Vasa	b. 1496 d. 1560
1523–1560	King	Gustavus I	
		Gustavus fought against Christian II of Denmark and was captured and held as a hostage. Following his escape, Christian beheaded Gustavus' father and brother-in-law. Gustavus suffered great privations before defeating the Danes and becoming King.	
1560–1568	King	Eric XIV, son of Gustavus I	b. 1533 d. 1577
1568–1592	King	John III, son of Gustavus I	b. 1537 d. 1592
1592–1599	King	Sigismund, son of John III	b. 1566 d. 1632
1599–1604	Regent	Charles IX, son of Gustavus I	b. 1550 d. 1611
1604–1611	King	Charles IX	
1611–1632	King	Gustavus II Adolphus, son of Charles IX	b. 1594 killed 1632
		Gustavus II, "Lion of the North," supported the Protestant cause against the Catholic League in the Thirty Years War.	

He saved Protestantism in Germany and won the Battle
of Lützen against Wallenstein, but was mortally wounded
in the hour of success.

1632–1654	Queen	Christina, daughter of Gustavus II	abdicated 1654 b. 1626 d. 1689

■ Palatinate Dynasty

1654–1660	King	Charles X Gustavus, nephew of Gustavus II	b. 1622 d. 1660
1660–1697	King	Charles XI, son of Charles X	b. 1655 d. 1697
1697–1718	King	Charles XII, son of Charles XI	b. 1682 killed 1718
1718–1720	Queen	Ulrica Eleonora, sister of Charles XII abdicated 1720	b. 1688 d. 1741
1720–1751	King	Frederick I of Hesse, husband of Ulrica Eleonora	b. 1676 d. 1751

■ Holstein-Gottorp Dynasty

1751–1771	King	Adolphus Frederick	b. 1710 d. 1771
1771–1792	King	Gustavus III, son of Adolphus Frederick	b. 1746 assassinated 1792
1792–1809	King	Gustavus IV Adolphus, son of Gustavus III	abdicated 1809 b. 1778 d. 1837
1792–1796	Regent	Charles, son of Adolphus Frederick	b. 1748 d. 1818
1809–1818	King	Charles XIII	

Sweden united with Norway from 1814 to 1905

■ Bernadotte Dynasty

1818–1844	King	Charles XIV John (Bernadotte)	b. 1763? d. 1844
1844–1859	King	Oscar I, son of Charles XIV	b. 1799 d. 1859
1859–1872	King	Charles XV, son of Oscar I	b. 1826 d. 1872
1872–1907	King	Oscar II, son of Oscar I	b. 1829 d. 1907
1907–1950	King	Gustavus V, son of Oscar II	b. 1858 d. 1950
1950–1973	King	Gustavus VI Adolf, son of Gustavus V	b. 1882 d. 1973
1973–	King	Charles XVI Gustavus	b. 1946

■ Statesmen

1290–1306	Marshal	Tyrgils Knutsson	
1375–1386	Marshal	Bo Jonsson Grip	
1653–1660	President of Treasury Board	Herman Klasson Fleming	
1680–1685	President of Treasury Board	Klas Hermansson Fleming	b. 1649 d. 1685
1676–1680	Chief Counsellor	Johan Gyllenstierna	b. 1635 d. 1680

1685–1697	President of Estates Restitution Board	Fabian Wrede	b. 1641 d. 1712
1680–1702	Chancellor President	Bengt Gabrielsson Oxenstierna	b. 1623 shot 1702
1715–1718	Charles XII's Minister	Georg Henrik von Görtz	b. 1668 executed 1719
1710–1719	Prime Minister	Arvid Bernhard Horn	b. 1664 d. 1742
1719–1720	Prime Minister	Gustav Cronhjelm	d. 1737
1720–1738	Prime Minister	Arvid Bernhard Horn	
1739–1746	Prime Minister	Carl Gyllenborg	b. 1679 d. 1746
1747–1752	Prime Minister	Karl Gustav Tessin	d. 1770
1752–1761	Prime Minister	Anders Johan von Hopken	d. 1789
1761–1765	Prime Minister	Klas Ekeblad	d. 1771
1765–1768	Prime Minister	Karl Gustav Lowenhielm	d. 1768
1769–1771	Prime Minister	Klas Ekeblad	
1772	Prime Minister	Joachim von Duben	d. 1786
1772–1783	Prime Minister	Ulrik Scheffer	b. 1716 d. 1799
1783–1785	Prime Minister	Gustav Philip Creutz	b. 1731 d. 1785
1785–1787	Prime Minister	Emanuel De Geer	d. 1803
1787–1789	Prime Minister	Johan Gabriel Oxenstierna	b. 1750 d. 1818
1788–1790	Prime Minister	Carl Wilhelm von Duben	d. 1790
1792–1797	Chancellor	Frederick Sparre	d. 1803
1792–1796	Counsellor	Gustav Adolf Reuterholm	b. 1756 d. 1813
1801–1809	Chancellor President	Fredrik Vilhelm von Ehrenheim	d. 1828
1801–1810	Earl Marshal	Hans Axel von Fersen	b. 1755 murdered 1810
1834–1844	Earl Marshal	Magnus Brahe	d. 1844
1858–1870	Chancellor	Louis Gerhard de Geer	b. 1818 d. 1896
1870–1874	Chancellor	Axel Gustav Adlercreutz	d. 1880
1874–1875	Chancellor	Edvard Henrik Carleson	d. 1884
1875–1876	Chancellor	Louis Gerhard de Geer	
18/6–1880	Prime Minister	Louis Gerhard de Geer	
1880–1883	Prime Minister	Arvid Rutger F. Posse	d. 1901
1883–1884	Prime Minister	Carl Johan Thyselius	d. 1891
1884–1888	Prime Minister	Oskar Robert Themptander	d. 1897
1888–1889	Prime Minister	Didrik A. G. Bildt	d. 1894
1889–1891	Prime Minister	Joh. Gustav N. S. Akerhielm	d. 1900
1891–1900	Prime Minister	Erik Gustav Boström	b. 1842 d. 1907
1900–1902	Prime Minister	Fredrik Wilhelm von Otter	d. 1910
1902–1905	Prime Minister	Erik Gustav Boström	
1905	Prime Minister	Johan Olof Ramstedt	b. 1852 d. 1935

1905	Prime Minister	Christian Lundeberg	b. 1842	d. 1911
1905–1906	Prime Minister	Karl Albert Staaff	b. 1860	d. 1915
1906–1911	Prime Minister	Salomon Arvid Achates Lindman	b. 1862	d. 1936
1911–1914	Prime Minister	Karl Albert Staaff	b. 1860	d. 1915
1914–1917	Prime Minister	Knut Hjalmar Hammerskjöld	b. 1862	d. 1953

Prime Minister Hammarskjöld was the father of Dag Hammarskjöld, the economist, who became secretary-general of the United Nations and who died tragically in a plane crash while on a peace-making trip to the Congo.

1917	Prime Minister	Carl Johan Gustav Swartz	b. 1858	d. 1926
1917–1920	Prime Minister	Nils Eden	b. 1871	d. 1945
1920	Prime Minister	Karl Hjalmar Branting	b. 1860	d. 1925
1920–1921	Prime Minister	Louis de Geer	b. 1854	d. 1935
1921	Prime Minister	Oskar Fredrik von Sydow	b. 1873	d. 1936
1921–1923	Prime Minister	Karl Hjalmar Branting		
1923–1924	Prime Minister	Ernst Trygger	b. 1857	d. 1943
1924–1925	Prime Minister	Karl Hjalmar Branting		
1925–1926	Prime Minister	Richard Johannes Sandler	b. 1884	d. 1965
1926–1928	Prime Minister	Carl Gustav Ekman	b. 1872	d. 1945
1928–1930	Prime Minister	Salomon Arvid Achates Lindman	b. 1862	d. 1936
1930–1932	Prime Minister	Carl Gustav Ekman		
1932	Prime Minister	Felix Teodor Hamrin	b. 1875	d. 1937
1932–1936	Prime Minister	Per Albin Hansson	b. 1885	d. 1946
1936	Prime Minister	Axel Alarik Pehrsson-Bramstorp	b. 1883	d. 1954
1936–1946	Prime Minister	Per Albin Hansson	b. 1885	d. 1946
1946–1969	Prime Minister	Tage Erlander	b. 1901	d. 1985
1969–1976	Prime Minister	Sven Olof Joachim Palme		
1976–1978	Prime Minister	Thorbjörn Fälldin		
1978–1979	Prime Minister	Ola Ullsten		
1979–1982	Prime Minister	Thorbjörn Fälldin		
1982–1986	Prime Minister	Sven Olof Joachim Palme		
1986–1991	Prime Minister	Ingvar Gösta Carlsson		
1991–1994	Prime Minister	Carl Bildt		
1994–1996	Prime Minister	Ingvar Gösta Carlsson		
1996–	Prime Minister	Göran Persson		

Switzerland (Swiss Confederation)

The Swiss Confederation was founded in 1291, and a Federal Constitution was adopted in 1848. Switzerland's government is a collegiate body of seven members called the Federal Council. There is no individual head of state. The Federal Councillors each take the Chair, in turn, for one year, during which he or she holds the title of President of the Swiss Confederation and discharges his or her normal duties.

1848–1849	President	Jonas Furrer	b. 1805 d. 1861
1850	President	Daniel-Henri Druey	b. 1799 d. 1855
1851	President	Martin Joseph Munzinger	b. 1791 d. 1855
1852	President	Jonas Furrer	
1853	President	Wilhelm Mathias Naeff	b. 1802 d. 1881
1854	President	Friedrich Frey-Herosee	b. 1801 d. 1873
1855	President	Jonas Furrer	
1856	President	Jakob Stämpfli	b. 1820 d. 1879
1857	President	Charles-Emmanuel-Constant Fornerod	b. 1819 d. 1899
1858	President	Jonas Furrer	
1859	President	Jakob Stämpfli	
1860	President	Friedrich Frey-Herosee	
1861	President	Melchior Joseph Martin Knüsel	b. 1813 d. 1889
1862	President	Jakob Stämpfli	
1863	President	Charles-Emmanuel-Constant Fornerod	
1864	President	Jakob Dubs	b. 1822 d. 1879
1865	President	Karl Schenk	b. 1823 d. 1895
1866	President	Melchior Joseph Martin Knüsel	
1867	President	Charles-Emmanuel-Constant Fornerod	
1868	President	Jakob Dubs	
1869	President	Emil Welti	b. 1825 d. 1899
1870	President	Jakob Dubs	
1871	President	Karl Schenk	
1872	President	Emil Welti	
1873	President	Paul Ceresole	b. 1832 d. 1905
1874	President	Karl Schenk	
1875	President	Jakob Scherer	b. 1825 d. 1878
1876	President	Emil Welti	
1877	President	Joachim Heer	b. 1825 d. 1879
1878	President	Karl Schenk	
1879	President	Bernhard Hammer	b. 1822 d. 1907
1880	President	Emil Welti	
1881	President	Numa Droz	b. 1844 d. 1899

1882	President	Simeon Bavier	b. 1825 d. 1896
1883	President	Louis Ruchonnet	b. 1834 d. 1893
1884	President	Emil Welti	
1885	President	Karl Schenk	
1886	President	Adolf Deucher	b. 1831 d. 1912
1887	President	Numa Droz	
1888	President	Wilhelm Friedrich Hertenstein	b. 1825 d. 1888
1889	President	Bernhard Hammer	
1890	President	Louis Ruchonnet	
1891	President	Emil Welti	
1892	President	Walter Hauser	b. 1837 d. 1902
1893	President	Karl Schenk	
1894	President	Emil Frey	b. 1838 d. 1922
1895	President	Joseph Zemp	b. 1834 d. 1908
1896	President	Adrien Lachenal	b. 1849 d. 1918
1897	President	Adolf Deucher	
1898	President	Eugène Ruffy	b. 1854 d. 1919
1899	President	Eduard Müller	b. 1848 d. 1919
1900	President	Walter Hauser	
1901	President	Ernst Brenner	b. 1856 d. 1911
1902	President	Joseph Zemp	b. 1834 d. 1908
1903	President	Adolf Deucher	
1904	President	Robert Comtesse	b. 1847 d. 1922
1905	President	Marc-Emile Ruchet	b. 1853 d. 1912
1906	President	Ludwig Forrer	b. 1845 d. 1921
1907	President	Eduard Müller	
1908	President	Ernst Brenner	
1909	President	Adolf Deucher	
1910	President	Robert Comtesse	
1911	President	Marc-Emile Ruchet	
1912	President	Ludwig Forrer	
1913	President	Eduard Müller	
1914	President	Arthur Hoffmann	b. 1857 d. 1927
1915	President	Giuseppe Motta	b. 1871 d. 1940
1916	President	Camille Decoppet	b. 1862 d. 1925
1917	President	Edmund Schulthess	b. 1868 d. 1944
1918	President	Felix Ludwig Calonder	b. 1863 d. 1952
1919	President	Gustave Ador	b. 1845 d. 1928

1920	President	Giuseppe Motta	
1921	President	Edmund Schulthess	
1922	President	Robert Haab	b. 1865 d. 1959
1923	President	Karl Scheurer	b. 1872 d. 1929
1924	President	Ernest Chuard	b. 1857 d. 1942
1925	President	Jean-Marie Musy	b. 1876 d. 1952
1926	President	Heinrich Häberlin	b. 1868 d. 1947
1927	President	Giuseppe Motta	
1928	President	Edmund Schulthess	
1929	President	Robert Haab	
1930	President	Jean-Marie Musy	
1931	President	Heinrich Häberlin	
1932	President	Giuseppe Motta	
1933	President	Edmund Schulthess	
1934	President	Marcel Pilet-Golaz	b. 1889 d. 1958
1935	President	Rudolf Minger	b. 1881 d. 1955
1936	President	Albert Meyer	b. 1870 d. 1953
1937	President	Giuseppe Motta	
1938	President	Johannes Baumann	b. 1874 d. 1953
1939	President	Philipp Etter	b. 1891
1940	President	Marcel Pilet-Golaz	
1941	President	Ernst Wetter	b. 1877
1942	President	Philipp Etter	
1943	President	Enrico Celio	b. 1889
1944	President	Walter Stämpfli	b. 1884
1945	President	Eduard von Steiger	b. 1881 d. 1962
1946	President	Karl Kobelt	b. 1891
1947	President	Philipp Etter	
1948	President	Enrico Celio	b. 1889
1949	President	Ernst Nobs	b. 1886 d. 1957
1950	President	Max Petitpierre	b. 1899
1951	President	Eduard von Steiger	
1952	President	Karl Kobelt	
1953	President	Philipp Etter	
1954	President	Rodolphe Rubattel	b. 1896 d. 1961
1955	President	Max Petitpierre	
1956	President	Markus Feldmann	b. 1897 d. 1958
1957	President	Hans Streuli	

284

1958	President	Thomas Holenstein
1959	President	Paul Chaudet
1960	President	Max Petitpierre
1961	President	Friedrich Wahlen
1962	President	Paul Chaudet
1963	President	Willy Spühler
1964	President	Ludwig von Moos
1965	President	Hans-Peter Tschudi
1966	President	Hans Schaffner
1967	President	Roger Bonvin
1968	President	Willy Spuler
1969	President	Ludwig von Moos
1970	President	Hans-Peter Tschudi
1971	President	Nello Celio
1972	President	Roger Bonvin
1973	President	Ernst Brugger
1974	President	Pierre Graber
1975	President	Rudlof Gnagi
1977	President	Kurt Furgler
1978	President	Fritz Honegger
1979	President	Hans Hurlimann
1980	President	Georges-Andre Chevallaz
1981	President	Kurt Furgler
1982	President	Fritz Honegger
1983	President	Pierre Aubert
1984	President	Leon Schlumpf
1985	President	Kurt Furgler
1986	President	Alphons Egli
1987	President	Pierre Auber
1988	President	Otto Stich
1989	President	Jean-Pascal Delmuraz
1990	President	Arnold Koller
1991	President	Flavio Cotti
1992	President	René Felber
1993	President	Adolg Ogi
1994	President	Otto Stich
1995	President	Kaspar Villiger
1996	President	Jean-Pascal Delmaruz

1997	President	Ârnold Koller
1998	President	Flavio Cotti
1999	President	Ruth Dreifuss
2000	President	Adolf Ogi
2001	President	Moritz Leuenberger
2002	President	Kaspar Villiger
2003	President	Pascal Couchepin
2004	President	Joseph Deiss
2005	President	Samuel Schmid

Syria (Syrian Arab Republic)

732–605 B.C.		Under Assyria	
605–539		Under Babylonia	
539–333		Under Persia	
333–323	Conqueror	Alexander the Great son of Philip II of Macedon *(See* Macedonia*)*	b. 356 d. 323 B.C.
323–301	King	Antigonus I	b. 382 killed 301

■ Seleucid Dynasty

301–281	King	Seleucus I Nicator	b. 356? assassinated 281
281–261	King	Antiochus I Soter, son of Seleucus I	b. 324 killed 261
261–246	King	Antiochus II Theos, son of Antiochus I	b. 286 d. 246
246–226	King	Seleucus II, son of Antiochus II	b. 247 d. 226
226–223	King	Seleucus III, son of Seleucus II	assassinated 223
223–187	King	Antiochus III (the Great), son of Seleucus II	b. 242 d. 187
187–176	King	Seleucus IV, son of Antiochus III	b. 217? assassinated 176
175–164	King	Antiochus IV Epiphanes, son of Antiochus III	d. 164
164–162	King	Antiochus V Eupator, son of Antiochus IV	b. 173 killed 162
162–150	King	Demetrius I Soter, son of Seleucus IV	b. 187 killed 150
150–145	King	Alexander Balas	
145–138	King	Demetrius II Nicator, son of Demetrius I	killed 125
138–129	King	Antiochus VII, son of Demetrius I	b. 158? d. 129?
129–125	King	Demetrius II	
125–96	King	Antiochus VIII, son of Demetrius II	d. 96
96–95	King	Antiochus IX, son of Antiochus VII	d. 95
95–94	King	Antiochus X, son of Antiochus IX	d. 92
	King	Demetrius III, cousin of Antiochus X	d. 88

| 69–64 | King | Antiochus XIII, son of Antiochus X | |
| | King | (Syria became a Roman province in 64 B.C.) | |

■ Modern Syria (Ruled by Turks from 1517 to 1918)

1831	Conqueror	Mehemet Ali	b. 1769 d. 1849
1878–1880	Governor-General	Midhat Pasha	b. 1822 d. 1884
		French Mandate from 1923 to 1946	
1925–1927	High Commissioner	Henri de Jouvenel	b. 1876 d. 1935
1928	High Commissioner	Henri Ponsot	
1939	High Commissioner	Gabriel Puaux	
1940	High Commissioner	Jean Chiappe	b. 1878 killed 1940
1940	High Commissioner	Henri Dentz	
1941	President	Sheikh Taj-ed-Dine-el-Hassani	
1943–1950	President	Shukri el-Kuwatli	
1950–1955	President	Hashim el-Atassi	
1951–1954	President	Adib Shishakli	
1954–1955	President	Hashim el-Atassi	
1955–1958	President	Shukri el-Kuwatli	
1958–1961		*Syria Linked with Egypt in the United Arab Republic*	
1958–1961	President	Gamal Abdel Nasser	b. 1918
1961–1963	President	Nazi M. el-Kudsi	
		Army coup in 1963	
1963–1966	President	Amin al Hafiz	
1966–1970	President	Nureddin Atassi	
1970–2000	President	Hafiz al-Asad	
2000–	President	Bashar Al-Asad	

Taiwan

While Taiwan is no longer a member of the United Nations and enjoys formal diplomatic relations with fewer than twenty-six nations, it still functions as a truly independent nation in almost every other respect.

1948–1949	President	Chiang Kai-Shek
1949–1950	President	Li Tsung-jen
1950–1975	President	Chiang Kai-Shek
1975–1978	President	Yen Chia-kan
1978–1988	President	Chiang Ching-kuo
1988–2000	President	Lee Teng-hui
2000–	President	Chen Shui-bian

Tajikistan (Republic of Tajikstan)

Having gained its independence during the breakup of the Soviet Union in 1999, Tajikistan was soon overtaken by a civil war that lasted until 1997.

| 1994– | President | Emomali Rahmonov | b. 1952 |

Tanzania (United Republic of Tanzania)

Tanzania was created in 1964 by the union of Tanganyika and Zanzibar.

1964–1985	President	Julius Kambarage Nyerere	b. 1921 d. 1999
1985–1995	President	Ali Hassan Mwinyi	b. 1925
1995–	President	Benjamin William Mkapa	b. 1938

■ Tanganyika

Tanganyika was a German colony from 1885 until World War I, after which it became a British mandate under the League of Nations and a British trusteeship under the United Nations. It attained independence in 1961.

| 1962–1964 | President | Julius Kambarage Nyerere |

■ Zanzibar

Zanzibar, a sultanate under British protection until 1963, became a republic in 1964.

| 1964 | Sultan | Seyyid Jamshid bin Abdullah bin Khalifa | deposed |
| 1964– | President | Abeid Amani Karume | |

Thailand (Kingdom of Thailand)

Thailand broke away from the Khmer Empire and became a unified state around 1350. Kings of the modern Thai dynasty are listed below.

■ Chakri Dynasty

1782–1809	King	Buddha Yod Fa	b. 1737 d. 1809
1809–1824	King	Buddha Loes La Nabhalai, son of Yod Fa	b. 1768 d. 1824
1824–1851	King	Nang Klao, son of Loes La Nabhala	b. 1788 d. 1851
1851–1868	King	Chom Kloa (Mongkut), brother of Nang Klao	b. 1804 d. 1868
1868–1910	King	Chula Chom Klao (Chulalongkorn), son of Chom Klao	b. 1853 d. 1910
1910–1925	King	Mongkut Klao (Vajiravudh), son of Chula Chom Klao	b. 1881 d. 1925
1925–1935	King	Prajadhipok (Phra Pok Klao), brother of Mongkut Klao abdicated 1935	b. 1893 d. 1941
1935–1946	King	Ananda Mahidol, nephew of Prajadhipok	b. 1925 assassinated 1946
1946–	King	Bhumibol Adulyadej, brother of Ananda	b. 1927

Togo (Togolese Republic)

The Republic of Togo is part of the former German colony of Togoland, mandated to France by the League of Nations after World War I. It was held by France under a United Nations trusteeship from 1946 until 1960, when independence was achieved.

1961–1963	President	Sylvanus Olimpio	assassinated 1963
1963–1967	President	Nicolas Grunitsky	b. 1915
1967–2005	President	Etienne Eyadama	d. 2005
2005–	President	Abass Bonfoh	

Tonga (Kingdom of Tonga)

The first ruler to unite all the Togan islands, King George Tupou I also established the dynasty that still rules the archipelago after more than a century and a half.

1845–1893	King	George Tupou I
1893–1918	King	George Tupou II
1918–1965	Queen	Salote Tupou III
1965–	King	Taua'ahau Tupou IV

Transjordan *See* Jordan

Trinidad and Tobago (Republic of Trinidad and Tobago)

Trinidad and Tobago became an independent state and a member of the British Commonwealth in 1962.

1961–1981	Prime Minister	Eric Eustace Williams	b. 1911 d. 1981
1981–1986	Prime Minister	George Michael Chambers	
1986–1991	Prime Minister	Arthur N.R. Robinson	
1991–1995	Prime Minister	Patrick A.M. Manning	
1995–2001	Prime Minister	Basdeo Panday	
2001–	Prime Minister	Patrick A.M. Manning	

Tripolitania *See* Libya

Tunisia (Tunisian Republic) *See also* Carthage; Vandal Empire

Tunisia was a French Protectorate from 1881 to 1956. It became an independent sovereign state in 1956.

1957–1987	President	Habib Ben Ali Bourguiba
1987–	President	Zine El-Abidine Ben Ali

Turkey (Republic of Turkey)

■ Seljuk Empire

The Seljuk Empire was established by Turkic invaders from Central Asia, which included much of what is modern-day Turkey, Iran, Iraq, and Syria.

1037–1063	Grand Sultan	Toghrul Beg
1063–1073	Grand Sultan	Alp Arslan
1073–1092	Grand Sultan	Malik Shah
1092–1104	Grand Sultan	Barkiarok
1104–1116	Grand Sultan	Mohammed
1116–1157	Grand Sultan	Sandjar

The Seljuk Empire was partitioned among four heirs.
Of these successor states, Roum, or Anatolia, lasted the longest.

■ Seljuk Empire (Sultans of Roum)

1092–1106	Sultan	Kilidy Arslan I
1107–1117	Sultan	Malik Shah
1117–1156	Sultan	Masoud I
1156–1193	Sultan	Kilidy Arslan II
1193–1211	Sultan	Khaikhosru II
1211–1222	Sultan	Azeddin Kaikus I
1222–1237	Sultan	Alaeddin Kaikobad
1247–1261	Sultan	Azeddin Kaikus II
1261–1267	Sultan	Kilidy Arslan III
1267–1276	Sultan	Kaikhosru III
1276–1283	Sultan	Masoud II
1283–1307	Sultan	Alaeddin

Seljuk Rule in Anatolia Replaced by Ottomans

■ Ottoman Empire

1299–1326	Emir	Osman I (Othman)	b. 1259 d. 1326
1326–1359	Sultan	Orkhan, son of Osman	b. 1279 d. 1359
1359–1389	Sultan	Murad I (Amurath), son of Orkhan	b. 1319 killed 1389
1389–1403	Sultan	Bajazet I (Bayazid), son of Murad 1	b. 1347 d. 1403
1403–1411	Sultan	Suleiman (Solyman), son of Bajazet I	d. 1411
1411–1413	Sultan	Prince Musa	
1413–1421	Sultan	Mohammed I, son of Bajazet I	b. 1387 d. 1421
1421–1451	Sultan	Murad II, son of Mohammed I	b. 1403? d. 1451
1451–1481	Sultan	Mohammed II, son of Murad II	b. 1430 d. 1481

1481–1512	Sultan	Bajazet II (Bayazid), son of Mohammed II	b. 1447 d. 1513
1512–1520	Sultan	Selim I, son of Bajazet II	b. 1467 d. 1520
1520–1566	Sultan	Suleiman I (or II), son of Selim I	b. 1496? d. 1566

Turkey reached the apex of its power during the reign of Suleiman "the Magnificent," who added greatly to the Turkish territories, conquering Belgrade, Budapest, Rhodes, Tabriz, Baghdad, Aden, and Algiers. He reorganized the country's administration, encouraged arts and sciences, and improved the conditions of his Christian subjects.

1566–1574	Sultan	Selim II, son of Suleiman I	b. 1524? d. 1574
1574–1595	Sultan	Murad III, son of Selim II	b. 1546 d. 1595
1595–1603	Sultan	Mohammed III, son of Murad III	b. 1566 d. 1603
1603–1617	Sultan	Ahmed I (Achmet), son of Mohammed III	b. 1589 d. 1617
1617–1618	Sultan	Mustafa I (Mustapha), son of Ahmed I	b. 1591 d. 1639
1618–1622	Sultan	Osman II, brother of Mustafa I	b. 1604 murdered 1622
1622–1623	Sultan	Mustafa I	abdicated 1623
1623–1640	Sultan	Murad IV, nephew of Mustafa I	b. 1609 d. 1640
1640–1648	Sultan	Ibrahim I, brother of Murad IV	b. 1615 murdered 1648
1648–1687	Sultan	Mohammed IV, son of Ibrahim	b. 1641 d. 1691
1687–1691	Sultan	Suleiman II (or III), brother of Mohammed IV	b. 1641 d. 1691
1691–1695	Sultan	Ahmed II, brother of Suleiman II	b. 1642 d. 1695
1695–1703	Sultan	Mustafa II, brother of Ahmed II	b. 1664 d. 1704
1703–1730	Sultan	Ahmed III, brother of Mustafa II	b. 1673 d. 1736
1730–1754	Sultan	Mahmud I (Mahmoud), nephew of Ahmed III	b. 1696 d. 1754
1754–1757	Sultan	Osman III, brother of Mahmud I	b. 1696 d. 1757
1757–1773	Sultan	Mustafa III	b. 1717 d. 1773
1773–1789	Sultan	Abdul-Hamid I, brother of Mustafa III	b. 1725 d. 1789
1789–1807	Sultan	Selim III, nephew of Abdul-Hamid I	b. 1761 murdered 1808
1807–1808	Sultan	Mustafa IV	b. 1779 assassinated 1808
1808–1839	Sultan	Mahmud II, brother of Mustafa IV	b. 1785 d. 1839
1839–1861	Sultan	Abdul-Medjid I, son of Mahmud II	b. 1823 d. 1861
1861–1876	Sultan	Abdul-Aziz, son of Mahmud II	b. 1830 d. 1876
1876	Sultan	Murad V, son of Abdul-Medjid	b. 1840 d. 1904
1876–1909	Sultan	Abdul-Hamid II, son of Abdul-Medjid	b. 1842 d. 1918
1909–1918	Sultan	Mohammed V (Mehmed), brother of Abdul-Hamid II	b. 1844 d. 1918
1918–1922	Sultan	Mohammed VI, brother of Mohammed V	b. 1861 d. 1926

Sultanate Abolished in 1922
Republic Proclaimed in 1923

■ *Republic*

1923–1938	President	Kemal Atatürk (Mustafa Kemal Pasha)	b. 1881 d. 1938

> *After entering military college, the future "Father of Turkey" received the prophetic name of Kemal, meaning "perfection." After resisting the Greek army's occupation of Turkey and defeating the Greeks, he became the first president of the Turkish Republic.*

1938–1950	President	Ismet Inonü	b. 1884
1950–1960	President	Celal Bayar	b. 1884
1960–1966	President	Cemal Gürsel	b. 1895
1966–1973	President	Cevdet Sunay	b. 1900
1973	Acting President	Tekin Ariburun	
1973–1980	President	Fahri Sabri Koroturk	
1980	Acting Pr.	Ihsan S. Caglayangil	
1980–1989	President	Kenan Evren	
1989–1993	President	Turgut Ozal	
1993	Acting Pr.	Husamettin Cindoruk	
1993–2000	President	Suleyman Demirel	
2000–	President	Ahmet Necdet Sezer	

Turkmenistan (Official U.N. Name)

With the breakup of the Soviet Union in 1991, Turkmenistan declared its independence under the leadership of Saparmurat Niyazov, who continues to exercise ultimate political authority.

Tuvalu (Official U.N. Name)

A parliamentary democracy with the British monarch as its head of state, this Polynesian nation has been independent since 1978.

Uganda (Official U.N. Name)

Uganda, a former British Protectorate, became an independent republic in 1963.

1963–1966	President	Sir Edward Mutesa II
1966–1971	President	Apollo Milton Obote
1971–1979	President	Idi Amin Dada
1979–1979	President	Yusufu Kironde Lule
1979–1980	President	Godfrey Lukongwa Binaisa
1980	President	Military Commission
1980	President	Presidential Commission
1980–1985	President	Apolo Milton Obote

1985–1986	President	Tito Okello	
1986–	President	Yoweri Museveni	

Ukraine (Official U.N. Name)

During the Middle Ages, the Ukraine came under Polish and Lithuanian rule. By the end of the 18th century, it was largely under Russian rule. In 1917 an autonomous republic was declared. The Ukraine became independent in 1918.

1917	Chief Minister	Vsevolod Holubovich	
1917	President (of Central Rada)	Michael Hrushevsky	b. 1866 d. 1934
1917	Prime Minister	Volodymir Vinnichenko	b. 1880 d. 1951
1917	War Minister	Simon Petlyura	b. 1879 assassinated 1926
1918	Chief of Directorate	Volodymir Vinnichenko (Under German occupation)	
1918	Hetman	Paul Skoropadsky	
1918	Chief of Directorate	Simon Petlyura (Communist coup)	
1919	Chief of State	Christian Rakovsky	b. 1873 d. ?

In 1920 Ukraine forcibly became a republic of the Soviet Union. Independence was reachieved in 1991.

1991–1994	President	Leonid Kravchuk
1994–2005	President	Leonid Kuchma
2005–	President	Victor Yushchenko

United Arab Emirates (Official U.N. Name)

Consisting of sheikhdoms formerly under British protection on the Arabian Peninsula, the United Arab Emirates continue as a loose confederation since achieving full independence in 1971.

United Kingdom (United Kingdom of Great Britain and Northern Ireland)

ENGLAND

Invaded in ancient times by successive migrations of Celtic races, England was under the Romans from 43 to 410 and then divided into petty kingdoms during the period before Egbert.

■ Saxon Rulers of England

828–839	King of Wessex	Egbert	d. 839
839–858	King of Wessex	Ethelwulf, son of Egbert	d. 858
858–860	King of Wessex	Ethelbald, son of Ethelwulf	
860–866	King of Wessex	Ethelbert, son of Ethelwulf	
866–871	King of Wessex and Kent	Ethelred I, son of Ethelwulf	d. 871

| 871–899 | King of Wessex and Overlord of England | Alfred the Great, son of Ethelwulf | b. 849 | d. 899 |

Alfred the Great was sent to Rome at the age of five and confirmed by Leo IV. He began his battles with the Danes during the reign of his brother Ethelred. In the succeeding years, he saved England and Western Europe from Scandinavian domination. By 896, the Danes realized he had prevailed. During the last years of his reign, Alfred became known for his contributions to scholarship and learning, reversing a decline occasioned by the Danish invasions.

| 899–924 | King of Angles and Saxons | Edward the Elder, son of Alfred | | d. 924 |

With the Danish invasions of the 9th century, West Saxon rule was extended to all of England.

924–940	King of Angles and Saxons	Athelstan, son of Edward	b. 895?	d. 940?
940–946	King of England	Edmund I, brother of Athelstan	b. 922	d. 946
946–955	King of England	Edred, brother of Athelstan		d. 955
955–958	King of England	Edwy, son of Edmund I	b. 940	d. 958
959–975	King of England	Edgar, brother of Edwy	b. 944	d. 975
975–978	King of England	Edward the Martyr, son of Edgar		d. 978
978–1016	King of England	Ethelred II the Unready, brother of Edward	b. 968	d. 1016
1016	King of England	Edmund II Ironside, son of Ethelred II	b. 993?	d. 1016

■ Danish Rulers of England

| 1016–1035 | King of England | Canute, son of Sweyn Forkbeard | b. 1000 | d. 1035 |

Son of Sweyn Forkbeard, King of Denmark, Canute took part in his father's conquest of Wessex at the age of seventeen or eighteen. The first Danish king to coin money, he brought order to England. As King of Denmark, he defeated the combined fleets of Norway and Sweden.

| 1035–1040 | King | Harold I Harefoot, son of Canute | | d. 1040 |
| 1040–1042 | King of England | Hardicanute, son of Canute | b. 1019? | d. 1042 |

■ Saxon Rulers Restored

| 1042–1066 | King of England | Edward the Confessor, son of Ethelred II | b. 1004? | d. 1066 |
| 1066 | King of England | Harold II, brother-in-law of Edward | b. 1022? | killed 1066 |

■ House of Normandy

| 1066–1087 | King of England | William I the Conqueror | b. 1027 | d. 1087 |

William the Conqueror had three strong claims to the throne of England. His cousin, Edward the Confessor, probably promised

*the succession to him; his wife, Matilda, was a descendant of
King Alfred; and his rival, Harold, had earlier promised to
support his claim.*

| 1087–1100 | King | William Rufus, son of William the Conqueror | b. 1059 killed 1100 |
| 1100–1135 | King | Henry I Beauclerc, son of William the Conqueror | b. 1068 d. 1135 |

■ House of Blois

| 1135–1154 | King | Stephen, nephew of Henry I | b. 1094? d. 1154 |

■ House of Anjou (later called Plantagenet)

1154–1189	King	Henry II, grandson of Henry I	b. 1133 d. 1189
1189–1199	King	Richard I Coeur de Lion, son of Henry II	b. 1157 killed 1199
1199–1216	King	John Lackland, son of Henry II	b. 1167 d. 1216
1216–1272	King	Henry III, son of John	b. 1207 d. 1272
1272–1307	King	Edward I Longshanks, son of Henry III	b. 1239 d. 1307
1307–1327	King	Edward II, son of Edward I	b. 1284 murdered 1327
1327–1377	King	Edward III, son of Edward II	b. 1312 d. 1377
1377–1399	King	Richard II, grandson of Edward III	b. 1367 murdered 1400

■ House of Lancaster

| 1399–1413 | King | Henry IV Bolingbroke, grandson of Edward III | b. 1367 d. 1413 |
| 1413–1422 | King | Henry V, son of Henry IV | b. 1387 d. 1422 |

*Henry V is famous for the victory he won over the French
at Agincourt, when five thousand French nobles were killed
against the loss of one hundred and thirteen English.*

| 1422–1461 | King | Henry VI, son of Henry V | b. 1421 murdered 1471 |
| 1470–1471 | King | Henry VI (restored) | |

■ House of York

| 1461–1470 | King | Edward IV, great-great-grandson of Edward III | b. 1442 d. 1483 |
| 1471–1483 | King | Edward IV (restored) | |

*Edward IV was a tyrannical despot, yet he had a remarkable
ability to win popularity with ordinary citizens through his
pleasant manners and fondness for the good things of life.*

| 1483 | King | Edward V, son of Edward IV | b. 1470 murdered 1483 |
| 1483–1485 | King | Richard III, brother of Edward IV | b. 1452 killed 1485 |

■ House of Tudor

1485–1509	King	Henry VII, son-in-law of Edward IV	b. 1457 d. 1509
1509–1547	King	Henry VIII, son of Henry VII	b. 1491 d. 1547

Though many of his actions were inspired by selfish motives, Henry VIII performed vitally important services for his country. Although quite ruthless in dealing with his many wives and political opponents, he prevented religious civil war; strengthened national unity; developed the navy; and extended the powers of Parliament. The Church of England's independence from Rome was also established.

1547–1553	King	Edward VI, son of Henry VIII	b. 1537 d. 1553
1553	Queen (for 9 days)	Jane (Lady Jane Grey)	b. 1537 beheaded 1554
1553–1558	Queen	Mary I, daughter of Henry VIII	b. 1516 d. 1558
1558–1603	Queen	Elizabeth I, daughter of Henry VIII	b. 1533 d. 1603

■ House of Stuart

1603–1625	King	James I, son of Mary, Queen of Scots	b. 1566 d. 1625
1625–1649	King	Charles I, son of James I	b. 1600 beheaded 1649

Commonwealth from 1649 to 1660

1653–1658	Lord Protector	Oliver Cromwell	b. 1599 d. 1658
1658–1659	Lord Protector	Richard Cromwell, son of Oliver Cromwell	b. 1626 d. 1712

With the execution of Charles I, Oliver Cromwell thought the monarchy had been abolished forever. Yet three years after Cromwell's death, Charles's son, whom Cromwell had defeated at Worcester, was King of England. Cromwell's body was disinterred from honorable burial in Westminster Abbey and hung on the gallows.

■ House of Stuart

1660–1685	King	Charles II, son of Charles I	b. 1630 d. 1685
1685–1688	King	James II, son of Charles I	abdicated 1688 b. 1633 d. 1701

■ Houses of Orange and Stuart

Revolution in 1688

		William III of Orange	b. 1650 d. 1702
1689–1702	Joint Rulers	Mary II, daughter of James II	b. 1662 d. 1694

■ House of Stuart

1702–1714	Queen	Anne, sister of Mary	b. 1665 d. 1714

■ House of Hanover or Brunswick

1714–1727	King	George I, great-grandson of James I	b. 1660 d. 1727
1727–1760	King	George II, son of George I	b. 1683 d. 1760
1760–1820	King	George III, grandson of George II	b. 1738 d. 1820

Although most of his subjects probably supported his policy, George III is perhaps best known today as the king who lost the American colonies. At the age of fifty, he became emotionally insane.

1820–1830	King	George IV, son of George III	b. 1762 d. 1830
1830–1837	King	William IV, son of George III	b. 1765 d. 1837
1837–1901	Queen	Victoria, grand-daughter of George III	b. 1819 d. 1901

The reign of Queen Victoria is unparalleled in the annals of imperial power, yet the early death of her husband was an emotional blow from which she never fully recovered.

■ House of Saxe-Coburg-Gotha

1901–1910	King	Edward VII, son of Victoria	b. 1841 d. 1910

■ House of Windsor (from 1917)

1910–1936	King	George V, son of Edward VII	b. 1865 d. 1936
1936	King	Edward VIII, son of George V	abdicated 1936 b. 1894
1936–1952	King	George VI, brother of Edward VIII	b. 1895 d. 1952
1952–	Queen	Elizabeth II, daughter of George VI	b. 1926

■ Statesmen

1216–1219	Regent	William Marshall, Earl of Pembroke	b. 1146? d. 1219
1377–1408	Earl Marshal	Henry Percy, Earl of Northumberland	b. 1342 d. 1408
1454–1460	Protector	Richard Plantagenet, Duke of York	b. 1411 killed 1460
1515–1529	Lord Chancellor	Thomas Cardinal Wolsey	b. 1475? d. 1530
1529–1532	Lord Chancellor	Sir (Saint) Thomas More	b. 1478 d. 1535
1533–1553	Archbishop of Canterbury	Thomas Cranmer	b. 1489 burned at stake 1556

Thomas Cranmer was chiefly responsible for compiling the first Book of Common Prayer, a document whose influence on the spirituality and language of the English-speaking world is impossible to overestimate.

1533–1540	Chief Minister	Thomas Cromwell, Earl of Essex	b. 1485? beheaded 1540
1547–1550	Protector	Edward Seymour, Duke of Somerset	b. 1506? beheaded 1552
1572–1598	Lord High Treasurer	William Cecil, Baron Burghley	b. 1520 d. 1598

1623–1628	Chief Minister	George Villiers, Duke of Buckingham	b. 1592 assassinated 1628
1628–1640	Chief Adviser	Thomas Wentworth, Earl of Strafford	b. 1593 beheaded 1641
1702–1710	Lord High Treasurer	Sidney Godolphin, Earl of Godolphin	b. 1645 d. 1712
1710–1714	Head of Ministry	Robert Harley, Earl of Oxford	b. 1661 d. 1724
1714	Lord High Treasurer	Charles Talbot, Duke of Shrewsbury	b. 1660 d. 1718
1714–1715	Prime Minister	Charles Montagu, Earl of Halifax	b. 1661 d. 1715
1715	First Lord of Treasury	Charles Howard, Earl of Carlisle	b. 1674 d. 1738
1715–1717	Prime Minister	Robert Walpole, Earl of Orford	b. 1676 d. 1745
1717–1718	First Lord of Treasury	James Stanhope, Earl Stanhope	b. 1673 d. 1721
1718–1721	First Lord of Treasury	Charles Spencer, Earl of Sunderland	b. 1674 d. 1722
1721–1742	Prime Minister	Robert Walpole, Earl of Orford (Whig)	
1742–1743	First Lord of Treasury	Spencer Compton, Earl of Wilmington (Whig)	b. 1673? d. 1743
1743–1754	Prime Minister	Henry Pelham (Whig)	b. 1695? d. 1754
1754–1756	Prime Minister	Thomas Pelham-Holles, Duke of Newcastle, brother of Henry Pelham (Whig)	b. 1693 d. 1768
1756–1757	Prime Minister	William Cavendish, Duke of Devonshire (Whig)	b. 1720 d. 1764
1757–1762	Prime Minister	Thomas Pelham-Holles, Duke of Newcastle (Whig)	
1762–1763	Prime Minister	John Stuart, Earl of Bute (Tory)	b. 1713 d. 1792
1763–1765	Prime Minister	George Grenville (Whig)	b. 1712 d. 1770
1765–1766	Prime Minister	Charles Watson-Wentworth, Marquess of Rockingham (Coalition)	b. 1730 d. 1782
1766–1768	Privy Seal	William Pitt, Earl of Chatham (Whig)	b. 1708 d. 1778
1768–1770	First Minister	Augustus Henry Fitzroy, Duke of Grafton (Whig)	b. 1735 d. 1811
1770–1782	Prime Minister	Frederick North, Earl of Guildford (Tory)	b. 1732 d. 1792
1782	Prime Minister	Charles Watson-Wentworth, Marquess of Rockingham (Whig)	
1782–1783	Prime Minister	William Petty, Earl of Shelburne (Whig)	b. 1737 d. 1805
1783	Prime Minister	William Henry Cavendish Bentinck, Duke of Portland (Coalition)	b. 1738 d. 1809
1783–1801	Prime Minister	William Pitt the Younger (Tory)	b. 1759 d. 1806

Considered by many to be England's greatest Prime Minister, the Younger Pitt was responsible for the First (1793), Second (1798), and Third (1805) Coalitions against Napoleon.

1801–1804	Prime Minister	Henry Addington, Viscount Sidmouth (Tory)	b. 1757 d. 1844
1804–1806	Prime Minister	William Pitt (Tory)	
1806–1807	Prime Minister	William Wyndham Grenville, Lord Grenville, son of George Grenville (Whig)	b. 1759 d. 1834
1807–1809	Prime Minister	William Bentinck, Duke of Portland (Tory)	
1809–1812	Prime Minister	Spencer Perceval (Tory)	b. 1762 assassinated 1812
1812–1827	Prime Minister	Robert Banks Jenkinson, Earl of Liverpool (Tory)	b. 1770 d. 1828

1827	Prime Minister	George Canning (Tory)	b. 1770 d. 1827
1827–1828	Prime Minister	Frederick John Robinson, Viscount Goderich (Tory)	b. 1782 d. 1859
1828–1830	Prime Minister	Arthur Wellesley, Duke of Wellington (Tory)	b. 1769 d. 1852
1830–1834	Prime Minister	Charles Grey, Earl Grey (Whig)	b. 1764 d. 1845
1834	Prime Minister	William Lamb, Viscount Melbourne (Whig)	b. 1779 d. 1848
1834–1835	Prime Minister	Sir Robert Peel (Tory)	b. 1788 d. 1850
1835–1841	Prime Minister	William Lamb, Viscount Melbourne (Whig)	
1841–1846	Prime Minister	Sir Robert Peel (Tory)	
1846–1852	Prime Minister	John Russell, Earl Russell (Whig)	b. 1792 d. 1878
1852	Prime Minister	Edward George Geoffrey Smith Stanley, Earl of Derby (Tory)	b. 1799 d. 1869
1852–1855	Prime Minister	George Hamilton Gordon, Earl of Aberdeen (Peelite)	b. 1784 d. 1860
1855–1858	Prime Minister	Henry John Temple, Viscount Palmerston (Liberal)	b. 1784 d. 1865
1858	Prime Minister	Edward Stanley, Earl of Derby (Conservative)	
1858–1865	Prime Minister	Henry John Temple, Viscount Palmerston (Liberal)	
1865–1866	Prime Minister	John Russell, Earl Russell (Liberal)	
1866–1868	Prime Minister	Edward Stanley, Earl of Derby (Conservative)	
1868	Prime Minister	Benjamin Disraeli, Earl of Beaconsfield	b. 1804 d. 1881

Disraeli's maiden speech as a member of Parliament was a failure—he was laughed down—yet he went on to become prime minister and the intimate friend and adviser of Queen Victoria. Perhaps his greatest service to Britain was his acquisition of control of the Suez Canal. After his death, the Queen visited his grave to lay a wreath, an unprecedented act.

1868–1874	Prime Minister	William Ewart Gladstone (Liberal)	b. 1809 d. 1898
1874–1880	Prime Minister	Benjamin Disraeli (Conservative)	
1880–1885	Prime Minister	William Ewart Gladstone (Liberal)	

Gladstone was a member of Parliament for sixty years. As Chancellor of the Exchange, he aimed to abolish income tax completely, and he succeeded in reducing it to threepence per pound. He was, perhaps, the greatest orator of the nineteenth century.

1885–1886	Prime Minister	Robert Arthur Talbot Gascoyne-Cecil, Marquess of Salisbury (Conservative)	b. 1830 d. 1903
1886	Prime Minister	William Ewart Gladstone (Liberal)	
1886–1892	Prime Minister	Robert Arthur Talbot Gascoyne-Cecil, Marquess of Salisbury (Conservative)	
1892–1894	Prime Minister	William Ewart Gladstone (Liberal)	
1894–1895	Prime Minister	Archibald Philip Primrose, Earl of Rosebery (Liberal)	b. 1847 d. 1929
1895–1902	Prime Minister	Robert Arthur Talbot Gascoyne-Cecil, Marquess of Salisbury (Conservative)	
1895–1903	Colonial Secretary	Joseph Chamberlain	b. 1836 d. 1914

1902–1905	Prime Minister	Arthur James Balfour (Conservative)	b. 1848 d. 1930
1905–1908	Prime Minister	Sir Henry Campbell-Bannerman (Liberal)	b. 1836 d. 1908
1908–1915	Prime Minister	Herbert Henry Asquith, Earl of Oxford and Asquith (Liberal)	b. 1852 d. 1928
1915–1916	Prime Minister	Herbert Henry Asquith (Coalition)	
1916–1922	Prime Minister	David Lloyd George, Earl of Dwyfor (Coalition)	b. 1863 d. 1945

*In the First World War, Lloyd George occupied the position of
semi-dictator of England from 1916 until victory in 1918.
His desire for a conciliatory policy toward Germany placed him
in opposition to Clemenceau, but press-led criticism at home made it
impossible for him to successfully oppose French policy.*

1922–1923	Prime Minister	Andrew Bonar Law (Conservative)	b. 1858 d. 1923
1923–1924	Prime Minister	Stanley Baldwin, Earl Baldwin of Bewdley (Conservative)	b. 1867 d. 1947
1924	Prime Minister	James Ramsay MacDonald (Labour)	b. 1866 d. 1937
1924–1929	Prime Minister	Stanley Baldwin (Conservative)	
1929–1931	Prime Minister	James Ramsay MacDonald (Labour)	
1931–1935	Prime Minister	James Ramsay MacDonald (Coalition)	
1935–1937	Prime Minister	Stanley Baldwin (Coalition)	
1937–1940	Prime Minister	Arthur Neville Chamberlain (Coalition)	b. 1869 d. 1940
1940–1945	Prime Minister	Winston Leonard Spencer Churchill (Coalition) (Conservative)	b. 1874 d. 1965
1945–1951	Prime Minister	Clement Richard Attlee (Labour)	b. 1883
1951–1955	Prime Minister	Sir Winston Churchill (Conservative)	

*Sir Winston Churchill was a great writer as well as a great statesman.
His books on the Second World War are magnificently written accounts
of those historical events in which he played a major part.*

1955–1957	Prime Minister	Anthony Eden, Earl of Avon (Conservative)	b. 1897
1957–1963	Prime Minister	Harold Macmillan (Conservative)	b. 1894
1963–1964	Prime Minister	Sir Alec Douglas-Home (Conservative)	b. 1903
1964–1970	Prime Minister	James Harold Wilson (Labour)	b. 1916
1970–1974	Prime Minister	Edward Heath	
1974–1976	Prime Minister	Harold Wilson	
1976–1979	Prime Minister	James Callaghan	
1979–1990	Prime Minister	Margaret Thatcher	
1990–1997	Prime Minister	John Major	
1997–	Prime Minister	Tony Blair	

SCOTLAND

No authentic information is available for the period before Kenneth MacAlpine united the Picts and Scots.

846–858?	King	Kenneth I MacAlpine	d. 858?
943–954	King	Malcolm I MacDonald	d. 954
971–995	King	Kenneth II, son of Malcolm I	assassinated 995
997–1005	King	Kenneth III, nephew of Kenneth II	
1005–1034	King	Malcolm II Mackenneth, son of Kenneth II	d. 1034
1034–1040	King	Duncan I, grandson of Malcolm II	killed 1040

Scots, Picts, Angles, and Britons united in Kingdom of Scotland in 1034.

1040–1057	King	Macbeth	killed 1057

Macbeth was immortalized by Shakespeare. In the play, he was incited by his wife to murder Duncan by treachery. Historically, it is known that he did indeed kill Duncan and seize the kingdom, but he was also later defeated and killed by Duncan's son, Malcolm III.

1057–1093	King	Malcolm III MacDuncan, son of Duncan I	killed 1093
1093–1094	King	Duncan II, son of Malcolm III	d. 1094
1094–1097	King	Donald Bane, brother of Malcolm III	
1097–1107	King	Edgar, son of Malcolm III	d. 1107
1107–1124	King	Alexander I, son of Malcolm III	b. 1078? d. 1124
1124–1153	King	David I, son of Malcolm III	b. 1084 d. 1153
1153–1165	King	Malcolm IV the Maiden, grandson of David I	b. 1141 d. 1165
1165–1214	King	William the Lion, brother of Malcolm IV	b. 1143 d. 1214
1214–1249	King	Alexander II, son of William the Lion	b. 1198 d. 1249
1249–1286	King	Alexander III, son of Alexander II	b. 1241 d. 1286
1286–1290	(Queen)	Margaret ("The Maid of Norway"), granddaughter of Alexander III	b. 1282? d. 1290

Interregnum from 1290 to 1292

1292–1296	King	John de Baliol or Balliol	abdicated 1296 b. 1249 d. 1315

Scotland Became Dependency of England from 1296 to 1306

1306–1329	King	Robert I the Bruce	b. 1274 d. 1329
1329–1371	King	David II, son of Robert I the Bruce	b. 1324 d. 1371

■ House of Stuart

1371–1390	King	Robert II, nephew of David II	b. 1316 d. 1390
1390–1406	King	Robert III, son of Robert II	b. 1340? d. 1406
1406–1437	King	James I, son of Robert III	b. 1394 assassinated 1437
1437–1460	King	James II, son of James I	b. 1430 killed 1460
1460–1488	King	James III, son of James II	b. 1451 assassinated 1488

1488–1513	King	James IV, son of James III	b. 1473 killed 1513
1513–1542	King	James V, son of James IV	b. 1512 d. 1542
1542–1567	Queen	Mary Stuart, daughter of James V	b. 1542 beheaded 1587

Mary Queen of Scots succeeded her father when she was six days old. She married her Catholic cousin, Lord Darnley, and gave him the title of King. Mary probably connived Darnley's murder, which allowed her to marry the Earl of Bothwell. Accused of plotting Queen Elizabeth's assassination, she was held prisoner for nearly twenty years, and finally beheaded.

1554–1560	Regent	Mary of Guise, consort of James V and mother of Mary Stuart	b. 1515 d. 1560
1567–1625	King	James VI, son of Mary Stuart and Henry, Lord Darnley	b. 1566 d. 1625

Scottish Crown United with the Crown of England in 1603
(See England, House of Stuart)

WALES

Wales was subdued by Agricola after 78. No authentic information is available for the period before Rhodri.

■ Welsh Sovereign Princes

844–878	Prince	Rhodri the Great (Rhodri Mawr)	
878–916	Prince	Anarawd, son of Rhodri	
916–942	Prince	Idwal the Bald, son of Anarawd	
942–950	"King of all the Welsh"	Hywel Dda the Good	
950–979	Prince	Iago ap Idwal (or Ieuaf)	
979–985	Prince	Hywel ap Ieuaf the Bad, nephew of Iago	
985–986	Prince	Cadwallon, brother of Hywel	
986–999	Prince	Maredudd ab Owain ap Hywel Dda	
999–1005	Prince	Cynan ap Hywel, son of Hywel	
1005–1023	Prince	Llewelyn ab Seisyll	
1023–1039	Prince	Iago ap Idwal, son of Idwal ap Meurig	
1039–1063	Prince	Gruffydd ap Llywelyn ap Seisyll	
1063–1075	Prince	Bleddyn ap Cynfyn, brother of Gruffydd	
1075–1081	Prince	Trahaearn ap Caradog, cousin of Bleddyn	
1081–1137	King of North Wales	Gruffyd ap Cynan ab Iago	
1137–1170	Prince	Owain Gwynedd, son of Gruffydd ap Cynan (Civil War, 1170–1175)	d. 1170
1175–1194	Prince	Dafydd ab Owain Gwynedd	d. 1203
1175–1194	Prince	Rhodri ab Owain	
1194–1240	Prince	Llywelyn Fawr the Great, son-in-law of King John	b. 1173 d. 1240

| 1240–1246 | Prince | Dafydd ap Llywelyn | |
| 1246–1282 | Prince | Llywelyn ab Gruffydd ap Llywelyn, grandson of Llywelyn the Great | killed 1282 |

Llywelyn allied himself with Simon de Montfort and was later recognized as overlord of Wales. He was attacked by Edward I for refusing to do him homage and forced, through hunger, to submit. The last champion of Welsh liberty, he was killed in a skirmish.

Conquered by England from 1277 to 1283

| 1400–1415 | Prince | Owen Glendower | b. 1359? d. 1416? |

■ English Princes of Wales

Created in 1301

| 1301 | Prince | Edward of Carnarvon (Edward II) | b. 1284 murdered 1327 |

Edward II was born at Carnarvon Castle, but the story that Edward I presented his newborn son to the people of Wales as their future native prince is untrue. An unsatisfactory monarch, frivolous, and incompetent, Edward suffered defeat at the hands of Robert Bruce at Bannockburn. His wife, Isabella of France, deposed him and had him put to death.

1343	Prince	Edward the Black Prince, son of Edward III	b. 1330 d. 1376
1377	Prince	Richard of Bordeaux (Richard II), son of the Black Prince	b. 1367 murdered 1400
1399	Prince	Henry of Monmouth (Henry V), son of Henry IV	b. 1387 d. 1422
1454	Prince	Edward of Westminster, son of Henry VI	b. 1453 killed 1471
1471	Prince	Edward of Westminster (Edward V), son of Edward IV	b. 1470 murdered 1483
1483	Prince	Edward of Middleham, son of Richard III	d. 1484
1489	Prince	Arthur Tudor, son of Henry VII	b. 1487 d. 1502
1503	Prince	Henry Tudor (Henry VIII), son of Henry VII	b. 1491 d. 1547

Wales United with England from 1536 to 1547

1610	Prince	Henry Stuart, son of James I	b. 1594 d. 1612
1616	Prince	Charles Stuart (Charles I), son of James I	b. 1600 beheaded 1649
1638?	Prince	Charles Stuart (Charles II), son of Charles I	b. 1630 d. 1685
1688	Prince	James Francis Edward Stuart, son of James II ("The Old Pretender") (attainted 1702)	b. 1688 d. 1766

"The Old Pretender" was one Prince of Wales who did not become King.

1714	Prince	George Augustus (George II), son of George I	b. 1683 d. 1760
1727	Prince	Frederick Louis, son of George II	b. 1707 d. 1751
1751	Prince	George William Frederick (George III), grandson of George II	b. 1738 d. 1820

1762	Prince	George Augustus Frederick (George IV), son of George III	b. 1762 d. 1830
1841	Prince	Albert Edward (Edward VII), son of Queen Victoria	b. 1841 d. 1910
1901	Prince	George (George V), son of Edward VII	b. 1865 d. 1936
1911	Prince	Edward Albert Christian George Andrew Patrick David (Edward VIII—Duke of Windsor), son of George V	b. 1894
1958	Prince	Charles Philip Arthur George, son of Elizabeth II	b. 1948

Union of South Africa *See* South Africa

Union of Soviet Socialist Republics *See* Russia

United Arab Republic *See* Egypt

United States of America

■ *Presidents*

| F = Federalist | D = Democratic | W = Whig |
| D/R = Republican party, later Democratic | R = Republican | |

1789–1797	President	George Washington (F)	b. 1732 d. 1799
1797–1801	President	John Adams (F)	b. 1735 d. 1826
1801–1809	President	Thomas Jefferson (D/R)	b. 1743 d. 1826
1809–1817	President	James Madison (D/R)	b. 1751 d. 1836
1817–1825	President	James Monroe (D/R)	b. 1759 d. 1831
1825–1829	President	John Quincy Adams (D/R)	b. 1767 d. 1848
1829–1837	President	Andrew Jackson (D)	b. 1767 d. 1845
1837–1841	President	Martin Van Buren (D)	b. 1782 d. 1862
1841 (31 days)	President	William Henry Harrison (W)	b. 1773 d. 1841
1841–1845	President	John Tyler (W)	b. 1790 d. 1862
1845–1849	President	James Knox Polk (D)	b. 1795 d. 1849
1849–1850	President	Zachary Taylor (W)	b. 1784 d. 1850
1850–1853	President	Millard Fillmore (W)	b. 1800 d. 1874
1853–1857	President	Franklin Pierce (D)	b. 1804 d. 1869
1857–1861	President	James Buchanan (D)	b. 1791 d. 1868
1861–1865	President	Abraham Lincoln (R)	b. 1809 assassinated 1865
1865–1869	President	Andrew Johnson (R)	b. 1808 d. 1875
1869–1877	President	Ulysses Simpson Grant (R)	b. 1822 d. 1885

1877–1881	President	Rutherford Birchard Hayes (R)	b. 1822 d. 1893
1881 (6 mos.)	President	James Abram Garfield (R)	b. 1831 assassinated 1881
1881–1885	President	Chester Alan Arthur (R)	b. 1830 d. 1886
1885–1889	President	Stephen Grover Cleveland (D)	b. 1837 d. 1908
1889–1893	President	Benjamin Harrison (R)	b. 1833 d. 1901
1893–1897	President	Stephen Grover Cleveland (D)	
1897–1901	President	William McKinley (R)	b. 1843 assassinated 1901
1901–1909	President	Theodore Roosevelt (R)	b. 1858 d. 1919
1909–1913	President	William Howard Taft (R)	b. 1857 d. 1930
1913–1921	President	Thomas Woodrow Wilson (D)	b. 1856 d. 1924
1921–1923	President	Warren Gamaliel Harding (R)	b. 1865 d. 1923
1923–1929	President	Calvin Coolidge (R)	b. 1872 d. 1933
1929–1933	President	Herbert Clark Hoover (R)	b. 1874 d. 1964
1933–1945	President	Franklin Delano Roosevelt (D)	b. 1882 d. 1945
1945–1953	President	Harry S. Truman (D)	b. 1884 d. 1972
1953–1961	President	Dwight David Eisenhower (R)	b. 1890 d. 1969
1961–1963	President	John Fitzgerald Kennedy (D)	b. 1917 assassinated 1963
1963–1969	President	Lyndon Baines Johnson (D)	b. 1908 d. 1973
1969–1974	President	Richard M. Nixon (R)	b. 1913 d. 1994
1974–1977	President	Gerald R. Ford (R)	b. 1913
1977–1981	President	James E. "Jimmy" Carter (D)	b. 1924
1981–1989	President	Ronald Wilson Reagan (R)	b. 1911 d. 2004
1989–1993	President	George H.W. Bush (R)	b. 1924
1993–2001	President	William J. "Bill" Clinton (D)	b. 1946
2001–	President	George W. Bush (R)	b. 1946

■ Vice Presidents

1789–1797	Vice President	John Adams (F)	b. 1735 d. 1826
1797–1801	Vice President	Thomas Jefferson (D/R)	b. 1743 d. 1826
1801–1805	Vice President	Aaron Burr (D/R)	b. 1756 d. 1836
1805–1812	Vice President	George Clinton (D/R)	b. 1739 d. 1812
1813–1814	Vice President	Elbridge Gerry (D/R)	b. 1744 d. 1814
1817–1825	Vice President	Daniel Tompkins (D/R)	b. 1744 d. 1825
1825–1832	Vice President	John C. Calhoun (D/R)	b. 1782 d. 1850
1833–1837	Vice President	Martin Van Buren (D)	b. 1782 d. 1862
1837–1841	Vice President	Richard M. Johnson (D)	b. 1780 d. 1850
1841–1841	Vice President	John Tyler (W)	b. 1790 d. 1862

1845–1849	Vice President	George M. Dallas (D)	b. 1792 d. 1864
1849–1850	Vice President	Millard Fillmore (W)	b. 1800 d. 1874
1853–1853	Vice President	William R. King (D)	b. 1786 d. 1853
1857–1861	Vice President	John C. Breckinridge (D)	b. 1821 d. 1875
1861–1865	Vice President	Hannibal Hamlin (R)	b. 1809 d. 1891
1865–1865	Vice President	Andrew Johnson (R)	b. 1808 d. 1875
1869–1873	Vice President	Schuyler Colfax (R)	b. 1823 d. 1885
1873–1875	Vice President	Henry Wilson (R)	b. 1812 d. 1875
1877–1881	Vice President	William A. Wheeler (R)	b. 1819 d. 1887
1881–1881	Vice President	Chester Alan Arthur (R)	b. 1830 d. 1886
1885–1881	Vice President	Thomas A. Hendricks (D)	b. 1819 d. 1885
1889–1893	Vice President	Levi P. Morton (R)	b. 1824 d. 1920
1893–1897	Vice President	Adlai E. Stevenson (D)	b. 1835 d. 1914
1897–1899	Vice President	Garret A. Hobart (R)	b. 1844 d. 1899
1901–1901	Vice President	Theodore Roosevelt (R)	b. 1858 d. 1919
1905–1909	Vice President	Charles W. Fairbanks (R)	b. 1852 d. 1918
1909–1912	Vice President	James S. Sherman (R)	b. 1855 d. 1912
1913–1921	Vice President	Thomas R. Marshall (D)	b. 1854 d. 1925
1921–1923	Vice President	Calvin Coolidge (R)	b. 1872 d. 1933
1925–1929	Vice President	Charles G. Dawes (R)	b. 1865 d. 1951
1929–1933	Vice President	Charles Curtis (R)	b. 1860 d. 1936
1933–1941	Vice President	John Nance Garner (D)	b. 1868 d. 1967
1941–1945	Vice President	Henry A. Wallace (D)	b. 1888 d. 1965
1945–1945	Vice President	Harry S. Truman (D)	b. 1884 d. 1972
1949–1953	Vice President	Alben W. Barkley (D)	b. 1877 d. 1956
1953–1961	Vice President	Richard M. Nixon (R)	b. 1913 d. 1994
1961–1963	Vice President	Lyndon Baines Johnson (D)	b. 1908 d. 1973
1965–1969	Vice President	Hubert H. Humphrey (D)	b. 1911 d. 1978
1969–1973	Vice President	Spiro Agnew (R)	b. 1918 d. 1996
1973–1974	Vice President	Gerald R. Ford	b. 1913
1974–1977	Vice President	Nelson Rockefeller	b. 1908 d. 1979
1977–1981	Vice President	Walter Mondale	b. 1928
1981–1989	Vice President	George H.W. Bush	b. 1912
1989–1993	Vice President	Dan Quayle	b. 1947
1993–2001	Vice President	Al Gore	b. 1948
2001–	Vice President	Richard Cheney	b. 1941

■ Statesmen (Secretaries of State)

1784–1789	Secretary of State	John Jay	b. 1745 d. 1829
1789–1793	Secretary of State	Thomas Jefferson	b. 1743 d. 1826
1794–1795	Secretary of State	Edmund Randolph	b. 1753 d. 1813
1795–1800	Secretary of State	Timothy Pickering	b. 1745 d. 1829
1800–1801	Secretary of State	John Marshall	b. 1755 d. 1835
1801–1809	Secretary of State	James Madison	b. 1751 d. 1836
1809–1811	Secretary of State	Robert Smith	b. 1757 d. 1842
1811–1817	Secretary of State	James Monroe	b. 1758 d. 1831
1817	Secretary of State	Richard Rush	b. 1780 d. 1859
1817–1825	Secretary of State	John Quincy Adams	b. 1767 d. 1848
1825–1829	Secretary of State	Henry Clay	b. 1777 d. 1852
1829–1831	Secretary of State	Martin Van Buren	b. 1782 d. 1862
1831–1833	Secretary of State	Edward Livingston	b. 1764 d. 1836
1833–1834	Secretary of State	Louis McLane	b. 1786 d. 1857
1834–1841	Secretary of State	John Forsyth	b. 1780 d. 1841
1841–1843	Secretary of State	Daniel Webster	b. 1782 d. 1852
1843–1844	Secretary of State	Abel Parker Upshur	b. 1791 d. 1844
1844–1845	Secretary of State	John Caldwell Calhoun	b. 1782 d. 1850
1845–1849	Secretary of State	James Buchanan	b. 1791 d. 1868
1849–1850	Secretary of State	John Middleton Clayton	b. 1796 d. 1856
1850–1852	Secretary of State	Daniel Webster	
1852–1853	Secretary of State	Edward Everett	b. 1794 d. 1865
1853–1857	Secretary of State	William Learned Marcy	b. 1786 d. 1857
1857–1860	Secretary of State	Lewis Cass	b. 1782 d. 1866
1860–1861	Secretary of State	Jeremiah Sullivan Black	b. 1810 d. 1883
1861–1869	Secretary of State	William Henry Seward	b. 1801 d. 1872
1869	Secretary of State	Elihu Benjamin Washburne	b. 1816 d. 1887
1869–1877	Secretary of State	Hamilton Fish	b. 1808 d. 1893
1877–1881	Secretary of State	William Maxwell Evarts	b. 1818 d. 1901
1881-1881	Secretary of State	James Gillespie Blaine	b. 1830 d. 1893
1881–1885	Secretary of State	Frederick Theodore Frelinghuysen	b. 1817 d. 1885
1885–1889	Secretary of State	Thomas Francis Bayard	b. 1828 d. 1898
1889–1892	Secretary of State	James Gillespie Blaine	
1892–1893	Secretary of State	John Watson Foster	b. 1836 d. 1917
1893–1895	Secretary of State	Walter Quintin Gresham	b. 1832 d. 1895
1895–1897	Secretary of State	Richard Olney	b. 1835 d. 1917

1897–1898	Secretary of State	John Sherman	b. 1823 d. 1900
1898-1898	Secretary of State	William Rufus Day	b. 1849 d. 1923
1898–1905	Secretary of State	John Milton Hay	b. 1838 d. 1905
1905–1909	Secretary of State	Elihu Root	b. 1845 d. 1937
1909-1909	Secretary of State	Robert Bacon	b. 1860 d. 1919
1909–1913	Secretary of State	Philander Chase Knox	b. 1853 d. 1921
1913–1915	Secretary of State	William Jennings Bryan	b. 1860 d. 1925
1915–1920	Secretary of State	Robert Lansing	b. 1864 d. 1928
1920–1921	Secretary of State	Bainbridge Colby	b. 1869 d. 1950
1921–1925	Secretary of State	Charles Evans Hughes	b. 1862 d. 1948
1925–1929	Secretary of State	Frank Billings Kellogg	b. 1856 d. 1937
1929–1933	Secretary of State	Henry Lewis Stimson	b. 1867 d. 1950
1933–1944	Secretary of State	Cordell Hull	b. 1871 d. 1955
1944–1945	Secretary of State	Edward Reilley Stettinius, Jr.	b. 1900 d. 1949
1945–1947	Secretary of State	James Francis Byrnes	b. 1879
1947–1949	Secretary of State	George Catlett Marshall	b. 1880 d. 1959
1949–1953	Secretary of State	Dean G. Acheson	b. 1893
1953–1959	Secretary of State	John Foster Dulles	b. 1888 d. 1959
1959–1961	Secretary of State	Christian Archibald Herter	b. 1895
1961–1969	Secretary of State	Dean Rusk	b. 1909 d. 1994
1969–1973	Secretary of State	William P. Rogers	b. 1913 d. 2001
1973–1977	Secretary of State	Henry A. Kissinger	b. 1923
1977–1980	Secretary of State	Cyrus Vance	b. 1917 d. 2002
1980–1981	Secretary of State	Edmund Sixtus Muskie	b. 1914 d. 1996
1981–1982	Secretary of State	Alexander Meigs Haig, Jr.	b. 1924
1982–1989	Secretary of State	George P. Schultz	b. 1920
1989–1992	Secretary of State	James Addison Baker, III	b. 1930
1992–1993	Secretary of State	Lawrence S. Eagleburger	b. 1930
1993–1997	Secretary of State	Warren M. Christopher	b. 1925
1997–2001	Secretary of State	Madeleine Korbel Albright	b. 1937
2001–2005	Secretary of State	Colin L. Powell	b. 1937
2005–	Secretary of State	Condoleeza Rice	b. 1954

■ Other Statesmen

1776–1785	Ambassador to France	Benjamin Franklin	b. 1706 d. 1790
1789–1795	Secretary of the Treasury	Alexander Hamilton	b. 1755 d. 1804

1801–1814	Secretary of the Treasury	Albert Gallatin	b. 1761 d. 1849
1877–1881	Secretary of the Interior	Carl Schurz	b. 1829 d. 1906
1918–1946	Presidential Adviser	Bernard Baruch	b. 1870 d. 1965
1924–1925	Attorney General	Harlan Fiske Stone	b. 1872 d. 1946
1933–1936	Ambassador to Russia	William Christian Bullitt	b. 1891 d. 1967
1936–1941	Ambassador to France	William Christian Bullitt	
1941–1942	Ambassador-at-Large	William Christian Bullitt	
1939–1950	Personal Representative of President to the Vatican	Myron Charles Taylor	b. 1874 d. 1959
1945–1953	Delegate to United Nations	Anna Eleanor Roosevelt	b. 1884 d. 1962
1961	Delegate to United Nations	Anna Eleanor Roosevelt	
1946–1953	Ambassador to United Nations	Warren Austin	b. 1877 d. 1962
1952	Ambassador to Russia	George Frost Kennan	
1953–1960	Ambassador to United Nations	Henry Cabot Lodge	
1961–1965	Ambassador to United Nations	Adlai E. Stevenson (grandson of Vice President of the same name)	b. 1900 d. 1965
1965–1968	Ambassador to United Nations	Arthur J. Goldberg	b. 1908 d. 1990
1968–1968	Ambassador to United Nations	George W. Ball	b. 1909 d. 1994
1968–1969	Ambassador to United Nations	James Russell Wiggins	b. 1903 d. 2001
1969–1971	Ambassador to United Nations	Charles W. Yost	b.1907 d. 1981
1971–1973	Ambassador to United Nations	George H. W. Bush	b.1924
1973–1975	Ambassador to United Nations	John A. Scali	b. 1918 d. 1995
1975–1976	Ambassador to United Nations	Daniel P. Moynihan	b. 1927 d. 2003
1976–1977	Ambassador to United Nations	William W. Scranton	b. 1917
1977–1979	Ambassador to United Nations	Andrew Young	b. 1932

1979–1981	Ambassador to United Nations	Donald F. McHenry	b. 1936
1981–1985	Ambassador to United Nations	Jeane J. Kirkpatrick	b. 1926
1985–1989	Ambassador to United Nations	Vernon A. Walters	b. 1917 d. 2002
1989–1992	Ambassador to United Nations	Thomas R. Pickering	b. 1931
1992–1993	Ambassador to United Nations	Edward J. Perkins	b. 1928
1993–1997	Ambassador to United Nations	Madeleine K. Albright	b. 1937
1997–1998	Ambassador to United Nations	Bill Richardson	b. 1947
1998–1999	Ambassador to United Nations	A. Peter Burleigh (acting)	b.1942
1999–2001	Ambassador to United Nations	Richard C. Holbrooke	b. 1941
2001	Ambassador to United Nations	James B. Cunningham (acting)	
2001–2004	Ambassador to United Nations	John D. Negroponte	b. 1939
2004–2005	Ambassador to United Nations	John C. Danforth	b.1936
2005	Ambassador to United Nations	Anne W. Patterson (acting)	b. 1949
2005–	Ambassador to United Nations	John R. Bolton	b.1948

■ Confederate States of America

1861–1865	President Jefferson Davis	b. 1808 d. 1889

The Confederate States consisted of eleven states that seceded from the United States of America in 1861. Full control was regained by the Unionist northern states at the conclusion of the Civil War in 1865.

■ Hawaii

Hawaii was an independent kingdom and republic before annexation to the United States.

1810–1819	King	Kamehameha I	b. 1758 d. 1819
1819–1824	King	Kamehameha II (Liholiho)	b. 1797 d. 1824
1824–1854	King	Kamehameha III (Kauikeaouli)	b. 1814 d. 1854
1855–1863	King	Kamehameha IV (Alexander Liholiho)	b. 1834 d. 1863

1863–1872	King	Kamehameha V (Lot Kamehameha)	b. 1830 d. 1872
1872–1874	King	Lunalilo (William Charles)	b. 1835 d. 1874
1874–1891	King	Kalakaua (David)	b. 1836 d. 1891
1891–1893	Queen	Liliuokalani (Lydia)	b. 1838 d. 1917
1893–1900	President	Sanford Ballard Dole	b. 1844 d. 1926

■ Republic of Texas

The Republic of Texas seceded from Mexico in 1836, became an independent republic from 1836 to 1845, and joined the United States in 1845.

1836–1838	President	Sam Houston	b. 1793 d. 1863
1838–1841	President	Mirabeau B. Lamar	b. 1798 d. 1859
1841–1844	President	Sam Houston	

Upper Volta *See* Burkina Faso

Uruguay (Oriental Republic of Uruguay)

Uruguay gained independence from Spain in 1811, along with Argentina. The struggle to resist Argentine domination led to Brazilian occupation from 1820 to 1827. A constitutional government was achieved in 1830.

1813–1820	Protector	José Gervasio Artigas	b. 1764 d. 1850
1830–1835	President	José Fructuoso Rivera	b. 1789 d. 1854
1835–1838	President	Manuel Oribe	b. 1790 d. 1857
1838–1842	President	José Fructuoso Rivera	
1843–1852	President	Joaquin Suarel	
1852–1853	President	Juan Francisco Giró	b. 1781 d. 1863
1854–1855	President	Venancio Flores	b. 1808 d. 1868
1855–1856	President (provisional)	Manuel B. Bustamante	b. 1785 d. 1863
1856–1860	President	Gabriel Antonio Pereira	b. 1794 d. 1861
1860–1864	President	Bernardo Prudencio Berro	b. 1803 d. 1868
1864–1865	President (provisional)	Atanasio Cruz Aguirre	b. 1801 d. 1875
1865–1868	President	Venancio Flores	
1868	President (acting)	Pedro Varela	b. 1837
1868–1872	President	Lorenzo Batlle	b. 1810 d. 1887
1872–1873	President (acting)	Tomás Gomensoro	b. 1810 d. 1900
1873–1875	President	José Ellauri	b. 1839 d. 1897
1875–1876	President	Pedro Varela	b. 1837
1876–1880	President	Lorenzo Latorre	b. 1844 d. 1916

1880–1882	President	Francisco A. Vidal	b. 1827 d. 1889
1882–1886	President	Máximo Santos	b. 1847 d. 1889
1886–1890	President	Máximo Tajes	b. 1852 d. 1912
1890–1894	President	Julio Herrera y Obes	b. 1876 d. 1912
1894–1897	President	Juan Idiarte Borda	b. 1844 d. 1891
1897–1903	President	Juan Lindolfo Cuestas	b. 1837 d. 1905
1903–1907	President	José Batlle y Ordóñez	b. 1856 d. 1929
1907–1911	President	Claudio Williman	b. 1863 d. 1934
1911–1915	President	José Batlle y Ordóñez	
1915–1919	President	Feliciano Viera	b. 1870 d. 1929
1919–1923	President	Baltasar Brum	b. 1883 d. 1933
1923–1927	President	José Serrato	
1927–1931	President	Juan Campisteguy	b. 1859 d. 1937
1931–1938	President	Gabriel Terra	d. 1942
1938–1943	President	Alfredo Baldomir	b. 1884 d. 1948
1943–1947	President	Juan José Amézaga	
1947–1947	President	Tomas Berreta	b. 1875 d. 1947
1947–1951	President	Luis Batlle Berres	
1951–1955	President of the National Council	Andres Martinez Trueba	
1955	President of the National Council	Luis Batlle Berres	
1956	President of the National Council	Alberto Zubiria	
1957	President of the National Council	Arturo Lezama	
1958	President of the National Council	Carlos Z. Fisher	
1959	President of the National Council	Martin R. Echegoyen	
1960	President of the National Council	Benito Nardone	
1961	President of the National Council	Eduardo Victor Haedo	
1962	President of the National Council	Faustino Harrison	
1963	President of the National Council	Daniel Fernandez Crespo	
1964	President of the National Council	Washington Beltram	

1965	President of the National Council	Carlos Maria Penades	
1966	President of the National Council	Alberto Heber	
1967	President of the National Council	Oscar Gestido	
1967	President	Oscar Diego Gestido Pose	
1967–1972	President	Jorge Pavheco Areco	
1972–1976	President	Juan Maria Bordaberry Arocena	
1976	Acting Pres.	Pedro Alberto Demicheli	
1976–1981	President	Aparicio Mendez Manfredini	
1981–1985	President	Gregorio Conrado Alvarez Armelino	
1985–1990	President	Julio Maria Sanguinetti Coirolo	
1990–1995	President	Luis Alberto Lacalle de Herrera	
1995–2000	President	Julio Maria Sanguinetti Coirolo	
2000–2005	President	Jorge Luis Batlle Ibanez	
2005–	President	Tabare Ramon Vasquez Rosas	

Urundi *See* Burundi

Uzbekistan (Republic of Uzbekistan)

This nation declared its independence from the Soviet Union in 1991. In the same year, the former First Secretary of the Communist Party, Islam Karimov, was elected president. The election was not viewed as fair or free by foreign observers, and as of 2005 Karimov was still in office.

Vandal Empire

In 409 the Vandals entered Spain from Gaul. In 428 the entire Vandal nation migrated from Spain to Africa.

428–477	King	Genseric (Gaiseric)	d. 477
		Genseric conquered Carthage, the city destroyed by Scipio the Younger nearly six centuries earlier, and made it the Vandal capital. When he sacked Rome in 455, it seemed that the ancient Carthaginians were being avenged.	
477–484	King	Hunneric, son of Genseric	d. 484
484–496	King	Gunthamund, cousin of Hunneric	
496–523	King	Thrasamund, brother of Gunthamund	d. 523
523–531	King	Hilderic, son of Hunneric	murdered 533
531–534	King	Gelimer, nephew of Thrasamund	
		Belisarius conquered the Vandal Empire, which became a province of the Byzantine Empire in 534.	

Vatican, The *See* Holy See, The

Vanuatu (Republic of Vanuatu)

This Polynesian island-state became independent in 1980.

1980–1991	Prime Minister	Walter Hadye Lini
1991	Prime Minister	Donald Kalpokas Masikevanua
1991–1995	Prime Minister	Maxime Carlot Korman
1995–1996	Prime Minister	Serge Rialuth Vohor
1996	Prime Minister	Maxime Carlot Korman
1996–1998	Prime Minister	Serge Rialuth Vohor
1998–1999	Prime Minister	Donald Kalpokas Masikevanua
1999–2001	Prime Minister	Barak Tame Sope Maautamata
2001–2004	Prime Minister	Edward Nipake Natapei Tua
2004	Prime Minister	Serge Rialuth Vohor
2004–	Prime Minister	Ham Lini

Venezuela (Bolivarian Republic of Venezuela)

Venezuela became independent from Spain in 1811 as part of Greater Colombia under the presidency of Simón Bolivar. In 1830 Venezuela seceded and became a separate nation.

1830–1846	President	José Antonio Paez	b. 1790 d. 1873
1846–1851	President	José Tadeo Mónagas	b. 1784 d. 1868
1851–1855	President	José Gregorio Mónagas, brother of José Tadeo Mónagas	b. 1795 d. 1858
		Civil War 1858 to 1863	
1863–1868	President	Juan Crisóstomo Falcón	b. 1820 d. 1870
1868–1870	President	José Ruperto Mónagas, son of José Tadeo Mónagas	
1870–1889	President	Antonio Guzman Blanco	b. 1829 d. 1899
1888–1890	President (provisional)	José Pablo Rojas Paul	
1890–1892	President	Raimundo Andueza Palacio	
1892–1898	President	Joaquín Crespo	b. 1845 killed 1898
1898–1899	President	Ignacio Andrade	
1899–1908	President	Cipriano Castro	b. 1858? d. 1924
1908–1914	President	Juan Vicente Gómez	b. 1857? d. 1935
1915–1922	President (provisional)	Victorio Marquez Bustillos	
1922–1929	President	Juan Vicente Gómez	

1929–1931	President (provisional)	Juan Bautista Pérez	
1931–1935	President	Juan Vicente Gómez	
1935–1941	President	Elcazar Lopez Contreras	
1941–1945	President	Isaías Medina Angarita	b. 1897 d. 1945
1945–1947	President	Rómuló Betancourt	
1948	President	Rómuló Gallegos	
1948–1950	Military Junta	Carlos Delgado Chalbaud	assassinated
1950–1952	Government Junta	G. Suarez Flamerich	
1953–1958	President	Marcos Pérez Jiménez	
1958	President	Wolfgang Larrazabal Ugueto	
1958–1959	President	Edgard Sanabria	
1959–1964	President	Rómulo Betancourt	
1964–1969	President	Raúl Leoní	
1969–1974	President	Rafael Caldera Rodríguez	
1974–1979	President	Carlos Andrés Pérez Rodríguez	
1979–1984	President	Luis Herrera Campins	
1984–1989	President	Jaime Ramón Lusinchi	
1989–1993	President	Carlos Andrés Pérez Rodríguez	
1993–1993	President	Octavio Lepage Barreto	
1993–1994	President	Ramón José Velásquez Mujica	
1994–1999	President	Rafael Caldera Rodríguez	
1999–2002	President	Hugo Rafael Chávez Frías	
2002–2002	President	Diosdado Cabello Rondón	
2002–	President	Hugo Rafael Chávez Frías	

Venice *See* Italy

Vietnam (Socialist Republic of Vietnam)

Under Chinese rule from the 3rd century B.C. to A.D. 15th century, Vietnam came under French administration in the 19th century as part of French Indo-China. Monarchs from the French colonial period are listed below.

■ Annam

1889–1914	Emperor	Than Thoi
1914–1916	Emperor	Duy Than
1916–1926	Emperor	Khai Dinh
1926–1940	Emperor	Bao Dai

Japanese Occupation from 1940 to 1945

Vietnam, composed of the former French possessions of Cochin-China, Annam, and Tonkin, came into being as an Associated State of Indo-China in 1949. French rule ended in 1954, and the country was partitioned along the line of the 17th parallel into South and North Vietnam.

■ Southern Zone

1949–1955	Head of State	Bao Dai	
1955–1963	President	Ngo Dihn Diem	b. 1901 murdered 1963
1963–1964	President	Duong Van Minh	
1964–1965	President	Nguyen Khanh	
1965–1975	President	Nguyen Van Thieu	

Saigon, the capital city of South Vietnam, fell to the military forces of North Vietnam in 1975, with formal reunification under the communist regime the following year.

■ Northern Zone

1945–1969	President	Ho Chi-Minh	b. 1890 d. 1969

■ Socialist Republic of Vietnam

1976–1980	President	Ton Duc Thang
1980–1981	Acting Pres.	Nguyen Huu Tho
1981–1987	Chair, Council	Truong Chinh
1987–1992	Chair, Council	Vo Chi Cong
1992–1997	President	Le Duc Anh
1997–	President	Tran Duc Luong

Yemen (Republic of Yemen)

In ancient times, Yemen was the home of the Minaean and Sabaean Kingdoms.

1904–1948	Imam	Yahya Hamied Alddien	b. 1871 murdered 1948
1949–1962	Imam	Ahmed, son of Yahya Hamied Alddien	b. 1898 d. 1962
1962–1962	Imam	Muhammed al Badr, son of Ahmed Hamied Alddien	b. 1928 Deposed

Revolutionary government Established in 1962

Republican Regime Recognized by United Nations

1962–1967	President	Abdullah as-Sallal
1967–1974	President	Abdul Rahman al-Iryani
1974–1977	President	Ibrahim Muhammad al-Hamadi

1977–1978	President	Ahmad al-Ghashmi
1978	President	Abdul Karim Abdullah al-Arashi
1978–1990	President	Ali Abdullah Saleh

The Republic of Yemen, uniting the northern and southern regions with their differing political and economic systems, was established in 1990. Although a renewed civil war ensued, the unified nation attained considerable stability under a democratic regime in the early years of the twenty-first century.

| 1990– | President | Ali Abdullah Salih |

Yugoslavia *See also* Bosnia and Herzegovina; Croatia; Macedonia; Serbia and Montenegro; Slovenia

Kingdom proclaimed on December 1, 1918

1919–1921	King	Peter I (of Serbia)	b. 1844 d. 1921
1918–1921	Regent	Alexander, son of Peter I	b. 1888 assassinated 1934
1921–1934	King	Alexander I	

Alexander I, King of the Serbs, Croats, and Slovenes, served with distinction in the Balkan War and held the position of commander-in-chief of the Serbian army when World War I began. He succeeded his father as king six weeks after an attempt on his life. On a visit to France thirteen years later, he was killed by a Croat assassin.

1934–1941	Regent	Paul, cousin of Alexander I	b. 1893
1934–1945	King	Peter II, son of Alexander I	b. 1923
1945		*Communist Republican Regime Installed*	
1945–1980	Premier	Josip Broz Tito	b. 1892 d. 1980

Tito established a policy of "national communism" that allowed for considerable economic freedom domestically. He also pursued a line of foreign policy that was independent from Soviet control. Political freedom, while greater compared to the nations of the Soviet bloc, was still severely restricted. With the death of Tito, Yugoslavia began to disintegrate as a political state, and for all intents and purposes ceased to exist in the early 1990s.

Zambia (Republic of Zambia)

Zambia, formerly the British Protectorate of Northern Rhodesia, became an independent republic in 1964.

1964–1991	President	Kenneth David Kaunda	b. 1924
1991–2002	President	Frederick J.T. Chiluba	b. 1943
2002–	President	Levy Patrick Mwanawasa	b. 1948

Zimbabwe (Republic of Zimbabwe)

Zimbabwe is the successor state to Rhodesia, the former British colony of Southern Rhodesia, which had unilaterally declared its independence from Great Britain in 1965.

■ *Rhodesia*

1966–1979	Prime Minister	Ian Douglas Smith	b. 1919

■ *Zimbabwe Rhodesia*

Between 1979 and 1980, as part of a transition to black majority rule, the nation returned temporarily to colonial status under Great Britain.

1979–1979	Prime Minister	Abel Tendekayi Muzorewa
1979–1980	Governor	Christopher John Soames

■ *Zimbabwe*

1980–	Prime Minister/ President	Robert Gabriel Mugabe

About the Editor

Having grown up in Japan, Brazil, Canada, and the United States, and holding a Ph.D. in Latin American history from Columbia University, Mark Hillary Hansen was a natural choice to revise and update this unique reference volume. Since obtaining his bachelor's degree (also from Columbia), Dr. Hansen has gained publication credits as an author, translator, and researcher, and continues to pursue his intellectual interests as an independent scholar in the fields of history and religion.